Lincolnshire History & Archaeology

Being the journal of the
Society for Lincolnshire History and Archaeology

Volume 53
2019

SOCIETY FOR
LINCOLNSHIRE
HISTORY &
ARCHAEOLOGY

Published by the Society
Jews' Court
Steep Hill
Lincoln
LN2 1LS

Articles in this journal refer to sums of predecimal British currency. The currency changed to the present decimal system in 1971. The predecimal coinage used pounds, shillings and pence (£.s.d. – e.g. £12 16s. 8d.). There were twenty shillings in one pound and twelve pence in one shilling. One guinea was twenty-one shillings or one pound and one shilling.

Measures of weight, length, volume and area may be given in imperial measurements in this journal. Many imperial measurements ceased to be used in the 1970s/80s although some sectors have retained them. For reference, the following approximate conversions apply:
1 ounce = 28.35g; 1 pound (16 ounces) = 0.45kg; 1 stone (14 pounds) = 6.35kg;
1 hundredweight (8 stones) = 50.8kg; 1 ton (20 hundredweight) = 1016kg.
12 inches (1 foot) = 0.305m; 1 yard (3 feet) = 0.91m; 1 mile (1760 yards) = 1.61km.
1 pint = 0.57l; 1 gallon (8 pints) = 4.55l.
1 acre (4840 square yards) = 0.405 hectares.

ISBN 978 0 903582 65 0

ISSN 0459-4487

Printed and bound in the United Kingdom by Henry Ling Ltd, at the Dorset Press, Dorchester DT1 1HD

Lincolnshire History & Archaeology

VOLUME 53, 2019

Contents

OBITUARIES

Maggi Darling   7

Alan Rogers   8

Beryl George   9

DAVID STOCKER   11
Dennis Mills – An Introduction

KATE TILLER   21
Dr Dennis Mills: An Overview of his Work and Legacy

BERYL GEORGE   29
The Encourager: A Case Study of Dennis Mills in his Eighties

VICTORIA THORPE   45
The Swan Family of Lincoln, 1754–1946

MARTIN WATKINSON   75
Reflections on 'Closed Parishes'

JOHN BECKETT   95
The Victoria County History of Lincolnshire

ROB WHEELER   121
Padley's Great Map of Lincoln

ANDREW WALKER   129
Interrogating the Growth of a City: Exploring Lincoln's Building Application
Database, 1866–1939

SHIRLEY BROOK   151
'Inviting Inspection in Order, by Force of Example, to Give an Impulse to
Improved Cultivation': J. J. Mechi's Experimental Farm at Tiptree in Essex and
Networks of Improvers in Nineteenth-Century Lincolnshire

MICHAEL TURNER   175
2022: Centenary of the Last Lincolnshire Yeoman

SARAH HOLLAND   195
'Wizards of the Soil': Constructing and Challenging the Institutional Rhetoric of
an Asylum Farm, Lincolnshire County Asylum, 1852–1902

ANDREW J. H. JACKSON   213
Co-operation in the Face of Conflict: The Lincoln Society and the First World
War, 1914–15

SHIRLEY BROOK   229
Dennis Mills: A Bibliography

THE HISTORIC ENVIRONMENT IN LINCOLNSHIRE 2018:   237
ARCHAEOLOGY AND HISTORIC BUILDINGS

BIBLIOGRAPHY   265

NOTES ON CONTRIBUTORS

JOHN BECKETT

Professor John Beckett taught history at the University of Nottingham for more than forty years until his retirement in 2021. A specialist in the history of the East Midlands, his many positions included Chair of the History of Lincolnshire Committee 1988-2021. His books included histories of the East Midlands and of the open field village of Laxton, Nottinghamshire. Between 2005 and 2010 he was Director of the Victoria County History (VCH) based at Senate House, University of London. During that period, he discovered that much work had been done for the VCH on Lincolnshire, which had never been published. In its original form this article was given as the Jim Johnston Memorial Lecture at Bishop Grosseteste University College in 2010.

SHIRLEY BROOK

Shirley Brook initially studied drama and taught in local schools. Later, part-time study led to a Certificate in Local History from the University of Nottingham followed by a BA(Hons) in Local and Regional History from the University of Hull. A scholarship from Hull enabled her doctoral research project on how new sources of funding and the mid-nineteenth century culture of improvement shaped Lincolnshire farm buildings. Shirley taught Local and Regional History for the University of Hull and was a tutor on the Heritage Studies course at Bishop Grosseteste from its inception in 1994 until it was discontinued in 2014. She is Vice Chair of the History of Lincolnshire Committee.

BERYL GEORGE †

Beryl George, a local history researcher based in Lincoln, died in May 2023. After a BA in History at Lancaster University and a career in university administration, Beryl arrived in the East Midlands in 1995 and in Lincoln two years' later. After working at Lincolnshire Archives, she undertook an MA in Local and Regional History at Nottingham University, with a dissertation on the provision of underground sewers in Lincoln 1848-76. She has since been involved in a number of local history projects and organisations and contributed to seven of the Survey of Lincoln's booklets. Between 2016 and 2021 she worked for the Lincolnshire Co-op on historical research into the Cornhill Quarter project and produced two books: *Lincoln's Cornhill Quarter: a surprisingly rich history* (2018) and *Lincoln's Cornhill Quarter: Riverside to Railway* (2020).

SARAH HOLLAND

Dr Sarah Holland is Assistant Professor at the University of Nottingham and is author of *Communities in Contrast: Doncaster and Its Rural Hinterland, c.1830-1870* (2019), which engaged extensively with Dennis's work on open and closed villages. Sarah's current work explores health and the countryside, which is the focus of her forthcoming book, *Farming, Psychiatry and Rural Society, England 1845-1955* (Routledge).

ANDREW JACKSON

Dr Andrew Jackson is a Reader in History, and the Head of Research and Knowledge Exchange at Bishop Grosseteste University. Andrew's background is in both history and geography, with research and publication interests including: nineteenth and twentieth-century rural and urban change; theory and practice in community, local and regional, and public history; newspaper and media history; the history of the English countryside in landscape art and regional fiction; the histories of Lincoln, Lincolnshire, and Devon; the development of the Lincolnshire Cooperative; and the life and work of Lincolnshire author Bernard Samuel Gilbert. Andrew regularly gives public lectures for local and regional historical societies.

DAVID STOCKER

David has published many books and articles on medieval architecture, archaeology and landscape, and his most recent book is on Anglo-Saxon stone sculpture in Cambridgeshire and Huntingdonshire (co-author with Paul Everson). Having retired from English Heritage in 2012, he is now Hon. Visiting Professor at the University of Leeds and a member of the Council of the National Trust since 2017. In 2018 he was appointed a Trustee of the National Heritage Memorial Fund/National Lottery Heritage Fund by the Prime Minister. During the pandemic he has served on a number of central government advisory panels dealing with the culture and heritage sectors.

VICTORIA THORPE

Victoria Thorpe was born in Melbourn, Cambridgeshire, when her father, Dennis Mills, was completing his PhD. The family moved to be near to Walton Hall, the headquarters of the Open University, in 1969. In her teens Victoria helped input population data into Cambridge University's main frame, for a research project that Dennis was involved with, and then assisted with transcribing census information, for other projects. Victoria has spent nearly forty years working for the supply chain and procurement departments of just three businesses in Buckinghamshire. Currently, she is assisting her husband, Graham, (ex RAF Scampton) to collect and upload information on war memorials, for the Imperial War Museum's database. Whilst Dennis was writing *Effluence and Influence* in 2011, he asked Victoria to research into the Swan family because Robert Swan was on the committee for commissioning Lincoln's new sewage system, and the article in this volume evolved.

KATE TILLER

Kate Tiller's academic fields are British local and social history, with particular research interests in English rural change post-1750, and religion and community in Britain since 1730. A third edition of her *English Local History: An Introduction* was published by Boydell in 2020. Her latest publication is *Communities of Dissent 1850-1914* (The Chapels Society, 2023). Dr Tiller is Reader Emerita in English Local History, University of Oxford and a founding Fellow of Kellogg College. In 2019 she was appointed OBE for services to local history. She and Dennis Mills long shared historical interests and aspirations to further participation in local history and in the recognition of its significance, including working together from their bases in Oxford University Department for Continuing Education and the Open University.

MICHAEL TURNER

Michael Turner is Emeritus Professor of Economic and Social History at the University of Hull where he has been a teacher and researcher since 1979. He is widely published in agrarian history including editing a book on the subject of the eighteenth-century land tax with Dennis Mills. Michael Turner spent his early career on the subject of parliamentary enclosure. He has also published work on agricultural rent and agricultural production including a major chapter and the statistical appendix in volume seven of *The Agrarian History of England and Wales 1850-1914* (2000). More recently he has concentrated his research on the subject of land tenure. His contribution to the present volume returns to his earlier work on parliamentary enclosure, specifically on Lincolnshire, but in the context of his recent findings on land tenure.

ANDREW WALKER

Dr Andrew Walker was Vice Principal of Rose Bruford College between 2010 and 2020 and before that worked for the University of Lincoln and its predecessor institutions from 1992, where, latterly, he was Head of the School of Humanities and Performing Arts. Andrew is series editor of The Survey of Lincoln's neighbourhood and thematic volumes, exploring the history of the city. He is currently Chair of the Society for Lincolnshire History and Archaeology.

MARTIN WATKINSON

Martin worked for The Open University in Milton Keynes for thirty-five years, latterly as Director of Strategy and Government Relations. He took early retirement in 2011 and moved back to his native Lincolnshire in 2018. He has an undergraduate degree from Keele University and an MPhil and PhD from the Centre for English Local History at Leicester University. His research interests centre on the social history of rural England and the microhistory of communities in north and east Lincolnshire after 1500.

ROB WHEELER

A statistician by training, Rob Wheeler has edited, jointly or solely, three volumes for the Lincoln Record Society. Two of these were cartographic in nature. He has also written extensively on Ordnance Survey maps, including most recently an examination of the large-scale revision processes employed in the early twentieth century. His investigations into J. S. Padley's activities as a contractor were published in a *festschrift* that marked Dennis Mills's eightieth birthday in 2011.

~

EDITOR'S REMARKS AND ACKNOWLEDGEMENTS

The death in 2020 of the Lincolnshire historian and geographer, Dennis Mills, inspired a day conference in December 2021 which celebrated his life and work. The papers presented on that day were so valuable and informative that the Society resolved to dedicate the whole of this volume of *Lincolnshire History and Archaeology* (vol. 53) to their publication, in Dennis's memory. Accordingly, the articles presented in this volume are based on the papers given at that conference, supplemented by several other contributions made by scholars who had worked closely with Dennis at some time during his career.

The editor is grateful to his associates, Andrew Walker and Naomi Field, who have shared and facilitated the editorial processes that have brought this journal to production. David George kindly consented to the publication of the paper by his wife Beryl, who died during the final stages of preparation of the volume. The editor would also like to thank all those colleagues listed below who have assisted with the publication of this volume: Lisa Brundle; Dawn Heywood; Louise Jennings; Mick Jones; Richard Watts; Alison Williams.

MARGARET J DARLING
(1939 – 2021)

Distinguished Roman pottery expert Margaret ('Maggi') Darling FSA died in Lincoln County Hospital on 23 December 2021, after a short illness.

Maggi came relatively late into archaeology, initially inspired by Graham Webster, then based in the extra-mural department of Birmingham University. She was particularly interested in the legionary-period pottery from Wroxeter and the related problem of supply to the Roman army. She moved to join the Lincoln Archaeological Trust in 1974 as its Roman pottery specialist and while based there produced a Nottingham University M.Phil thesis on her established area of interest.

Over the next few decades Maggi went on to become a highly-respected scholar and to compile a large number of reports on the material from excavations in Lincoln, now published in a wide range of books and monographs. She also wrote several scholarly articles on particular aspects of pottery study. Her Lincoln expertise culminated in the publication in 2014 of the substantial *Corpus of Roman Pottery from Lincoln* (written jointly with Barbara Precious).

While based at Lincoln, Maggi produced the pottery reports on the legionary material from Wroxeter, from Kingsholm (Gloucester), and from the fortress at Inchtuthil, Perthshire. In 1977, she was seconded for a couple of years to Norfolk Museums to produce a report on the 1950s excavations at the late Roman site at Caistor-on-Sea (written jointly with David Gurney). More recently, she supplied reports on developer-funded work on both sides of the Humber.

Maggi was a Fellow of the Society of Antiquaries of London (elected 1995), and also a past-president and valued member of the Study Group for Roman Pottery. She produced and edited its first *Guidelines for the Archiving of Roman Pottery* in 1994.

ALAN ROGERS
(1933 – 2022)

Professor Alan Rogers, Lincolnshire author and local history lecturer, and later the founding Secretary General of the Commonwealth Association for the Education and Training of Adults, died on 5 April 2022.

Born in 1933, Alan Rogers attended the University of Nottingham as an undergraduate from 1951. In 1959 he joined Nottingham's Department of Adult Education as Lecturer in Local History, first as resident tutor in South Lincolnshire and later as Director of the University's Centre for Local History. In 1965 he published *The Making of Stamford* and, in 1972, the important and much-read *Approaches to Local History*. He served as Chairman of the History of Lincolnshire Committee from 1965 to 1979 and authored the hugely popular book *A History of Lincolnshire* in 1970, updating it with a second edition in 1985.

In 1980 Alan moved to Ireland to be Director of the Institute of Continuing Education at Magee University College, Derry, and later Dean at the University of Ulster. He subsequently worked at the University of Reading where he increasingly moved into work on adult education and international development. He continued to be closely associated with Nottingham and was an honorary professor from 1998 until his death, giving lectures and advising doctoral students on a regular basis.

Alan was the founding secretary general of the Commonwealth Association for the Education and Training of Adults and also founded the Uppingham Seminar series of international adult education residentials. He published very influential books in the field of adult education such as *Teaching Adults* (1986), *Adults Learning for Development* (1992) and *Non-formal Education* (2007). Alan continued to be an active scholar and practitioner until his death, his work including projects for the Afghani police force and the Tanzanian Folk Development Colleges.

BERYL GEORGE
(1960 – 2023)

Beryl George made an important contribution to the writing of Lincoln's history in the early twenty-first century. Beryl served as the Reviews Editor for *Lincolnshire Past & Present* from Spring 2021 and was also a member of the Editorial Committee of *Lincolnshire History & Archaeology* from 2016 until her death in May 2023. In addition, to her work for the Society for Lincolnshire History and Archaeology, Beryl played an important role in The Survey of Lincoln, of which she was Vice Chair. She was also a valued volunteer for the International Bomber Command Centre's Digital Archive and part of the team engaged in listing Lincoln's buildings and structures of local importance.

Beryl was born and raised in Bedfordshire. She had a long-term interest in history which she studied at Lancaster University between 1979 and 1982. Following her degree, Beryl worked at the Cranfield Institute of Technology (later University), where she became a Student Research Administrator. She moved to Lincoln in the later-1990s and worked at Lincolnshire Archives as a Heritage Assistant until 2002. Here, she gained a tremendous familiarity with the county's archive holdings and was always willing to pass on her knowledge to researchers.

Beryl's first history-related publication was 'The Silk Factories of Chippenham – 1825-1900', published in the *Buttercross Bulletin* (Chippenham Civic Society, No 104 (Summer 2002, pp. 13-18).

Her Lincoln-based history publications first appeared in 2010 and 2011 in respectively *Lincolnshire Past and Present* and *Lincolnshire History and Archaeology*. These two articles, drawing upon her MA thesis research, explored Lincoln's Corporation and its sewer provision between 1848 and 1876. From 2013 until 2022, Beryl contributed thirteen chapters to The Survey of Lincoln's books, including two pieces co-authored with her husband, David.

Between 2016 and 2018 Beryl was employed as a researcher by Lincolnshire Co-op and she produced two highly regarded historical works, published by the Co-op, *Lincoln's Cornhill Quarter: A Surprisingly Rich History* (2018), and *Lincoln's Cornhill Quarter: Riverside to Railway*, (2020).

Amongst Beryl's many qualities as a local historian was her ability to work very successfully in partnership with others. The collaborative work she undertook with Dennis Mills on the city's population history is just one example of this.

Dennis Mills with Kate Tiller at the launch of a festschrift in his honour on 26 March 2011 at a party at Branston Village Hall celebrating Dennis's 80th birthday.
(Photo: Ken Redmore).

DENNIS MILLS – AN INTRODUCTION

David Stocker

In his delightful and perceptive 'Appreciation' introducing SLHA's celebratory 2011 volume of essays for Dennis,[1] Nigel Goose framed his comments around three vignettes. Recognising a good idea, then, what follows is a series of personal perspectives that I hope will encapsulate my own impression of what makes Dennis's contribution to our scholarly world particularly distinctive. Like Nigel, I'm also tempted to start in Trumpington Street, Cambridge, in the mid 1970s. Though I did not realise it, I too was in Cambridge that day when Dennis lectured to the famous CAMPOP Institute, setting before them procedures he had developed during research on the social history of Melbourn, in southern Cambridgeshire. But I'm afraid I did not go to hear him. In fact, I was a little frightened by that sort of history; 'Structuralism' was in everyone's thoughts and my undergraduate Tudor-and-Stuart module seemed dominated by studies of bread-price indices.[2] As I walked down Trumpington Street then, I was much more likely to back-off, to the right, into the Fitzwilliam Museum opposite, than to turn left into CAMPOP's offices. I now wish I had turned left to hear about Dennis's distinctive work on Melbourn of course: I've grown much more appreciative of such historical approaches, and now know that I missed a chance to hear how large data-sets could be used to write absorbing local history – and could be combined with interesting ideas – before the digital database was invented.

But I need not regret my right-turn, as many people have heard Dennis's message in the generation since the publication of his Melbourn conclusions – and the extension of his approach across the nation – in his well-known *Lord and Peasant … * book in 1980.[3] Kate Tiller explains below how influential this book has been and how Dennis's innovative teaching methods developed throughout his career, using large data-sets in novel ways. The paper by Beryl George below, exploring the population statistics for Lincoln city, represents the transformation of Dennis's thinking, by a younger generation of scholars. It is a terrible irony, then, that – sadly - this was amongst the final pieces that Beryl wrote, and that local history has - unexpectedly – been deprived of a rising talent. But the papers by Brook, Holland, Thorpe, Walker and Watkinson in this volume also fall squarely within this tradition of local history studies, which Dennis first advocated in his work at Melbourn and in this seminal book more than forty years ago, and which these days tends to be described as 'systems analysis'.

The papers by Brook and Thorpe below, in particular, are keen to explore individuals who can be side lit by such datasets, and something similar could also be said of Professor Turner's contribution here. Such papers follow Dennis in deploying biography alongside a variety of different categories of evidence: economic, social, cartographic. I remember Dennis becoming interested in the social background and circumstances of his own ancestors working on the Revesby Abbey estate, which led to lengthy discussions about the archaeology and architectural history of the abbey and house, and how they compared with similar county structures in the nineteenth century.[4] He knew that I had a personal investment here, as my home (a former farmhouse) contained a room of just the type that he was seeking at Revesby; typically, it was also originally accessible only from outside (Fig. 1). Learning from Dennis, Brenda Coulson

Fig.1
Manor Farm House, Thorpe on the Hill, from NE, c.1960. This (poor quality) air photograph shows the external back stairs rising to the white dormitory door exclusively for the male farmhands. This room had no other doorway and was probably a 'bothy' as defined by Dennis.
(Photo: David Stocker)

had used census returns to establish that there were five or six farm workers accommodated here in the mid-nineteenth century, where they were kept physically separated from the female staff who worked in the farmhouse kitchen. But how common were such buildings? Well, I think that remains to be established.

Inter alia, I also tried to persuade Dennis that the so-called 'prehistoric barrows' between the Red Lion and the hall in Revesby were – in fact – rabbit-warrens, and that therefore his ancestors would have been managing coneys there as part of their responsibilities ... I don't think I was successful! Nevertheless, it was entirely typical of Dennis that he wanted to understand the 'bothy' in which his father had been accommodated on the Revesby estate; where it was, what it might have looked like, and how many similar examples could be found within similar agricultural settings.

Answering Kate Tiller's call for the integration of local historical studies into the national debate, Dennis's enthusiasm for such 'total history' – recruiting all available sources of information in pursuit of a single narrative – is nowhere better exemplified than in his marvellous *Effluence and Influence*.[5] It is perhaps the ambitious vision of this book that strikes the reader first, before s/he is impressed with the detail. The intricacies of mid nineteenth-century local politics can be a little dull, so why not enliven it by telling the story through the rumbustious campaign to provide Lincoln with a working sewer system? And then, to provide appropriate academic context, why not include discursive summaries of the battle in other comparable cities? In telling this engaging story, geology, archaeology, structural and civic engineering and cartography are all recruited, alongside more conventional sources of political history and genealogy. My own engagement with Dennis regarding this book was trivial, exchanging information about the archaeology of High Bridge, but the book itself is an excellent specimen of Dennis's ability to combine sources from different fields to construct a compelling – fully rounded – historical narrative. It even serves a more didactic purpose, as it places several important original sources for the nineteenth-century city into print. This is local history at its liveliest and most worthwhile – a truly great book!

One of many innovative aspects of *Effluence* ... is its skilful use of cartographic sources as primary evidence – an important category of evidence, often overlooked by historians. This is an interest that Dennis passed on to his daughter, Victoria Thorpe, as is evidenced by her valuable paper on the Swan family below. Here cartographic evidence is thoroughly integrated with more conventional documentary analysis to generate a richer account of one of Lincoln's most important families. Prior to *Effluence* ..., of course, Dennis had also previously enjoyed a fruitful collaboration in cartographic history with Rob Wheeler, when the two of them produced their collection of historic maps of Lincoln.[6] And *Effluence* ... shows how well Dennis had absorbed lessons in critical cartography from his co-author (an acknowledged expert in this field). The comparison between the two books is instructive; whilst *Effluence* … is scrupulous in its use of cartography, it proceeds from the maps themselves to draw large-scale conclusions, and to blend this form of evidence with many others. This is a less prominent feature of the important (and still best-selling) earlier volume of City maps and Rob Wheeler's remarkable paper below, demonstrating the value of maps as evidence in their own right, ensures that Dennis's life-long devotion to cartography is recognised appropriately here.[7]

Indeed, Dennis was an early pioneer in using maps as primary evidence, not just for locating places, but also for identifying historical trends and establishing historical 'character'. As Kate Tiller explains, he described his landscape work as following the tradition of Darby and Hoskins, though attempting to apply their approach to periods of more modern history – particularly to episodes of enclosure from the sixteenth to the nineteenth centuries.[8] This interest in the 'character' of past landscapes actually began with

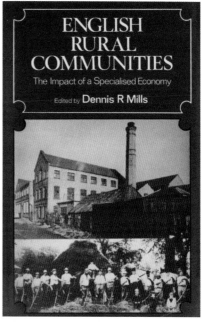

Fig.2
Cover of English Rural Communities, *Macmillan, London & Basingstoke 1973.*

his MA, which dealt with northern Kesteven – and was published as long ago as 1959.[9] Dennis continued to be interested in this rigorous and discursive approach to historical geography, and his influence on the topic, as it developed, was marked by his master-minding and editing the important collection of papers *English Rural Communities*, published in 1973 (Fig. 2).[10] I feel the significance of this book has been somewhat unjustly overlooked in all the excitement over *Lord and Peasant* … and Dennis's subsequent achievements. The volume was conceived by Dennis, he selected the papers, and most importantly he wrote the Introduction. This text is only eighteen pages long, but this short piece of writing remains one of the most lucid explorations of the interdisciplinary study of landscape since the Second World War; combining archaeology, historical geography and social, political and economic history. In his section on methodology there, he makes one of the earliest pleas I know that the goal of all such studies should be an explanation of landscape '*Character*'.[11] Even if this aspect of Dennis's work has been somewhat overlooked by subsequent local historians, it has been highly influential on a whole generation of historical geographers and landscape archaeologists, who have subsequently developed models and analytical techniques based on this search for historic 'character', using datasets from every conceivable source. This process culminated, perhaps, in the development of the suite of approaches now called 'Historic Landscape Characterisation' (Fig. 3).[12] Historic Landscape Characterisation has become an influential movement within the developing heritage sector, as history and heritage have entered the Planning mainstream and played their part in government activity more widely. Indeed, Dennis recognised that this would be the case in his reference to Ted Heath's forthcoming (1974) local government reforms. The important recent collection of

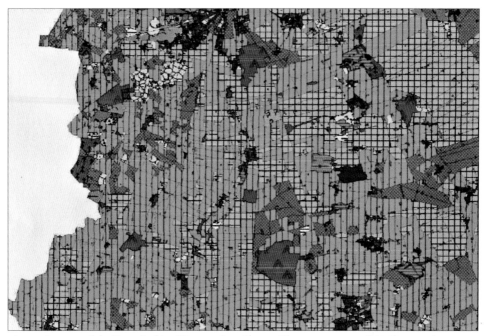

Fig.3 Section of the Lincolnshire Historic Landscape Characterisation (HLC) map showing 'modern types'. The excerpt covers an area south-west and south of Lincoln (for orientation, the magenta-coloured areas represent airbases). NB this is a greatly reduced print-out from a digital map.

'Historic Characterisations' of twenty-nine Lincolnshire towns, by Nicola Grayson and her team at the County Council, demonstrates how fundamental such thinking has become in historic-environment Planning.[13] Furthermore – as all these reports were generated in collaboration with groups of local historians – it also demonstrates how local historians are becoming involved in deciding the future of their heritage. Dennis would have approved of that! But the point I want to emphasise here is that somewhere at the roots of this significant development in local history, feeding into Planning and government, lies Dennis's short 'Introduction' to his 1973 book.

Historic Landscape Characterisation work nationally has a direct relationship with the world of Town and Country Planning; it is where historical ideas meet the contemporary world. Consequently, it is appropriate that several papers in this volume also have a direct relationship with contemporary planning; Andrew Walker's paper, for example, shows how mutually beneficial the study of local history and the consideration of planning issues can (and should) be. Led perhaps by Dennis's experience and belief in this activity, he and Andrew recognised the great value of the City of Lincoln Council's archive of planning applications, as historical evidence, and – assisted by crucial understanding and effort by John Herridge – this vital project has seen most of this archive made usable and transferred to the County Archives. This, then, was a classic Dennis Mills style project – recognising the value of an unrecognised resource, recruiting colleagues to make the material accessible, and then leading the way by showing (often in jointly authored papers) how it could be exploited both academically, and politically.[14]

I'm proud to say that Dennis's work on the assessment of local Historic Landscape Character, and indeed on the village's recent agricultural history, was used in Thorpe on the Hill's *Neighbourhood Plan*. Dennis's work on Thorpe was undertaken in the 1950s and 60s, though we found it still valid today (Figs 4a & 4b). Even the excellent maps that he

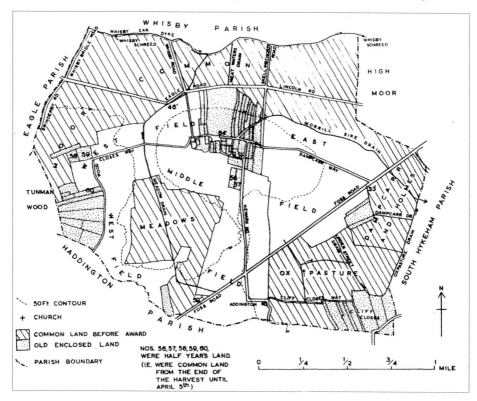

Fig.4a (above)
Dennis Mills's 1959 plan of Thorpe on the Hill (Mills, D. 'The Development of Rural Settlement around Lincoln', East Midlands Geographer, 11, 1959, 3-15).

Fig.4b (left)
The Thorpe on the Hill Neighbourhood Plan 'Proposals Document' (2014).

produced – depicting the 'character' of different zones of agricultural activity in the parish in the post Medieval period – have been developed and reproduced in the formal supporting documentation.[15]

Dennis's approach as editor to his Introduction for the 1973 book also caused him to point out (for the first time?) that, in many parts of England with mineral resources, 'miners' were not a monolithic group, dedicated only to mining.[16] He was amongst the first commentators to identify the importance of a 'miner-farmer economy', where mining was something that farmers also undertook in quiet times during the agricultural year. In the 1990s, the hunt for such 'miner-farmers' became one of the most urgent activities in landscape history in Northern England – yet Dennis had advocated such work twenty years before.[17] In this sense, Dennis was precursor to a more recent generation of Industrial Archaeologists, who have set aside the premise of much work undertaken during the period of maximum de-industrialisation in England in the 1960s and 70s, that industrial history was essentially a technocratic exercise. This younger generation prefer to see industrial manufacturing, as did Dennis, as one aspect of a wider geographical and social history, rather than a separate, isolated, subject.[18]

Fig.5 Knitting machines in their custom-built knitting lofts at the remarkable Ruddington Framework Knitters Museum south of Nottingham. (Photo: David Stocker)

*Fig.6 Remains of possible 'Moffrey' at Manor Farm, Thorpe on the Hill.
(Photo: David Stocker)*

Questions surrounding impact of industry in the countryside in the pre-steam age (after which point industry of all types tended to gravitate towards the coalfields) underlay Dennis's study of the early-modern rural textile industries in Leicestershire and Nottinghamshire (Fig. 5). His East-midland studies thus became worked examples of his enlightened, interdisciplinary, approach – which now seems considerably ahead of its time. In this work, Dennis united his exploration of material culture with statistical evidence, one of the first scholars to attempt such an approach. His various papers reporting his findings, culminated in his piece in *Textile History* for 1982.[19] This original and innovative study brought an interdisciplinary understanding, uniting documentary history with industrial archaeology. But, in fact, Dennis's approach – which still seems adventurous today – was already mature in his paper on rural knitting industries in Nottinghamshire, combining the geography of settlement with population data, in his second contribution to his 1973 book.[20]

Dennis's interest in exploiting the value of Industrial Archaeology to understand wider questions of social and landscape history is echoed particularly in Shirley Brook's paper here, where she sets the practicalities of agricultural techniques against surviving documentation for the career of Alderman Mechi. Shirley, then, is standing in the tradition established by Dennis, that aims to generate farm-specific studies as a mechanism for exploring broader issues in social and economic history.[21]

Dennis's willingness to be interested in everything around him led to his eventual recognition as expert in the archaeology – as well as the conservation - of agricultural machinery. When I returned to live in the county in 2007, purchasing my former farmhouse at Thorpe on the

Hill, I accidentally acquired my own collection of ancient agricultural machinery. Seeking advice about its care, I was delighted to discover that my wreck of a farm vehicle (Fig. 6) might be the remains of a hermaphrodite cart – a 'Moffrey'. That is to say, a humble, all-purpose, two-wheeled cart for most of the year, but built to accommodate a removable set of front wheels and higher sides for conversion to a wain at harvest time. Indeed, Dennis – my advisor – happened to be the world-expert on this type of vehicle; his seminal article in *Folk Life* appeared that very year, in 2007–8, summarising a string of earlier papers.[22] After an afternoon's debate, Dennis thought mine could have been the rear half of a Moffrey, but – if so – it was also an unusual type of muckspreading cart, because several constructional details indicated that role. This much was obvious in the lie of the planks and the underlying frame structure, apparently … and, by the way, my plough was a ridging-plough for potatoes and not for grain cultivation. Both observations offered useful insights into Manor Farm's economy, prior to the era of EU subsidies, which became the topic of discussion for the remainder of the afternoon. For me, that afternoon was an object lesson in the application of object biography to local history, made more enjoyable because unexpected.

On that occasion, or on another, Dennis revealed that he had actually included Thorpe on the Hill in his research and teaching with his local groups at Collingham and Swinderby, reminding me that Dennis was also an innovative educationalist.[23] His analysis of my agricultural vehicles, and their integration with larger issues of history and economy were examples of the humane and dedicated teaching for which he was renowned. Such abilities had been evident in his establishment of the committed group at Melbourn, and continued during his time at the Open University, so when he and Joan moved north again, he continued to inspire local history groups in the Lincoln locality. I never experienced Dennis's teaching in formal settings myself (though it is considered in Kate Tiller's paper), but surely his all-embracing studies of 'total history' were just ideally suited to such learning groups?

A career in such formal teaching also led Dennis to consider the systematic publication of discoveries made by his local history groups, and such considerations led him directly to promoting the successful completion of the Society for Lincolnshire History and Archaeology's *History of Lincolnshire* project.[24] According to the volumes' prefaces themselves, Dennis was involved in producing the final five volumes in the series (volumes III, VII, IX, XI & XII) – a role 'behind the scenes' that also deserves recognition, and he stepped into the full limelight as editor of the final volume in the series, in 1989.[25] This major series of volumes, is some recompense for the lack of a conventional Victoria County History for Lincolnshire, although it covers the material that – in other counties – would be reserved for the first few volumes.[26] The series never intended to usurp what is seen, these days, as VCH's most valuable contribution to a given county's history – detailed and accurate 'parish accounts'. The long and convoluted tale of how the Lincolnshire Victoria County History found itself in such a parlous situation is recounted with marvellous care, wit and wisdom here by John Beckett.

Looking back over Dennis's long life, Kate Tiller's assessment below is clearly correct – it is his extraordinary 'range' that is so distinctive and inspiring about Dennis's scholarship. He was interested in literally everything around him, and was capable of recruiting methods, ideas and material from many disciplines, probing the entire historic environment, to create innovative studies. Some such studies, like landscape 'characterisation', have subsequently inspired discrete activities and continuing scholarly enquiry. And finally, like all our contributors here, I always found Dennis a wonderfully helpful and generous scholar, who was always prepared to encourage and assist younger colleagues ... and, usually, he was prepared to share some of his enormous archive of research results.[27]

So, Dennis's loss is to scholarship in general, and not just to Lincolnshire scholarship, significant though his contribution to Lincolnshire was, and it is not simply to documentary history, significant though that was too. His loss diminishes us all – scholars working in many fields. We no longer have his humane good humour and disinterested helpfulness to inspire us and to link together our various fields of research.

NOTES

1. Goose, N., 2011, 'Dennis Mills An Appreciation', in *Lincoln Connections. Aspects of City and County since 1700. A Tribute to Dennis Mills*, eds. Brook, S., Walker, A., and Wheeler, R., Lincoln, pp.10-11.

2. For example: Laslett, P., 1965, *The World we have lost*, London; Ramsey, P. H. (ed.), 1971, *The Price Revolution in Sixteenth Century England*, London; Chambers, J. D., 1972, *Population, Economy and Society in Pre-Industrial England*, Oxford.

3. Mills, D. R., 1980, *Lord and Peasant in Nineteenth Century Britain*, London and Totowa N.J.

4. Mills, D. and Thorpe, V., 2018, 'Bothy Boys', *Lincs Past and Present* 112, Summer, p.13-8. Stocker, D. A., 2008, 'A Tenant Farmhouse with Two Good Parlours. Manor Farm House, Thorpe on the Hill', unpublished ms. in author's possession.

5. Mills, D. R., 2015, *Effluence and Influence. Public Health, Sewers and Politics in Lincoln 1848-50*, Lincoln.

6. Mills, D. R. and Wheeler, R. C. (eds), 2004, *Historic Town Plans of Lincoln, 1610-1920*, LRS 92, Lincoln.

7. In fact, Rob Wheeler followed Dennis in combining cartographic evidence with other categories of information in his remarkable book: Wheeler, R. C. (ed.), 2008, *Maps of the Witham Fens from the Thirteenth to the Nineteenth century*, LRS Vol. 96.

8. Dennis explained his position at the start of his 'Introduction' to Mills, D. (ed.), 1973, *English Rural Communities. The Impact of a Specialised Economy*, London and Basingstoke, pp.9-27.

9. Mills, D., 1959, 'The Development of Rural Settlement around Lincoln', *East Midlands Geographer* 11, pp.3-15.

10. Mills, *English Rural Communities* ... (note 8 above).

11. *Ibid.*, p.11.

12. Fairclough, G., Lambrick, G. and McNab, A. (eds.), 1999, *Yesterday's World, Tomorrow's Landscape* ..., London; Clark, J., Darlington, J. and Fairclough, G., 2004, *Using Historic Landscape Characterisation*, London; Fairclough, G., 2006, 'Chapter 12: The United Kingdom – England', in Fairclough, G. and Grau Møller, P. (eds.), *Landscape as Heritage. The Management and Protection of Landscape in Europe, A Summary by the COST A27 Project < Landmarks>*, Geographia Bernensia, G. 79, Berne, pp.269-299. The Lincolnshire HLC project (2007-2011) was one of the last and most comprehensive county projects to be completed, directed by Alastair Mackintosh. It deployed both fundamental thinking and research derived from Dennis's work.

13. Grayson, N. and Robertson-Morris, G. (eds.), 2002, *The Lincolnshire Extensive Urban Survey*, 29 vols, Lincoln.

14. Many papers during Dennis's final decade of research make use of this archive – See Shirley Brook's bibliography here for details.

15. Thorpe on the Hill Parish Council 2014, *Thorpe on the Hill. Our Neighbourhood Plan – Proposals Document*; [Nigel McGurk] 2017, *Thorpe on the Hill, Neighbourhood Plan 2016-2036*. Report by Independent Examiner, to North Kesteven District Council.

16. Mills, *English Rural Communities* … (note 8 above), p.13.

17. Cranstone, D., 2001, 'Industrial Archaeology – Manufacturing a New Society', in Newman, R., Cranstone, D. and Howard-Davis, C., *The Historical Archaeology of Britain, c.1540-1900*, Stroud, 183-210, at pp.201-3.

18. For commentary on this debate, see Cranstone, 'Industrial Archaeology … ' (note 17 above), pp.183-6.

19. Mills, D., 1982, 'Rural industries and social structure: Framework knitters in Leicestershire, 1670-1851', *Textile History* 13, pp.183-203.

20. Mills, D. R., 1973, 'The Geographical Effects of the Laws of Settlement in Nottinghamshire: an analysis of Francis Howell's report', in Mills, *English Rural Communities* … (note 8 above), pp.182-191.

21. E.g., Mills, D., 2007, 'Titus Kime, entrepreneur of Mareham le Fen 1848-1931, and the Eldorado Potato Boom of 1903-4', in Howard, J. and Start, D. (eds.), *All Things Lincolnshire. A collection of papers and tributes to celebrate the 80th birthday of David N Robinson OBE MSc*, Lincoln, pp.139-50.

22. Mills, D., 2007-8, 'Recording and interpreting moffreys: hermaphrodite cart/wagons of Eastern England', *Folk Life: Journal of Ethnological Studies* 46, pp.99-122.

23. Mills, D. and Tinley, R., 1991, 'The People of Swinderby in 1771 and 1791: A study in population mobility', *Lincolnshire History and Archaeology* 26, pp.7-11.

24. See Rogers, A., 1976, 'Preface to the Series' in May, J., *Prehistoric Lincolnshire*, History of Lincolnshire I, Lincoln 1976, p.iv.

25. Mills. D., (ed.), 1989, *Twentieth Century Lincolnshire*, The History of Lincolnshire Volume XII, Lincoln.

26. A single volume was published, about half of which is dedicated to Lincolnshire's religious history, but with sections on Politics, Society and Economics, Industry, Agriculture, Forestry, Education and Sport – Page, W. (ed.), 1906, *The Victoria History of the County of Lincoln, Volume II*, London.

27. Personally, I am grateful for notes and maps Dennis gave me about Thorpe on the Hill, Swinderby and Collingham, shortly following my return to the county.

DR DENNIS MILLS: AN OVERVIEW OF HIS WORK AND LEGACY

Kate Tiller

Following his death in March 2020, there have rightly been many tributes to Dennis Mills, the man, and his long and productive life. It was a life during which he influenced very many people and was a frequent and often pathfinding contributor on a varied range of historical themes including work significant both in his home city and county of Lincolnshire and nationally. Dennis Mills was indeed 'a local historian of all England,'[1] This volume, and the online conference in December 2021 on which it draws, are welcome opportunities to assess that contribution.[2] I am honoured to have been asked to offer an opening overview. I should like to reflect particularly on the distinctive features of Dennis's work, its legacies for local history, and the challenges it sometimes poses for us in taking local history forward.

AN INTERDISCIPLINARY APPROACH

Dennis Mills was notably interdisciplinary in his approach. This can be a rather superficial tag, perhaps entailing some cross reference to work from parallel disciplines but leading to no deeper integration or change of practice. In the hands of Dennis, it was far more than this. He read Geography with History at Nottingham University in the early 1950s.[3] He taught geography in his early career and referred to himself as a historical geographer. He brought a spatial and social scientific approach to his concept of local studies and if understanding people in their place is at the core of local history, what alliance of disciplines could be more appropriate and enriching to both partners?

Out of this, for example, he proposed locating individuals, families and households literally in their place and demonstrated how this could be done, using predominantly nineteenth- and twentieth-century sources for house re-population. He then explored people's living circumstances, their houses and outbuildings, their household goods, worked out the composition of their households, where they lived in a settlement and who their neighbours were. He interpreted his spatial findings, relating them to economic activities, occupations, service functions, transport links and key relationships between villages and towns (their relative functions, size, distance and direction), drawing on geographical concepts such as settlement hierarchy and central place theory.

The resulting local history was not about single places approached as in an isolated bubble. Whilst Dennis was certainly often interested in a particular place his approach to its history reflected his interdisciplinary thinking throughout his long career. An outstanding example is his studies of the village of Melbourn in Cambridgeshire, where he was a school teacher in the 1960s. Melbourn was part of his postgraduate research on landownership and was to feature in his later, most widely-known published work, where its local evidence contributed to discussion of wider themes.[4] The village featured in his work in other ways. Characteristically, Dennis as a school teacher sought to encourage pupils to undertake investigations of their own locality as part of their history or geography studies. In 1968 he published a book[5] on the English village in a series aimed at fourteen-to-sixteen year olds and providing a practical guide to potential projects they might undertake, including those for 'the Certificate of Secondary Education'. Throughout its succinct pages there is a distinctive emphasis on understanding the historical and recent experience of their chosen place through a range of original sources and in the context of surrounding landscape and settlements. Maps feature prominently and Melbourn is one of the cases included, as seen in Fig.1. Yes this is a map! It shows the relative position of neighbouring villages (amongst them Melbourn). To this spatial relationship is added census data on their population size, shown in a graphic which emphasises the varying size of the villages and sparks a series of points for further investigation as to why this was the case. Varied acreage, land use, land holding, employment, services, how many people go to work outside the village are all raised as suggested questions. The distinctive Mills approach is clear to see in an interdisciplinary marriage of history and geography, the use of local studies combining documentary and field evidence, and the involvement of a range of practitioners and audiences. Melbourn featured in his national and international books and articles as well as in work published in local and regional journals, guides, trails and pamphlets (often presented collaboratively with the students and local historians who he did so much to encourage).

Also typical was Dennis's attention to how the practicalities of research and recording might be managed with limited outlay. In 1968 the map making (as in Fig.1) involved tracing and graph paper, then pencilled versions made permanent with Indian ink. At this point he adds that 'If Indian inks are used it is possible to scratch out mistakes with a razor blade'.[6] This was the lot of a local historian in the 1960s. Dennis continued to be alert to the practicalities of research and presentation and, as we shall see, was an early adopter and disseminator of the developments in computing and information technology which expanded so much during his career. He was a keen and practical advocate of ways in which local historians could use and benefit from them.

These have been rural examples but the same interdisciplinarity is very relevant to towns as Mills demonstrated. For example, market towns and their hinterlands, next up in those

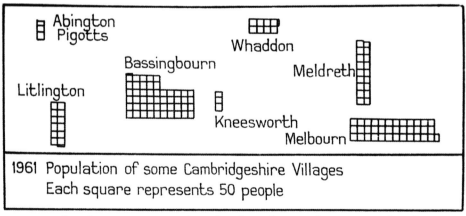

Fig.1 Interdisciplinary perspectives: Spatial and population information combined in a map from The English Village *(1968), p.47. The villages are considered as a group, also adding to understanding of individual places, which include Melbourn one of Dennis Mills's most intensive and sustained local case studies.*

village settlement hierarchies, were a theme of his work. So too was the study of larger towns and suburbanisation. Again, he took perspectives and methods from historical geography and employed local studies of which those of Lincoln and its hinterland are notable examples.[7] He saw suburbanisation as a key area of change and development in many local experiences, particularly of the late nineteenth and twentieth (and now the twenty-first) centuries. It has blurred the once separate physical, economic and social identities of rural and urban whilst generating patterns of living separated by class and ethnicity, cultural and immigrant difference.

Dennis's concept of local studies was developing at the same time as the flowering of landscape history, a subject particularly associated with W. G. Hoskins and his influential *The Making of the English Landscape*, first published in 1955. It is interesting to compare their approaches and impact. Hoskins drew strongly on social and economic history approaches, whilst both he and Mills were concerned with demographic trends and the use of fieldwork investigations in association with more traditional reliance on documentary evidence. This latter emphasis in landscape studies generated strong links between history and archaeology, particularly in the use of non-intrusive topographical and building survey work. Whilst there was overlap and complementarity between their formulations of local studies in important ways their approaches were very different. Hoskins's view of local history was rooted in a strong agenda based on a teleological narrative of the history of local communities from prehistory to the early twentieth century. It spanned their origins, growth, maturity and decline, and then inevitable collapse in the face of industrialisation and urbanisation. It is an agenda that hits the buffers when it reaches the later nineteenth and twentieth centuries; times when Hoskins saw traditional communities being destroyed by forces of modernisation. He viewed changes in the twentieth-century landscape with vehement, anti-modernist rejection. Mills's geographical, historical and social scientific approach was very different. He embraced the need to extend the scope of local history into the twentieth century and recent past. Not only did he champion this cause but, as we shall see, pioneered the practice of local research on the twentieth century in Lincolnshire and elsewhere.

APPLIED HISTORICAL STUDIES

A key concept in developing such additional aspects of local history was applied historical studies. As we have seen in his 1968 book for schools, it was an abiding feature of Dennis's work to spell out the evidence and how to use it. This fostered active engagement by a range of historians in doing original research for themselves. The focus was often on shared questions and trends and this encouraged comparative local studies of different localities. The use of comparison is one of the particular strengths of good local history and Dennis was a notable exemplar and enabler of this. (I sometimes wonder why do we not use the term 'citizen historian' in parallel with 'citizen scientist' to describe developments in the practice of local history since the 1960s).

As Dennis aimed his work and activities at varied audiences, family historians became important. The late Jeremy Gibson, doyen of genealogy and family history, recalled his collaborations with Dennis in producing volumes for the 'Gibson guides', inexpensive and widely available pamphlet guides to original documentary sources for family and local history.[8] He remembered Dennis's help with the very first of the series in 1979, *Census Returns 1841, 1851, 1861, 1871 on Microfilm.*[9] *A directory of local holdings.* This was an indication of Dennis's

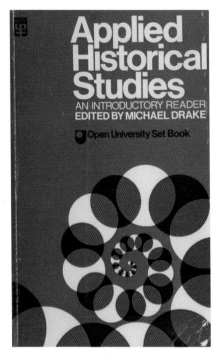

Fig.2
Cover of Michael Drake (ed.), 1973,
Applied Historical Studies: An
Introductory Reader.

up to date attitude to then recent technology, making available key resources beyond their original archive repositories. The guides series subsequently 'sold several hundred thousand' in those pre-internet days. Dennis was equally active in using them to spread awareness of less well-known evidence, and to widen the scope of local researchers, as in the case of the guide to Land Tax Assessments, which included a county gazetteer of surviving assessments.[10] It was very difficult to say no to supporting Dennis's projects and I recall being 'volunteered' to compile the Berkshire entry. It was also typical that Dennis jointly edited a volume of scholarly essays on land tax assessments and their significance,[11] his involvement again spanning both accessibility and advanced research.

This focus on accessibility and research found expression in his work at the Open University (OU) where he was Staff Tutor and then Senior Lecturer on the central staff in the 1970s and 1980s. Dennis played a major role, with Michael Drake, Ruth Finnegan and others, in creating and running the undergraduate programme Family and Community History, a course still fondly remembered by its many participants as 'DA301'. This OU coding signalled the programme's distinctive interdisciplinary and cross-faculty character (combining Arts and Social Sciences). DA301 was very much an exercise in Applied Historical Studies.[12] Many were the OU degrees gained and the individual lives transformed as students tasted opportunities for original research. Numbers of students went on to postgraduate research and to active roles in local history, including the ongoing Family and Community History Research Society. Dennis helped bring together individual student projects for publication, as for example studies of migration in the pamphlet *Victorians on the Move*.[13]

A consequence of Dennis's wide contacts and engagement was that he initiated, edited or contributed to a myriad of local history publications, ranging from full length books to local guides and trail leaflets. (Shirley Brook's bibliography of his published work in this volume (see pp. x-y) is an invaluable record of much of this range). This myriad was part of an explosion in local history publication, much of it by definition regional, county or 'one place' in content and production. It represented expansion and progress but it also posed, and still poses, a major challenge for local history. This is to ensure that local history research and publications do not disappear into a void of scattered and unconnected fragments. Whilst outcomes often offer original, significant contributions to the history of a place or a theme like migration, they can too frequently fall into an unacknowledged or underestimated mass of little-known material. Some such publication falls outside the formal systems of ISBNs and commercial and academic publication, and this so-called 'grey literature' may not be picked up in centralised bibliographies, copyright libraries and online library catalogues.

Is local history still failing to do itself justice by allowing this important literature (which Dennis did so much to encourage) to disappear from view? Getting an ISBN and including a date and place of publication help. Authors and local groups can ensure that copies of their publications go to the principal relevant local studies repository (library, archive, museum or heritage centre or these days some combination thereof), which collects local publications and maintains online catalogues of them. Some county history organisations publish annual lists of new publications relating to their area. However, all these initiatives are on a small, relatively local scale. Is an accessible, overall system allowing authors or groups producing accounts of local research to deposit copies in an online archive a way forward? In field archaeology, which has a parallel issue with 'grey literature' that falls below the horizon of formal publication, the OASIS project provides an online system for reporting local investigations, archiving the reports in an overall collection hosted by the

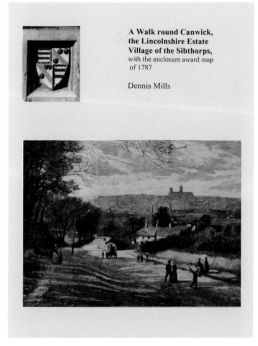

Fig.3
One of Dennis's pieces of 'grey literature': A Walk Round Canwick, the Lincolnshire Estate Village of the Sibthorps *(2003).*

Archaeology Data Service, and linking the information with area Historic Environment Records, museums and national heritage organisations. Might a similar system, adapted to patterns of local history activity, capture the subject's wealth of research outputs and make them better known and available both to practitioners and an interested public?

INNOVATION AND ANALYSIS

Dennis Mills was often innovative in his work. If he saw a gap, for example in period coverage or use of a type of evidence, he would not be shy of filling it, or getting others to do so. One major instance is that he was early in addressing the limited local historical coverage of the twentieth century. This is notably seen in Volume XII of the History of Lincolnshire series, *Twentieth Century Lincolnshire* (1989), which he edited and to which he contributed.

The local history of the twentieth century poses particular demands and challenges.[14] Many staple local historical themes remain sensitive or controversial, uncomfortably close in personal memories and connections, whilst the comparative perspectives and conceptual bases on which objective studies of other periods can draw were relatively little developed. Different sources had to be used, especially oral history, whilst familiar earlier staple information is sometimes absent or restricted in access for reasons of confidentiality. The presentation of recent history has taken on new emphases to which local history has

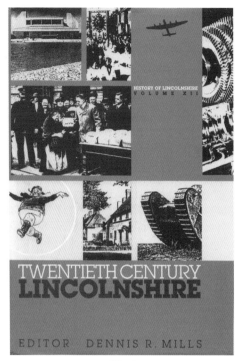

Fig.4
Cover of History of Lincolnshire Vol.XII,
Twentieth Century Lincolnshire.

increasingly had to relate, as in the case of family history, public history and the heritage industry. A limited number of themes have sometimes dominated the views taken of the century, for example the two world wars, and other areas for investigation have needed to be identified and developed.

Dennis was well aware of these possible pitfalls but firm in his opinion that they should not be allowed to prevent local historians from beginning to engage seriously and more comprehensively with the twentieth century, even if this would inevitably be a first attempt which others would need to 'rewrite as new perspectives emerge...but to leave the writing of history entirely to succeeding generations is to abandon our duty at least to capture factual records made and the view of events and periods held by those who lived through them.[15]Dennis would relish the efforts of his successors in preserving recent and contemporary records, in revising or expanding earlier accounts and in opening up new themes in twentieth-century history.

Close-focused, deep-rooted and specific research was, as we have seen, characteristic of Dennis. Yet he also analysed and discussed findings in the context of big ideas. His book *Lord and Peasant in Nineteenth Century Britain* (1980) is perhaps the best known example of what was a general approach of his. Also apparent are his interdisciplinary roots. Indeed, *Lord and Peasant* first appeared as a volume in the Croom Helm Historical Geography Series, edited by R. A. Butlin. It is a mark of its significance that it was reprinted in 2016 (including an e-book version) as a volume in the Routledge Library Editions: *The Victorian World*.[16] By then it had become a widely cited work across social, rural, nineteenth-century and local historical studies, particularly for its typology of open and closed settlements.

It is the lot of authors of such seminal studies for their work to be diffused over the years by generations of students, tutors and supervisors and sometimes to become diluted and over simplified along the way. It is always important to go back to the original. There we will find that we are not dealing with a deterministic view that landownership unilaterally caused a settlement to be open or closed, nor with an open/closed model and categorisation based on a single black and white dichotomy. Rather, a wider spectrum of types is suggested and related to underlying systems of rural society, peasant and estate. In a chapter on 'How and Where the Model Works' you will find a table of Open and Closed Township Characteristics.[17] This shows the various elements, expressed as on the ground features, which may be found in actual settlements. They range from large populations to poachers (in open villages) and small populations to gamekeepers (in closed villages). It is a summary that has often been quoted and employed by local researchers. I recall Dennis telling me that he added poachers and gamekeepers as a light-hearted final comparison but found it solemnly taken up, investigated and debated. Overall it is part of a holistic view of village types, not offered as a rigid binary labelling of rural experience but as a categorised spectrum which can be used as a basis to investigate features discernible from a combination of qualitative and qualitative evidence. *Lord and Peasant* is also a book of further extensive scope, including chapters on rural Wales and rural Scotland, a contrast of town and country, and considerations of villages overtaken by industrialisation and urbanisation and of socio-spatial segregation and the roles of urban landowners in different types of town.

When Dennis returned, in 2006, to the open and closed model[18] he was engaging with many subsequent studies sparked by his book. Typically, he illustrated his points by comparative local case studies, of a closed and an open village. The open village is none other than Melbourn. He also reflected generally, reiterating the original and continuing need to counter any received assumption that the structure of nineteenth-century rural society was essentially tripartite, made up of landowners, tenant farmers and landless labourers. This neglected a significant presence of small landowners, small farmers, craftsmen, traders, often dual occupationists, with an interest in the soil. Many relied substantially on family labour and their economic activities engaged with an open rather than a subsistence market. They were neither large capitalist farmers nor landless labourers but a 'peasantry' which found opportunities to survive and flourish in particular localities and were at the core of open village societies. As to location, in broad terms estate villages were more likely to occur in arable areas and open communities in pastoral zones but in practice local studies revealed many exceptions, including groups of varying village types in proximity to each other. Here a system of interacting village types, working symbiotically in key areas such as the supply of labour and housing, might be observed. Whilst sole causes in the creation of open and closed, for example poor law policy, could no longer be argued patterns of landownership remained important in assessing the processes of open and closed at work. In typical style Dennis urged continuing work at different scales, including on the one hand large area databases for statistical analysis (he debated the conclusions of some such studies made following his own formulations of 1980) and on the other a behavioural approach using local case studies. As contributions to this volume show, the rich perspective on village typology highlighted by Dennis Mills continues to provide local and national historians with significant focuses for debate and investigation.

Rural social structure, including open and closed settlements, was just one of the areas of 'big ideas' in which Dennis made influential contributions. Others include definitions of community; migration; rural and urban differences and connections; the historical treatment of the twentieth century, all of them overarched by the transition from traditional to modern society. As I hope these reflections have shown these contributions were achieved in a distinctive style. They were the fruit of active interdisciplinarity; of expanded and combined use of both documentary and fieldwork evidence; of innovation and expansion in major fields of study; of applied historical studies: and of the use of local studies by widened range of participants and practitioners, of readers and recipients. Dennis, through his own distinguished scholarship and his generous sharing of his knowledge and enthusiasm, achieved an involving yet rigorous way to historical understanding that has left a lasting legacy and the challenge of following in his footsteps.

NOTES

1   Nigel Goose in Brook, S., Walker, A. and Wheeler, R. (eds), 2011, *Lincoln Connections. Aspects of City and County since 1700. A Tribute to Dennis Mills*. Lincoln: The Society for Lincolnshire History and Archaeology. p.11.

2.   This chapter is based on a paper delivered to an online day conference on 4 December 2021, organised jointly by the British Association of Local History, Lincoln Record Society, The Survey of Lincoln and the Society for Lincolnshire History and Archaeology, to celebrate Dennis's life and work.

3.   For further details see Jackson, A. J. H. and Walker, A., 2021, 'Dennis Mills (1931-2020): an appreciation and assessment', *The Local Historian*, 51.1, pp. 56-61.

4.   See for example, Mills, D. R., 1980, *Lord and Peasant in Nineteenth Century Britain*, pp.70-3; Mills, D., 2006, 'Canwick (Lincolnshire) and Melbourn (Cambridgeshire) in Comparative Perspective within the Open-Closed Village Model' in *Rural History*, 2006, 17, pp.1-22.

5.   Mills, D. R., 1968, *The English Village*

6.   *Ibid.*, p. viii.

7.   Mills, D. R., 1994, 'Community and Nation in the Past: perception and reality' in Drake, Michael (ed.), *Time, Family and Community. Perspectives on Family and Community History*. Milton Keynes, Open University Press in association with Blackwell, pp. 261-85. In a broad-ranging discussion of the impact on communities of the urbanisation of the British population followed by its suburbanisation Mills employs a case study of Lincoln and its surrounding villages from 1850 into the late twentieth century (pp. 261-272). He writes 'in a deliberately descriptive and personalised form' (p.261) to get his readers thinking about parallels in the development of areas they know, before going on to put his case study 'into the national context of economic, demographic, and social change' (p.272).

8.   Personal communication. Letter from Jeremy Gibson to the author, 3 November 2021.

9.   Gibson, J. S. W. (comp.),1979, Plymouth. *Census Returns 1841, 1851, 1861, 1871 on Microfilm. A directory of local holdings.*

10. Gibson, J. S. W. and Mills, D., (eds.), 1983 (repr. 1984), *Land Tax Assessments c.1690 – c.1950*, Plymouth.

11. Mills, D. and Turner, M., (eds), 1986, *Land and Property: the English Land Tax 1692-1832*, Gloucester.

12. Drake, M., 1973, *Applied Historical Studies: an introductory reader*. Open University Press, Milton Keynes.

13. Mills, D. with Philip Aslett et al.,1984, *Victorians on the Move: Research in the Census Enumerators' Books 1851-81*. Buckingham, 1984.

14. See Tiller, K., 2010, 'Local History and the Twentieth Century: an overview and suggested agenda' in *The International Journal of Regional and Local Studies*, Series2, Vol., 6.2, pp.16-47.

15. Mills, D., (ed.), 1989, *Twentieth Century Lincolnshire*, History of Lincolnshire Series, 12, Lincoln. p.12.

16. Mills, D. R., 2016 reprint, *Lord and Peasant in Nineteenth Century Britain*, Routledge Library Editions: The Victorian World, p. 34.

17. Mills, 1980, *Lord and Peasant.* p.117.

18. Mills, 2006, *Rural History*, see note 4.

THE ENCOURAGER: A CASE STUDY OF DENNIS MILLS IN HIS EIGHTIES

Beryl George

Having got to work with Dennis Mills for the first time in 2009, the author was involved in several projects, usually as part of a small group, right up until his death in 2020. This case study of the production of a section of The Survey of Lincoln website on the population of Lincoln 1801-2011, is intended to reflect Dennis's method of working and 'people skills' in his last decade. It is also intended to provide a rare example of a local history collaborative project as it played out in real time. The case study is based on email trails and working notes.

INTRODUCTION

Although historical research is usually conducted by an individual, there is a lot to be gained through collaboration with others: a larger amount of data collected and assessed; the benefit of a wider field of knowledge and contacts; the pooling and discussion of ideas and, above all, the encouragement of working in a small team.

Collaboration between different researchers in local and community history has its origins earlier than might be thought, but from the latter part of the twentieth century clearly owes a big debt to Open University modules, including those taught by Dennis Mills himself.[1] Organisations like the Family and Community Historical Research Society (FACHRS) and the History Workshop are just two current examples of organisations encouraging such collaboration.[2]

Many people worked with Dennis over his long career: colleagues, students and volunteers, but apart from the odd reminiscence given in passing during a memorial event, or mentions in the various obituaries, very little of his working process has been recorded. Indeed, it is difficult to find published material on how any local history projects were conducted in reality, rather than a sanitised version for a completion report.

In order to illustrate Dennis's working process, the 'Population of Lincoln' project was chosen.[3] This was for a number of reasons: the author was part of the core team; it was one of Dennis's last projects and as such could give an idea of his working method in later life; and there was a complete email trail and associated working papers.

THE IDEA

Since its publication in 1974, *Victorian Lincoln* by Sir Francis Hill, has been used by many historians of Lincoln as a definitive work, especially the seemingly useful appendices of population and housing figures from 1801 to 1901.[4]

Dennis had his doubts, however. When describing how his initial project on the nineteenth century population of Lincoln came about, he wrote: '...the whole 19C enterprise started with my finding too many errors for comfort in Hill's table – no doubt one of his office juniors was at fault (and to think that I turned down that job in 1946!).'[5]

Dennis's background in population and census research stretched back to at least the 1970s and he wrote and taught on different aspects of it, especially census enumeration.[6] The nineteenth-century population of Lincoln had been written up by Dennis (DM) originally in 2007, following a seminar in 2003.[7] There was also information in the introduction to the plans in *Historic Town Plans of Lincoln* (2004).[8] Using these nineteenth-century figures in November 2014 to help a former Bishop Grosseteste University (BGU) student, DM added some for the twentieth century which are also published in *Twentieth Century Lincolnshire.*[9] It appears from this book that DM had studied census figures from 1801 up to 1921 and from 1971 onwards. He wrote in an email in November 2014 that 'it was the lack of internet resources of the right kind for the 20th century that prompted the situation arising last week' [i.e. helping the former BGU student].[10] Tables sent at that time give clear information on what DM had so far: Lincoln population figures up to 1921, national up to 1981 (except 1966). He had also a table of population by Lincoln parish for the nineteenth century.[11] Populations for Lincoln by ward for the twentieth century had not been obtained.

At the launch of The Survey of Lincoln's book *Birchwood, Hartsholme and Swanpool: Lincoln's Outer South-Western Suburbs*, in late November 2014, DM met David George (DGG) and the topic of twentieth-century population statistics came up.[12] The author (BRG) and DGG had been studying the development of the Birchwood and Doddington Park estates in Lincoln (1959-2012), so had looked at the population and housing figures in great detail. DM realised that DGG could probably provide information which had been difficult to access, making a complete run of population totals (down to a parish/ward level) for every census a viable prospect. Being an historical geographer, DM always envisaged maps to show the location of parishes and wards. Using The Survey of Lincoln website would enable anyone to get the information easily. The website states 'We considered that there was no readily accessible collation of material about the changing population of Lincoln so we have prepared these webpages to start to improve that.'[13]

THE TEAM

The initial team was made up of: the author (BRG), a local historian with recent research focussing on post-war Lincoln history; her husband David George (DGG), a Lincolnshire County Council planner, then working in planning policy, but formerly in demographic projections, lead roles on handling census data etc. and Geoff Tann (GT), freelance archaeological and historical researcher, secretary of The Survey of Lincoln between 2009 and 2019, and its website editor. Plus, of course, DM himself, with all his wealth of knowledge and experience. Rob Wheeler (RW) joined the team in March 2015. With expertise in statistics and maps (and extensive knowledge of Lincoln's history and geography), RW's eye for detail was invaluable.

Also involved were John Herridge (JH) (formerly a staff member of the City of Lincoln Heritage Team) and Alastair MacIntosh (AM) (City Archaeologist, City of Lincoln) who helped with the ward boundary information and the options for maps. Miriam Smith (MS) the editor of *The Lincoln Enquirer* also worked with DM and BRG on the article submitted to that publication.

ISSUES TO RESOLVE
Data Issues
The main issues were: obtaining data at the correct level (parish or extra-parochial areas, wards); making comparisons between censuses; and tackling problems relating to a specific census.

Data issues in the nineteenth century concerned mainly large institutions within parishes and extra-parochial (or 'xp') areas. Extra-parochial places were not within any ecclesiastical

Date: Tuesday, 25 November 2014 at 12:01 GMT

Dear Geoff and Dennis

Had a good look around the internet last night and a discussion with David. Our conclusions are as follows:

1.   It will be possible to give census totals for wards in Lincoln from 1901-2011 (no census 1941).
2.   With district and ward boundary changes, it will be tricky to give anything other than a broad indication of population change within a number of the wards. Sometime ward changes between censuses have been calculated by the Office of National Statistics (ONS), so these could be used.
3.   The paperwork associated with boundary changes - Boundary Commission etc - should be available in the Central Library and ought to have maps. I'm yet to check Lincs to the Past for anything which might be in Lincoln City Council's deposited papers at LAO.
4.   Hist Pop (http://www.histpop.org/ohpr/servlet/Show?page=Home) will cover the period up to 1937; 1951-61 vols are in the Central Library; 1971-81 seem to be only on fiche there (but need to recheck this); 1991 is on a number of formats and I know there are ward level statistics because David prepared them on behalf of Lincs County Council. (Incidentally, the 1991 census figures were considered unreliable, so we would have to mention that and give David's alternatives.) 2001 and 2011 are available via the Lincolnshire Research Observatory (http://www.research-lincs.org.uk/population.aspx) and ONS's Neighbourhood Statistics site - but I'll have to get David to explain to me how to use these sites properly.
5.   We will probably end up with a small table of population figures by ward and quite a bit of explanation and a number of diagrammatic maps. It should be enough for someone who is interested to work out what was going on and point them in the direction of further research - which sounds OK really!

This will take a bit of time to complete, but I'm quite happy to do the donkey work (and David is happy to advise). Would it be worth putting the 1801-1901 figures on asap and then adding the 20th century ones? Incidentally, the 1901 census gives both parish and ward totals, but I haven't worked out yet the connection between them (were all the wards made up from parishes or did any cross parish boundaries?).

best wishes

Beryl

Fig.1 Copy of email from BRG to DM and GT, 25 November 2014.

parish, as the name implies. Several xp areas had, however, been treated as enumeration districts (EDs) since 1841 so, for data purposes, were the same as parishes.

The complications of people resident in institutions at a census were mostly sorted out prior to the start of the project. For example, notes on the 1891 census from the same paper:

1891
* Pp 680 and 758 of the Report lists the transfers made under the Divided Parishes Acts to eliminate detached areas of parishes or to eliminate extra-parochial places:
Under 1882 Act, 24 March 1888 – Entire area of Holmes Common added to St Mary-le-Wigford to become St Mary and Holmes Common, 2 houses and 10 persons affected in 1891 census.
From St Peter-in-Eastgate, 10 houses and 52 people transferred to St Margaret, 65 houses in two areas and 627 persons to St Paul (see also note 7 below).
Entire area of Castle Dykings (45 houses and 179 persons) transferred to St Paul.
From Monks Liberty 3 houses and 15 persons transferred to St Peter-in-Eastgate.
Under 1882 Act, no date given, 1 house and 4 persons from St Nicholas to St Peter.
3. This population was in the County Hospital in a detached area of St John. The union of St Nicholas and St John had occurred by Order in Council, 4 June 1841 (LAO

Faculty Book 5, p. 433). However the census authorities ignored this until 1891 when they probably added the Newport portion of St John to St Nicholas.

4. St Martin included 105 persons in the County Asylum (Lawn).

5. St Mary-le-Wigford and Holmes Common included three persons in the Small Pox Hospital on Holmes Common.

6. St Nicholas included 262 in the Barracks and 156 persons in the Prison, therefore normal residents numbered 4,982.

7. St Paul included 312 in the Workhouse, therefore normal residents 1,262.[14]

There continued to be minor issues. For example, an email on 27 May 2015 mentioned a slight discrepancy between the source map for the nineteenth century and the transfer of a small amount of land to another parish.[15]

Census data in the twentieth century had another problem: the changes in technology meant that the ways of accessing it varied. There was extensive census (and related) information available online up to 1937 on the HistPop site; census reports in printed form for 1951

Ward Name	Created	Changed	Abolished
Abbey	1900	1967, 1979, 1999, 2007	
Birchwood	1979	1999, 2007	
Boultham	1967	1979, 1999, 2007	
Bracebridge	1967	1979, 2007	
Carholme	1900	1967, 1979, 2007	
Castle	1900	1967, 1979, 2007	
Ermine	1967		1979
Foss	1920	1959	1967
Glebe	1999	2007	
Hartsholme	1967 & 1999	2007	1979
Longdales	1979		1999
Minster	1900	1967, 1979, 1999, 2007	
Moorlands	1967	1979, 1999	
Park	1900	1967, 1979, 1999, 2007	
Tritton	1979		1999
Witham	1900		1967

Fig.2 Lincoln Wards 1900–2015 from George and Mills, 'Population of Lincoln', Table 5. The wards were current for 2015 – Birchwood and Hartsholme wards changed again in 2016.

and 1961 at the Lincoln Central Library; for 1971 and 1981 these were on microfiche at the same place; the 1991 census was accessible via DGG and 2001 and 2011 online via the Lincolnshire Research Observatory.[16] This information was outlined in an email to DM and GT at the start of the project (see Fig. 1).[17]

In addition to the different sources for twentieth-century census data, comparisons between censuses threw up a variety of issues.

1.   The move from parishes to wards as the main output area
Although censuses were taken from 1841 using enumeration districts (EDs) as their smallest unit, geographical data provided by the enumerators included both parish (or township) and ward from 1861.[18] Census reports continued to use parishes or townships as 'output areas' until 1901. From 1911, wards were used, but the reports for that census helpfully contained a comparative table linked to the civil parishes showing the change in population on the older boundaries. DM speculated on how the change might have been undertaken: 'A subsequent hypothesis for B and D to test out please is that each ward was made up of a multiple of parishes/EDs, so perhaps they effectively used the parishes again for the last time in 1911 (not 1901), added them together as appropriate to get the ward totals, then in 1921 used the wards only, with some appropriate subdivisions for enumerators.'[19]

It was decided that, in light of the difficulties of comparison beyond 1911, it would be better to give parish figures for the nineteenth century and ward ones for the twentieth.

2.   The Lincoln boundary extensions of 1920, 1959 and 1967
Lincoln experienced a significant boundary extension in 1920, when Bracebridge and Boultham and smaller parts of Bracebridge Heath, North Hykeham and Skellingthorpe were incorporated into the county borough. Fortunately, the 1921 census included comparative figures for these areas.[20] Similarly, when the Lincoln boundary was extended to include the former RAF Skellingthorpe in 1959, the 1961 census included a comparison to the 1951 census, taking this into account.[21] In 1967, the boundary change to the north-east of the city, was dwarfed by the changes in wards, but once again there was a comparative figure for the newly included area.[22]

3.   The lack of a census in 1941
No census was conducted in 1941, owing to the war, but the 1939 National Registration was used (with suitable caveats). Population figures immediately post-war were rather tenuous. DM questioned the reduction in population indicated in the 1939 National Registration saying: 'The reliability of the 1939 data is questionable. Did Lincoln really lose as many people in the 1930s and then have a sharp revival in the 1940s because of war, and postwar conditions? The only other decade of absolute decline was to be the 1960s.'[23]

This was investigated in more detail, using local newspaper reports of population and housing figures published by Lincoln Corporation used for calculating rates (and obtaining Government funding).[24] The National Registration figure was found to be largely in line with other estimates.

4.   Changes in ward boundaries especially from 1967 onwards
The largest problem with data proved to be the changes in ward boundaries, especially from 1967 onwards. These are summarised in Fig. 2.

DM gave his reaction to initial populations by ward in a draft dated 15 January 2015: 'Population by Ward – quite an effort here. The Victorian period was much easier as they

Survey of Lincoln
DRAFT OF CONTENTS FOR WEBSITE ENTRY re LINCOLN POPULATION

26.2.15

Visuals to illustrate the wide contrast in population totals between 1801 and 2011,
eg Pugin's painting of early 19C High St (central part), very few people about, cf.
modern photo from the same spot.
Simple introductory NOTE
Possible repeat of the simple table 1801-2011 from the article.

Present TABLE 1, Lin. popn. 1801-2011, totals and changes, with national
comparison.
Present TABLE 2, similar for England and Wales to nearest 1000.

Nineteenth century
NOTE on census taking and reports
Present TABLE 3, Lin. parishes and XP areas, pop totals, 2pp.
Present NOTES (footnotes) to table 2pp.
MAP of parishes from Mills and Wheeler.

Twentieth century
Present TABLE 4 Pop of civil parishes, 1901 and 1911 (this is a sort of transitional
table between the centuries, or between parishes and wards).
NOTE on Changes in Lincoln Wards, 1901-2011, probably also note on the main
functions of wards.
TABLES
Lincoln pop totals by ward 1901-2011
4 tables of comparisons (changes) by ward for four different periods, the first being
1901-67.
MAPS if available:
eg, 1901-67 and current situation , with some extra detail for wards that came and
went between 1967 and 2007.
----

*Fig.3 DM's first layout of website, dated 26 February 2015 sent with email from DM to BRG
and DDG, 26 February 2015.*

stuck rigidly to the ED boundaries. What I did, among other things, was to add Foss and
Witham 1961 together (25,975) and then added the five new wards together (39,041) and
discovered that there was a 'deficit' of 13,066 to 'explain'. I found that Castle lost 13,076,
and Carholme and Park lost a few 100s. Does that get us somewhere near what happened.
Obviously 'real' change was going on in that decade as well, but it just happens to be a decade
of relative stability …'[25]

But with a variety of inputs (especially from DGG), it was possible to make some comparisons
across censuses.[26]

5.   Compiling information for the ward maps

By early March 2015, much of the data had been compiled, but decisions needed to be made about how to display the twentieth-century ward material in map form. This involved two issues: obtaining the information on the exact boundaries of the wards from 1900 to 2015 and working out how to display these on a clear map or maps.[27] DM contacted JH to see whether a ward map for 1900 had been created prior to his retirement as an overlap for the Lincoln Heritage Database. It had been and the useful map was then made available by AM.[28]

Information on the other ward boundaries was found from a variety of sources: from mapping held by the County Council (provided by DGG); information on the Local Government Boundary Commission website; and ward maps deposited in Lincolnshire Archives by the City of Lincoln Council.

Technical Issues

Once the information had been obtained, how to display the twentieth-century changes to ward and district boundaries became a complex technical issue. After BRG raised the issue, DM turned his attention to this point in late March 2015, saying 'Obviously you need some help, so we must all rally round.'[29] There were two decisions to make: what to use as a base map and how to represent the wards on it. A number of options for the age of the base map were suggested by DM, JH, AM and RW from c.1900 to the modern day.[30] DM was aware of the drawbacks of any given date, emailing after he had worked on a mock up: 'I found it rather anachronistic to be putting names on a map where the colours relate to 1900, but the streets relate to about 2000! That sort of thing will probably be a problem whatever strategy we adopt. For the 19C we have a map that shows boundaries only, no streets.'[31]

The technique for display was also complex. The GIS system used by the City of Lincoln Council which produced the Lincoln Heritage Database was used under licence to that organisation. Other possibilities were to use the resources on the Ordnance Survey site or other free GIS software available online. It rapidly became obvious, however, that these would involve technical skills beyond BRG's capabilities. At a meeting of the team at DM's home on 23 May 2015, RW suggested using Google maps as the base, and adding on each map as a layer. This proved an ideal solution, with the organisation of the map layers decided within a few weeks. DM called it a 'natty proposal'.[32] The maps were completed by early July.[33]

Another technical issue was the layout of the website, with GT as website editor trying to come up with solutions to layout issues. There were decisions to be made about how to organise the information, since every table required explanation. There needed to be a balance of both information sections explaining why the changes (or otherwise) in the population might have occurred and tables giving the data in a clear and precise way. It was also necessary to have a lot of background for the tables and maps for the twentieth-century material to emphasise the changes to both district and ward boundaries.

A preliminary version of the layout was prepared by 6 January 2015, but this was intended as a basic structure to organise the (rapidly escalating) number of tables and explanatory notes.[34] DM prepared a first draft of website contents in late February 2015 (see Fig. 3). He described it as: '...a bit vague in a few places and you may like to tighten these up, where possible (or disagree, delete, add etc)'.[35]

Around the end of March 2015, there was a lot of discussion about how the information should be presented: what should be seen first and how the links should work. In response to

SUGGESTED RE BOXING, 20 March 2015   *Also a lot of text changes so use the versions below.*

Preliminaries

1.I suggest deleting the article now that Miriam has accepted it.
2.On home page install button: 'The population of Lincoln 1801-2011', possibly placed immediately above Giles 40"
3. Repeat this at the top of the screen that opens up at the press of the button.
4. Box 1 to appear below the title:

Introduction

Britain was later than many developed nations of the day in not taking a census until 1801. For several decades there had been arguments as to whether the number of poor people was increasing, either as an absolute figure, or as a proportion of the total population. Censuses were needed to make possible an analysis of the actual situation, but it was the threat of renewed war against France that brought about the first census in the spring of 1801. Since then, with the wartime exception of 1941, there have been censuses at every ten-year interval down to 2011, as well as a ten per cent 'sample' census in 1966.

5. We then need some device to get readers to move either on to 1801-1901 or 1901-2011. I am, of course, now going to concentrate on a sequence for the first period. I would like to see buttons corresponding to the box titles, eg on RH side of the Introduction or below it.

Box 2 with a new title as follows:

Nineteeth-century census-taking

In 1901 the Home Office set up the machinery for counting the people, which was based on a body of enumerators visiting each house in their enumeration districts in order to obtain answers to a very limited number of questions. In Lincoln, as in country areas and many other towns, the ancient parishes were much the most convenient areas for this purpose.

Fig.4 DM's suggestions for boxes in nineteenth century section, dated 20 March 2015 sent with private correspondence by email from DM to GT (copied to BRG, DGG and RW), 20 March 2015

GT's suggestion about using text boxes to help separate the material, DM prepared a version of how the various sections could be boxed (see Fig. 4 for extract), explaining his reasoning: 'But to begin at the beginning, which is what I did in order to help myself visualise what it would be like for the uninitiated. You will find that although I started out thinking only a few adjustments would be necessary, in fact in some ways I have done a root-and-branch job.'[36]

DM then had further thoughts: 'No doubt I would have been found out pretty soon, but overnight it occurred to me that there should be a button early on, e.g. in the Introduction

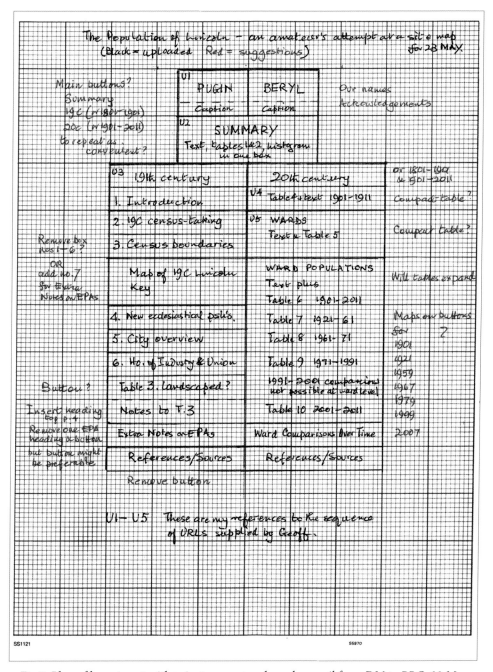

Fig.5 Plan of layout sent with private correspondence by email from DM to BRG, 22 May 2015.

box of the download, which allows the reader to go the summary tables, which, in many, probably most cases, may be all (s)he wants.'[37]

The organisation of the Population section went through a number of iterations. Before a meeting of the team held in late May, DM produced a plan to represent the structure as agreed by that time (see Fig. 5), which was very similar to the layout of the final webpages.

Working Methods

It may seem an obvious point to anyone who knew DM that he had researched and published with other people throughout his career and was not an academic who jealously guarded his personal status.[38] DM's interest in bringing together researchers in order that they could both challenge and encourage one another is also mentioned in his obituaries.[39] He was also keen that research should be published in some form, otherwise what really was the point?[40]

Another important factor was that everyone might make mistakes or take data at face value. A good example from this project was when he brought RW in to check for mistakes, misinterpretations or unclear points.[41]

DM was prepared to persevere if he was not happy with something. An example from this project was BRG taking a modern photograph of Lincoln's High Street from the same viewpoint that A. C. Pugin used for his painting which dated from *c.* 1819 (both the painting and modern photograph are displayed on the front page of the Population section). In the end, this took three occasions to get exactly what DM wanted. The changes to the High Street in Lincoln have been so great over 200 years (including dismantling St Peter at Arches church, the construction of the Waterside Centre and the installing of street furniture), it was very difficult to stand in the right place for the shot. There was also the possibility that Pugin 'cheated': that he used (literally) artistic licence. DM was always keen to say what he liked about the photographs, but still push towards confirming, or otherwise, the idea that Pugin painted what he saw. 'Just before the third round of photographs were taken, DM concluded: 'I would suggest that you try a shot from near the Nationwide BS and if the Stonebow is invisible we can say that Pugin "cheated".[42] In the event, the Stonebow was (just) visible, so Pugin was let off the accusation.

DM was keen on sending confirming emails after conversations or meetings so that everyone was clear about what had been decided and what the next steps might be.[43] He also copied emails of interest around to the team, so we all had the same information.[44] The team meeting on 23 May 2015 was planned in great detail, including how everyone was going to fit into his study with their laptops and who was to park on the drive![45]

Everyone involved in the project had other things to do and DM tried to make sure he allowed for other people's lives getting in the way. BRG had a child at primary school, so had to cover school holidays, GT had a work schedule and DM himself was occupied from mid-January to the latter part of February 2015 on editing his latest book.[46]

Although the primary communication method for this project was by email, DM made occasional telephone calls to talk through a point. There was one meeting of the team (DM, GT, BRG, RW) on 23 May 2015 at the Millses' home, and a further one on 8 June between DM and BRG. But there were also informal meetings at two of The Survey of Lincoln meetings (28 March 2015 and 9 June 2015) and a Research Seminar on 25 April 2015. DM

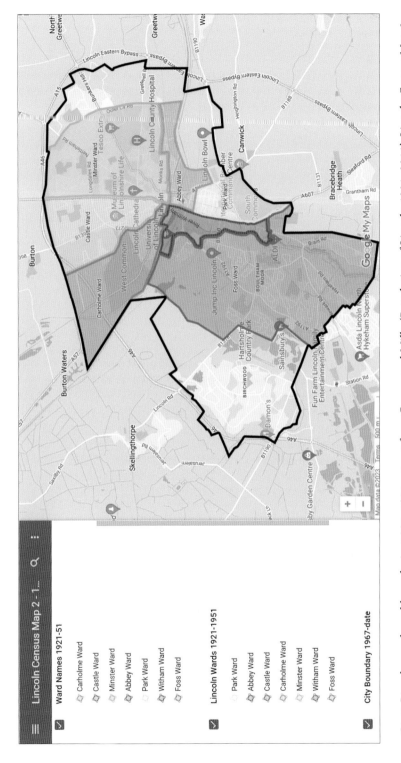

Fig.6 Lincoln wards and boundaries 1921–1951 extract from George and Mills, 'Population of Lincoln 1801–2011', Lincoln Census Map 2.

was a great believer in people informally chatting at meetings to help with specific queries or spark off new ideas.

NEW CHALLENGES

DM was quite open about when things were new to him. One example involves website construction, where he said: 'I don't find website construction very straightforward, this being my 1st experience…'[47]

It is clear from earlier emails that DM had a format in mind but was not sure if it was possible or not (and whether it would cause a huge amount of work). In the last stages of creating the online maps, DM concluded: 'I have been following the learned chat since your first email in the sequence, but I have nothing to add to that, being only an amateur in such matters. So please (all) accept my congratulations on a job so splendidly done.'[48] In general, DM was happy to try out new things in the software he had if these were explained sufficiently. He was aware that he may not always have the features on his (slightly earlier) version of the software.

ENCOURAGEMENT

Throughout the project, DM was keen to provide encouragement to keep everyone motivated. His initial reaction at the start was that he was: '… pleased that D [DGG] and G [GT] are so willing to take up the challenge – quite a stiff one from my own experience. The 19C is much easier!'[49]

With the courtesy of an earlier time, DM acknowledged emails if he had no time to reply and apologised for changing his mind. One example of this was an email titled 'Second Thoughts', in which he said: 'Quite a few second thoughts. Hope I've not wasted any of your time and that this effort is also not too premature.'[50] And then went on to outline his idea for a histogram to represent the increase in population to draw people in.

When the nineteenth-century parish population tables were uploaded onto the website in mid-March and niggles in the layout ironed out, DM replied to GT and BRG: 'Thanks very much for all the progress you have made.'[51] No doubt all the attention to getting every detail correct involved GT in a lot of extra work. This was especially true ahead of the team meeting in May, and DM was keen to encourage him, remarking on progress 'There is some jolly good stuff…' and 'I was especially pleased to see the parish boundary map.'[52]

Following the meeting, DM wrote: 'Many thanks for yesterday. I think we made splendid progress under your tutelage and have now broken the back of the work.'[53] DM also thanked the author on a number of occasions, for 'technical expertise' (on laying out a Word table); 'splendid progress' (on finding a solution for displaying the maps); and for the completed maps.[54]

BATON PASSING

Linked to the idea of encouragement was DM's inclusion of relevant snippets of information in his conversations or emails. Examples included: the ending of Enumerators' Books with 1901 census; the size of enumeration districts; his memories of the 1939 National Registration ('There were no household schedules as far as I can remember, just a bloke walking round, or so it seemed') and the work situation immediately after the war ('I turned down two offers I hadn't sought').[55] These were links to DM's previous work or reminders of the importance of personal memory as a source of pertinent historical information.

On the latter point, DM wrote in his introduction to *Twentieth Century Lincolnshire* that even though recent history will always have to be re-evaluated: 'to leave the writing of history entirely to succeeding generations is to abandon our duty at least to capture factual records made and the views of events and periods held by those who lived through them.'[56]

To the author it felt like passing the baton and there is nothing more encouraging than feeling that you need to take things forward yourself.

FRUITION
The website section was completed at the end of July 2015, some eight months after it was first proposed. Despite a website migration, the project remains on The Survey of Lincoln website and a possible update following the release of 2021 census data is being considered.

PUBLICITY
It is reasonable to suggest that DM was most keen for people to use published research: but they had to know it was available. So, publicity was important. As early as late November 2014, he proposed sending some kind of note drawing attention to the website pages, to be published in *The Lincoln Enquirer*, the members' newsletter of The Survey of Lincoln, which carries a number of short articles.[57] This became an article providing an overview of the entire population history of Lincoln, although concentrating on the 1801-2011 period.[58] Working with the editor, Miriam Smith, it went through a number of versions but helped to shape the background information which was to go on the website.

Once the website pages went live, DM sent emails around to his friends and former colleagues etc., drawing their attention to it.[59] If he had been from a younger generation and if social media had been more developed, no doubt DM would have been able to publicise it further, but his intention was clear.

CONCLUSION
The working methods DM used are illustrated here using one of his final projects. It is likely, however, that those who worked with him in earlier decades would recognise certain characteristics. A bringing together of a small team to collaborate; calling on other specialists where necessary. A strong work ethic (despite his years) and expecting the same of others. Attention to detail and wanting everything to be right. A willingness to accept new technology where this was a sensible option. Above all, enthusiasm for a huge variety of subjects and encouragement of others. Rob Wheeler said in his obituary:

> Not the least of the benefits Dennis conferred on Lincolnshire historical work was his encouragement of researchers from a wide range of backgrounds. A natural teacher, he had the gift of posing productive questions that can test or transform a hypothesis. He always set himself exacting standards and he encouraged others to live up to them, but in a gracious manner that exhorts rather than commands.[60]

I hope that many of these characteristics are clear from this case study. It is a good model for others to follow.

NOTES
1.   See a useful history in Weinbren, Daniel, 2019, '"To Support Active Empirical Research at the Grassroots": The Family and Community Historical Research Society', *Family & Community History*, Vol 22/1, April, pp. 4-21.

2.   See Weinbren, 2019 and History Workshop, 2023, 'About HWO' https://www.historyworkshop. org.uk/about-us/ [accessed 5 January 2023]. Obviously, there are many other current examples of organisations encouraging collaboration between historians from different types of background.

3.   George, Beryl and Mills, Dennis, 2015, 'The Population of Lincoln, 1801-2011', https://sites. google.com/site/thesurveyoflincoln/Projects/pop?authuser=0, [accessed 16 November 2022].

4.   Hill, Francis, 1974, *Victorian Lincoln*, Cambridge University Press, Appendices 1 and 2.

5.   Private correspondence by email from DM to BRG and GT on 6 December 2014.

6.   For example, Mills, Dennis and Schürer, Kevin, (eds), 1996, *Local Communities in the Victorian Census Enumerators' Books*, Leopard's Head Press, Oxford.

7.   Private correspondence by email from DM to BRG (for DGG as well) and GT on 24 November 2014.

8.   Mills, D. R. and Wheeler, R. C., 2004, *Historic Town Plans of Lincoln 1610-1920*, Lincoln Record Society, 92, Woodbridge, p. 12.

9.   Mills, Dennis R., (ed), 1989, *Twentieth Century Lincolnshire*, History of Lincolnshire, XII, Lincoln, p. 23.

10.   Private correspondence by email from DM to BRG (for DGG as well) and GT on 26 November 2014 (13.44 GMT).

11.   Three draft tables by DM received by the author on 6 December 2014 showing Lincoln's population totals 1801-1921 from census reports and the population of England and Wales 1801-1981 taken from Mitchell, B. R., 1988, *British Historical Statistics*, Cambridge, p. 9. Both of these tables included some notes on sources and decadal increases by number and percentage. The third table was of parish population totals from 1801-1901 from census reports.

12.   George, Beryl and George, David 'The Birchwood Estate: planning a neighbourhood' and 'Doddington Park: the second front' in Walker, Andrew (ed), 2014, *Birchwood, Hartsholme and Swanpool: Lincoln's Outer South-Western Suburbs*, The Survey of Lincoln, Lincoln, pp. 54-57 and pp 58-61. Unusually, we were both at the book launch.

13.   George and Mills, *Population of Lincoln*, home page.

14.   Mills, Dennis, 2014 'Lincoln Parishes and Extra-Parochial Areas, 1801-1901, Population Totals' unpublished paper, p. 3.

15.   Private correspondence by email from DM to BRG on 27 May 2015.

16.   Hist Pop is available at: http://www.histpop.org/ohpr/servlet/Show?page=Home [accessed 18 November 2022]; General Register Office, 1955, *Census 1951 England and Wales: County Report. Lincolnshire and Rutland*, HMSO; General Register Office, 1964, *Census 1961 England and Wales: County Report. Lincolnshire (Parts of Lindsey)*, HMSO; 1971 and 1981 census reports turned out to be available in printed form at the Lincoln Central Library; Lincolnshire Research Observatory is available at: : https://www.research-lincs.org.uk/Home.aspx [accessed 18 November 2022].

17.   Private correspondence by email from BRG to DM, GT copied to DGG on 25 November 2014.

18.   See Mills and Schürer, *Local Communities*, p. 17 and Higgs, Edward, 1989, *Making Sense of the Census*, HMSO, p.133.

19.   Private correspondence by email from DM to BRG and GT on 6 January 2015.

20.   See *Census of England and Wales, 1921, County of Lincoln [and Rutland]*. Table 6: Intercensal Changes in Boundaries of Administrative and Registration Areas in between 3 April 1911 and 19 June 1921, Lincolnshire and Rutland, BPP 1923/4, p. 21.

21.   See General Register Office, 1964, *Census 1961, England and Wales County Report, Lincolnshire (Parts of Lindsey)* Table 4: Intercensal Changes of Boundary (between 8 April 1951 and 23 April 1961), HMSO, p. 8.

22. See Office of Population, Censuses and Surveys, 1973, *Census 1971, England and Wales County Report, Lincolnshire (Parts of Kesteven and Lincoln CB) Part 1.* Table 2: Population 1951-1971 and intercensal variations, HMSO, p. 1.

23. Private correspondence by email from DM to BRG on 18 January 2015, contained in note on draft version of Table 1.

24. For example, *Lincolnshire Echo*, 4 November 1938, p. 4, col. 5. Mid-Year Estimates were used for rate support calculations from 1930 onwards.

25. Private correspondence by email from DM to BRG on 18 January 2015.

26. Private correspondence by email from BRG (copied to DGG) to DM on 14 February 2015.

27. Private correspondence by email from BRG to GT (copied to DGG and DM) on 3 March 2015.

28. Private correspondence by email from DM to JH (copied to AM) and AM to DM and JH on 21 April 2015.

29. Private correspondence by email from DM to BRG (copied to GT and RW) on 25 March 2015 (16:13 GMT).

30. See private correspondence by email from RW to BRG (copied to DM) on 28 March 2015; from BRG to DM on 21 April 2015 and from DM to BRG on 21 April 2015.

31. Private correspondence by email from DM to BRG (copied to RW) on 28 April 2015.

32. Private correspondence by email from DM to BRG on 11 June 2015.

33. Private correspondence by email from BRG to DM, RW, GT and DGG, 8 July 2015.

34. Private correspondence by email from GT to DM, BRG (and DG), 6 January 2015.

35. Private correspondence by email from DM to BRG and DGG, 26 February 2015.

36. Private correspondence by email from DM to GT (copied to BRG, DGG and RW), 20 March 2015.

37. Private correspondence by email from DM to GT, BRG, DGG and RW, 21 March 2015.

38. See, for example, the bibliography in Brook, Shirley, Walker, Andrew and Wheeler, Rob, (eds) 2011, *Lincoln Connections: aspects of City and County since 1700*, Society for Lincolnshire History and Archaeology, Lincoln, pp. 12-15 which contains numerous examples of collaborative publications.

39. For example, Jackson, Andrew J. H., and Walker, Andrew, 2021, 'Dennis Mills (1931-2020): an appreciation and assessment', *The Local Historian*, January, Vol 51: 1, pp. 57-61 and Wheeler, Rob, 2020, 'Dennis Mills (1931-2020): Death of a notable Lincolnshire historian', http://www.slha.org.uk/news/index.php?year=2020#apm1_6 [accessed 5 January 2023]. The obituary by Rob Wheeler was adapted from the biography included in Brook, Walker and Wheeler, 2011 *Lincoln Connections*.

40. The author remembers that at one of her earliest meetings with DM, he came along with a note of possible avenues for the publication of her MA thesis research.

41. First suggested in private correspondence by email from DM to BRG, 21 February 2015.

42. Private correspondence by email from DM to BRG, 11 May 2015.

43. For example, private correspondence by email from DM to BRG (for DGG as well) and GT on 24 November 2014.

44. For example, emails to and from JH and AH concerning possible ward maps on 21 April 2015.

45. Private correspondence by email from DM to GT, RW and BRG on 6 May 2015 and DM to BRG on 14 May 2015.

46. Mills, Dennis R, 2015, *Effluence and Influence: Public Health, Sewers and Politics in Lincoln, 1848-1850*, Society for Lincolnshire History and Archaeology, Lincoln.

47. Private correspondence by email from DM to BRG, 15 May 2015.

48. Private correspondence by email from DM to BRG, RW and GT, 21 July 2015.

49. Private correspondence by email from DM to BRG, DGG and GT on 26 November 2014 (13.53 GMT).

50. Private correspondence by email from DM to BRG and DGG, 22 February 2015.

51. Private correspondence by email from DM to GT and BRG, 18 March 2015.

52. Private correspondence by email from DM to GT (copied to BRG and RW), 19 May 2015.

53. Private correspondence by email from DM to GT, 24 May 2015.

54. Private correspondence by email from DM to BRG (copied to DGG, GT and RW), 12 March 2015; from DM to BRG and AM, 29 April 2015, (15:35) and from DM to BRG, RW and GT (copied to DGG), 9 July 2015.

55. Private correspondence by email from DM to BRG, 11 December 2014 (16.04); DM to BRG and GT, 6 January 2015; DM to BRG, 18 January 2015; DM to BRG, 26 January 2015.

56. Mills, 1989, *Twentieth Century Lincolnshire*, p. 12.

57. First mentioned in private correspondence by email from DM to GT and BRG, 26 November 2014 (13.44).

58. George, Beryl and Mills, Dennis, 2015, 'The Population of Lincoln', *The Lincoln Enquirer*, 29, pp. 4-6

59. Private correspondence by email from DM to various individuals, 22 July 2015.

60. Wheeler, 2020, 'Dennis Mills'.

THE SWAN FAMILY OF LINCOLN, 1754 – 1946[1]

Victoria Thorpe

This article consolidates research that my father, Dennis Mills, and myself have undertaken to examine the history of the Swan family of Lincoln. It begins with the arrival of the Swan family in Lincolnshire and the first records of the family in the Cornhill area of Lincoln in 1754. The article then examines how, across several generations, the Swan family established itself in the city, first in Cornhill and then latterly in a number of uphill residences. Attention is paid to the lives and professional careers of a number of key members of the family including Robert Swan the elder, John Swan and Robert Swan II and his wife Lucy. The Swan family's central involvement in the residential development of nineteenth-century Lincoln is explored, as is its engagement in varied activities ranging from dairying to brickmaking. The ways in which the family maintained its position amongst the city's most prominent citizens, in part through a series of significant marriage alliances, is also examined.

INTRODUCTION

This consideration of one family across two centuries reveals how social and economic status could be maintained within one urban centre and also demonstrates the impact a single family could have upon the development of a city. The Swans are purported to have arrived from Scotland to Swinderby. The family story is that Henry Swan acquired property and land from funds gained whilst serving as surgeon to Charles Edward Stuart.[2] However, Burke's Family Records states that they came from Glasgow with General Monck, some seventy years earlier.

The earliest reference found to a Henry Swan being resident in Swinderby was from the Register of Duties Paid for Apprentices of 1715, where he is listed as a carpenter with an apprentice from Swinderby.

Henry Swan I (1687-1755) founded a dynasty of surgeons, four of whom were also named Henry. When Henry I died at Swinderby, he left considerable property, some of it in that parish.[3] His sons Francis and Henry II (1715-82) were both surgeons, Francis at Collingham, and Henry II at Swinderby, later at Lincoln

THE SWAN FAMILY'S EARLY YEARS IN CORNHILL, LINCOLN:
THE HENRY SWANS AND ROBERT SWAN THE ELDER, c.1754-1828

The first reference found to a Swan occupying property in the Cornhill area of Lincoln occurs in 1754 as one of the abutments of a property on the site of the present Halifax Bank and W. H. Smith's.[4] More detail emerges in an auction sale of 1762, held for the Peart family, when Henry Swan II was the highest bidder for one of six lots, for which he paid the substantial sum of £605. This comprised a freehold messuage, an adjoining piece of leasehold ground in the Cornhill, and a grass close, all in St Mary-le-Wigford parish. The leasehold was a very small area, 'taken out of the Corn Market Hill', twenty-two by six yards. This ran north-south, putting six yards between the messuage and the stalls on the market hill.[5]

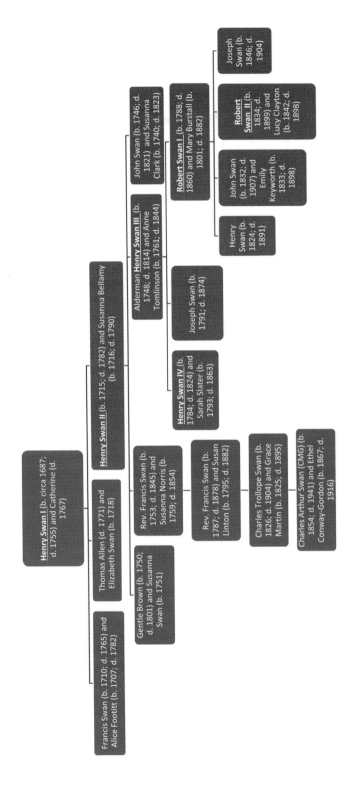

Fig.1 The Swan family tree – simplified over five generations, c.1687 – 1900

Fig.2 A 2013 view of the Corn Exchange of 1848 looking east. The site of the Swan residence probably stretched from the back of Thornton's shop (far left in St Benedict parish), southwards to the road in front of W H Smith's (right hand side). To the rear and eastwards the grounds reached Elder Lane, now Sincil Street. The 'necessary' mentioned in the text may be represented by a small building shown on Padley's plan on the site of the new Corn Exchange of 1879, the building with the distinctive tower. Photo: Dennis Mills.

In 1792 **Henry Swan III** insured his whole estate in Lincoln and a number of villages and the account gives details of the Cornhill property.[6] The buildings were all brick and tiled and comprised (1) a dwelling house, (2) stable and chamber over, and (3) a (second) house and shop 'under one roof with building and offices adjoining', the house occupied by Robert Green. Then follows 'Chiphouse only near, brick and stone and tiled; and coach house and chamber over in St Mary's Lane', both of which need elucidation. Carpenters were sometimes known as chippies, which might be a clue as to the use of the 'chiphouse'. Perhaps it was where a servant sawed logs and chopped sticks for the house. 'Only near', meaning 'close by', is probably to point out the contrast with the coach house. Later evidence shows the latter would have been approached from the dwelling by a drive down the garden to Elder Lane (Sincil Street) thence into St Mary's Lane (now Street). This property is most probably that shown as belonging to Swan on a map of 1792.[7] We have placed this at the east end of the present station forecourt, but it had gone before J. S. Padley drew his 1842 plan.

The next relevant document occurs in 1814 in the form of the will of Henry Swan III, (1749-c.1814).[8] He was a surgeon and apothecary, who had been mayor in 1779, 1785 and 1797.[9] His trustees were his brothers John and Francis Swan, as well as his brother-in-law George Gordon, Dean of Lincoln Cathedral, 1809-45.[10] So, although Henry III lived in a below-hill parish, he had become a member of the 'cathedral set'. This was an advantage to his son Robert, of whom more later, who was to become chapter clerk.

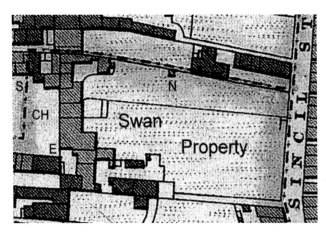

Fig.3
From Padley's 1842 map.
CH = Cornhil, E = Entrance,
N = possible position of the
'necessary', S = Stable. The
broken line running north -
south between S and CH is
the parish boundary with St
Benedict's to the W (left) and
St Mary le Wigford. This turns
east at the top of the extract, the
boundary of the Swan property
following it to Sincil Street

Henry's residence was described in his will as 'my messuage and dwelling house with the garden and other appurtenances... and so much of my piece of leasehold land as lies in front thereof'. 'Robert is to have part of the garden'. He is said to 'occupy the room part of the house as an office; and the stable, [the] bedchamber over the shop and surgery and [the] chambers over the [apothecary's] shop'.

The whole messuage was to pass to two of Henry's sons, Henry IV (the eldest son) and Robert. Probably they were each to inherit the rooms they currently occupied, plus in due course the small number of rooms continued to be occupied by their parents, followed by their widowed mother. Henry and Robert were directed to take down an outshot in Robert's share, as they were to construct 'a wall at least six feet high … from the northeast corner of the dwelling house … in a straight easterly direction to the top of the slope being in length about thirty feet and from thence in a northerly direction to the necessary [the toilet].'

When the lease of the small area in front of the residence was renewed in 1821, it shows that Mrs Ann Swan, Henry's widow, was living in the southerly part of the dwelling, her eldest son in the northerly part. The plan suggests that Mrs Swan's gateway at the south end of the building corresponded approximately to the modern street between Santander Bank and W. H. Smith's.[11]

The 1828 Valuation used in conjunction with Padley's 1842 plan, confirms the Cornhill as the location.[12] The north side of the Cornhill from the High Street to the site of Thornton's shop was in the parish of St Benedict, and the remainder of the Swan property was situated in St Mary-le-Wigford. The Valuation contains the following relevant entries:

> St Mary-le-Wigford.
>
> Within 'Boundary no 1 – The Cornhill West and North, the High-Street West, St Mary's Lane South, Elder Lane East, the parish of St Benedict North':

Robert Swan's entry is the first:

> House, &c., and Garden occupied by T. Clark, Surgeon, annual value £30.

Surgery, with small Warehouse, occupied by J. Swan & Co. Surg, £8.

House, Stables, Gardens, &c, occupied by Sarah Swan, £70.

St Benedict.

Robert Swan, Esq., Stables, &c, and Yard at north-east corner of the
Cornhill, occupied by T. Clark, Surgeon, £7.

The total valuation came to over £100 at a date when small cottages were valued at less than
£5 each. The analysis can be started with the stables belonging to Robert Swan in the north-
east corner of the Cornhill within St Benedict's parish, which are assumed to be contiguous
with the properties listed under St Mary. Whilst one cannot assume that the authors of
the published valuation, Edward Betham and Edward Willson recorded their entries in a
geographical order, their sequence does suggest that the Swan territory, including the two
gardens, comprised most of the block facing the east end of the Cornhill and running
through to Elder Lane (Sincil Street).

Henry Swan IV died in 1824 having been both sheriff and mayor of the city. He left his widow
Sarah in a dwelling which he had presumably bequeathed to his brother Robert, the couple
being childless. In White's 1826 directory the medical practice is described as Swan and
Macaulay but is given as Swan and Clark in Pigot's 1828-29 directory. The surgery was also
used by Joseph Swan, a younger brother. He had been surgeon at Lincoln County Hospital
1814-2 but gave up that post in order to move to London.[13] According to the Valuation, Mrs
Ann Swan, Henry III's widow was living in Minster Yard by 1828.

However, Mrs Sarah Swan was still at the Cornhill in 1828-29, but in April 1835 she was
advertising the property to let from an address in Minster Yard. It was described as:

> A Capital Messuage on the Cornhill, with stables for six horses, coach
> house, saddle room and brewhouse, and other extensive buildings in
> the yard, together with a very large garden well stocked with fruit trees,
> and an excellent hot house. The House comprises dining, drawing and
> breakfast rooms, two kitchens, storerooms, pantries, and very good
> arched cellars,[14] nine excellent bedrooms, besides a dressing room and
> water closet, servants' bedrooms, and other conveniences.[15]

There seems to have been a large number of bedrooms compared with downstairs rooms,
which might be explained by the use of some of the latter as a surgery and shop. In the
following December Mrs Capp announced that she had rented the property from Mrs
Swan so that she could move her 'ladies' seminary' into it. As she made the point that 'The
sleeping apartments are peculiarly airy and commodious', Mrs Capp had probably been
attracted by the numerous bedrooms.[16] Until the property was taken down, according to
frequent press advertisements, it continued to be used by both a school and a medical
practice.

In 1821, the lease had cost the Swans an extra £1 fine for being in arrears with renewal
by eleven years, and they were late again with the renewal, due in 1831, which became an
issue in 1835. After some disagreeable exchanges of views between Robert Swan and the
corporation, the latter in 1839 decided to risk a court action by removing the posts and
chains and throwing the land into the vegetable market.[17]

Clearly the demands of commerce were getting close to the Swan house. A good deal of modernisation occurred in Lincoln in the 1840s, including efforts to accommodate the markets more suitably and the three livestock markets were removed to a site along Monks Road. In 1844 Robert Swan decided to put his property up for sale by auction on 21 November, including:

> Lot 1. All that Messuage, being No. 5. Cornhill in the parish of St. Mary le Wigford, with the Out-buildings Yard and large Garden belonging thereto, now in the occupation of Mr. Roome, and a room belonging to the same house in the occupation of Mr. Howitt, surgeon.
>
> Lot 2. Another Messuage, being Nos. 3 and 4. Cornhill, North of the above, with the Surgery, Stables, Coach house, and Garden thereto belonging, now in the occupation of Mr. Howitt.[18]

Mr and Mrs Roome were the owners of the school first brought to the building by Mrs Capp. The buyer was not the corporation, since the *Stamford Mercury* reported that:

> The spacious premises at the back of the Cornhill which the Town Clerk at a recent meeting of the Lighting and Paving Commissioners intimated it was very desirable should be secured for the purpose of providing a Corn Exchange for Lincoln, have, it is stated, been purchased by Mr. Mackinder, Mere Hall. The late Mayor is also stated to be connected with the purchase; and, as report goes, the old premises are to be taken down, and a splendid inn erected. Whether, in conjunction with the inn, a Corn Exchange is to be provided, we do not hear.[19]

However, in 1845 there was more discussion about the possibility of 'providing more comfort for farmers and corn merchants' and the chief merchants, William and Edward Rudgard and Charles Seely offered to pay [rent] for standing. A public company was set up with corporation approval and it laid the foundation stone of the Corn Exchange in September 1847, the building opening the next year with merchants' stalls set out.[20]

Robert Swan (1788-1860) is presumed to have been born in the family's Cornhill property. He was sent to the Grammar School, then in Greyfriars. In 1804, at the age of sixteen, Robert was articled to George Tennyson, an attorney of Grimsby, with whom the Swans had a distant marriage connection. Tennyson was deeply involved in the Grimsby Haven scheme to improve port facilities, a company in which Henry Swan had invested money mentioned in his will. Robert Swan probably lived in Grimsby during his clerkship, but at that time Tennyson lived in part of Deloraine Court, James Street.[21]

When Swan died in 1860, an obituary indicated that he was admitted to his profession at the usual age, after seven years as an articled clerk with Tennyson.[22] At the very early age of twenty-four, he was appointed clerk to the Witham Navigation Company at the First Meeting of Proprietors, 11 June 1812. Proprietors present included Mr Swan, Rev F. Swan, Robert Swan, and Henry Swan. Rev F. Swan was also attending as proxy of Mr James Tomlinson Terrinist. Swan was a member of the Navigation Commissioners prior to the 1812 Act coming into effect to replace the Commissioners with the Company.[23]

Fig.4 Number 20 Minster Yard is the house with two bay windows, with an extension to the right served by a second black door (perhaps giving access to the rear). In the 1828 Valuation the house, said to be next to the arch, making it number 19, was valued at £16; Robert Swan's at £45, which would fit number 20 if it was as now. Photo: Dennis Mills, 2013.

In 1826 Robert Swan, as clerk to the Company, obtained the Bill under which the navigation of the River Witham was improved.[24] Although he was to receive most of his high income from such clerkships, Swan also undertook a certain amount of work in private practice as a solicitor, as from at least 1811 there were several notices a year in the *Stamford Mercury*, in which he was acting in property sales.[25]

On 2 October 1816 he had acquired the clerkship to the Lincoln Court of Sewers which administered the drainage of the city and the surrounding countryside. He was to relinquish this post in May 1831. In 1817 he was appointed clerk to the Lindsey magistrates (Lincoln District).[26]

Robert Swan's most important appointment came in 1821, when he was appointed chapter clerk and deputy registrar of the Diocese of Lincoln, effectively the man who did the work on behalf of the registrar and was able to add to these various other fee-paying posts within the diocese. According to his obituary he gained the appointments because of the influence of the Gordon family.[27] George Gordon, the Dean, was the husband of one of his maternal aunts. Perhaps Gordon's influence amounted to introducing Swan and John Fardell jun. to each other when the latter wished to retire. On 26 March 1821 Swan paid Fardell the considerable sum of £7000 for his business as a proctor (an ecclesiastical lawyer) 'and divers other employments he had exercised', including the registrar-ship and the chapter clerkship.[28]

This seems hardly credible to the modern mind, but such nepotism was the general practice with many public posts at this time. Swan was to live through a period of great change in this respect, and when he was obliged in 1858 to relinquish the proctorship of the Lincoln Probate Court, one of the most lucrative of his posts, he acquired in compensation a pension approaching £2000.[29]

In the late eighteenth century the Register Office was in the north gatehouse of the Close, on the site of the present Priory Gate.[30] Swan may have worked there for a time, but his directory entry in 1822 was as an attorney in Eastgate. By 1826 he was in the Exchequergate, using freehold offices, now Exchequergate Lodge (to the west of the Arch).[31] The Exchequergate was to be the registrar's office for many years.

Swan was a member of the old unreformed council in 1825-26, and was elected to the reformed council in 1837-40 and 1843-59, becoming an alderman in 1847. He was the first Conservative elected to the reformed council but was said to be an 'enlightened reformer', with interests in education and a prominent advocate of underground sewerage, member of the sanitary committee, 1847-50, chairman during this critical period of debate.[32] There is a memorial window in Robert Swan's name in the south aisle of the cathedral nave (SG45).

MOVING UPWARDS: ROBERT SWAN THE ELDER, HIS CONTEMPORARIES AND THEIR UPHILL RESIDENCES, c.1828-60

It is not until 1828 that we have found any evidence as to where Swan lived, although there are plenty of reasons to think that it was in the Close. According to the Valuation of that year, Robert owned a house near the Exchequergate, number 20, one of the 'Number Houses' north of the Gate (see Fig. 4).

Fig.5 Number 12 Minster Yard, the northern part of the property formerly known as Graveley Place. It is L-shaped with an east-west range running back from the right hand side of the streetside range. Photo: Dennis Mills, 2013.

Fig.6 Number 13 Minster Yard. According to Stanley Jones (The Survey of Ancient Houses in Lincoln - II), *the right hand and smaller part in a darker rendering was built about 1750, the remainder towards the east at various dates over the next 100 years. Photo: A. Walker, 2023.*

The annual value was put at £45, greater than the figure for nearby houses.[33] Although the Valuation described Swan as the proprietor, he was in fact leasing the property from the Dean and Chapter, a restriction that applied to the other houses he later owned in the Close. In 1831 he was advertising a house in his own occupation in Minster Yard for sale or to let. It contained 'dining, drawing, and breakfast rooms, bedrooms, with 3 dressing-rooms, servants' rooms, kitchens, store-room, excellent cellars, and other conveniences, also a Coach house and Stable'.[34] In 1834 Swan obtained a piece of ground of 142 square yards, south of the White Hart stables and west of 'premises' already belonging to him, suggesting that his offer of 1831 had at least not led to a sale.[35] These references were probably all to the same house, and it is not until the 1841 census that more solid ground is reached with the first reference to 12 Minster Yard on the east side of the cathedral. His household consisted of fourteen people: Swan and his wife, six children, a governess and four female servants and one male.

In 1851 the address is given as 12b, whilst at 12a there lived John G. S. Smith, Judge of the Lincoln County Court. The judge had a household of only four persons, but now Swan had no less than seventeen in his house: Swan himself and his wife, five children, a governess, his sister-in-law with a daughter, and five female servants and two male, a groom and a footman. A lease plan of 1820 shows that the whole house contained only two 'low' rooms and an entrance, three chambers, three garrets and a wash house; a little larger in 1855.[36] The property hardly seems to have been big enough for twenty-one people. In 1856 Swan's address was given as 13 Minster Yard, across the road from number 12 and on the south

Source	Robert Swan	Mrs Ann Swan	Revd Francis Swan	Mrs Sarah Swan (widow of Henry IV)
1790 Poll book			Silver St, see Sarah's column later.	
1826 White (county)		Mrs Swan, no initial - Cornhill	Grecian Place now Greestone Place	Mrs Swan, no initial - Cornhill
1828 City Valuation	Probably 20 Minster Yd, a 'number house'. Office in Exchequergate	Minster Yd Proprietor	Grecian Place (sequence suggests no.2) FS = proprietor	Cornhill, but Robert was proprietor
1828-29 Pigot (county)	Minster Close	Minster Yd	Grecian Place	
1835 Pigot (county)	Chapter Clerk, Minster Close	Minster Yd 1836 D&C lease for no. 7 shows her at no. 8	Grecian Place	Cornhill, later in Minster Yd as letting Cornhill
1841 Census	12 Minster Yd. 14 in household	8 Minster Yd – 6 people in household	2 Grecian Place – 6 people in household	Not found anywhere in Lincoln
1842 White (county)	12 Minster Yd	8 Minster Yd	2 Grecian Place	14 Silver St
1843 Victor and Baker (city)	12 Minster Yd (Office 3 Exchequergate)	8 Minster Yd (d. 25 May 1844)	2 Grecian Place	14 Silver St
1849 Kelly (county)	Minster Yd	Deceased	Mrs F Swan at 2 Grecian Place (Francis had died in 1845)	Silver St house for sale, February 1845
1851 Census	12b Minster Yd. 17 in household.		No further entries	Rock Park, Higher Bibbington, Wirral, Cheshire
1856 White (county)	13 Minster Yd			
1861 Census	Minster Yd – Mrs Mary A. Swan, Robert's widow – 14 in household			Rock Park, Higher Bibbington, Wirral, Cheshire

Fig.7 Swan addresses from 1790 poll book, directories, 1828 Valuation, and census enumerators' books to 1861.

side of the cathedral.[37] In 1861, after his death in 1860, his widow Mary Ann was still living somewhere in the Minster Yard, quite probably in this house, which in 1872 was occupied by their eldest son John, who had become diocesan registrar.[38] Mrs Swan was listed in the census enumerator's book as a landed proprietor; she still had five unmarried adult children living with her, the same sister with a daughter, and six servants including a groom and a butler.

So far we have talked about Swan's property in Cornhill and The Close. Robert Swan's contemporaries' houses were 'above hill', except for 15 Silver Street, which one could describe as a step in that direction. Robert Swan's sister-in-law, Mrs Sarah Swan (the widow of Henry Swan IV), was still at the Cornhill in 1828-29, but in April 1835 she was advertising the property to let from an address in Minster Yard. Evidently the latter was only temporary, as that year she had already on 28 March bought the lease on 15 Silver Street from the Corporation. It was on the south side of Silver Street, between Free School Lane and Broadgate, separated from the Lane by one other property, and now part of the NCP car park. In 1828, 15 Silver Street had been occupied by Robert Bousfield, a surgeon, and he had a garden and stables.[39] At this date, the upper end of Silver Street was much less commercialised than the lower end near the High Street. Indeed, the block of territory between Free School Lane and Bank Street, long the property of the Lincoln Co-operative Society, was still a large residence called Palfrey Place, set in grounds and occupied by Thomas Brogden, an auctioneer and later the owner of the *Lincolnshire Chronicle*.[40] Sarah Swan sold number 15 in 1845 for £1100 having paid only £525 for it in 1835. It was described in the following terms:

> SILVER-STREET, LINCOLN. VALUABLE FREEHOLD ESTATE. To be SOLD by AUCTION
>
> By Mr. Hitchins, At the Saracen's Head, Lincoln, on Tuesday the 4th day of March next, at Six o'clock in the Evening, unless previously disposed of by private contract, of which due notice will be given, ALL that excellent DWELLING-HOUSE, with Garden, Stables, and convenient Out-buildings adjoining, situate Silver-street, in the city of Lincoln, as now in the occupation of Mrs. Henry Swan. This desirable residence comprises Dining and Drawing Rooms, Store-room, Two Kitchens, Five good Lodging-rooms, Water-closets, excellent Cellars, Forcing Pumps, and replete with every convenience for a genteel family. The property Freehold, and being pleasantly situated, is very eligible. For view apply at the house, and for further particulars, to Mr. ROBERT OWSTON, solicitor, Brigg. 11th Feb., 1845.[41]

No further references to Mrs Sarah Swan in Lincoln have been found. She later moved to Rock Park, Higher Bibbington on The Wirral in Cheshire, where she was enumerated in the censuses of both 1851 and 1861. She died in 1863. Her late husband's uncle, the Revd Francis Swan, the younger brother of Henry Swan III, was baptised at Swinderby in 1753. He was living in Silver Street in 1790, but all the other addresses we have for him from 1826 are in Grecian Place (now Greestone Place), said to be number 2 in 1841, 1842 and 1843, the latter just before he died in 1845 at the great age of 92 years. This was a large house even before the north extension erected after Francis's death. The size was more than big enough for the household, as Francis and his wife Susanna Norris had only two children. At the 1841 census there were only six people in the house: Francis and Susanna, three servants and a ten-year-old child, Mary Swan, presumably their grand-daughter Mary Charlotte Swan, born around 1832. Francis held several livings in Lincoln and elsewhere, and he is remembered in a memorial window in the north aisle of the Cathedral suggesting that he left his family well-endowed.[42]

Francis Swan was followed as head of the family by his son, another Revd Francis, who had migrated to the countryside, buying the advowson of Sausthorpe near Spilsby in 1819. He was instituted to the living as rector and in 1822 built the New Hall on the site of an earlier house. In 1838 Francis II bought the manor and estate of Sausthorpe, thus becoming the village's squarson.'[43] On his mother's death after 1849, this branch of the Swans was without a house in Lincoln, but nevertheless very active as developers of land in the lower city.[44]

Robert Swan's mother Ann was widowed in 1814, and her husband, Henry III, had willed that his chief heirs, his sons Henry IV and Robert, were to share the Cornhill property in such a way that their mother also had accommodation within it.[45] Perhaps the area had become less salubrious than it had been in 1760s, with the markets expanding in front of the house. Ann had moved from Cornhill by 1828, when she is first recorded as living in the Minster Yard. Not only was she then near her brother-in-law Francis, but more pertinently

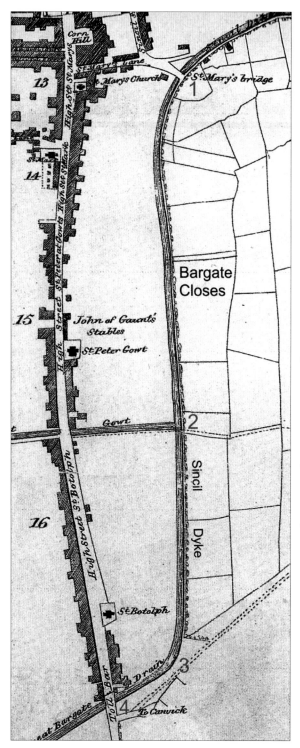

near her sister Sarah who, as Mrs George Gordon, was mistress of the Deanery.[46] When a precise address became available in 1836 it was 8 Minster Yard. Again, this is a very large house, of which Robert was the head lessee. He appeared to have been intent on making it even larger at that date by adding number 7 to it.[47] However, at the 1841 census Mrs Swan was occupying only number 8 which seems under-populated. It contained only Mrs Swan, four servants, and her daughter Sophia, aged 'about 35', but actually almost forty.

Mrs Swan died on 25 May 1844 and her son Robert took the opportunity to offer numbers 7 and 8 for sale at the same time as he sold the Cornhill property. She is referred to as the late occupier of one of the messuages, with a Bromhead as sub-lessee in the other:

> LINCOLN. — To be SOLD by AUCTION, By Mr. Melton, the City Arms Inn in Lincoln, on Thursday the 21st day of November, 1844, at 4 o'clock in the Afternoon …
>
> Lot 3. Two Messuages, being Nos. 7 & 8 Minster Yard in the parish of St. Margaret, with the Stable and Garden at the back thereof, one of which Messuages was lately in the occupation of Mrs. Swan, and the other now in the occupation of Mr. Alexander Bromhead.[48]

Perhaps number 8 did not get sold, as it is associated with the Swan family at dates later than 1844. In 1872, White's Directory of Lincolnshire gave Mrs Swan, Robert's widow, as occupier. In 1892 White listed the occupiers as the Misses A. C. and A. M. Swan. Even in 1901 the census recorded the occupier as Annie Caroline Swan, aged 72, spinster daughter of Robert, with a cook and housemaid.

THE CLERICAL SWANS AND THE DEVELOPMENT OF LINCOLN'S BARGATE CLOSES: BUILDING BRIDGES AND RESIDENTIAL STREETS

Now we move on to look at the clerical Swans, who migrated to Sausthorpe, but nevertheless completely changed the face of the Bargate Closes. In order for their development to go forward, the lack of bridges over the Sincil Dyke had to be solved.

The first Revd Francis Swan (1753-1845), who lived in Greestone Terrace, held a number of livings in the city and county, his clerical income being estimated in 1838 at about £1000 p.a..[49] He owned property in the Bargate Closes – for example, six relatively small closes in St Peter at Gowts parish, on the east bank of the Sincil Dyke, the lease of which he bought from the Corporation for £860 in 1789.[50]

His son, Revd Francis II, BD, (1787-1878) bought the living at Sausthorpe in 1819 and built the Hall in 1822.[51] Nevertheless, he took a close interest in the development of property in Lincoln, which was continued by his second surviving son, Revd Charles Trollope Swan (1826-1904).

Several articles have been written about the building of streets in the Bargate Closes between Canwick Road and the Sincil Dyke.[52] One key to understanding their development is the access to them especially from the High Street direction across the Sincil Dyke. In 1842 when Padley drew his first large-scale survey, there was still no means of crossing the Sincil Dyke with a horse and cart or a number of animals, between St Mary's Bridge and Bargate, a distance of about three-quarters of a mile. (See Fig. 8.) Canwick Road, laid out in 1843 by

Date	Applicant	Street names: first applications by the Swans	Street names: further building or re-application
1871	Revd F. Swan	Portland (which part not clear)	
1872	Revd F. Swan	Kesteven, Cross	
1875	Revd F. Swan	St Andrew's	
1876	Revd F. Swan	Chelmsford, Ripon, Sincil Bank, Canwick Rd	Cross, St Andrew's, Portland,
1881	Revd C. T. Swan	Trollope, Linton, Thesiger,	
1882	Revd C. T. Swan		Thesiger, Cross
1883	Revd C. T. Swan	Hope, Arthur, Norris	St Andrew's
1890	Revd C. T. Swan		Hope, Norris
1897	Revd C. T. Swan	Scorer, Grace, Martin, Kirkby	
1900	Revd C. T. Swan	Sausthorpe, Hood, Henry, Dunlop	Scorer, Cross, Kirkby, Thesiger
1906	Col. C. M. G. Swan	Bridge in Scorer St	Scorer (probably High St end)

Fig.9 Swan applications in St Andrew's parish from Register of Plans of Buildings, Heritage Services, City of Lincoln.

Padley himself as the turnpike surveyor, made little difference to the development of the Bargate Closes, probably because of the danger of flooding.[53] By 1851 Padley could only show the Chaplin's Arms inn opposite a few houses still distinguishable by being out of alignment with later building.

In 1848, after his father's death in 1845, Revd Francis Swan II bought the Tentercroft, and it was connected to the east bank of the Dyke by a bridge.[54] In order to make good use of this bridge, he and his mother (Susanna Maria) conducted a ferocious correspondence with the Manchester, Sheffield and Lincolnshire Railway (built 1848) from 1848 to 1868. They wished to have the crossing over this line (and just east of the bridge) converted from an unmanned to a manned crossing, to make it more attractive to develop land roughly on the site of the west section of the future Kesteven Street.[55]

Meanwhile, by the time of Padley's 1868 revision, the Dyke had been bridged at the east end of Monson Street and a new street leading all the way to Canwick Road had actually been named (as Ripon Street), but it contained no houses. Possibly its construction was prompted by the establishment of Robey's works in Canwick Road in 1854 and the holding of the Royal Agricultural Society's show on the Cow Paddle in the same year.[56]

In his 1872 directory White was still able to give only sixteen house numbers in Ripon Street, probably on the north side and near the bridge, compared with 130 numbers on both sides by 1892. Portland Street with its bridge does not appear on the 1868 Padley map, but some buildings on its future course can be seen west of Sincil Dyke and just south of the boundary between the parishes of St Mark and St Peter at Gowts. A discussion in the Corporation in June 1871 revealed that these buildings belonged to the Revd Francis Swan I, who was proposing to knock them down in order to drive a new street through the property, over the Sincil Dyke, and all the way to Canwick Road. Would the Corporation consider giving him a grant of £50 towards the cost of the bridge, the same figure as granted for the Monson Street Bridge? This phraseology hints at the possibility that it was Swan who had organised its construction. The following points arose in the discussion:

(1) Swan's road would cost him £2200, including pulling down the buildings and the loss of the income from them.

(2) It was proposed to make the road 40 feet wide, except unfortunately only 30 feet to the west of the Dyke where it was to connect with the High Street which would be the busiest section.

(3) The bridge would enable Swan to bring a large area on to the market for building land.

(4) Nevertheless, it would be a great boon to everyone. A committee was formed and when it reported in August it recommended approval of the grant. The Corporation agreed to this, should the road be made 40 feet wide throughout, and indeed that is how it appears on Padley's 1883 plan.[57]

In September 1871 Swan moved swiftly forward to register plans for houses in Portland Street. The 1877 Kelly directory recorded fifty-eight addresses in the street, and the 1892 White's directory reported 107. The table in Fig. 9 demonstrates a considerable level of planning, the streets broadly speaking being developed in a sequence from north (Kesteven Street) to south (Sausthorpe and Norris Streets), The last development was apparently the laying out of the western part of Scorer Street after the Sincil Dyke had been bridged for that street in 1906.[58] In total, three bridges were necessary for the peopling of the Bargate Closes.

A quite striking feature of this very large Swan development was the provision of a church and a school situated at the north end of St Andrew's Street, on the corner with Portland Street and Canwick Road. This choice of location suggests that the Swans saw both the latter roads as leading to their 'urban village'. The new church was built on land donated by Canon Swan in 1876-78 for the new parish of St Andrew's created in 1883. It was demolished in 1970, but the associated parish school (or parts of it) survive as an auction house.[59] Even the name of the new parish replicated the dedication of the church in their estate village east of Horncastle.

The Swans also put their stamp on this district through the use of their own Christian names and the surnames of in-laws for several of the streets – for example, Charles and Arthur Streets (C. T. Swan and his son Charles Arthur); Grace Street, his wife, also their daughter Grace Eleanor; Martin Street (Grace's maiden name); Linton Street (wife of Revd Francis Swan II); Dunlop Street (Agnes, daughter of C. T. Swan, married Major Archibald Dunlop).[60] Some of the in-laws might have been disappointed by the sizes of 'their' streets. For instance, Major Dunlop, who was in charge of a whole barracks at the 1911 census, had been assigned a street of only about a dozen workers' houses.

JOHN AND EMILY SWAN OF STONEFIELD HOUSE: DAIRYING, BUILDING AND BRICK MAKING

John Swan, born 7 June 1831, was the fourth child of Robert Swan I and Mary Ann Burstall. Robert was a solicitor, and held the registrarship of the Lincoln Diocese among several other prestigious public offices, and John had joined him in the family practice by 1856.[61] In 1901 he published a pedigree of the family in which he described himself as:

> Registrar of the Diocese of Lincoln, and two Archdeaconries; District
> Registrar of H M Court of Probate; Chapter Clerk; Clerk to County

Figs10 (left) and 11 John Swan and Emily Swan (née Keyworth) (images courtesy of His Honour Judge John Machin).

Justices, Captain Commandant of the Lincoln Volunteer Corps to April 1871; member of the Carlton and Coaching Clubs (in London).

Swan married Emily Keyworth in January 1863, the daughter of John Kirk Keyworth, a miller and corn merchant (see Figs 10 and 11).[62]

It is reasonable to assume that both John and his father, and also later his brother Robert II, had a substantial staff to carry out the work these offices entailed, as well as conventional legal practice. Nevertheless, the number of other responsibilities John sustained is quite remarkable, as is their diversity, although some synergies between them will be demonstrated.

The Swans lived at Stonefield House, Church Lane, which he started to build in the mid-1860s (see Figs 12 and 13). It is set back from Church Lane by about eighty yards (75m) and immediately behind it were the horse stables usually found in association with a large residence. The farmstead was located a little further north, with what can be assumed as the 'home' closes to the west as far as the site of Stonefield Avenue and as far north as the cow stables, an area approaching only about twelve acres. However, the dairy enterprise, begun in 1870, must have ranged over other fields as the herd in 1887 was over seventy-head of pure-bred Jerseys, a well-known milk breed. Some indication of the greater extent of the farm was revealed in 1894 when the enterprise was being sold off. At this point thirty-eight acres of growing lucerne and rye were advertised for sale in lots of about one acre in four fields between Riseholme Road and Nettleham Road, a location that might have been as much as a mile away from the farmstead.[63]

Some indications of the facilities of the farmstead occur in building applications approved by the City Council: for additions to the dairy in 1884 (ledger number 1516) and 1886 (number 1738); and to the farm buildings including the cow stables with two silos in 1883–84 (numbers 1428 and 1621). In 1884 permission for new build was sought for three more silos used for the preparation of silage (number 1659).[64]

The near-column length article on the dairy herd that appeared in the *Lincolnshire Chronicle* in 1887, apparently reprinted from the *Live Stock Journal*, describes its management in considerable detail. The salient facts are that the cows in milk were tied up in all seasons, having a constant supply of water, chopped oats and hay, chaff and a little bran and cake. Peat moss was used for litter (bedding).

This description possibly relates to the seventy-four foot long building, for which plans were drawn up in April 1883 (number 1428). These included a cow house, thirty by thirty-four feet, in the centre with four loose boxes to the west taking up a further twenty feet of the south elevation. A liquid manure tank was to be shared by the cow house and the loose boxes. Two silos taking up the remaining twenty feet were to be erected at the east end of the building.

Only eighteen months later, in September 1884, what appears to be a quite separate cow house plan was registered. It was to be sixty by fifty feet overall, with standings about four feet six inches across, for four rows of eleven cows taking up the fifty-foot dimension, the rows themselves being fifteen feet wide. As before there was to be a liquid manure tank

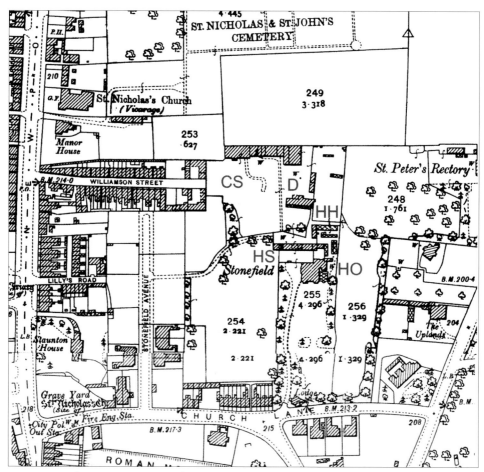

*Fig.12 Ordnance Survey 25-inch plan of 1894 showing Stonefield House (HO) and Farm.
CS = Cow Stables; D = Dairy; HS = Horse Stables and HH = Hothouses. Not to scale. The
6-inch Ordnance Survey map, surveyed in 1886, marked the cow stables as 'Stonefield Dairy'.*

*Fig.13 Stonefield House, 2014. The former horse stables to the left and rear, with new build
extension to the house to the right. Photo courtesy of Franklin Ellis architects.*

observing '*conditions that the tank to receive the drainage … is made watertight.*' That might
have dealt with the liquid waste, but the solid must have been a liability, suggesting that there
was land available to the north on which to spread it.

The three later silos whose plans were registered in 1884 were intended to be housed in
a separate building, fifty-five by thirty-three feet, each silo about ten feet wide, the iron
roof supported by two sets of pillars over two feet thick. The depth below the surface was
to be eight feet, the height above ground twelve feet, plus six foot of roof height. These
measurements are near enough to those reported in the *Lincolnshire Chronicle* in 1887,
which also reported the other two earlier silos. They had brick walls rendered in Portland
cement to give a smooth surface. It was estimated that they could contain 576 tons of silage.[65]

Mucking out started at five in the morning, followed by the arrival of the women milkers
at six o'clock. They were required to cleanse their hands before starting work, and also to
cleanse the cows' udders. The yield of each cow was weighed and a continuous record kept,
to inform changes in the food supply. A 2½ hp stationary (steam) engine was used for
various processes. Butter production was described as if it was the only main product, and
the skimmed milk was taken into the town by contractors' carts. The making of butter was
achieved without it ever being touched by human hand.

This was undertaken in a building whose plans had been registered in January 1884 and
extended in January 1886, making it approximately sixty by twenty-four feet, with an upper
storey above a small central portion. The walls were to be brick, the damp course to be of
asphalt; and the sanitary pipes to be jointed in cement. A chimney is shown. Subsequently
the dairy was converted into a dwelling, further extensions to which were approved by the
City Council in 2009. Photographs in the application, taken as the house was in 2009 before
new work was started, show a front elevation which appears to match the original designs

approved in 1884-86. Its appearance could be described as that of a cottage orné.[66]

An interesting aspect of the dairy enterprise is that another main product, at least in 1885, was *koumys*, an effervescent preparation of milk, which had undergone a natural process of fermentation (i.e., something similar to putrefaction). In that year, John Swan was advertising this drink in the *Lincolnshire Chronicle* at 1s. 3d. for a quart champagne bottle, 10d. for a pint. The advantage of these bottles was that the drink could be drawn safely with a champagne tap, although beer bottles with patent stoppers could also be used. Swan stated that doctors recommended *koumys* for pulmonary disease and for those of delicate health. It was said to be for dyspepsia and Bright's disease, water-brash, stomach acid and acid eructations. It was suitable for children and aged persons and was invaluable in the sick room. 'It may be obtained from all chemists, and at Stonefield Dairy, Lincoln; Post Office orders payable to John Swan, telegraphic address "Above Hill", Lincoln'.[67] A modern account of *koumys* and similar drinks is available on the internet.[68]

The buying of land and sometimes the building of houses are activities in which one is not surprised to find solicitors being involved, although going as far as brick manufacture is possibly unusual. In 1871 John Swan had registered plans for the development of what became Chaplin, Hermit and King Streets off the lower High Street immediately south of Portland Street. By 1872 the Swans had taken Thomas Bourne into partnership with them in the legal practice and it was Swan and Bourne who in 1882 registered plans for Albany, Waldeck and Turner Streets to the west of Burton Road south of its junction with Yarborough Road.[69]

At the 1881 census John Swan gave as one of his occupations, 'brick manufacturer employing 59 men and 16 boys'. In 1882 White's Directory recorded Swan Bros and Bourne as brick and tile manufacturers at West Cliff brick works, Burton Road, with E. Handley as manager. The company also appears in Kelly's directories for 1876, 1885 and 1889, the latter being the year which Hill gives as the date when the company was amalgamated with the Bracebridge Brick and Tile Company to become the Lincoln Brick Company, with Francis Bennett as the manager, from a very well-established family of brick manufacturers in Derby and Nottingham. It is also of interest that Robert Toynbee, another solicitor, financed a brickyard (See Figs 14 and 15).[70]

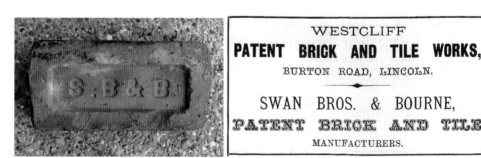

Left: Fig.14 Brick manufactured by Swan Bros and Bourne at West Cliffe brickworks. Photo by Martyn Fretwell.
Right: Fig.15 Advertisement from White's Directory of Lincolnshire, 1882. The term 'patent' was used to indicate that the bricks were made on a patented machine. The bricks themselves were not patented.

John and Robert Swan might have concentrated on matters in which they had immediate expertise, such as the buying of land, access, the capital required and the keeping of company accounts. They would also have been party to information about building developments going on at a rapid pace in Lincoln between about 1850 and 1890.

As young men the Swan brothers were also officers in the First Lincolnshire Rifle Volunteers, which one could interpret as a patriotic way of expressing a spare time interest in rifle shooting as a sport. Following the Crimean War (1853-56), the government decided that the regular army could not cope with all the responsibilities the Empire might thrust upon it. The existing militia force was modernised, and Lincoln, like many cities, acquired a new militia barracks in 1857, now the Museum of Lincolnshire Life. This housed a permanent staff whose principal task was to recruit and train men over significant periods. The latter received pay and could be called up to join the regular army (i.e., the Lincolnshire Regiment) in times of emergency. In 1859, it was decided to supplement these measures with the national formation of a Rifle Volunteer Force, who were not only volunteers but also provided their own uniforms and, so long as they conformed to War Office regulations, also their rifles.[71]

The Lincoln force was formed in June 1859 and on 19 February 1861 the *Illustrated London News* depicted them skating down the River Witham. In 1863 they were under the command of Joseph Shuttleworth, who was also at the head of the first company, with John Swan as the captain in charge of the second company and Robert Swan of the third of the three companies. Further down the list was T. C. Bourne as a sergeant. The drill shed provided by Charles Seely, Lincoln's MP, was situated behind 181-82 High Street, probably part of one of his steam mill premises. They had a shooting range of 600 yards at the west end of the South Common. In 1872, there were said to be 220 men in the force, many being mechanics in the engineering works, and since 1850 over 800 men had been 'drilled'. In 1872 the government brought in measures to draw the Rifle Volunteers into a greater degree of contact and organisation with the regular Army, and this prospect may have been what prompted John Swan to resign in 1871 (as recorded in his Swan pedigree), having succeeded Shuttleworth as commandant.[72]

Emily Swan died in April 1898 and John in October 1907, leaving no children. John's estate passed to his sister Frances who had married Dr George Mitchinson, thence on to their children, but was sold to Jane Ruston, widow of Joseph Ruston in 1910. After passing through the ownership of Hannah Swan, John's niece, and her husband Captain Francis Boothby, Stonefield was sold in 1930 to a builder, Walter Middleton, after whom Middleton's Field was named.[73] Today, the Preparatory Department of Lincoln Minster School is situated in Stonefield House. The dairy has survived as a dwelling with Stonefield Close as the address and was extended in 2009. The cow stables, in association with a builder's yard, survived until at least 1969 but have since disappeared, making way for the building of Oakbrook Court. The small building shown between them on the OS 1894 plan (see Fig. 12) has also gone, but the site is now occupied by a house known simply as Stonefield.[74]

ROBERT SWAN II AND LUCY SWAN OF QUARRY HOUSE

Robert Swan II, of Quarry House married Lucy Clayton at St James', Westminster, by special licence on 21 January 1864. The ceremony was conducted by Revd J. A. Jeremie, DD, subdean of Lincoln Cathedral. Lucy's two sisters, Fanny and Mary, were bridesmaids along with Robert's sister Alice. Lucy was attended by both her parents, Nathaniel and Hannah Clayton.

Also present were Mr and Mrs Joseph Shuttleworth. Other significant guests were the MP Charles Seely and his wife; Mr and Mrs John Swan (Robert's elder brother and partner in the family solicitors' practice); Dr George and Mrs Frances Mitchinson (nee Swan, Robert's sister); William Swan (Robert's younger brother); Mr Cockburn (most likely William Yates Cockburn, who married Lucy's sister Fanny, later the same year); Mr Thomas Greetham, Robert's uncle by marriage to his aunt Louisa Swan, and Mr John Greetham, their son. The reception was held at the Burlington Hotel. Robert and Lucy Swan then honeymooned in Paris.

This marriage was very significant. Not only were Nathaniel Clayton and Joseph Shuttleworth business partners; they were also related by the marriage of Nathaniel's sister, Sarah Grace, to Shuttleworth in 1842.[75] In the next generation, Lucy was to become one of Nathaniel's three co-heiresses, there being no sons to inherit. As Hill pointed out, both Clayton and Shuttleworth were of humble origins, but the firm they started in 1842 became much the biggest firm of iron founders in Lincoln. The 'new money' of Clayton was now to join the 'old money' of the Swan family, with its long-established and prominent social position in the city. Similarly, the bridegroom's brother John had married into the Keyworth family who, along with Seely, were partners in the firm of Clayton and Shuttleworth.[76]

Robert Swan II attended Rugby School and Trinity College, Cambridge, graduating with a BA in 1857. He worked with his elder brother John in the family legal practice, one of the principal functions of which was as registrars of the diocese. He was also JP, captain in the Royal North Lincolnshire Militia, and registrar of births, marriages and deaths in Lincoln. After their marriage Robert and Lucy first lived in 13 Minster Yard with Robert's widowed mother. There was plenty of room for two households, as it was virtually two semi-detached houses. Subsequently they moved to 9 Minster Yard.[77]

Fig.16 Regimental photograph of the North Lincolnshire Militia, 1870, outside The Quarry. Robert Swan is third from the right of the standing row, Mrs Swan is third from the left of the seated row. From the Museum of Lincolnshire Life, Reg. Photo Box 6 LR Album 900p, MLL9971, courtesy of Lincolnshire County Council.

The couple had a stone-faced, four-storey house known as The Quarry or Quarry House built in a secluded location on a plot of land, once St Nicholas's quarry, bounded by Wragby Road and Sewell Road. They moved into this house sometime between 1867 and 1870. The *Lincolnshire Chronicle* reported in 1867 an incident that might be related to preparations for the building: a fatal accident at a pit between Wragby Road and Sewell Road; Edward Rushton, a labourer working for Mr W. Huddleston, a builder, died from his injuries. He had been clearing earth from the pit and wheeling it on a raised plankway and he had been working there for three weeks.[78] The *Stamford Mercury* reported on 21 May 1869:

> Robert Swan, Esq. treated the men employed in the building of his new house, Wragby Road, to a dinner at the Dolphins Inn, on Saturday last, Mr. T. Pilkington, plumber, taking the chair, and Mr. Hewson, plasterer, the vice-chair. About 60 persons were present, and after dinner a variety of toasts were drunk.

There is no extant building application for the house, but additions were approved in August 1875, July 1878, and March 1883 and are all included in the footprint shown by Padley in the latter year.

The application for the two-bedroom lodge was approved in October 1869, the architects being Bellamy and Hardy. Robert had some stables built on the opposite side of Wragby Road, the application being approved in June 1872, with architects Goddard and Son. Additions and alterations to the stables were approved in August 1879, June 1881 and January 1892.[79]

By the 1871 census, Lucy, wife of Robert Swan, had given birth to six of their eight children, the eldest being six and the youngest ten months. There were seven servants living in the house, and a gardener and his family in the lodge. By 1881 the servants had increased to nine, including a governess for the home education of the girls. The eldest son, Robert Clayton-Swan attended Eton and matriculated at Trinity College, Cambridge, but did not graduate. The second son, Nathaniel Clayton-Swan, attended Rugby and Trinity, graduating with a BA in 1895; Harold was 'privately educated'.

The Swans lived at The Quarry for the rest of their lives, Lucy dying in 1898, Robert in 1899 and this led to a series of sales. The Quarry was put up for sale in September 1899 by Swan and Bourne, solicitors. The grounds were stated to be over three acres with stabling for ten horses. A sale of carriages and harness at the stables on 11 October included a Landau and a Victoria carriage, as well as a dog cart, luggage cart and associated harness. Robert was a keen collector of orchids; of which 600 were sold in pots in April 1899, doubtless having been grown in the conservatory at the side of the house, or possibly in the greenhouses. There was a separate sale of the greenhouse and gardening equipment in November 1900 which took place at a paddock off Eastcliff Road.

Robert was a very keen lawn tennis player and is purported to have been key in introducing the sport to the city. To ensure he could practise all year round he built a covered court, opposite The Quarry, presumably in Wragby Road, which in later times was converted to a cottage.[80] In 1902, after the death of Robert Swan in 1899, the property was purchased by the Revd Edward Giles.[81] The house more recently became accommodation for students of the Lincoln Minster School.

DESCENDANTS OF ROBERT SWAN II AND LUCY SWAN

So, what happened to Robert and Lucy's children? The short answer to this question is that they mostly left Lincoln, if not straight after marriage, then later on – and eventually there was no one in the male line of the Swans living in the city. Before moving on to the children of Robert II and Lucy (nee Clayton), it is worth noting members of their own generation who survived for many years after Robert II and Lucy had died.

William Swan was born in November 1840 and became a doctor, MB Oxon and MRCSE, and it was probably he who is listed as Dr W. Swan, 64 Bailgate in 1919 and 1922 (but not in Lincoln at earlier dates). His sister, Alice, survived from April 1843 until at least 1926 in 8 Minster Yard, which, in 1892, she had shared with another Miss Swan (possibly her sister Ann Caroline, born in November 1828). This was the house occupied in 1872 by Mrs Mary Ann Swan, their mother. John and Emily Swan had no children, but Robert II and Lucy more than made up for that with eight children born between 1864 and 1874, five girls and three boys.

Turning to Robert and Lucy's children, Robert Clayton Swan, the first born (November 1864), was separated by the girls from the other two boys, Nathaniel Clayton Swan (born September 1872) and Harold Clayton Swan (born December 1874). In 1901, Robert was living at Gallowshill Hall in Northumberland, having married Mildred Mary Elliot, second daughter of Sir George Elliott, Bt., of Houghton Hall, Durham in October 1892. In 1911 Nathaniel was living at Atherstone House, Eastgate, with his sister Lucy Clayton Swan where they kept five servants. Neither of them married.

They were still there in 1922, but were at D'Isney Place, Eastgate when Nathaniel died. The youngest son, Harold was living at Reepham Manor in 1903 when he married Lettice Huntsman, daughter of a Yorkshire clergyman, who died in 1912, leaving no children. Harold stayed there until about 1919-20 when he moved to Heighington Hall, remaining there until his sudden death in 1925.[82]

At the 1901 census Robert II's house, The Quarry, was occupied by three of his children (Beatrice, Lucy and Nathaniel, with Lucy as head of household). They were still living there in 1902, before the handover to Revd Edward Giles.[83] The four girls who married all spent some of their married lives in Lincoln, though in the case of Agnes this was probably only a short time around the birth of her first child, the mother-to-be perhaps wishing to be near her own mother.

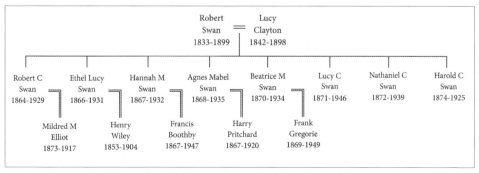

Fig.17 Descendants of Robert Swan II

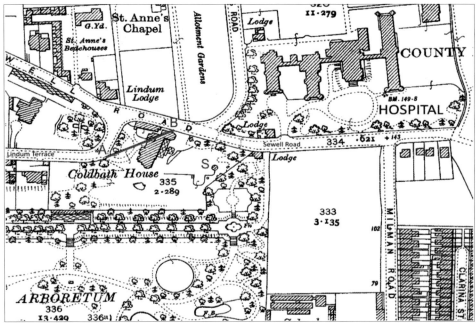

Fig.18 *The Cold Bath House had long been an extra parochial area when in 1857 it became a civil parish, although never containing more than eleven people in the Boothby household in 1911. This miniscule parish had an area of 2.289 acres as shown by this extract from the 1932 edition of the Ordnance Survey 25-inch plan. Note the proximity of the County Hospital and the size of Mr Hebb's mansion in comparison to the hospital. The line A-B is the approximate position of the current NW boundary established in 1953; S=the surviving summerhouse – for the cold bath itself.*

Ethel Lucy (born January 1866) married Henry Wiley, an Army officer from Ireland, in 1890, and by the time of the 1891 census they were living in Newport Cottage, next to the Arch. In 1892 the address given for them by White was a house in Sewell Road not far from The Quarry. They next moved to Southsea, where Henry died in 1904, Ethel living in Ashley Gardens, Westminster until her death in 1931.[84]

In August 1893 Hannah Mildred (born August 1867) also married a soldier – Francis Boothby, a captain in the Lincolnshire Regiment, which necessitated several moves, but one was to Skellingthorpe and they were at The Cottage, Swallowbeck from 1897 to 1902.[85] On 4 November 1908 Boothby with four other directors (some more suitably qualified) issued a prospectus for a new company called the Reliance Taxi-Cab Co. Ltd to operate in London with a share capital of £195,000. The company was described in ambitious terms but did not last beyond 2 November 1909.[86]

The Boothbys had obtained the lease of Cold Bath House in 1907. This dwelling was built in 1857 by Henry Kirke Hebb, a solicitor who was clerk to Lincoln Sanitary Authority from 1866 to 1899.[87] This was a property said to contain a room big enough to receive the whole Corporation, as well as eleven bedrooms and dressing rooms; it had a stable block next to Sewell Road. It was very privately situated with a high wall on one side and adjoined the Arboretum on two further sides. In 1914 Captain Boothby transferred the lease to the Lincoln School, whose Wragby Road premises had been commandeered for use as a military hospital and in the 1930s it became a nursing home run coincidentally by an unrelated Mrs (Sister) Swan. By the outbreak of the Second World War, Cold Bath House was a Nurses' Home, containing offices occupied by soldiers. On 2 August 1942 it was totally destroyed by a German bomb, possibly intended for the County Hospital; one soldier was killed and other soldiers as well as nurses were injured. The grounds were added to the Arboretum in 1953 as the Coronation Gardens.[88]

In 1914, the Boothbys had bought Stonefield House, Church Lane, which had once belonged to John Swan, Hannah's uncle. They were there in December 1928 when their son John Clayton Swan died. They stayed there until 1930 when the property was sold to Walter Middleton.

Agnes Mabel (born October 1868) married yet a third Army officer in 1898, Captain Harry Pritchard, their first son being born in Lincoln.[89] They were at Syston Old Hall at the 1901 census and at Peatling Parva, Leicestershire, in 1911.

Beatrice Mary (born January 1870) married Frank Gregorie, a land agent and surveyor, in January 1904. As the wedding presents included a silver tea caddy from the servants at Atherstone House, this suggests that Beatrice was living there (with her brother and sister Nathaniel and Lucy – see above) from the sale of Quarry House in1902 until the wedding. At the time of the 1911 census the couple were living at the Burghersh Chantry, James Street, Lincoln, which they had left by 1919.[90] During the First World War he had 'kept up' with his military brothers-in-law by serving in the Army, reaching the rank of captain. In 1922 the Gregories were at 13 Minster Yard, the house in which Beatrice's father and grandfather Swan had lived. It seems likely that they moved later that year, as Stone's Place, Skellingthorpe (now Skellingthorpe Road, Lincoln), was to let in August 1922, with the move out of the house by the Wells-Cole family followed by Mr Frank Gregorie until at least 1930. A letting advertisement on behalf of Lord Liverpool describes the house as having three sitting rooms and ten bed and dressing rooms, with stabling that appears to have been used to accommodate the hunting fraternity, gardens including a walled kitchen garden, an orchard, a paddock and a motor house. Frank Gregorie outlived his wife and in 1949, at his death, he was living at Harmston to which they had moved by January 1934, Beatrice dying soon afterwards.[91]

Frank was a partner in the land agents James Martin for fifty years and during that time clients of the firm included the Jarvises of Doddington Hall, Cockburn of Harmston, the Tennyson d'Eyncourt family at Tealby, the Earl of Liverpool at Hartsholme Hall and Captain Ellison at Boultham Hall.[92]

Lucy Clayton (born February 1871) never married but it was she who kept the name of the Swan family alive in Lincoln longer than anyone else in the family. She had lived with her unmarried brother Nathaniel, first at Atherstone House, then at D'Isney Place, both in Eastgate, which he left to Lucy on his death there in 1939.

She died 10 October 1946 and the sale of her effects at the Central Market on 4 February 1947 is recorded; also the fact that the house was sold the next month for £4000 to Mr G. Mason of North Hykeham.

So ends the story of the Swan family in Lincoln. It may be remembered that the clerical Swans, who developed the Bargate Closes, turned themselves into country gentry in 1822 by building Sausthorpe Hall (between Horncastle and Spilsby). Late Victorian and Edward generations became army officers, but the family maintained a presence at Sausthorpe into the 1960s.[93] In the city of Lincoln itself, over a period of two centuries, the Swans' varied involvement in its economy and society reveals how one family could retain its prominent position in constantly changing times.

NOTES

1. Previous articles examining aspects of the history of the Swan family by Dennis Mills and Victoria Thorpe have included: 'The Cornhill residence of the Henry Swans and Robert Swan the elder', *The Lincoln Enquirer*, 25 (November 2013), 2-5; 'The career of Robert Swan the elder and his uphill residences', *The Lincoln Enquirer*, 26 (May 2014), 4-6; 'The houses of the contemporaries of Robert Swan the elder', *The Lincoln Enquirer*, 27 (November 2014), 2-4; 'John Swan and Stonefield House, Church Lane' *The Lincoln Enquirer*, 34 (November 2017), 2-5; 'John Swan of Stonefield House', *Lincolnshire Past and Present*, 110 (Winter 2017-18), 18-21; 'Robert Swan II, Quarry House', *The Lincoln Enquirer*, 35 (May 2018), 7-9; and 'Where the children of Robert Swan II and Lucy Swan went to live', *The Lincoln Enquirer*, 36 (November 2018), 2-5.

2. See www.wikipedia.org/wiki/Charlie_Swan_(horse_trainer)

3. Genealogical information from Maddison, A. R., 1894, *Lincolnshire Pedigrees*, Publications of the Harleian Society, vol. LII, pp. 941-944 and from www.Ancestry.co.uk

4. Lincolnshire Archives Office MISC DON 104/1.

5. LAO LPC/1/1/33; LAO *Archivists' Report*, vol. 10, 1958-59, p. 20.

6. Sun Insurance Schedule: Henry Swan, 1792, 583629.

7. Map 47 by Robert Stickney in Wheeler, R. C., (ed), 2008, *Maps of the Witham Fens from the thirteenth to the nineteenth century*, Lincoln Record Society, vol. 96.

8. TNA/PROB11/1555, ff 289-298.

9. Maddison, *Lincolnshire Pedigrees*, p. 942.

10. Gordon was the husband of Sarah, nee Tomlinson, the sister of Ann, nee Tomlinson, Henry's wife, i.e., he was Henry's wife's brother-in-law. One of several press references to this relationship occurred in the *Stamford Mercury*, 30 March 1838, when Robert Swan was referred to as the Dean's nephew. Our thanks to John Herridge for assistance with the extraction of local press items from www.britishnewspaperarchive.co.uk

11. LAO, LC Charters 42/974.

12. Two copies in Lincoln Central Library simply entitled on their spines as 'Lincoln Valuation 1828', class mark L LINC 333.332. Inside, the proper title is Edward Betham and Edward J. Willson, *Particulars and Valuation of the Parishes of Lincoln in the year 1828*.

13. *Dictionary of National Biography*, old edition. Some of the accommodation seems to have been continuously let to one or more surgeons after the death of Henry Swan IV, the last surgeon of that name, judging by directory and press references, including advertisements.

14. It is worth noting that there is an arched cellar underneath part of the Corn Exchange building which, until recently, was occupied by Waterstones.

15. *Stamford Mercury*, (*SM*) 10 April 1835.

16. *SM*, 18 December 1835.

17. *SM*, 18 December 1835, 16 June 1837, 22 and 29 March 1839 and 19 April 1839. In 1835 all leaseholds from the corporation had become freeholds under an Act of that year, so Robert Swan could have brought the corporation to court for taking over this part of his property.

18. *SM*, 15 November 1844.

19. *SM*, 29 November 1844.

20. Hill, Sir Francis, 1948, *Victorian Lincoln,* Cambridge. pp. 49-50.

21. Information from Peter Harrod; and The National Archives (TNA), KB 105-107, Court of King's Bench, Articles of Clerkship, Series I, II, III via www.Ancestry.com. George Tennyson was the poet's grandfather. The will is at TNA, PROB11/1555, ff289-298. E. Gillett, *A History of Grimsby,* 1992, pp.164-67, 182; Sir Francis Hill, *Georgian Lincoln,* 1966, p.272. Tennyson was in the Close in 1797 when the marriage settlement of his daughter Elizabeth was prepared: Lincolnshire Archives (LAO) TDE/A/Miscellaneous/3/21.

22. *The Law Times,* 2 June 1860, pp.141-42. This passage was a repeat of the *Lincolnshire Chronicle,* 18 May 1860, p.6. On 7 December 1810, the *Stamford Mercury* reported that Robert Swan of Lincoln had been appointed 'attorney at law, a Master Extraordinary in his Majesty's High Court of Chancery'.

23. TNA, RAIL 885/1. Our thanks to Rob Wheeler for looking up this information especially for us. In the June 1812 list Mr Swan can be identified with Henry, Robert's father; Henry Swan as his elder brother; and the Rev. F. Swan as his father's brother. It would have been the elder Henry Swan who was a Commissioner. The Swans seem to have been there in force for a purpose. Terrinist was a misspelling for the unusual name of Terrewest. James Tomlinson Terrewest was born at Lincoln 1781; major in 34th Foot 30 April 1807; retired 1 February 1810; died Newark 10 October 1854. http://www.napoleon-series.org/military/organization/Britain/Infantry/Regiments/c_34thFoot.html. The Tomlinsons were also connected to the Swans by marriage – see note 9 of D. Mills and V. Thorpe, 'The Cornhill residence of the Henry Swans and Robert Swan the elder', *The Lincoln Enquirer,* no. 25, November 2013, p. 5.

24. *The Law Times, loc. cit.*

25. See, for instance, *SM,* 8 November 1811. See www.britishnewspaperarchive.co.uk. Our thanks to John Herridge for help in handling this source; Ambler, R. W., (ed.), 2006, *Lincolnshire Correspondence of John Kaye, Bishop of Lincoln, 1827-53,* Lincoln Record Society, vol. 94, p. 4, note 35.

26. LAO, UWIDB 5/3/2, Court Minute Book for the period 1792-1825; SM, 27 May 1831; *Lincolnshire Chronicle,* 18 May 1860, p. 6.

27. *The Law Times, loc. cit.*

28. *Correspondence of John Fardell, Deputy Registrar, 1802-1805,* ed. Mary E. Finch, Lincoln Record Society, vol. 66, 1973, especially p.50; LAO, Misc Don 238/124 and DIOC/RAC/3/7 and *SM,* 6 April 1821. John Fardell, jun. had 'inherited' the post from his father in 1805 and made money so quickly he retired in 1821 at the age of 37.

29. *The Law Times, loc. cit.*, but the *Lincolnshire Chronicle, loc. cit.*, put the pension at £1500.

30. Finch, p. 46.

31. *Pigot and Co's Directory of Lincolnshire,* 1822-23 and *White's Directory of Lincolnshire,* 1826. Stanley Jones *et al., The Survey of Ancient Houses in Lincoln, II, Houses to the South and West of the Minster,* 1987, p. 103.

32. 3 LAO, Misc Dep 531/1/29, Winifred Craven's biographical notes on councillors prepared for Sir Francis Hill. Also *The Law Times, loc. cit.*

33. Edward Betham and Edward J. Willson, *Particulars and Valuation of the Parishes of Lincoln in the year 1828,* Lincoln Central Library, L LINC 333.332. Stanley Jones *et al., Survey of Ancient Houses, II,* p. 103.

34. *SM,* 28 October 1831.

35. *SM,* 23 July 1834.

36. Stanley Jones *et al.,* 1984, *The Survey of Ancient Houses in Lincoln, I, Priorygate to Pottergate,* p. 69.

37. White's *Directory of Lincolnshire,* 1856.

38. White 1872. Unfortunately, the 1861 enumerator did not record house numbers.

39. *SM,* 9 April 1835. Our thanks to John Herridge for help with this reference. www.britishnewspaperarchive.co.uk; (LAO), HILL 42/4/8, 9 and 11.

40. In Venables, E., 1887, 'A survey of houses in the Minster Close…1649 with additions', *Associated Architectural Societies' Reports and Papers*, vol. xix, pt.1, p. 73-74; the site was about one and a half roods in 1649.

41. *Lincolnshire Chronicle*, 21 February 1845. The property had become freehold in 1835 under the Municipal Corporations Act of that year, which enfranchised all the Corporation leaseholds.

42. His total clerical income was estimated as about £1000 p.a. by the *SM*, 12 October 1838, p.2. In addition to this considerable sum, he also had an income from the rents of many of the Bargate Closes, e.g., in 1789, LAO, BS V/1/12/1.

43. Leach, T., 1968, *Sausthorpe*, Lincolnshire Local History Society, p. 14.

44. Wheeler, R., 2011, 'Housing development between Sincil Dyke and Canwick Road', in Walker, A., (ed.), *South-East Lincoln: Canwick Road, South Common, St Catherine's and Bracebridge*, The Survey of Lincoln, pp.18-20.

45. TNA, PROB11/1555, ff289-298.

46. Taylor, B., 1999, *A Sign of the Times: the story of Nettleham, a Lincolnshire village*, Carillon Press, p. 51. Ann and her sisters were heiresses under their father's will.

47. LAO, LL7/24. The lease and plan show that in 1836 Robert Swan was the new head lessee of no.7 Minster Yard, next on the north to his mother, Ann Swan, with her name down to be the occupier after the interest (i.e. the decease) of three spinsters of 6 Cheyney Walk, Chelsea.

48. *SM*, 15 November 1844, p. 1.

49. *SM*, 12 October 1838, p.2. He has resigned from the incumbency of St Peter-at-Arches (the church used by the Corporation, *SM*, 16 April 1830, p. 3.

50. LAO. BS V/1/12/1.

51. Leach, 1968, *Sausthorpe*, pp. 14, 16.

52. Hodson, M., 'Eastwards from Swan's Paddock' (pp. 14-17) and Wheeler, R., 'Housing development between Sincil Dyke and Canwick Road' (pp. 18-20) in Walker, A., (ed.), 2011, *South-East Lincoln*, A Walker 'Workers' housing between Sincil Dyke and Canwick Road, c. 1870-1914'. *The Lincoln Enquirer*, 22, May 2012, pp. 2-4. See also his article on similar housing developments west of the Sincil Dyke and in St Botolph's parish. 'Residential development. 1875-1939', in Walker A., (ed). 2016, *Lincoln's City Centre south of the River Witham; from High Bridge to South Park*, Survey of Lincoln, pp. 55-59.

53. For example, as late as 1877 there were serious floods in Canwick Road and the east end of Ripon Street. See Hodson, M., 1984, *Lincoln Then and Now, vol.2*, p. 47; and Elvin, L., 1976, *Lincoln As it Was, vol.2*, p. 3, the latter showing the absence of houses from this part of Ripon Street.

54. According to Sir Francis Hill, *Victorian Lincoln*, p. 128. See also Hodson and Wheeler, as in note 30.

55. LAO BS V/2/2/A 1-74. Most of these 74 items were specifically concerned with the crossing. Lincoln Central Library Map 385 is a sketch map dated 2 February 1850 showing roughly how such a development might have been laid out. It was only in 2016 that the creation of a lengthened Tentercroft Street has materialised.

56. Hill, *Victorian Lincoln*, 1974, p. 120 and White. 1856; Mills, D., 2001, 'An "edge-land" the development of the Witham valley east of Canwick Road', in Walker, A., (ed) *Aspects of Lincoln, discovering local history*. Barnsley, p. 139.

57. *Lincolnshire Chronicle*, 16 June 1871, p. 6 and 4 August 1871, p. 6. William Cooling, who spoke for Swan in the Corporation meeting, was mentioned in Swan's will, proved on 2 February 1878 as his agent of thirty years.

58. We are most grateful to John Herridge for extracting from the Register of Plans of Buildings enough data to give an overview of the Swan developments, but there is much more detail available, e.g., as in Walker, 2012, pp. 2-4 – information on builders, with plans of a house in Kirkby Street.

59. Eventually four schools were built and in 1916 they had a combined roll of 1166 children, based on Arthur Ward's note in Walker, (ed.), *South-East Lincoln*, p. 68, Kelly's Directory of Lincolnshire, 1916 and LAO, Lincoln St Andrew PAR 16/1.

60.   Our thanks to Maurice Hodson for this suggestion.

61.   Except where otherwise stated our sources are various directories for the city and county; census enumerators' books; probates; John Swan's pedigree of the family printed in 1901 and information found on www.Ancestry.co.uk.

62.   J. K. Keyworth was born in Lincoln but lived away from the city for most of his life. His brother, Thomas Michael Keyworth, was a much better known Lincoln miller and corn merchant in partnership with Charles Seely. All three were also in partnership with Clayton and Shuttleworth, the iron founders (1851 Census), when J. K. Keyworth was living at Chorley, near Alderley Edge, Cheshire; *London Gazette*, January 1861, and information from Dr Rob Wheeler.

63.   Acreage of farm from Lincolnshire Archives (LAO), MISC Dep 575/57 and 612/12 and figure 3. Also based on *Lincolnshire Chronicle,* 11 May 1894, Report of sale, p.8; *LC,* 23 September 1887, 'The Stonefield Dairy Herd', p.6, and *LC,* 13 April 1894, Advert of sale, p. 1. This advertisement was repeated on 27 April, p. 1, along with an advert for the sale of the dairy equipment. A herd of 70 was very large in this period, when the many cowkeepers in and close to Lincoln would have got a decent living as producer-retailers from a dozen cows.

64.   We wish to thank John Herridge for supplying information from the Lincoln Building Applications collection in Lincolnshire Archives; see www.thesurveyofLincoln.co.uk for an introduction and calendar.

65.   Silage making was an innovation of the 1880s following the wet summers of the 1870s which made hay harvesting very difficult. However, it was mainly confined to gentlemen farmers such as Swan and the home farms of the larger estates. General adoption only came in the middle of the twentieth century: Collins, E., (ed.), 2000, *Cambridge Agricultural History*, vol. VII, pp. 571-2. We owe this information to the kindness of Dr Shirley Brook.

66.   City of Lincoln Council, planning application 2009/0459/F.

67.   *LC,* 6 November 1885, p. 8.

68.   http://www.henriettes-herb.com/eclectic/usdisp/kefir.html

69.   LAO, *Archivists' Report,* 10, 1958-59, p. 21, where it is described as the area to the south of Portland Street, west of the Sincil Dyke and east of the High Street. This development appears to have been capitalised by raising a mortgage of £5000 in 1873, which was not paid off until 1897 – LAO, MISC DEP 612/11/1-3.

70.   Hill, *Victorian Lincoln*, 1974, p. 125. Hill also mentions a shortage of bricks in Lincoln in 1857 and that bricks could be bought more cheaply from Nottingham; Stocker, D., (ed.), 2003, *The City by the Pool*, p. 357, contains the suggestion that the West Cliff works was one of the two biggest inside the city, probably opening 1860 and demolished 1911. Our thanks to Martyn Fretwell for assistance with this passage. https://eastmidlandsnamedbricks.blogspot.co.uk/2014/09/bennett-brickmakers-in-derby-nottingham.html

71.   Based on Wikipedia articles, which appear to be reliable enough for this brief statement.

72.   According to Akrill's *Lincoln City Directory* of 1863 and White's *Lincolnshire Directory* of 1872.

73.   LAO, MISC DEP 612/1/3/1 and 572/57.

74.   Kelly's *Directory of Lincoln*, 1969; Lincoln City Council Planning Application 2009/0459/F and LAO, 5MARTIN/ 398, p. 5.

75.   She died on 9 October 1849. His second wife was Caroline Ellison from Boultham Hall whom he married on 4 December 1861 in London. Our thanks to Miriam Smith for this additional information emphasising the way in which the Lincoln business class was interwoven by marriages.

76.   Hill, *Victorian Lincoln*, 1974, pp. 73-74 and 121, Miriam Smith 'Joseph Shuttleworth's homes', *The Lincoln Enquirer*, 17, November 2009, pp. 8-11. We have mentioned the two elder Clayton sisters (Lucy and Fanny); there was also a third – Mary Anne, who married Alfred Shuttleworth, eldest son of Joseph, who inherited Hartsholme Hall from his father. Except where otherwise stated our sources are various directories for the city and count, census enumerators' books; probates; John Swan's pedigree of the family printed in 1901 and information found on www.ancestry.co.uk

77.   Morris and Company's *Commercial Directory and Gazetteer of Lincolnshire*, 1868 listed Robert at 13 Minster Yard but Akrill's *City Directory* 1867 listed him at 9 Minster Yard in 1867.

78.   *LC*, 26 January 1869, p. 4. We are indebted to Geoff Tann for this extract.

79.   Lincoln City Council, Building Applications numbers 665, 974 and 1400 for the house and 365, 1075, 1225 and 2129 for the stables. The stables went through many different occupiers, the last being the Ricari Emiliani garage down to 2005, when the premises were demolished and replaced by The Cloisters, a block of apartments. Our thanks to John Herridge for making these documents available and for the quotation from the *Stamford Mercury*.

80.   *Lincolnshire Echo*, 9 March 1899 and *Lincolnshire Chronicle*, 21 April 20 September and October 1899 and 13 November 1900.

81.   Maurice Hodson, 'The house in the hallow': 'The Quarry', in Walker, A., (ed.) 2010, *Uphill Lincoln II; the North-Eastern Suburbs*, The Survey of Lincoln, pp. 42-3. This describes another of the uses to which the property was put after that.

82.   Atherstone House is probably 12 Eastgate. There is a comprehensive guide to Atherstone House and Atherstone Place in Jones, S., *et al.*, 1990, *The Survey of Ancient Houses in Lincoln, vol. III*, pp. 105-26. See also various directories and inquest notes for Harold's death.

83.   *Lincolnshire Chronicle*, 19 December 1902.

84.   *Lincolnshire Echo*, 13 June 1931.

85.   Geoff Tann, 'The Cottage, Swallowbeck', *The Lincoln Enquirer*, 31, May 2016, pp. 8-9.

86.   Lease for sale in *Lincolnshire Chronicle*, 29 November 1907. *Morning Post*, 4 November 1908, p. 11 and *Manchester Courier*, 3-4 November 1908, p. 1 and company records 2 November 1909.

87.   Lease of Cold Bath House advertised in *Lincolnshire Chronicle*, 29 November 1907 by the Sills family, Sir Francis Hill, *Victorian Lincoln*, 1974, p. 171.

88.   Arboretum interpretation panel on the site; 'The Gossiper', *Lincolnshire Echo*, 28 November 1950, p.4; Hurt, F., 1991, *Lincoln during the War*, pp. 56-59, including photograph of damage.

89.   Perhaps these soldiers found their wives through the regimental connections of Robert Swan II. See earlier on this article.

90.   See Jones *et al.*, *The Survey of Ancient Houses III*, 1990, pp. 94-104 in note 3 on the Burghersh Chantry.

91.   *Stamford Mercury*, 4 August 1922, p.1; information from Dr Rob Wheeler, letter from Gervase Wells-Cole to Ruth Tinley, 1970. Our thanks to Beryl George for these. See also George, B. and Tinley, R., 2014, '"A gentlemanly style of residence": Stone's Place through time', in Walker, A., (ed.) *Birchwood, Hartsholme and Swanpool, Lincoln's Outer South-Western Suburbs*, The Survey of Lincoln, pp. 20-23.

92.   Lincolnshire Archives Report, 21, 1969-70 and information from Dr Rob Wheeler.

93.   Leach, *Sausthorpe*, 1968, pp. 14,16.

REFLECTIONS ON 'CLOSED PARISHES'

Martin Watkinson

Dennis Mills's work on 'open' and 'closed' parishes has influenced a whole generation of historians writing about social conditions in the Victorian countryside. This article celebrates that legacy and seeks to build on the foundations that Mills has laid. In particular, it reflects on and develops his model of 'closed' parishes.

'Closed' or 'close' parishes were generally dominated by one or two major landowners who owned all the farms and cottages in the village and let them to a small and strictly controlled number of tenants. In some instances, the landlord of a closed parish was resident in that parish. He was regarded as 'the squire' of the village and typically exercised tight control over village affairs. In other cases, the landlord lived elsewhere. Such 'absentee' landlords were often seen as remote figures with less opportunity, and perhaps less inclination, to intervene in parish business.

This distinction between closed parishes with resident and absentee landlords is an important one and is often made. Nevertheless, the differences between them – economically, socially, politically and culturally – are seldom explored in detail. This article seeks to identify those features more clearly with reference to the county of Lincolnshire and to the parish of Humberston in particular. The analysis suggests that Mills's model of closed parishes requires some minor revision and merits further development.

OPEN AND CLOSED PARISHES

The terms 'open' and 'closed' parishes were originally adopted in the nineteenth century to explain differences in the way that power and authority were exercised in the countryside.[1] A closed parish was taken to be one in which the ownership of land and housing was concentrated in the hands of one or, at most, two or three proprietors. Open parishes were those in which property was divided between several or many owners.

These differences between parishes were seen to have important implications for the administration of poor relief and the laws of settlement. In closed parishes, the landowner (or the landowners acting together) had the ability, if they were so inclined, to limit settlement in the parish and to exclude or remove those who were potentially chargeable to the poor rates. In open parishes, landowners could less easily apply limits on settlement because property holders were more numerous and had different interests: for example, small farmers might seek to limit the numbers of those dependent on poor relief but cottage owners, petty tradesmen and speculative builders might be receptive to the influx of newcomers because they could profit from the increased demand for housing and goods. As a consequence, poor families were often drawn (and sometimes driven) into open parishes where they created a ready pool of casual labour from which farmers in closed parishes could draw.[2]

Mills took this simple distinction between open and closed villages and from it created a more sophisticated typology of rural settlement. He developed the model in two important ways. First, he suggested that open and closed parishes occupied the opposite ends of a broad spectrum. Between these two extremes were ranged a number of other (intermediate) parish types, including open parishes which contained a mix of large and small landowners and closed parishes in which the landlord was an absentee or was non-resident.[3]

Second, he argued that each of these parish types was associated with differences in other variables. So closed parishes tended not only to have smaller populations and fewer numbers of poor people than open parishes, but also to have large farms, seasonal scarcities of labour, a limited number and range of craftsmen and tradesmen, good quality housing, and well-endowed churches, schools and charities. They were also highly regulated. Villagers there were said to be conditioned by landlord, parson and schoolmaster to be deferential to their superiors and accepting of their place in society. Open parishes, on the other hand, were the polar opposite of closed parishes.[4] Mills's characterisation of the differences between open and closed parishes is summarised in the table below (Figure 1).

As Sarah Banks and others have pointed out, these characteristics do not hold for all places at all times.[5] Nevertheless, the model provides a helpful framework for analysis and has been widely used by historians writing about nineteenth-century rural society. For example, the model has been used to examine and explain differences between parishes in the supply of labour, the distribution of housing, the administration of poor relief, the pattern of religious affiliation, and the incidence of popular protest.[6]

Open Parishes	Closed Parishes
Many small landowners	One or a few large landowners
Large populations	Small populations
Rapid population growth	Slow population growth
Small farms	Large farms
Several craftsmen	Few craftsmen
Several shops and pubs	Few or no shops and pubs
Housing plentiful but poor	Housing scarce but good
High poor rates	Low poor rates
Strongly Nonconformist	Strongly Anglican
Strongly radical and independent	Highly deferential

Fig.1 Characteristics of Open and Closed Parishes (based on Mills, D., 1980, Lord and Peasant in Nineteenth-Century Britain, p. 117, Table 6.1)

CLOSED PARISHES WITH NON-RESIDENT LANDLORDS

Mills did not define in detail the characteristics of his two intermediate parish types. He did, however, make two broad observations on closed parishes with absentee owners. The first was that landlords tended to intervene less in the affairs of closed parishes in the far reaches of their estates than in parishes close to their main house.[7] The second was that in parishes where the landlord lived elsewhere, social leadership was exercised not by the landlord but by the parson and the large tenant farmers.[8]

Mills was not alone in noticing these distinctions. A number of other historians have commented on the failure of absentee landlords to engage pro-actively with outlying villages. For example, those studying individual estates have noticed that landowners were prepared to invest greater sums in the physical infrastructure of estate villages than in closed parishes further from home. Heather Fuller observed this phenomenon in her study of the Yarborough estates in north Lincolnshire and used the term 'distance decay' to describe the tendency for farmhouses, cottages and other buildings to be progressively less stylish and ornamented the further they were from the main house at Brocklesby.[9] Shirley Brook noticed a similar feature on the Chaplin's estates in Blankney and Metheringham.[10] David Grigg, writing about South Lincolnshire, also suggested that landlords were sometimes disinclined to invest in agricultural improvement in parishes that were some distance from their main house.[11]

Others have remarked that non-resident landlords were less disposed to look after the moral and material welfare of their tenants in parishes where they themselves were not resident. In his study of landed estates on the Lincolnshire Wolds, Charles Rawding observed that absentee landlords were less likely than resident landowners to be directly involved in the provision of employment, the upkeep of estate cottages and the distribution of charity. As a consequence, they were less able to impose their authority on village affairs or exercise influence in matters of religion, politics or social conduct. The landlord's absence from the village, Rawding commented, removed many of the social obligations which were present in the area around the great house.[12] James Obelkevich similarly observed for South Lindsey that an absentee owner could exert little influence over the religious life of his parish, other than by screening out persons with unacceptable religious views when he or his agent selected new tenants.[13]

In these circumstances, it fell to others to perform many of the duties that absentee landlords were unable or disinclined to undertake. In South Lindsey, Obelkevich remarked that since there were so few resident squires, farmers acted as *de facto* rulers in most parishes, controlling village government (in the parish vestries) as tightly as they controlled the village economy.[14] Charles Rawding noted that the landlord's agent might also take a more active role in parishes where the landlord was non-resident.[15]

All of the studies cited above were conducted at a 'macro' level. In other words, they were concerned primarily with an examination of particular parts of the county or of individual estates. It is, therefore, instructive to see whether a more detailed study conducted at a 'micro', or parish, level can add to our understanding of the nature of landlord and tenant relationships in closed parishes.

The 'micro' analysis that follows arises from a detailed study of a single parish (Humberston in Lincolnshire) during a single century (1750-1850).[16] It is a well-documented village and

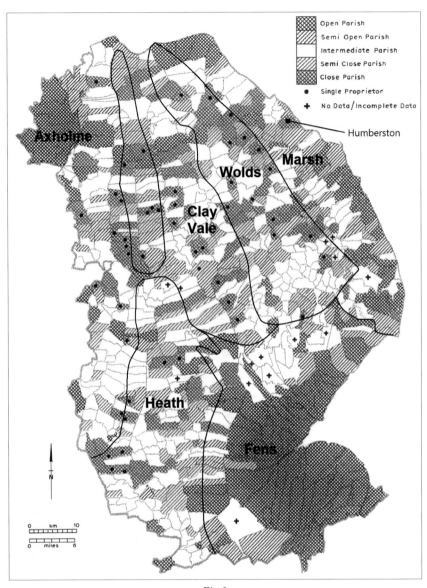

Fig.2

*The Distribution of Open and Closed Parishes in Lincolnshire, c.1830 (based on Bennett,
S., 'Landownership and parish type, c.1830' in Bennett, S. and Bennett, N., (eds), 1993, An
Historical Atlas of Lincolnshire, Hull, pp. 94-5). The classification is based on an analysis of
the Land Tax returns for 1831 and 1832 (and, in some cases, 1826). Open parishes are those
which had more than 55 landowners and where the largest paid less than 30 per cent of the
tax; semi-open parishes are those where just one of those criteria applied. Closed parishes are
those which had fewer than 5 proprietors and where the largest paid more than 85 per cent of
the tax; semi-closed parishes are those where just one of these criteria applied. Intermediate
parishes lie between these two extremes.*

reveals a great deal about the exercise of power and authority in a closed parish with an absentee landlord. In particular, it suggests that we need to add some caveats to Mills's hypothesis. First, it is necessary to set the parish in context.

HUMBERSTON IN LINCOLNSHIRE

Open and closed parishes were differently distributed across Lincolnshire in the nineteenth century. As is evident from Figure 2, there was a predominance of open parishes in the low-lying, ill-drained lands of the Fens and the coastal marshes, the Humber and the Isle of Axholme, where smallholders had traditionally been able to eke out a tolerable existence from arable and pasture farming, fishing and fowling. Closed parishes and intermediate parishes were located primarily on the better drained uplands of the Wolds and on the Lincoln Heath, close to the Great North Road, where the aristocracy and gentry had chosen to build their houses, lay out their parks and create estate villages.[17]

In north-east Lincolnshire, this pattern was disturbed by the presence of a small cluster of closed parishes in the Middle Marsh. These were parishes in which holdings had been progressively engrossed and consolidated by indigenous farmers in the sixteenth and early seventeenth centuries and which had subsequently been acquired by rising gentry families in search of good fattening pastures and by wealthy attorneys and merchants looking to invest in property.[18] By the mid-eighteenth century, these major landowners were living in grand houses on the Wolds or further afield. As a consequence, few Marshland parishes had resident squires. In their absence, agents managed their estates from a distance, the clergy filled their roles as JPs, and large tenant farmers exercised control of parish business.[19] Humberston was one such parish.

Humberston today is a large village immediately to the south of Cleethorpes and five miles from Grimsby. The northern half of the parish is largely residential but the southern part is still agricultural. In the nineteenth century, before the growth of Grimsby and Cleethorpes, Humberston was a much smaller settlement than it is today, containing just 200 to 250 people (see Figure 3). The parson and eight farmers dominated the parish. The rest of the working population was made up of agricultural labourers and farm servants and a handful of craftsmen.[20]

All the land and all the houses in the parish were owned by a single landlord. Between 1792 and 1836, the landlord was Robert Smith, a Midlands banker and London financier who became an MP for Nottingham and a friend of William Pitt. It was Pitt who raised him to the peerage as the first Lord Carrington in 1796.[21] His son Robert John, the second Lord Carrington, held the estate from 1836 until his death in 1868.[22] The third Lord Carrington sold it in 1920.[23]

During the period of the Carringtons' ownership, Humberston was administered as an outlying portion of a large estate that was centred on High Wycombe in Buckinghamshire. The estate included other property in Buckinghamshire as well as in London, Lincolnshire, and Wales.[24]

THE ROLE OF THE LANDLORD

An examination of the Carringtons' role in the management of their distant property in Humberston therefore provides an opportunity to evaluate Dennis Mills's claim that landlords tended to be less interventionist in peripheral parts of their estates than in villages close to their residence.

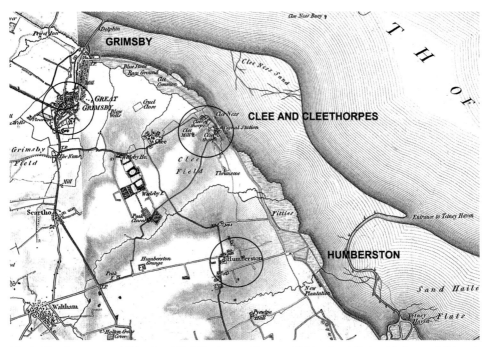

Fig.3 Humberston and District, 1824 (Ordnance Survey, Old Series, 1824, with later additions).

In some respects, it can be said that Mills's claim holds true for Humberston. It is clear, for example, that the Carringtons had little interest in the aesthetics of the village or its physical infrastructure. On the Wolds, resident landlords were busy creating neatly ordered villages in which their presence, status and authority were displayed in the regular layout of the village, the grandeur of the manor house, the landscaping of the park, and the architectural uniformity of the tenants' houses.[25] In Humberston, Carrington had little reason to spend money on a grand house or park since he decided fairly early on that he was not going to reside in the village. He therefore knocked down the old manor house in Humberston and replaced it with a farmhouse. He also built new brick farmhouses for four more of his farms (Field House, Midfield, Church, and South Sea Lane Farms). His son, Robert John, built a sixth (Whitehall Farm).[26] The houses had a broadly similar architectural style – symmetrical brick fronts with tall (occasionally square) sash windows capped with a flat brick arch or a white stucco lintel (see Figure 4). In contrast with many estate villages on the Wolds, these were relatively plain and simple buildings, employing none of the mock gothic designs, ornate barge boards, decorative finials and insignia for which the Yarborough and Heneage estate cottages became renowned. In Humberston, only two later buildings, a cottage and the smithy, had the Carrington arms on the front aspect or the gable end.[27]

The creation of these new farmsteads was intended, at least in part, to attract wealthy tenant farmers whose capital investment would be used to improve the land. The same considerations did not apply to labourers' cottages, not least because farmworkers were in ready supply and housing was in high demand. The Carringtons were, therefore, less concerned with the condition of the cottages belonging to the estate. Most of these were traditional thatched cottages of mud and stud which dated from the seventeenth or eighteenth centuries (see Figure 5). One, at least, was in a parlous condition: William Marshall reported in 1814 that 'it is so rotten & bad that I am affraid [sic] it will be difficult to make stand for much longer'.[28] Others were patched up or were encased in brick and roofed with tiles.[29] As a consequence, for most of the nineteenth century, old cottages and new farmhouses stood side by side in a haphazard arrangement of ill-matched buildings, in stark contrast with the regular and compact morphology of estate villages on the Lincolnshire Wolds.

The Carringtons also made only a modest contribution to the social and spiritual life of the village. When the first Lord Carrington acquired the Humberston estate, the funds that a previous landlord, Matthew Humberston, had bequeathed for the building and maintenance of almshouses and a school were languishing in the Court of Chancery where they had been for over eighty years. It took twenty years for Carrington to begin legal proceedings to have these monies released and applied to their intended purposes. Even then, the Master of Chancery believed that Carrington was motivated merely by 'a wish to benefit the estate' rather than from any 'nobler and more liberal feeling'.[30]

Neither were the first or second Lord Carrington conspicuous benefactors of

Fig.4
Brick and Tile Farmhouse on the Carrington Estate in Humberston (author's photograph).

Fig.5
Mud and Stud Cottage on the Carrington Estate in Humberston (Grimsby Public Library, Local History Library: H804/728).

the church, the school or the almshouses in Humberston. They were generous and regular subscribers to national organisations and to charities and societies in and around their home in High Wycombe but they contributed less frequently to good causes in Humberston and usually made one-off payments to meet particular circumstances rather than regular donations to support village charities.[31] When the first Lord Carrington wrote his will in 1836, he bequeathed £100 to the poor of High Wycombe but left nothing to the poor of Humberston.[32] The second Lord Carrington was even more divorced from the affairs of the parish. It was said, albeit by a political rival, that he declined to give a single penny to the school or the almshouses in Humberston.[33]

This reluctance to engage closely and directly with the affairs of Humberston may have been a reflection of the Carringtons' personal priorities and interests. Like other Whig aristocrats, they may have felt more inclined to exhibit a *laissez faire* attitude to social relations than adopt the paternalist views associated with many Tory landlords. But their close involvement

Fig.6 Post-Enclosure Farms in Humberston, c.1860 (constructed from Centre for Buckinghamshire Studies: D-CN 18/8/1/5, and Carrington Family Archive, Bledlow: Items 5-6).

in affairs in Buckinghamshire suggests that, as Mills supposed, it was more likely to have been a function of distance.

However, there were other aspects of the Carringtons' management of their Humberston estates which demonstrated a clear willingness to engage directly in the affairs of the parish. In this respect, they do not conform to Mills's stereotype. Two of these exceptions are examined below.

Caveat 1: Improving the Land

First, the Carringtons were very much concerned with those aspects of the estate that generated an income. The first Lord Carrington, in particular, took a very close and personal interest in the improvement of the land.

As soon as he acquired the estate in Humberston, Lord Carrington set about its improvement. In 1792 he engaged contractors to build a new sea wall and he began the process of reclaiming the saltmarsh lying behind it.[34] In the following two years, he completed the enclosure of the parish by repossessing and dividing up the common meadows, pasture and furze grounds (see Figure 6).[35] And in a series of letting agreements completed in 1792, 1794 and 1796, he required or authorised his tenants to plough up more than 276 acres of old pasture and scrub land, and to drain, pare and burn old meadow land.[36] An independent report, undertaken in 1796, spoke of the 'great improvements' that had been made throughout the parish and a survey taken in 1805 showed that the value of the agricultural land had increased by almost a third, rising from an average of 17s. 0d. an acre in 1792 to £1. 2s. 6d. an acre in 1805.[37]

In the years after 1800, Lord Carrington turned his attention to improving the system of husbandry in Humberston and introducing progressive farming methods. When he acquired the estate in 1792, the arable land in Humberston was still being cultivated on a traditional three-course rotation of wheat or barley, beans and fallow.[38] This was a typical crop cycle for the Middle Marsh at this time, but was quite out of step with the more progressive rotations adopted on the light soils of the Wolds and elsewhere, where rotation grasses and turnips had replaced bare fallows.[39] Lord Carrington used annual letting agreements to insist that clover and, where possible, turnips should be included in the standard system of crop rotation in place of a winter fallow. As a result, most farmers moved to a four-course rotation incorporating rotation grasses between 1796 and 1805, though it was not until the introduction of cheap mass-produced, pipe drains in the 1840s that turnips could be grown successfully in Humberston.[40]

In these respects, the first Lord Carrington was a diligent landlord. He replied promptly to letters, despite the many other calls on his time, and he was assiduous in ensuring that his instructions were carried out. It is evident from the estate papers that Carrington went through each one of the draft letting agreements with great care, annotating them where he felt they needed additions or corrections, and asking detailed questions when he required further information.[41] He not only introduced cropping covenants within the leases to stipulate the course of farming to be followed but he also commissioned and scrutinised cropping returns to ensure that the covenants were being strictly followed.[42] He also issued detailed instructions to individual farmers. In a single letter to his principal tenant, William Marshall, in 1809 he expressed regret that one of the tenants had not honoured a promise to sow seeds in one of his fields, he instructed Marshall to prevent another tenant ploughing up any more grass, and he urged Marshall to continue to experiment with warping.[43]

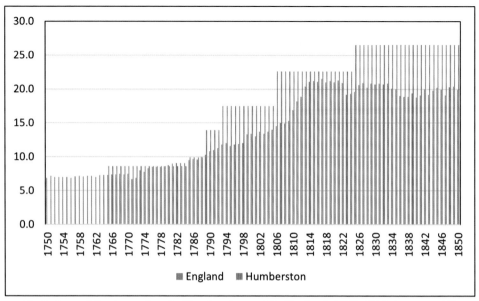

Fig.7 Annual Rents per Acre in Humberston and in England, 1750–1850 (see note 44).

As a result of his careful management of the estate, the first Lord Carrington was able to push rents in Humberston slightly ahead of the general rise in agricultural rents (see Figure 7).[44] This was a significant outcome for a landlord who, having relinquished his commercial interests, came to rely solely on his landed income. And it explains why Lord Carrington was singularly focused on the improvement of the estate and the enhancement of land values in Humberston.

Caveat 2: Empowering the Agent
The second caveat is that we should not discount the influence of the landlord's agent. The agent was likely to have had a greater degree of delegated authority in the administration of outlying properties than in the management of estate villages close to home. In these circumstances, the agent might well choose to act in areas where the landlord was negligent or uninterested.

In the case of Humberston, Lord Carrington employed his business associate and friend, Thomas Thompson of Hull, as his agent in north Lincolnshire. Thompson was an old-style agent – a professional man with business interests of his own who undertook estate management on a part-time basis. He had begun his working life as a clerk in the counting house of Wilberforce and Smith, a firm of Russian and Baltic merchants in Hull. He rose to become manager there in 1779 and eight years later also became managing partner of Smiths' bank in Hull. This brought him into a close working relationship with Robert Smith, the first Lord Carrington, who was a senior partner in the Hull bank.[45] A surviving portrait depicts him as a leading figure in the improvement of Hull Docks in the early nineteenth century (see Figure 8).

Thompson performed the role that many other stewards or agents undertook – he selected the tenants, managed the leases, collected the rents, and acted as intermediary in communications between Carrington and the tenant farmers.[46] But he was more than a cipher for Lord Carrington. He had considerable discretion to act on his own initiative. Thompson himself wrote that 'my noble friend, Lord Carrington, the owner of the estate, left me at liberty to fulfil his wishes and my own, in any way I thought best'.[47] This is evident in several initiatives for which Thompson himself took responsibility, the most important of which was the provision of cow pastures for the labouring poor.

Thomas Thompson had a deep concern for the welfare of the poor. He was known in Hull as a reforming poor law guardian, seeking to keep the poor out of the workhouse by providing them with work, out-relief and allotments.[48] In Humberston, Thompson persuaded Lord Carrington to set aside some sixty acres of pasture and meadow in the south of the parish for the use of the thirteen Cottagers who had lost their rights to common land when the parish had been finally enclosed in the 1790s. Thompson later extended this by the addition of another twenty-four acres in the north of the parish

Fig.8
Portrait of Thomas Thompson (1754–1828) by John Russell (1745–1806) (Maritime Museum, Hull, © Ferens Art Gallery/ Bridgeman Images).

to benefit five other families (see Figure 6). In 1825, he increased this number to eight.[49] The creation of cow pastures brought considerable benefit to these twenty-one families who not only used milk to enrich their diet, but also sold surplus milk and butter to generate income and accumulate savings. Examination of the vestry minutes and overseers' accounts for Humberston for the period up to 1834 reveals that no-one in possession of a cottage and a cow sought, or received, poor relief during that time.[50]

Thompson's successor as agent was James Henwood. Like Thompson, Henwood started as a clerk and rose in time to be a full partner in Smiths' bank in Hull. Also, like Thompson, he was an ardent Methodist – a local preacher, class leader, circuit steward and member of Conference – who gave practical support to the Methodist congregation in Humberston.[51] Though Carrington granted land for a Methodist chapel in Humberston, he declined to contribute to the building fund. According to the Methodists in Humberston, it was James Henwood who helped them overcome 'two years of difficulty' to get their chapel built. Henwood even delivered one of the two opening services in the chapel in 1835.[52]

It is apparent, therefore, that Carrington's agents were diligent in discharging many of the functions that in estate villages would have fallen to the landlord. Thomas Thompson appears to have had a genuine concern for the well-being of the tenants and was the driving force behind the provision of cow pastures for the poor. James Henwood was concerned for the spiritual welfare of the villagers and gave practical support to the Methodists. In many ways Carrington's firm managerial approach and his agents' humanitarian and religious sensibilities, complemented each other very well and provided firm and clear leadership in a parish in which neither landlord nor agent were resident.

THE INFLUENCE OF THE PARSON AND TENANT FARMERS

What, then, of Mills's second claim, that when the landlord was non-resident the parson and large tenant farmers assumed leadership of the parish? The experience of Humberston suggests that matters were not always this straightforward. As noted above, there were several aspects of village life in which landlord and agent played an active role, despite being non-resident. Moreover, the parson and the farmers could not always be relied upon to act for the landlord.

Caveat 4: The Parson

In the ideal Victorian parish, the squire and parson worked harmoniously together to regulate parish affairs, to maintain social order, and to minister to the poor and the sick.[53] Yet in Humberston, as in many other parishes in the eighteenth and early nineteenth centuries, the living was held by a succession of non-resident clerics who appointed curates to perform their duties. However, the curates were also non-resident and provided only a basic level of spiritual and pastoral support. In 1790, the curate conducted services just once a fortnight in summer and every third week in winter, and celebrated communion only three times a year.[54] The absence not only of a resident squire, but also of a resident parson, therefore, left a vacuum in the heart of the village community.

A new era was ushered in during the 1820s when Lord Carrington installed the Revd Joseph Gedge as the resident clergyman and schoolmaster.[55] Gedge was to teach in the charity school during the week and to conduct services in the church on Sunday. This put an end to a period of absenteeism but it did not usher in a new era of harmony. Carrington had hoped that Gedge would be a person of 'humble mind & studious disposition & of industrious habits'.[56] Instead, he discovered that he had appointed a strong-willed and ambitious young man who was prepared to challenge and confront him on a number of issues.

From the outset, Gedge complained about the inadequate size of the schoolhouse, the insufficiency of his stipend, and the onerous nature of his duties as both parson and schoolmaster.[57] The first Lord Carrington, for his part, was irritated by what he took to be Gedge's extravagant lifestyle, his social pretensions, and his refusal to perform his duties as schoolmaster as rigorously as he demanded.[58] This led to a running battle between the first and second Lords Carrington and the Revd J. Gedge which lasted for eighteen years and culminated in Gedge's dismissal as schoolmaster in 1838.[59] This sparked two protracted lawsuits in the Court of Chancery. In the first, Gedge petitioned the Court for unfair dismissal and won. In the second, he sought to remove Carrington and Carrington's friends and family from the Board of Trustees of the Humberston Charity. Though he was only partially successful in this second case, the first Lord Carrington and his son essentially withdrew from the Trust at that point and allowed Gedge free rein.[60]

Gedge did not, however, use his considerable power and authority to provide local leadership in the parish. The villagers complained that Gedge neglected his duties as both headmaster and priest, appointing a junior teacher to take his place in the school, on a fraction of his salary, and taking only one church service a week. Two of the leading farmers in the village alleged that it was a common opinion in Humberston and its neighbourhood that Gedge

Fig.9 Photograph of Henry Marshall and his Family, c.1870 (Grimsby Public Library, Local History Library: H804/728).

felt himself above being a schoolmaster. In addition, they grumbled that Gedge spent more of his time outside the village than he did within it – visiting family and friends, officiating as clergyman in a second parish, sitting as a clerical JP, and, after 1837, acting as a poor law guardian. When Gedge fell out with Lord Carrington and petitioned against him in the Court of Chancery, he was unable to muster any supporting affidavits from his parishioners in Humberston.[61] The residents of Humberston, it seems, were more inclined to take the side of their absentee landlord than their resident parson.

Caveat 5: The Tenant Farmers

If the clergy proved inadequate surrogates of the absentee landlord, what then of that other important group, the tenant farmers? In the absence of a resident landlord and a resident parson, and latterly of a resident but uninterested parson, the tenant farmers of Humberston exercised a high degree of authority.

At the time of enclosure, the first Lord Carrington created eight farms in Humberston. The smallest was 160 acres and the largest was 580 acres (see Figure 6). These were huge farms by local standards: elsewhere in the Marsh, farms generally averaged around forty to sixty acres in size.[62] Those who farmed these large acreages during the years of high prices between 1795 and 1815 and in the period after 1835, enjoyed significant prosperity. The most successful amongst them furnished their houses with linen, silver and china. They bought or rented small parcels of land in neighbouring parishes. They invested in shares in the new docks scheme in Grimsby and lent money out on mortgage. And they provided substantial annuities for their widows and significant cash bequests for their children.[63] Their wealth alone set them above others in the village. Figure 9 reproduces a wonderfully staged photograph of Henry Marshall, one of the leading tenant farmers, showing off his family and his fine house, his horse and his groom, and one of his farm servants.

The farmers' elevated social status was evident every week at church. Here, according to Revd J. Gedge's daughter, the farmers occupied the pews in the nave of the church whilst the farm servants and labourers sat up in the gallery, wearing their Sunday smocks (see Figure 10).[64] In the graveyard, the farmers were buried beneath substantial headstones close to the main (west) door of the church whilst others occupied graves with less permanent memorials elsewhere in the churchyard.

The farmers' social standing was given extra weight by their control of the vital components of parish life – employment, housing, and poor relief. Farmers were the major employers in the parish, providing work for more than three-quarters of the working population of Humberston in the century and a half after 1750.[65] They were also the principal managers of the housing stock, providing tied cottages for farm labourers and lodgings for farm servants who were hired for the year.[66] Farmers were also the main ratepayers in the parish – between them they contributed at least 95 per cent of the parish rate – and so they took it upon themselves to govern the parish.[67] They dominated the vestry meetings (which was the principal unit of local government at that time) and they monopolised the parish offices, serving exclusively as churchwardens, constables and overseers of the poor.[68] In this last capacity they determined who was eligible to receive poor relief from the parish and under what terms. There were, therefore, few residents of Humberston who did not depend on the farmers for a roof over their heads, food on their table, and wages or allowances in their pockets.

Fig.10 Interior of Humberston Parish Church showing the nave (with box pews now removed), where the farmers sat with their families, and the gallery to the west (with an organ now inserted) where the farm labourers and servants sat (author's collection).

The farmers, therefore, formed a natural and powerful oligarchy. Apart from the vicar, there were few others in the parish with the economic or social standing to challenge them. Yet they were not a homogeneous group and it should not be assumed that they always acted in unison. There were clearly gradations in status and wealth between, for example, John Walesby, who occupied the prestigious Manor Farm, cultivated 583 acres and employed fourteen men, and Lionel Wilson who lived in a thatched farmhouse, worked 180 acres, and employed four labourers.[69] Some, like William Marshall, were progressive farmers with well-managed farms and an established reputation in the locality as breeders of high-quality, long-wool sheep and short-horn cattle. Others, like Samuel Bee, struggled to keep their farms in a decent state of cultivation.[70]

There were also differences between them in matters of religion and politics. Most of the farmers in the village were Anglicans but three long-serving tenant families (the Tomlinsons, Bees and Kirbys) were staunch Methodists and had strong connections with other Wesleyans in the Grimsby Circuit.[71] Politically, the farmers generally voted for the Whigs after 1832 but there were occasional dissenting voices: Thomas Tomlinson and Robert Story took opposing sides in the acrimonious and corrupt parliamentary elections in Grimsby in 1819 and Thomas Mountain voted for the Tories in 1852.[72]

Neither should it be assumed that the tenant farmers acted in accordance with their landlord's wishes. Indeed, the values and interests of the tenant farmers were sometimes at odds with those of the absent landlord. The second Lord Carrington, for example, was greatly in favour of the new poor law and saw the workhouse as a vital means of supporting and protecting those who were unable to fend for themselves.[73] The tenant farmers in Humberston, however, preferred to keep the village poor in the parish. They circumvented the provisions of the new poor law by putting the able-bodied to work on the parish roads and sea banks, rather than sending them to the workhouse, and by distributing out-relief to the elderly and infirm in their own homes.[74]

Finally, there were others in the village who, from time to time, claimed a leadership role in the parish. They included the village craftsmen, the senior cottagers, and even those labourers who exercised a prominent role in the Methodist chapel, as local preachers or class leaders. Notable amongst this group was Thomas Richardson, the village grocer, tailor and draper who was at various times a school teacher, land surveyor and census enumerator, as well as a class leader and a society steward in the Methodist chapel in Humberston.[75] Though Richardson was a cottager, and not therefore a member of the Vestry, he played a major role in the dispute between the Carringtons and Revd J. Gedge, arguing publicly against Gedge's fitness to hold office.[76]

SUMMARY
So what, in summary, can we say about closed parishes with non-resident landlords?
Dennis Mills opened this discourse by mapping out the respective roles of landlords, clergy and farmers. He depicted absentee landlords as remote figures who, because of the constraints of distance and perhaps of temperament, were reluctant to get involved in the affairs of distant parishes that they owned. In their absence, he said, the resident clergy and the principal tenant farmers provided social leadership in the parish.

This has proved to be a perceptive analysis. The foregoing examination of life in Humberston, has confirmed that landlord, parson and farmer, together with the landlord's agent, were the major repositories of power and authority in the parish. The balance of power between these groups in Humberston was, however, slightly different from that which Mills mapped out. The landlord and his agent were considerably more interventionist, and the parson somewhat less supportive and active, than Mills's formulation might have suggested. And though the tenant farmers fully performed the leadership roles that Mills envisaged for them, they were not a homogeneous or compliant group and there were others in the village who held positions of influence. In Humberston at least, power and authority was shared between the principal stakeholders in quite specific ways and it was not uncommon for power to shift from one party to another as prevailing authority structures were successfully challenged by one faction or another.

Despite these nuances and caveats, this analysis adds substance to Dennis Mills's view that the sharing of functions between the landlord, the agent, the parson and the leading tenant farmers was the defining characteristic of a parish without a resident landlord. And it was, above all else, what distinguished it from a parish with a resident landlord, where a single authority figure ruled the roost.

NOTES:

1. Checkland, S. G. and E. O. A., (eds), 1974, *The Poor Law Report of 1834*, Harmondsworth, pp. 190-203; Mills, Dennis R., 1970, 'The Geographical Effects of the Laws of Settlement in Nottinghamshire: An Analysis of Francis Howell's Report, 1848', *East Midlands Geographer*, 5, pp. 31–8; Short, Brian, 'The evolution of contrasting communities within rural England', in B. Short (ed.), 1992, *The English Rural Community: Image and Analysis*, Cambridge, pp. 28-9. See also the evidence of Mr W. R. Flint, Relieving Officer for the Louth District, Lincolnshire, in British Parliamentary Papers (hereafter BPP), *Select Committee on the Irremovable Poor, Minutes of Evidence*, H.C. 1860 (520), pp. 167-79.

2. Short, 'Contrasting Communities', pp. 29-35; Mills, Dennis R., 1959, 'The poor laws and the distribution of population, *c.*1600-1860, with special reference to Lincolnshire', *Transactions of the Institute of British Geographers*, 26, pp. 185-95.

3. Mills, D. R., 1980, *Lord and Peasant in Nineteenth-Century Britain*, pp. 76-83. Mills defines closed parishes as those in which a single landlord paid more than half of the land tax (or two to three owners paid two-thirds) and open parishes as those with 50 owners or more (or 20 owners or more with an average density of less than 36 acres per owner). Other historians have sometimes used different labels and different methods of classification.

4. *Ibid.*, pp. 116-44.

5. Banks, Sarah, 1988, 'Nineteenth-century scandal or twentieth-century model? A new look at 'open' and 'close' parishes', *Economic History Review*, 41, pp. 51-73. See also Spencer, D., 2000, 'Reformulating the 'closed' parish thesis: associations, interests, and interaction', *Journal of Historical Geography*, 26, pp. 83–98, and Short, 'Contrasting communities', p. 39.

6. On labour supply see: Holderness, B. A., 1972, '"Open" and "close" parishes' in England in the eighteenth and nineteenth centuries', *Agricultural History Review*, 20, pp. 126-39; Sheppard, J. A., 1961, 'East Yorkshire's agricultural labour force in the mid-nineteenth century', *Agricultural History Review*, 9, pp. 19-39; Rawding, C. K., 1994, 'Village type and employment structure: an analysis in the nineteenth-century Lincolnshire Wolds', *Local Population Studies*, 53, pp. 53-68. On housing, see: Ayres, M., 2004, 'The provision of housing and power relations in rural England, 1834-1914' (unpublished PhD thesis, University of Leicester), pp. 27-72. On poor relief, see: Song, B. K., 2002, 'Parish typology and the operation of the poor laws in early nineteenth-century Oxfordshire', *Agricultural History Review*, 50, pp. 203-224; Digby, A., 1978, *Pauper Palaces*, pp. 89-92; Apfel, W., and Dunkley, P., 1985, 'English rural society and the new poor law: Bedfordshire, 1834-47', *Social History*, 10, pp. 37-68; Rawding, C. K., 1986, *Poor Relief and the Rural Workforce: A Case Study of North Lincolnshire, 1834-1861*, Sussex. On religion, see: Snell, K. D. M., and Ell,

P. S., 2000, *Rival Jerusalems: The Geography of Victorian Religion*, Cambridge, pp. 364-94; Everitt, A., 1972, *The Pattern of Rural Dissent: The Nineteenth Century*, Leicester, pp. 20-22; Obelkevich, J., 1976, *Religion and Rural Society: South Lindsey, 1825-1875*, Oxford, pp. 12-13. On popular protest, see: Hobsbawm, E. J., and Rudé, G., 1969, *Captain Swing*, pp. 182-3; Mills, D. R., and Short, B. M., 1983, 'Social change and social conflict in nineteenth-century England: the use of the open-closed village model', *Journal of Peasant Studies*, 10, pp. 253-62; Reed, M., 1984, 'Social change and social conflict in nineteenth-century England: a comment', *Journal of Peasant Studies*, 12, pp. 109-21; Mills, D. R., 1988, 'Peasants and conflict in nineteenth-century England: a comment on recent articles', *Journal of Peasant Studies*, 15, pp. 394-400. On the twentieth-century countryside, see: Jackson, A. J. H., 2012, 'The 'Open-Closed' settlement model and the interdisciplinary formulations of Dennis Mills: conceptualising local rural change', *Rural History*, 23, pp 121-136.

7. Mills, *Lord and Peasant*, pp. 39 and 76.

8. Mills, D. R., 1965, 'English villages in the eighteenth and nineteenth centuries: a sociological approach, Part 1', *Amateur Historian*, 6, pp. 271-8.

9. Fuller, H. A., 1976, 'Landownership and the Lindsey landscape', *Annals of the Association of American Geographers*, 66, pp.14-23.

10. Brook, A. S., 2005, 'The buildings of high farming: Lincolnshire farm buildings 1840-1910', (Ph.D. thesis, University of Hull, https://hydra.hull.ac.uk/resources/hull:14019), pp. 99-102.

11. Grigg, D., 1966, *The Agricultural Revolution in South Lincolnshire*, Cambridge, pp. 82-3. See also Holderness, B. A., 1972, 'Landlords' capital formation in East Anglia, 1750-1870', *Economic History Review*, 25, p. 436.

12. Rawding, C. K., 2001, *The Lincolnshire Wolds in the Nineteenth Century*, Lincoln, pp. 173-4. See also Rawding, C. K., 1992, 'Society and place in nineteenth-century north Lincolnshire', *Rural History*, 3, pp. 59-85, and *idem.*, 1990, 'The iconography of churches: a case study of landownership and power in nineteenth-century Lincolnshire', *Journal of Historical Geography*, 16, pp. 157-176.

13. Obelkevich, J., 1976, *Religion and Rural Society: South Lindsey, 1825-1875*, Oxford, p. 30.

14. *Ibid.*, p. 46.

15. Rawding, *The Lincolnshire Wolds*, p. 174.

16. Watkinson, M. A., 2017, 'The Microhistory of a Lincolnshire Parish: Humberston, 1750-1850' (PhD thesis, University of Leicester; http://hdl.handle.net/2381/40639).

17. Bennett, S., 'Landownership and parish type' and Mills, D., 'Country seats of the gentry' in S. and N. Bennett, (eds), 1993, *An Historical Atlas of Lincolnshire*, Hull, pp. 94-5 and 106-7 respectively; Obelkevich, *Religion and Rural Society*, pp. 8-22; Rawding, *The Lincolnshire Wolds*, pp. 51-6 and 170-1.

18. Young, A., 1799, *A General View of the Agriculture of the County of Lincoln*, p. 182; Thirsk, J., 1957, *English Peasant Farming: The Agrarian History of Lincolnshire from Tudor to Recent Times*, pp. 147-51, 154-5, 237-8 and 327-8; Beastall, T. W., 1978, *The Agricultural Revolution in Lincolnshire*, Lincoln, pp. 10-11, 17, and 92; Holderness, B.A., 1974, 'Aspects of inter-regional land use and agriculture in Lincolnshire, 1600-1850', *Lincolnshire History and Archaeology*, 9, pp. 35-42; Watkinson, M. A., 1984, 'Population change and agrarian development: the parishes of Bradley, Scartho and Humberston, c.1520-c.1730' (unpublished M.Phil. thesis, University of Leicester), pp. 143-248.

19. Thirsk, *Peasant Farming*, p. 237; Obelkevich, *Religion and Rural Society*, pp. 8-17 and 23-102; Gillett, E., 1982, *The Humber Region in the 19th Century*, Hull, p. 42; Davey, B.J., 1994, *Rural Crime in the Eighteenth Century: North Lincolnshire, 1740-80*, Hull, pp. x and 59; Davey, B.J., and Wheeler, R.C., (eds), 2012, *The Country Justice and the Case of the Blackamoor's Head*, Lincoln, pp. 1-23.

20. The National Archives (hereafter TNA): HO 107/637/15 and HO 107/2113.

21. Leighton Boyce, J. A. S. L., 1958, *Smiths the Bankers, 1658-1958*, pp. 54-7 and 128-29; Pollard, A. F., rev. S. M. Lee, 2009, 'Smith, Robert, first Baron Carrington (1752–1838)', *Oxford Dictionary*

of National Biography (www.oxforddnb.com); Symonds, P. A., and Thorne, R. G., 'Smith, Robert (1752-1838)', in R. Thorne, (ed.), 1986, *The History of Parliament: the House of Commons 1790-1820* (www.historyofparliamentonline.org).

22. Cokayne, G. L., et al., (eds), 1910, *The Complete Peerage of England, Scotland, Ireland, Great Britain and the United Kingdom*, 3, pp. 63-64.

23. Adonis, A., 2010, 'Carington, Charles Robert Wynn- , marquess of Lincolnshire (1843–1928)', *Oxford Dictionary of National Biography* (www.oxforddnb.com); *idem.*, 1988, 'Aristocracy, agriculture and Liberalism: the politics, finances and estates of the third Lord Carrington', *Historical Journal*, 31, pp. 871-97.

24. Centre for Buckinghamshire Studies (hereafter CBS): 'Family and Estate Papers of the Carington Family, Barons Carrington' [Calendar of the D-CN Deposit], p. 1, and Appendix 2.

25. Fuller, 'Landownership and the Lindsey landscape', pp. 16-19; Mitson., A., and Cox, B., 1995, 'Victorian estate housing on the Yarborough estate, Lincolnshire', *Rural History*, 6, pp. 29-45; Rawding, *The Lincolnshire Wolds*, pp. 56-68.

26. CBS: D-CN 18/8/1/2, letter dated 8 April 1817, D-CN 18/8/4/2, rentals for LD 1813 and LD 1818, D-CN 18/8/4/8, estimate for 1790, and D-CN 18/8/4/10, tenancy agreements for Thomas Kirby and William Marshall, 1796; *Lincoln, Rutland and Stamford Mercury (hereafter LRSM)*, 28 December 1810, p. 3, col. 3; Anon, 'White Hall Farm', English Heritage (http://www.pastscape. org.uk/hob.aspx?hob_id=1566622).

27. The cottage is no. 2 Cottage Yard Lane and the smithy is in Church Lane.

28. CBS: D-CN18/8/4/5, Cropping book, 1810-13.

29. Cousins, R., 2000, *Lincolnshire Buildings in the Mud and Stud Tradition*, Sleaford, pp. 34 and 45; Lincolnshire Archives Office (hereafter LAO): Misc Dep 145/10; North-east Lincolnshire Archives (hereafter NELA): 474/3; Historic England, 'Listing: Humberston', (https://historicengland.org.uk).

30. BPP, 1839, *32nd Report of the Commissioners of Inquiry into Charities, Part 4*, H.C. 1839 [194], p. 427; TNA: C 13/665/5; CBS: D-CN 18/8/4/7/3, Opinion of Mr Steele, 1804, and 18/8/4/7/9.

31. For High Wycombe, see: CBS: D-CN 21/6/1; Pollard, 'Smith, Robert', n.p.; Snoxell, D., n.d., 'Robert John Smith, 2nd Baron Carrington, 1796-1868', typescript, courtesy of Sarah Charlton, Archivist to Lord Carrington, p. 4; Leighton Boyce, *Smiths the Bankers*, p. 129; Ashford, L. J., 1960, *The History of the Borough of High Wycombe from Its Origins to 1880*, p. 283; Walpole, K. A., n.d., *From One Generation to Another: A Panorama of Wycombe Abbey, Buckinghamshire*, Wycombe, p. 12. For Humberston, see: CBS: D-CN 18/8/4/7/1/2 and D-CN 18/8/4/7/4, Gedge to Carrington, 17 February 1830; *LRSM*, 30 December 1842, p. 3, col. 5, and 27 December 1844, p. 3, col. 5; *Lincolnshire Chronicle*, 23 January 1846, p. 8, col. 2, 1 January 1847, p. 5, col. 4, and 31 December 1847, p. 5, col. 6; *The Hull Packet*, 12 January 1849, p. 6, col. 3; CBS: D-CN 18/8/4/7/2, certificate, 25 February 1840.

32. CBS: D-CN 17/1/35, m. 12.

33. NELA: 238/90.

34. CBS: D-CN 18/8/4/5 and 8-10; Young, *General View*, pp. 260-1.

35. CBS: D-CN 18/8/4/8, tenancy agreements.

36. CBS: D-CN 18/8/4/8, tenancy agreements.

37. CBS: D-CN 18/8/4/8, tenancy agreements and Beecroft's Report of Tillage, D-CN/18/8/4/3, and D-CN 18/8/4/9, Marshall to Carrington, 1798.

38. CBS: D-CN 18/8/4/8; Young, *General View*, p. 46.

39. Thirsk, *Peasant Farming*, pp. 244-9; Beastall, *Agricultural Revolution*, pp. 156-60 and 174; Perkins, J. A., 1976, 'The prosperity of farming on the Lindsey uplands, 1813-37', *Agricultural History Review*, 24, pp. 126-143; Darby, H. C., 1952, 'The Lincolnshire Wolds', *Lincolnshire Historian*, 9, pp. 315-24.

40. CBS: D-CN 18/8/4/2, Michaelmas 1796, and 18/8/4/8,11,12, and 14-19.

41. CBS: D-CN 18/8/4/8, tenancy agreements, and especially D-CN 18/8/4/11, questions re Humberston leases.

42. CBS: D-CN 18/8/4/3,5,6, and 8.

43. CBS: D-CN 18/8/4/4, 12 January 1809.

44. National Archives, Scotland (hereafter NAS): GD 46/1/12 and 324; CBS: D-CN 13/1/31, 18/1/5, ff. 90-3, 18/8/4/2, 6 and 12; Turner, M. E., Beckett, J. V., and Afton, B., 1997, *Agricultural Rent in England, 1690-1914*, Cambridge, pp. 314-18. Rent books for Humberston do not survive for the years after 1825: it is assumed here that rents were increased in 1826 in line with the revaluation undertaken in the previous year, as they had on similar occasions in the past.

45. CBS: D-CN 20/2/3 and 6; Robinson, A. R. B., 1992, *The Counting House: Thomas Thompson of Hull, 1754-1828, and His Family*, York, pp. 1 and 13; Leighton Boyce, *Smiths the Bankers*, pp. 160-3, 183-92 and 192-4; Jackson, G., 1972, *Hull in the Eighteenth Century: A Study in Economic and Social History*, Oxford, pp. 102-3.

46. CBS: D-CN 11/1/2, ff. 14-15, 11/2/1, 18/8/1/2, and 18/8/4/2, 4 and 10.

47. Thompson, T., 1805, 'Reasons for giving lands to cottagers, to enable them to keep cows', *Communications to the Board of Agriculture*, vol. 4, p. 425.

48. Robinson, *Counting House*, pp. 19-21, 55 and 68; Gillett, E., and McMahon, K. A., 1980, *A History of Hull*, Hull, p. 238. Thompson wrote a tract on 'Observations on the Improvement of the Maintenance of the Poor' in 1801.

49. Young, *General View*, pp. 494-5; Thompson, T., 1799, 'Extract from an account of a provision for cottagers keeping cows at Humberston, in the county of Lincoln', *The Reports of the Society for Bettering the Condition and Increasing the Comforts of the Poor*, 2, pp. 133-8, and *idem.*, 'Reasons for giving lands to cottagers', pp. 422-28; Gourlay, R., 1801, 'An inquiry into the state of the cottagers in the counties of Lincoln and Rutland', *Annals of Agriculture*, 37, 215, p. 591; BPP, 1906, *Departmental Committee on Small Holdings in Great Britain, Minutes of Evidence*, H. C. 1906 [Cd 3278], pp. 258-64.

50. Watkinson, M. A., 2016, 'Enclosure and the Cottager: "The Cottage System" in North Lincolnshire', *Lincolnshire History and Archaeology*, 51, pp. 121-40.

51. Ward, W. R., (ed.), 1976, *Early Victorian Methodism: The Correspondence of Jabez Bunting, 1830-1858*, p. 87 n.1; 'The late James Henwood, esq.', *Hull Packet*, 7 April 1854, p. 5, col. 4.

52. *LRSM*, 31 July 1835, p. 3, col. 3; Grimsby Public Library, Local History Library (hereafter GPL): Skelton Papers, 1835, f. 134.

53. Gilbert, A. D., 'The land and the church' in Mingay, G.E., (ed.), 1981, *The Victorian Countryside*, vol. 1, pp. 43-57.

54. LAO: Spec. 3., p. 60.

55. LAO: Reg 40/334; *LRSM*, 24 October 1823, p. 3.

56. NELA: 239/1, f. 61.

57. NELA: 239/8.

58. NELA: 239/7.

59. The details are set out in Watkinson, 'The Microhistory of a Lincolnshire Parish', pp. 93-111.

60. CBS: D-CN 18/8/4/7/11, Affidavit of Lord Carrington, 16 May 1850.

61. NELA: 239/1, ff. 104-113.

62. CBS: D-CN 18/8/1/5; Obelkevich, *Religion and Rural Society*, pp. 47-8.

63. LAO: LCC Wills 1781/185, 1814/130, 1817/151, 1819/237, 1822/172, 1826/328, 1829/21, 1839/378 and 1852/385; Jackson, G., 1971, *Grimsby and the Haven Company*, Grimsby, p. 86.

64. Cockburn, H. E., 1929, 'Notes upon Humberston', *Humberston Church Magazine*, Part 2, November 1929, n. p. (in NELA: 474/1).

65. BPP, 1802, *Abstract of Answers and Returns … (Enumeration Abstract), 1801*, H. C. 1801-2 (9), Part 1, pp. 193-4; *idem.*, 1833, *Abstract of Population Returns of Great Britain, 1831, Vol 1 (Enumeration Abstract)*, H.C. 1833 (149), pp. 342-3; TNA: HO 107/637/15, pp. 1-11, HO 107/2113, pp. 1-14, and RG 9/2390, pp. 1-14.

66. CBS: D-CN 13/1/2, 31 and 18/8/4/3, 6; NAS: GD 46/1/324.

67. LAO: Humberston Par. 13/1, Rate Assessment Book for 1825-1878.

68. LAO: Humberston Par. 10/1 and 2.

69. TNA: HO 107/2113, pp. 7 and 11.

70. CBS: D-CN/18/8/4/6, pp. 5-8 and 23-4; GPL: Skelton Papers, 1848, p. 50; *LRSM*, 24 March 1848, p. 2, col. 6, and 6 October 1848, p. 2, col. 7; *The Hull Packet*, 10 January 1845, p. 5, col. 6; CBS: D-CN 18/8/4/7/5, Marshall to Jalland, 24 June 1840.

71. Cockburn, 'Notes upon Humberston', n. p.; Hocken, J., 1839, *A Brief History of Wesleyan Methodism in the Grimsby Circuit*, Grimsby, pp. 48-9; Anon., n.d., *Amos Appleyard, Methodist Pioneer, 1750-1813*, Gainsborough, pp. 27-33; Baker, F., 1935, *The Story of Cleethorpes and the Contribution of Methodism through two hundred years*, Cleethorpes, pp. 65 and 117; LAO: Meth Recs 3/Grimsby 7 & 8, Grimsby Wesleyan Circuit Schedules, 1848-1894.

72. Jackson, *Grimsby and the Haven Company*, p. 86; Gillett, E., 1970, *A History of Grimsby*, Hull, pp. 196-201; *Poll Books for the North Division of Lincolnshire, December 1832*, p.104, *January 1835*, p. 118, *August 1841*, p. 127, *July 1852*, p. 109; *LRSM*, 21 July 1837, p. 2, col. 5, and 25 June 1841, p. 1, col. 3.

73. TNA: MH 12/489/256, ff. 374-375.

74. The details are set out in Watkinson, 'The Microhistory of a Lincolnshire Parish', pp. 207-15.

75. NELA: 474/1 and 478/71-73; LAO: Meth Records 3/Grimsby/7 and 8; Baker, *The Story of Cleethorpes*, pp. 65 and 117.

76. NELA: 239/1, ff. 108-11.

THE VICTORIA COUNTY HISTORY OF LINCOLNSHIRE

John Beckett

The Victoria County History (VCH) was founded in 1899 as a national project operating at a county level. It still exists, and in recent years has been active in counties proximate to Lincolnshire including Northamptonshire, Leicestershire, Derbyshire, Staffordshire, Nottinghamshire and Yorkshire East Riding. Lincolnshire has only one volume, which is still available to purchase, and a large part of its text is available free to view online. To the eternal regret of librarians, the 1906 volume was seen as part of a 'set' and numbered accordingly as volume II. This has caused confusion to those who, unsurprisingly, ask what has happened to volume I, let alone (as promised in volume II) volumes III, IV, V and VI. This article looks at the origins of the VCH in Lincolnshire, at the progress made, and its collapse in 1910.[1]

The Victoria County History (VCH) was launched in Spring 1899, and news of the venture reached Lincolnshire in April that year. Arthur Doubleday, the founding editor, had calculated that he could do little without the co-operation of local scholars. In the nineteenth century the gentleman scholar's natural home was the county society, whether archaeological, historical, natural historical, antiquarian, or some combination of all of these. It was to these men, and they tended to be exclusively men, that the VCH needed to appeal. Doubleday's concern was that they would need to be persuaded of the value of the VCH. His solution was the county committee, a listing, and perhaps a gathering of the great and the good, chaired by the lord lieutenant, and including the aristocracy and gentry, as well as leading antiquarians, many of whom were to be found on the committees of the local societies. Doubleday believed the committees were needed to break down what he characterised as 'the natural reluctance of provincial specialists to submit to any sort of control by [a London] body'. It was also hoped, of course, that the committees might play a role in fund raising and that the landowners would open their muniment rooms to the researchers, as well as 'inspiring with confidence the county archaeologists and others whose local knowledge would be needed to supplement the work of various experts at headquarters.'[2]

Doubleday approached individual counties through well-known local historians and people with whom he had come into contact in the past. For Lincolnshire he approached Alfred Atkinson of Brigg, Canon George Harvey, who had served as secretary to the Diocesan Architectural Society between 1867 and 1886, and who was a Fellow of the Society of Antiquaries (FSA), and Dr E. Mansel Sympson of Deloraine Court, Lincoln. Harvey responded on 22 April 1899 from Navenby, where he had held the rectory since 1893, to say that he had seen an announcement of the project in *The Times* 'and was glad to learn from your own letter of yesterday that the proposal had really taken definite shape. I shall be most glad to do anything in my power to help on so useful and necessary a work.'[3] Harvey agreed that 'the formation of a County Committee was a 'very important matter' and that he would send the names of some gentlemen 'who would, I think take up the matter very warmly'.[4] Mansel Sympson also promised help while noting that 'It is not an easy thing to suggest names of people for the Lincolnshire Committee and I am ignorant of the number you want.' He sent Doubleday 'a list of members of our local archaeological society with those members' names marked

Fig.1
Revd Arthur Roland Maddison (1843–1912)
c. 1905. From: Sturman, C.,ed., 1992, Some
Historians of Lincolnshire, *SLHA Occasional*
Paper 9, p.27.

(including all the Vice Presidents) who seem to me to be suitable. They represent, fairly well, most of the chief interests of the county.'[5]

Mansel Sympson's list included: Mr J Cordeaux is our leading authority on birds. Canon W. W. Fowler (Headmaster of the Upper Grammar School) on entomology, G. M. Lowe Esq (Castle Hill House) other branches of Natural History (with the Revd E. A. Woodruffe-Peacock, Cadney near Brigg, and Frederick Burton Esq. (Geology), Gainsborough.[6]

What happened to these recommendations is unclear, because nothing further seems to have taken place in relation to the VCH in Lincolnshire until the autumn of 1901. Quite likely, Doubleday was simply overwhelmed with the task he had set himself of trying to start work in all the English counties simultaneously.

On 31 October 1901 an invitation went out to members and guests of the Associated Architectural Societies inviting them to attend a meeting on 8 November 1901 of the Architectural Society at their rooms in Eastgate, Lincoln, 'with a view to making arrangements for the compilation of materials for the History of the County of Lincoln'.[7] The letter of invitation was signed by three of Lincolnshire's foremost scholarly parsons: Revd (later Canon) William Oswald Massingberd, rector of South Ormsby, Revd Arthur Roland Maddison (1843-1912), and Revd Arthur Sutton, who had been rector of Brant-Broughton, near Newark, since 1888. The initiative was driven by Massingberd and Maddison: two weeks before the official invitations were issued Massingberd had told another of the county's scholarly clerics, Revd Thomas Longley, rector since 1888 of Conisholme:

> We are expecting Mr Doubleday – the General Editor of the Victoria History of the Counties of England – at Lincoln next month to consult about Lincolnshire. It is a big undertaking. Still here is an opportunity that will never come again, as they print and undertake to send down to writers in the county some extracts from Inquisitions, Fines, and other records. Will you help us? Such work as you are engaged on, collating D[omesday] B[ook], Lindsey Survey and Testa [de Nevill], will be a great help to begin with.[8]

No minutes of the 8 November 1901 meeting have survived, and it seems not to have attracted the attention of the local press. We can reconstruct something of the business transacted on

8 November from what happened subsequently.[9] Two key decisions were taken: to form a county committee, and to start preparatory work on the proposed Lincolnshire 'set'. What did this mean in practice?

From the outset, the VCH was planned as a set of volumes for each county. The intention was to have two volumes of general essays, written by a variety of national and local experts, and two topographical volumes, which were in effect studies of the manorial descents, churches and advowsons of every parish in the county, researched and written on a Hundred by Hundred basis. When a local editor was signed up his tasks included providing names for the county committee, finding appropriate writers for essays in the general volumes, and masterminding or overseeing the topographical entries in volumes III and IV. Usually, the VCH Central Office sought out an appropriate editor, but the tone of the correspondence for Lincolnshire suggests that the initiative came from Massingberd and Maddison. The two men, and particularly Massingberd, became the leading players in promoting the VCH in Lincolnshire, with Massingberd as local editor.[10]

Massingberd took the lead because he was only too aware that Lincolnshire had never had a multi-volumed county history in the manner of a Thoroton for Nottinghamshire or Nichols for Leicestershire. For him the VCH was a means of filling the gap which had remained despite numerous attempts to set such a history in motion, of which the most recent had been in the 1870s.[11] Perhaps more than any of his fellow gentlemen-clerics, Massingberd felt this lack acutely.

Fig.2 Revd Thomas Longley (1843–1926) (standing) in 1906. From: Sturman, Some Historians..., *p.33.*

Fig.3 The Rectory at South Ormsby – Revd William Massingberd lived here with wife Emily and daughter Dorothy until his death in 1910. Photographed c. 2020. Photo courtesy South Ormsby Estate.

William Oswald Massingberd (1848-1910) was born in London in 1848, the second son of Francis Charles Massingberd (1800-1872) and his wife Fanny. William Oswald went to Magdalen College, Oxford, where he graduated with third class honours in Law in 1871. He returned immediately to Lincolnshire where he was ordained deacon and became his father's curate at South Ormsby. His father died in 1872, and the following year William was collated to be rector of South Ormsby with Ketsby, Calceby and Driby. The patronage was in the hands of Charles Francis Massingberd-Mundy of Ormsby Hall, his distant cousin.[12] With 3358 acres in and around South Ormsby, and an income of £4784, the Massingberd-Mundys were one of the largest landowners on the Wolds. Massingberd held the living of South Ormsby for thirty-seven years until he died in 1910. He was a rural clergyman par excellence, with only four or five hundred parishioners in the four places for which he was responsible, and a gross income of £690 (net £490) in addition to the rectory built by his father. He was created a justice of the peace in 1883 and sat regularly on the Horncastle Petty Sessional Bench. It was common for him to visit tenants in South Ormsby and Driby on a Sunday afternoon in order to cultivate good relations through the community.[13]

In 1884 Massingberd married Emily Sophia Soper, the youngest daughter of the rector of Somersby and Bag Enderby, with whom he had a daughter, Dorothy Emily. In 1901, when the VCH initiative was launched, Massingberd was fifty-three, and living in the rectory with Emily (46) and Dorothy (15) together with four female servants aged 28, 25, 17 and 16. This was the Trollopian rural clerical magistrate in action, and the Massingberds holidayed in the 1900s in Scotland, and on the continent.[14]

Massingberd's great love lay with his antiquarian interests. He was widely regarded in his own lifetime as one of the 'leading authorities on matters architectural and archaeological' in Lincolnshire, he read papers on local archaeological subjects to the Louth Naturalists' Antiquarian and Literary Society, and he was editor from 1899 with Maddison of *Lincolnshire Notes and Queries*, founded in 1888.[15] He edited for publication and added to his father's book on the *History of South Ormsby*, and he published in 1902 an edition of Ingoldmells court rolls.[16] With this background, it comes as no real surprise that Massingberd and his circle of leisured clergy with antiquarian interests saw the VCH as an opportunity to fill the gap where the county history should have been.

Following the meeting in Lincoln on 8 November 1901, and the decision to promote the VCH in the county, Massingberd was faced with two tasks: to recommend potential members of the county committee, for Doubleday to approach from London, and to recommend local authors, particularly for the two general volumes, and volunteers for the topographical entries destined for volumes III-VI. On 27 November Doubleday started the committee ball rolling by sending to Massingberd a list of potential members he was proposing to approach. In turn, Massingberd discussed the list with Maddison, and they added the names of 'gentlemen who have, or are likely to have charters and other documents which will be of use'.[17] Massingberd made an indirect approach to Lord Brownlow, the lord lieutenant, to check that he would be willing (as in other counties) to chair the county committee,[18] but it was left to Doubleday to approach the potential committee members requesting their support, and the first tranche of letters was sent out in the opening days of March 1902. Brownlow was named as the committee chairman, and the letter confirmed that 'the organizing of local work for the History has been undertaken by the Revd Canon Maddison and the Revd W. O. Massingberd who would act as general secretaries and editors.'[19]

Massingberd wanted to be sure of the support of the Lincolnshire committee and he called a meeting for 8 April 1902 in the Lincoln Guildhall. At the last minute Doubleday was unable to attend,[20] which annoyed Massingberd who saw it as a snub which might easily upset the whole project: 'If you could have been at the meeting you would have seen something of the feeling that prevails … We shall probably quite agree with them but shall be unable to meet their views. And so there will be more delay. Whereas it seems to me quite time something was done if it is to be done at all.'[21]

No minutes of the meeting on 8 April 1902 have survived but newspaper reports recorded that Maddison and Massingberd were confirmed as secretaries (in effect local editors), the general committee, and a smaller executive committee (Appendix 2), were appointed, a decision was taken to expand the general committee, and Doubleday signalled his agreement (following a pre-meeting with Massingberd and Maddison) that in view of the size of Lincolnshire there should be four volumes of topographical history, rather than the standard two.

Massingberd emerged from the meeting in a positive frame of mind, telling R. W. Goulding the day afterwards that 'the Lincolnshire committee [should have] control over the work so far as that we shall be able to see that the volumes are a history and not a directory, and that no poor illustrations are inserted. Altogether I am more hopeful. But it is a very big work. This [Doubleday] is beginning to realise and talks of possibly giving outside help in writing the topography.'[22] In the weeks following the Lincoln meeting, Doubleday sent out invitations to potential committee members. Mostly those contacted replied promptly, but Longley only submitted his formal (positive) response on 29 October, having lost the original letter: 'we were

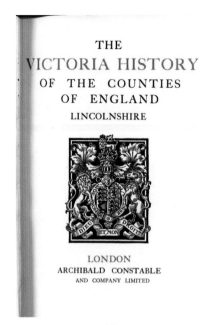

THE

VICTORIA HISTORY

OF THE COUNTIES
OF ENGLAND

LINCOLNSHIRE

LONDON
ARCHIBALD CONSTABLE
AND COMPANY LIMITED

Fig.4
The Victoria County History for
Lincolnshire II (1906) – Front cover with
dust cover. Author's photo.

in the midst of spring cleaning when papers are apt to go astray' he explained to Massingberd.[23]

While all this was going on Massingberd was also putting together lists of potential authors for the essays in the general volumes. In each county set the general volumes were written by a combination of national and local specialists. Volume I normally included natural history, pre-history and earthworks, the Romano-British and Anglo-Saxon periods, and Domesday with any associated survey such as the Lindsey Survey. Volume II began with religious history and religious houses, and was followed by economic and social history, industry, agriculture, forestry, political history, education and schools, and sport. The exact balance between the two volumes depended on what material was available when the VCH Central Office was ready to send a volume to the press. Contracted authors were remunerated at the rate of one guinea per 1000 words.[24]

As elsewhere authors were contracted to write the appropriate essays. For volume I national experts wrote on palaeontology (Richard Lydekker), molluscs B. B. Woodward, and crustacea Revd T. B. B. Stebbing. Local contributors included Frederick Burton, whose section on geology reached proof stage, J. O. Horley on marine zoology (16,500 words), C. H. C. Haigh on birds (12,500 words) and mammals (4000 words). Revd Edward Adrian Woodruffe-Peacock, vicar of Cadney, wrote on botany, A. Smith on fishes, and Revd A. Thornley on insects (35,000 words).[25] Massingberd recommended the Revd E. H. Tatham Claxby of Alford and Revd Alfred Hunt of Welton, Lincoln, who agreed to do the Roman material. William Page, who had by this time joined Doubleday in the role of General Editor, signed up Mr C. H. Bothamley, a Lincolnshire man living in Weston Super Mare to write on earthworks.[26] Massingberd prepared an edition of Lincolnshire Domesday, to which Frank (later Sir Frank) Stenton wrote an introduction (35,000 words). Stenton also prepared a guide to the Lindsey Survey (20,000 words).

Assigning chapters was relatively easy. More troublesome was the question of persuading authors to write the chapters. By the end of 1904 Page had still to receive the entries on Roman History and Domesday Book, and it was decided to publish volume II first, probably in 1906.[27] As a result, and because material was still unavailable in 1908, volume I was never published, and the authors were probably only partially paid.[28]

Volume II was published in 1906. It contained a similar mix of national and local specialists. The ecclesiastical history was written by Miss M. M. C. Calthrop, who was on the staff of the VCH Central Office, and Miss S. Melhuish, a graduate of Liverpool. The entries on religious houses were contributed by Sister Elspeth of All Saints' Community. She proposed to visit Lincoln in 1904 to consult the cathedral records, and Page approached the Bishop of Lincoln asking him to find her somewhere appropriate to stay: 'Sister Elspeth would like to be at some sisterhood or similar institution, while she is at Lincoln as she cannot go to an hotel or a boarding house'.[29] Shortly afterwards she retired to Illinois. This meant she had to be supplied with notes and records, and Massingberd was not over-impressed when he read the proofs of her work. He found various errors, which Page attributed to Sister Elspeth living abroad 'and so had not full opportunities of referring to original documents. We did as much as we could for her here, but this is of course not like the writer consulting the records herself'.[30] Even Sister Elspeth found Lincoln Cathedral too much to attempt from a distance, and Phyllis Wragge, another of the London staff, researched and wrote the section.

Other blips occurred along the way. Massingberd, not surprisingly, had his chapter on social and economic history ready for Page to comment on early in 1906, but then it transpired that Maurice Footman, who had been recommended to undertake

Fig.5
Revd William Oswald Massingberd
(1848–1910) c. 1905. From: Sturman, Some
Historians..., p.40.

the chapter on industry after Mr Turner Simonds dropped out, and who claimed in April 1905 already to be busy writing, had not actually written one of the supposed 50,000 words for which he was contracted. In the end, Footman passed on his notes (such as they were). Massingberd wrote the introduction to the industries section, and Miss Ethel Hewitt, who was on the London staff and wrote entries for a number of counties, completed the entry.[31] George Collins wrote the chapter on agriculture. He freely admitted that he needed the money and asked for 'my cheque at once as I am a very poor person and cannot afford to wait an indefinite period'. He also wrote several of the sections on hunting.[32] Alfred Welby found errors in the foxhunting section which he believed Collins should have recognised and corrected.[33]

Massingberd was critical of the chapter on Forestry written by Dr John Charles Cox. In the proofs he found a reference to a Graham Park, an 'inexcusable blunder' because 'when the error was pointed out he might have taken the trouble to correct it'.[34] Despite these difficulties, compounded by a long delay at the binder, the book was out before the end of 1906.[35] It included a fulsome tribute to Massingberd written by Page:

> The editor desires to express his great indebtedness to the Revd W. O. Massingberd, M.A. for his constant advice and assistance while passing this volume through the press. From his great knowledge of local history much important material has been added and small errors which would have escaped the attention of anyone less skilled in the topography of Lincolnshire have been corrected.[36]

Massingberd was indignant when he heard that Welby had his copy before him and he was still checking the post on 4 January 1907.[37]

Although Massingberd had given considerable support and help over the two general volumes (I and II), his main interest was in the topographical entries. His motivation was a combination of his enthusiasm for South Ormsby, and his hope that the VCH might turn out to be the be an adequate substitute for Lincolnshire's missing county history. His thinking was clear from his *History of South Ormsby*.[38] The book was originally drafted by Massingberd's father and advertised but not published in 1870. Massingberd considered publishing his father's book as it stood, but 'the more I looked into the original sources of information at Ormsby and the [Public] Record Office the more convinced I became that I must rewrite the whole account'. He added a great deal of material from the PRO, the Prerogative Court of Canterbury, and local family papers, and he pointedly noted on the title page that it was 'compiled from original sources'. He thanked both Maddison and also Mr William Boyd, a record agent, 'for help in reading documents'. Boyd had 'given me assistance and advice in my searches at the Record Office without which many records would have escaped my notice'. Boyd was one of a new generation of professional researchers who worked in the recently created Public Record Office (PRO) on behalf of distant researchers. As a result, the South Ormsby book was a records-driven book, reflected in its emphasis on Domesday, on family history, on landownership, including court rolls and agriculture, and on the parish church. It is a book which is scarcely readable today but it is typical of its time and reflected the sort of scholarly work that gentlemen-clergy could and did undertake. It also explains the thinking he brought to the VCH.

The VCH was set up at what now appears to have been break-neck speed, and little thought went into how the manorial histories would be compiled, beyond a rather vague hope that the local clergy would offer their services. When Doubleday looked more closely into this option he found that 'very few local people were competent for the task, and yet fewer had facilities to undertake it because they were too remote from London'.[39] Initially the VCH seems to have employed one or two record agents to look up particular documents on behalf of distant researchers. Massingberd knew of this arrangement in December 1901 when he referred in a letter to Doubleday to 'your workers when looking up Inquisitions post mortem for Manorial History', and he was also aware that as local editor it was his task to 'write the history of manors', or to recruit others for the task, although he warned Doubleday that 'it is impossible to find competent writers for 30 wapentakes'. At this stage the VCH was still thinking in terms of a system of 'local correspondents'.[40] They would be recruited by Massingberd to supply 'information concerning a particular wapentake and the parishes in it, e.g., the boundaries of the wapentake, the parishes it contains, and any alterations in the same'. For each parish the correspondents were to supply information on:

> The physical situation and acreage; hamlets
> Soil, minerals, stone quarries, sand and gravel pits etc.
> Pasturage or arable – chief crops
> Parks, commons, village green
> Roads and bridle paths
> Railway station and when opened
> Names of owners of land and their arms
> Gentlemen's seats
> Principal occupations, trades etc.

> Folklore, games or customs
> Field names, exceptional and of interest
> Antiquities (not to be described)
> Modern History of Manors, Court Rolls
> Fairs or Markets, Enclosure Award, Tithe Map
> Any buildings worth describing – only mention
> Present patrons of the Living and their immediate predecessors
> Monuments before 1550 – murals before 1700
> Church plate; Registers; Churchwardens' accounts; Charities, Schools etc.[41]

Massingberd enthusiastically distributed copies of the list among his fellow antiquaries, but their response was disappointing. As he admitted to Doubleday 'they are extremely willing to criticise but not to work'.[42]

R. W. Goulding's reaction was typical. On 14 February 1902 Massingberd wrote to Goulding, a Louth antiquary who was by this time the Librarian at Welbeck Abbey, to propose that he, together with Canon Charles Wilmore Foster and Longley 'could work on Louthesk and Ludborough ... most of the work can be done by correspondence'.[43] Goulding was less enamoured of the proposal than Massingberd might have hoped. He told Longley 'I have a letter from Canon Massingberd asking if you, Dr Foster and myself will be responsible for collecting information for Louthesk and Ludboro', and I have replied that between us I have no doubt we shall be able to do it.' He added a list of the particulars 'about which information is desired in each parish'. Massingberd noted that 'Several of the points are given in Kelly's Directory, but I scarcely think that a 'history' should follow the lines of a Directory or a Guide Book. Other instructions are distinctly disappointing, e.g.

> !   Antiquities (not to be discussed)
> !   Modern history of manors.
> But I hope that these are subject to modification.'[44]

When Goulding asked for more detail, Massingberd explained the system with greater clarity:

> The local editors write the history of the manors and advowsons, in fact are answerable for the topography. They obtain modern information through the Correspondents in the Wapentakes, and are sent extracts from Inquisitions, Fines &c from London. No doubt some of the information may be obtained from a Directory, but even so it has to be obtained and most ought to be obtained first hand. But the history would be incomplete without the facts. The experts describe the antiquities, and the local editors write the history of manors.

So far so good, but he concluded on a less positive note: 'Some of the correspondents would make a tremendous hash of either. It is impossible to find competent writers for 30 wapentakes ....
'I do not mean by this', he continued, that the History promises to be all I could wish, but it seems to me that we have here an opportunity not to be lost, but to be made the best of'.[45]

For Massingberd the main consideration was that there should be sufficient space to do justice to the manorial histories. Lincolnshire was allocated only two volumes for topography, which he considered inadequate. Because he believed the VCH to be worthwhile he fought a battle with Doubleday, and later with Doubleday's successor William Page, over space:

Fig.6

William Page (1861–1934) was general editor of the Victoria County History from 1902 to 1933. Photo VCH.

... and have obtained a considerable increase. The volumes devoted to topography are to be supplemented so as to contain, as I understand, double the space. Even this is not enough for so large a county, but it is better than nothing, and we have if left to ourselves no hope of a county history at all.

He added that 'as far as it goes, [the history] will be entirely based upon original documents. And the Parochial historians will be able to expand the History instead of, as now often, not knowing where to look for materials.'[46]

Massingberd occasionally gave the impression of working on the VCH single handedly, but this was not the case. In Spring 1902 Revd Robert Eden George Cole, rector of Doddington since 1861 and the author of a history of the village in 1897, prepared an outline of the history of the manor, which he sent to Doubleday for approval. The intention, according to Massingberd, was that 'when this is put into print with illustrations we shall have some notion of what is expected of us, and what Mr D[oubleday] will admit. Then we can have a Committee meeting and see what we can do next.'[47] In fact, there is little evidence of topographical work in the county going forward between 1902 and 1904, probably because Massingberd was tied up with his work for VCH Lincolnshire II.

In summer 1904 Doubleday left the VCH and handed over his responsibilities to William Page, with whom he had jointly shared the role of general editor since 1902. Page reorganised the London office and hired young male graduates from Oxford and Cambridge, and young women who had studied in the ancient universities but were not permitted to graduate. The young scholars took on a major search of the PRO classes to locate information likely to be of use at the local level. Searching PRO and British Museum sources on a county-by-county basis had proved time consuming and repetitious, and Page decided to blanket-search the topographical sources for all English counties before compiling the parish entries for any particular county or Hundred.

The knock-on effect was that the production of topographical volumes would have to wait until the searching had been completed, a task which took about a year to undertake. Through much of 1904 and 1905 work on individual topographical accounts was suspended while the graduates scoured the indexes and catalogues of the PRO. In December 1904, while visiting London, Massingberd offered to call on Page: 'I have nothing very particular in the way of County History on hand, and we might, perhaps, hit upon something useful.'[48] Evidently they did; indeed, it was at this meeting Page told Massingberd only one extra volume of topography could be allowed for Lincolnshire rather than the two offered by Doubleday. He also agreed to attend a meeting of the VCH Lincolnshire Executive Committee (appointed by the County Committee at the 1902 meeting – see Appendix 2) in Lincoln early in 1905. Massingberd set about rousing VCH supporters to attend 'to discuss with the General Editor the new scheme'.[49]

The Lincoln meeting was fixed for the Architectural Society rooms in Lincoln, on 27 January 1905, and Page attended with the VCH Business Manager, R. Meredith.[50] The meeting was chaired by Colonel (later Sir) Alfred Welby, MP (for Taunton), whose family home was in Grantham. Massingberd acted as secretary, and the other attendees were Maddison and Canon Foster, Revd Robert Cole, Revd Arthur Sutton, Revd Edward Adrian Woodruffe-Peacock, Colonel Williams and F. M. Burton. After some preliminary discussion of the state of play regarding the two general volumes, the meeting addressed the question of space for the topographical entries. Massingberd was furious about the change of thinking in regard to the number of volumes. He had previously (14 January) told Goulding:

> I call it 'new' because it is new to us and different from what we were promised, e.g. Doubleday promised to double the two topographical volumes (2 volumes were to be virtually four), now they have cut this down to three and the result is one volume for towns and 85 villages, 2 volumes for 600 villages, according to my estimate. 2 vols = 1200 pages, which gives 2 pages for each. At least a page will be filled by description of the Church and modern information, leaving less than a page for history. Is it worth working for? Is it a history or an 'illustrated guide book'?'[51]

Page told the Lincoln meeting that the plan was to handle the Lincolnshire topographical entries in three volumes, of which one would be in two parts. Collectively they would include 1950 pages, of which 200 would be reserved for the eight large towns, leaving 1750 pages for the smaller towns and villages, or nearly three pages each. The Executive Committee objected: in their view Doubleday had previously promised four topographical volumes, which Page had now cut to three. They circulated Mr Cole's sample history of Doddington which, they commented, would easily fill three pages. On this basis, they argued, more space would be needed to do justice to the county. Page and Meredith sought an agreement that if the space allocated turned out to be insufficient, they would 'in some way provide the additional space necessary'. The meeting also affirmed Massingberd's position as local editor, in effect joint editor with Page of the topographical volumes. He would not expect a fee, but he did ask for expenses of £10 a year.[52] Subsequently Massingberd told Goulding that the Lincolnshire party at the meeting were satisfied with Page's assurance that more space would be found if required, but he was never reconciled to the way in which he and his fellow antiquaries were being treated.[53]

Once the searching of indexes and catalogues had been completed by VCH Central Office staff, many of the women were re-deployed as topographers, drafting the manorial histories for the local editor to check. It was a while before they reached Lincolnshire, but on 9 August 1907, the draft parish histories for Yarborough Hundred, written in the London office, were sent to Massingberd to edit.[54] He immediately concluded that they were too condensed, and full of errors. He told Longley: 'I have been working on the MS relating to some 20 parishes in Yarborough sent to me by the Vict Hist people. There is much of interest, though I do not always follow the [manorial] descents given.'[55] There was much more as Massingberd dissected the entries using his knowledge of both the terrain and the documentation, before complaining again to Page that Lincolnshire needed more space. Page rejected his complaints.[56] For his part Massingberd continued to protest, citing the previous agreement with Doubleday that Lincolnshire should have four volumes of topography rather than the three which had been on offer since 1905. Massingberd pointed out that as he was not claiming a fee for his work, the VCH had fewer costs to meet and so should afford the extra volume. It was a battle he was not prepared to lose, and on 18 November, Page confirmed that the VCH had approved the additional volume.[57] Massingberd was sufficiently placated that he agreed to undertake further work for the VCH in Lincolnshire, this time on Corringham Hundred, but now as author rather than as editor checking other people's work. Page set out the situation in a letter to him on 6 December:

> In confirmation of our talk the other day I shall be glad if you will undertake to write the Topography of the Wapentake of Corringham with the Borough of Gainsborough at a rate of a guinea a thousand words. The average length for each parish so far as your part of it is concerned should not exceed 1,800 – 1,900 words, and the Borough of Gainsborough should not exceed 10,000 words so far as your part of it is concerned. I do not want you to trouble about the architecture or the charities, both of which I will supply.

To aid Massingberd in his work, Page agreed to send him 'all the papers which relate individually to [Corringham parishes], there is a great deal of material under what we call Miscellanea, which relates to two or more parishes; this I am having picked out and will send it to you as soon as it is ready'. He also sent Massingberd a copy of the *Guide*, prepared by himself and Doubleday, for local authors engaged in topography, and offered 'to have additional material from the PRO and British Museum looked up for him and to send him the references to the documents he needed to see required'.[58] This was standard VCH practice for local editors living a distance from London.

Massingberd took Corringham alone, although he did receive some useful material from Longley.[59] Clearly he could not edit the topography for thirty wapentakes and over 600 parishes in the county, especially now that he had to research and write them not just edit. As he told Longley, Central Office supplied: 'extracts from Inquisitions post mortem, feet of fines, and some other classes of documents and give references to others, e.g., Plea Rolls, Chancery Proceedings etc., and these the writer has to look up for himself in the [Public] Record Office'. This 'takes the gilt off the gingerbread, because the VCH paid only 1 guinea per 1000 words and allowed 1800 words per parish 'and expenses swallow up a large proportion of this. The writer has to look up for himself ... a good deal to make the history satisfactory'.[60]

Page was well aware that Massingberd could not write all the topographical entries for Lincolnshire, and in February 1908 he sent him a list of other potential contributors. Massingberd provided some rather mixed views of his fellow antiquaries:

> Canon Maddison, Major Poynton, and Messrs Cole and Goulding, are of course quite good and competent men for County History but will any of them do what you want? Is it at all possible Major Poynton would, no one knows more of the Plea Rolls and other records relating to Lincolnshire, but I feared he expected fuller work than you can give. Canon Maddison is prepared to work at the Genealogy. Mr Cole

is excellent but will he undertake hard work now? Mr Goulding is Librarian to the Duke of Portland, and I should fear has not time to spare, otherwise he would be just your man. J Philipps I know not, nor Joseph Medcalf. Mr Jebb is a Solicitor at Boston, and would hardly have the time, and I should think is not accustomed to the kind of thing. Mr C Moor was Vicar of Gainsborough and published in a Gainsborough paper an account of most of Corringham Wapentake. In this he rather falls between two stools, trying to write for the people, and for archaeologists at the same time. He can read records but did not make as good use of his time in London as one might have expected in the matter of searching records. Altogether I am doubtful about him.

One man stood out. This was Revd C.W. Foster of Timberland, Lincoln. Foster, wrote Massingberd, was 'a man who would do your work really well … if he can find the time. He is at present secretary to the Diocesan Education Committee. It might be worthwhile to write to him. He is really a good man and might possibly help.'[61]

Page also approached Alfred Welby for help. He wrote to him on 26 February 1908:

> … we are now taking in hand the 'Topography' for the county and I have been wondering whether you could assist me by writing some of the parish histories and manorial descents…. The wapentakes of Bradley, Well and Ludborough. We have collected a large amount of material necessary to writing these accounts from the records at the Public Record Office and elsewhere, and I would let you have the use of all this. We can give between 1500 and 2000 words for an ordinary parish. I should not want you to trouble about the architecture, for which I have a separate staff. The rate of remuneration we are offering is a guinea a thousand words. I should want anything that was undertaken for these wapentakes by the end of this year. In the next volume, the material for which I shall want early in 1910, we are taking in hand the wapentakes of Aslacko, Gartree, Lawress, Walshcroft and Wraggoe.[62]

A couple of days later Page reported to Massingberd that Welby 'is going to make a trial on two parishes of Well Hundred to see how he can tackle the work: if he finds he can manage it he will take up the whole Hundred. Mr Goulding is considering Louth Esk (Wold Division) and I am sending him further details of what we want. Mr Cole, will I hope undertake Boothby Graffoe … He mentioned the names of Revd C Moor of whom you told me, and of Dr Mansel Sympson.[63]

Massingberd approved of Sympson, although he was doubtful 'whether he is familiar with original records', but Revd Robert Cole turned down the approach because at the age of seventy-six he was unsure that he wanted to wait four years before there was any hope of seeing Boothby Graffoe in print. Meantime, Welby decided he wanted to write Ludborough rather than Well, Maddison turned down Page's overtures, and Goulding could not find the time to do Louth Esk. Revd Reginald Dudding, vicar of Saleby, near Alford, took on the Marsh Division of Louthesk, after Massingberd had checked that he could read records. Massingberd also asked Longley to show Dudding around the area, although his own view was that it would be preferable for Longley to do this area and Dudding to do parishes in and around Conisholme.[64] All this seemed positive but even as he was starting work on

Corringham a crisis was just around the corner.

In the summer of 1908 Massingberd offered to do another ten parishes once he had finished Corringham,[65] Longley was hard at work, 'Mr Cole is at work on Well and will not need correction; nor should Colonel Welby with Ludbro', but Marley [or Manley?] and Bradley the Ladies are at work on. And I know you have Louthesk done, as you sent it me years ago, and it is most useful to have it to refer to.[66] The architectural work was also in hand. This was undertaken by young men working to the architectural editor in London. In October 1908 Massingberd reported to Goulding that:

> Two young architects are going the round of Lincolnshire churches for the Victoria History. They report to their Boss, and he or they write the descriptions. They expect to be in the Louth neighbourhood next week, and ask if I can tell them of lodgings, which I cannot, can you? They would want them for about two weeks. They prefer them to hotels.[67]

Charles Peers was the architecture editor in the London office, and the two young men were one-third of his team of six assistants researching and writing architecture entries. They were expected to cycle around the countryside stopping off to write descriptions of churches. We know they were active because architectural narratives have survived for nine of the wapentakes in Lindsey, in the areas that Massingberd and his clerical colleagues were working on.

With work on the Lincolnshire topographical entries for VCH Lincolnshire well advanced the financial crisis which overtook the VCH in late autumn 1908 could not have come at a worse moment. Page wrote to Massingberd on 15 December 1908 with the bad news:

> I know you will be very sorry to hear that there are again financial difficulties on the History and we shall have to go slowly for a time. I cannot go into details in writing but there is no blame to be attached to anyone and I very much hope that in the course of a month or two the necessary funds will be forthcoming to replace what have been withdrawn. For the present I am now instructed not to proceed with any fresh work. If you like I can send you on some more of the Lincolnshire parishes but perhaps you would rather wait till things are more settled.[68]

Massingberd was devastated, unsurprisingly given that the squabbles over length had been resolved and 'just when we thought we were getting on with the Lincolnshire volume of topography'.[69] Quite what had happened in London was not clear, but it seems likely that one of the project's funders had withdrawn their support. Replacing them was problematic, despite the willingness of King Edward VII to bestow a baronetcy on anyone who came forward with an endowment for the project![70] While efforts were made to stabilise the financial position, publication paused.

Massingberd refused to be daunted by this news, and with Christmas out of the way he offered to visit Page in London to discuss continuing to put the Lincolnshire material into proper order in the hope and expectation that publication was only delayed, not stopped. Page was less sanguine, responding that 'at the present moment everything is in abeyance. If you will, under these circumstances, go on with the parochial histories I will have the papers got ready for you'. Massingberd offered to start work immediately on the parishes intended for volume III, which had yet to be allotted to other authors. The list included twelve parishes in Manley wapentake, thirteen in Bradley wapentake, and ten in Louth Esk wapentake, including Louth Borough, which Page was particularly keen for Massingberd to do.[71] In fact Massingberd passed the latter commission to Miss Henrietta Garbett because she had already done some work on the town and he had recommended her to Page for work in the London office in 1906.[72] Page offered to have some classes searched in the PRO.[73]

In April 1909 Page told Massingberd that 'the prospect for the History is more hopeful than it was a little while ago and I hope that we shall be able soon to go on with the work as before.'[74] In a follow up letter (now missing) he evidently told Massingberd that funding would probably need to be raised locally. For Massingberd this was a further

Fig.7
Canon Charles Wilmore Foster (1866–1935)
Photo c. 1930. From: Sturman, Some
Historians..., p. 57.

blow: 'Lincolnshire is unfortunately now a very poor county, and the landowners have no thousands to play with. I should think the first thing would be to communicate with Lord Brownlow and see what he says. I fear the very few who have any money have comparatively little interest in the work.'[75]

Massingberd continued to work on topography through 1909, and Page occasionally sent him notes relevant to the twenty-one parishes he had identified as needing to be completed before volume III could be published. Page was not optimistic that the notes would be of much use, telling Massingberd in August 1909 that 'I am afraid these notes are very incomplete for I have had to part with all my staff here and have no one to copy out the miscellanea which for Lincolnshire contains far the most important entries. I fear therefore you will not find them of much use.'[76] Massingberd was undaunted and told Longley on 5 February 1910 that:

> I have now been through the Coates entries again. As regards North Coates I am converted to your views and am very much obliged for your help altogether.... I quite agree that there are instances of land placed in the wrong wapentake, but this [Darcy land] appears to be right. The general result is that I may employ part of Lent in rewriting the early history of these parishes.[77]

The VCH was, in effect, relaunched in April 1910, following an agreement on funding which involved W. H. Smith and Sons, the booksellers. But this agreement only guaranteed funds for ten counties, and Lincolnshire was not one of them. Page asked Welby to visit him for 'a chat about getting a guarantee for the completion of the Lincolnshire vols', and he told

Massingberd that 'the matter was left that I should draw up a scheme which he could lay before one or two people'.[78] Massingberd responded with a proposal of his own:

> Can it be arranged to guarantee the loss, say £150 or £200 per volume of topography? Many of us would guarantee a small sum which we should expect to lose, who not fairly guarantee a capital sum which might embarrass our successors. You said once a 10 per cent loss might be expected. If a volume costs £1500 that would be £150. And surely if the Lincolnshire committee sent a volume to be printed the printers would print it without further difficulty.[79]

Page offered to consider the suggestion but he was not optimistic.[80] With Meredith, the Business Manager, he drew up a balance sheet which suggested that the cost of printing and publishing the missing five Lincolnshire volumes (I, III, IV, V, VI) would be £9191, but the sales revenue was predicted to total only £5000.[81] Massingberd's response has not survived, but Page subsequently sent the figures to Welby and F. M. Burton. He added in the letter to Burton that 'the cost of ten counties has been guaranteed, but Lincolnshire is not amongst the number, and that a small sum has been set aside for distribution among contributors to unpublished volumes other than the ten counties'. This had enabled Page to pay Burton for his unpublished work for volume II, but it probably would not lead to publication without further funds.[82]

Welby proposed to forward the financial details to Brownlow with the intention of persuading the lord lieutenant to call a meeting at which the financial issues could be considered at a county level. Perhaps inevitably, however, he asked questions about what was really needed: 'looking over the items I see a very large sum in each volume for the architecture of churches and old houses; could not this be greatly reduced?'[83] Page was not in favour of a meeting,[84] so Welby suggested that he and Page meet with Brownlow to discuss progress but he added ominously 'we have to consider that there is a feeling the local people have had no say in the publication and are now asked to find the funds.'[85]

Massingberd spent part of Lent editing histories of Great Coates and North Coates, prepared in the VCH Central Office, but during the summer his health broke down and on 11 September 1910, he died at South Ormsby rectory. Welby wrote to Page on 13 September 1910:

> You have probably seen in today's Paper the announcement of Mr Massingberd's death. He is the greatest possible loss to Lincolnshire antiquarianism. No one has the knowledge he had. I have heard from him several times lately, but beyond saying he was much tired by work and only partly rested by his holiday, there was nothing to make one think his life was in any danger.[86]

Massingberd had been the driving force behind the VCH in Lincolnshire, and with his death went any hope of it proceeding, given the financial conditions surrounding the whole project. In November 1910, after allowing a suitable length of time for mourning, Page approached Massingberd's widow to ask her to send to London all the VCH material, in return for which he would ensure that she was paid for the work her late husband had undertaken even though it was not published. The VCH eventually agreed to a payment of one-hundred guineas.[87] Page went through the papers when they arrived in London and was gratified to find how much work Massingberd had done on Louthesk and Corringham 'which will be of very great value to us when the history of Lincolnshire is again taken in hand'.[88]

Nothing further had happened when in March 1912 Longley told Goulding:

> I am afraid we may say good bye to the hope of seeing any further
> Victoria History of Lincolnshire. I have just had a letter from Mr
> Page, asking me to return the papers which were sent to me dealing
> with Conisholme, Grainthorpe and Cockerington, as there seemed
> no chance of any further step being taken at present, though they
> hoped that at some future time &c. &c – a rather unsatisfactory finish
> – but I learnt about two years ago indirectly that the whole future of
> the scheme was very uncertain, and then when Mr Massingberd died
> I felt quite certain that Lincolnshire at any rate would collapse.[89]

The VCH was revived after the First World War, but no further work has taken place in Lincolnshire. In August 1918 Canon Foster approached William Page with the offer of a deal on Domesday material:

> A friend of mine, the Rev T Longley, has been working on Domesday
> etc for a quarter of a century and he is finishing a volume of tables
> showing the modern equivalents of the DB places, the assessments,
> team-lands, teams, sokemen, villeins, bordars etc., and the
> corresponding entries in the Lindsey Survey etc, Professor FM
> Stenton, who thinks Mr Longley's work extremely valuable, will
> I think contribute an introduction. Mr Longley is also preparing a
> volume concerning the DB tenants, and the corresponding entries
> in the *Testa de Nevill*. Gouran Smith's translation of the Lincolnshire
> section of DB is useless, and for the purpose of Mr Longley's volumes
> he and I want to edit a new translation. Mr Stenton has promised
> his help, and we propose to follow the VCH plan. Stenton tells me
> that Massingberd prepared a translation for the VCH and that it
> was revised by Dr Round. I have also heard that the VCH publishers
> allowed a translation of the Cheshire DB which had been prepared
> for them to be edited locally.[90]

Behind the measured language lay a serious problem. Foster was requesting permission from the VCH to print Massingberd's translation of Domesday Book and to co-operate in any future relevant work produced by the VCH. Page was sceptical, telling Foster that 'as to our translation of the Domesday text of Lincolnshire made partly by Mr Massingberd and partly by Mr Round, I will have to talk to the managing Director of the VCH. I must say, however, I see considerable difficulties in giving you permission to print it in the publications of the Lincoln Record Society.'[91]

Foster was seemingly not offended, responding that 'I quite understand your position. What I wish most of all is that you could go on with the VCH and print your Lincolnshire material.'[92] Page had himself been responsible for the natural history and other material prepared for the abortive volume I in the Lincolnshire set. An attempt to publish some of it in the 1950s came to nothing, except for the natural history sections which were transferred in 1965 to the Natural History Museum and subsequently lost.[93] The remaining material stayed in the VCH archive until it was transferred to Lincolnshire Archives in autumn 2010.[94] In the 1960s, by which time the VCH no longer published natural history, the material was passed to the British Museum. Subsequently it was moved to the British Library.

In 1901, even before a VCH committee was formed for Lincolnshire, Massingberd wrote a long and rather prescient letter about the proposed VCH. We do not know to whom this was addressed (although it might have been Longley), but it is well worth quoting:

> As regards Lincolnshire Domesday Book, I am flattered by your offer. I have often desired to work with an expert on Lincolnshire history but I do not feel certain that I am justified in accepting the offer at once. There is the question of the History of Lincolnshire as a whole. What satisfied you ought to satisfy me. But are you satisfied that there is a reasonable hope that the Lincs part of the VCHs will be done well? I rather doubt whether the VCH authorities realise the difficulties. We have a large county, a huge mass of records, very little done, and very few workers. We have no laymen of means who take any active part in the work. We cannot maintain a Record Society, and a volume of records does not obtain sufficient subscribers to cover the expense of printing. I cannot therefore at present see how the history is to be written. As far as early records are concerned I am almost the only man in Lincolnshire who works at them, though fortunately Major Poynton now is able to do at the [Public] Record Office much more work than I, and would be of immense use if his services can be secured. As a rule, Lincs people try to get on too fast, and write their history without having collected the materials. That of course we want to avoid. But who is to write a history, say, of Bolingbroke, or Lincoln, or the Baronage.... there are 100s and even 1000s of records to be searched at the Record Office and British Museum, and how it is to be done I do not see. But the question has, I think, to be answered before we can talk of a History worthy of the County. As regards myself, I have always said that my services are at the disposal of the Lincs Committee when formed. But I do think that we should not attempt what we do not see our way to do well, and I am not sure that I am best employed on Domesday Book.... I had always thought that my business was to collect materials for other people to use and have tried to avoid premature conclusions. And I do not see who in Lincolnshire is to undertake the early parochial histories of this part of the county unless I do. However, this is perhaps for others more than for me to decide. I am willing to do what I can in any way for County History as long as I am satisfied that we have a prospect of the whole History of the county being satisfactory...

The VCH represented the last attempt at providing Lincolnshire with its missing county history although the Record Society, founded by Foster within months of Massingberd's death, stands as a memorial to a clergyman who did more than any other Lincolnshire man to make a county history happen – and nearly succeeded. Years later Dorothy Owen wrote of Massingberd that he could be:

> ...represented as almost the first local historian to benefit from the great developments in historical technique in the last thirty years of the nineteenth century; the first to use all available document sources, and to use them critically; to incorporate into his work the findings of genealogists and archaeologists; to encourage the development of important aids such as Place-Name Surveys, and to initiate the editing of fundamental texts for the history of the county.[95]

His untimely death in 1910 brought VCH Lincolnshire to a halt and ensured that much of his own work remained unpublished.

APPENDIX 1
The VCH Lincolnshire Committee[96]

Earl Brownlow	Chairman
Duke of Rutland	Belvoir
Duke of Portland	Welbeck
Marquess of Bristol	Ickworth Park, Bury St Edmunds
Earl of Yarborough	Brocklesby Park
Lord Bishop of Lincoln	Old Palace, Lincoln
Lord Welby	11 Stratton Street
Sir Hickman Bacon, Bart.	Thonock Hall, Gainsborough
Very Revd the Dean of Lincoln	The Deanery, Lincoln
The Venerable Archdeacon of Lincoln	
The Revd the Precentor of Lincoln	
The Revd the Chancellor of Lincoln Cathedral	
The Revd the Subdean of Lincoln Cathedral	
The Venerable the Archdeacon of Stow	
J. Banks Stanhope Esq.	Revesby Abbey, Boston
Rt Hon. Henry Chaplin, Esq.	Stafford House, Louth
J. L. Ffytche Esq., FSA	The Terrace, Freshwater, Isle of Wight
W. H. Smyth Esq.	Elkington Hall, Louth
W. D. Fane, Esq.	Fulbeck Hall, Grantham
Revd Canon Maddison FSA	Vicar's Court
Revd W. O. Massingberd	Ormsby Rectory, Alford
Revd A. F. Sutton	Brant Broughton
J. Goulton Constable, FSA	Walcot, Doncaster
Herbert Kirk Esq.	Sleaford
Revd Prebendary Andrews	Claxby, Market Rasen
Revd H. J. Cheales	Friskney, Boston
Revd R. E. G. Cole	Doddington, Lincoln
J. Cordeaux Esq.	Great Coates, RSO, Lincoln
Revd J. Fernie	Burton, Lincoln
Lt Col. Conway Gordon	Lynwode, Market Rasen
Revd R. D. Hemmans	Holbeach
Revd J. C. Hudson	Thornton, Horncastle
G. S. W. Jebb	Norton House, Boston
Revd Canon Jeudwine	Harlaxton Rectory, Grantham
Nevill Reeve-King Esq.	Ashby Hall, Sleaford
F. A. Larken, Esq.	Lincoln
A.S . Leslie-Quelville	Branston Hall, Lincoln
Col. Moor	Frampton Hall, Boston
Dr W. O'Neill	Lindum Road, Lincoln
E. A. Woodruffe-Peacock, Esq., FSA	Kirton in Lindsey
Gilbert Peacock Esq.	Greatford Hall, Stamford
H. A. Peake Esq.	Sleaford

Revd J. A. Penny	Wispington
Dr Martin Perry	Spalding
Revd J. W. Sale	Halton Holgate, Spilsby
W. Scorer Esq.	Bank Street, Lincoln
Coningsby C. Sibthorpe Esq.	Sudbrooke Holme, Lincoln
Very Revd the Dean of Stamford	Market Deeping
Revd A. F. Sutton	Brant Broughton
Revd C. J. Swan	Sausthorpe Hall
Dr E. M. Sympson	Deloraine Court, Lincoln
Major Tempest	Coleby Hall, Lincoln
Revd W. A. H. Thorold	Stainby, Grantham
James Thropp Esq.	Bailgate, Lincoln
Revd J. C. Walter	Langton Rectory
W. Watkins	Architect, Lincs.
Col Mildmay Willson	Rauceby Hall, Sleaford
R. W. Goulding Esq.	Ivy Cottage, Gospel Gate
Everard Green Esq. FSA (Rouge Dragon)	College of Arms
Revd Canon Harvey FSA	Navenby Rectory, Lincoln
W. Boyd Esq.	Record Office, Chancery Lane
Joseph Phillips	Stamford
Revd T. Longley	Conisholme Rectory, Grimsby
Col. Alfred Welby MP	House of Commons
Revd C. W. Foster	St Andrews Clergy House
Revd Canon Moor	Gainsborough
W. V. R. Fane Esq.	Fulbeck Hall, Grantham
J. Edwin Cole Esq.	Swineshead Hall, Boston
Gervase Carey Elwes Esq.	Brigg
F. M. Burton Esq.	Gainsborough

APPENDIX 2
Executive Committee 1902[97]
Canon Harvey
Canon Maddison
Revd W. O. Massingberd
Revd C. W. Foster
Revd R. E. Cole
Revd A. F. Sutton
[above all styled 'clerical']
W. V. Fane, Esq.
Col Welby
Col Williams
J. G. Runnard Moore Esq.
Geo. Jebb Esq.
J. Goulton Constable Esq.
Joseph Phillips Esq.
R. W. Goulding Esq.
E. Mansel Sympson Esq.

F. M. Burton, Geology
Revd E. A. Woodruffe-Peacock, Flora
Revd A. Thornley, Entomology
Mr Smith, Tetryology
Mr Cator Haigh, Ornithology

APPENDIX 3
List of Parishes in Yarborough Hundred sent to Mr Massingberd, 9 August 1907
Barrow on Humber
Barton on Humber
Bigby
Bonby
Croxton
East Halton
Elsham
Goxhill
Habrough
Horkstow
Immingham
Keelby
Killingholme
Kirmington
Great Limber
Little Limber
Riby
Saxby
Stallingborough
South Ferriby
Thornton Curtis
Ulceby
Wootton
Worlaby

APPENDIX 4
Contents of VCH Volume II (1906)
Ecclesiastical History (pp. 1–77) Miss M. M. C. Calthrop (to 1600) and Miss S. Melhuish (from 1600)
Religious Houses (pp. 78–244) – introduction by Sister Elspeth of All Saints' Community
Lincoln Cathedral – Miss Phyllis Wragge, Oxford Honours School of Modern History.
[The rest are by Sister Elspeth (93 entries), Miss Rose Graham FRHistS (13 entries) and A. G. Little MA (17 entries)]
Political History (pp. 245–292) by C. H. Vellacott
Social and Economic History (pp. 293–355) by William Oswald Massingberd
Table of Population (pp. 356–380)
Industry (pp. 381–396) – introduction by Massingberd; Deep Sea Fisheries and Fish Docks, Mines and Quarries, Agricultural Implement Manufacturers (Miss Ethel M Hewitt)
Agriculture (pp. 397–415) by G. E. Collins

Forestry (pp. 417–420) by J. C. Cox
Schools (pp. 421–492) by A. F. Leach
Sport (pp. 493–506)
　　　　　Ancient and Modern – ed. by E. D. Cuming
　　　　　Foxhunting (pp 493–506) by G. E. Collins and Rt. Hon Lord Monson
　　　　　Harriers and Beagles and otter hounds (p. 506) by G. E. Collins
　　　　　Racing and Polo (pp. 506–511) by Cuthbert Bradley
　　　　　Shooting (pp. 511–514) by Revd J. F. Quire
　　　　　Wild Fowling (pp. 514–518) by Henry Sharp
　　　　　Coursing (pp. 518–519 by J. W. Bourne
　　　　　Angling (pp. 519–525) by R. Mason
　　　　　Golf (pp. 525–527) by W. T. Warrener
　　　　　Athletics (p. 528) by J. E. Fowler Dixon

APPENDIX 5
Lincolnshire Material Transferred from the VCH Archives to Lincolnshire Archives, Autumn 2010
Lincolnshire Slips

The slips are in envelopes and parcels for all parishes – 619 envelopes
Slips for wapentakes　　　29 envelopes
Slips for ridings　　　　　Lindsey
　　　　　　　　　　　　Kesteven
　　　　　　　　　　　　Holland
(Slips usually contained references in public sources relating to Lincolnshire.)

Draft narratives for the Parts of Lindsey (Wapentake name in bold)
Well

Hill (Bag Enderby only)
Corringham – all parishes
Louthesk – all parishes except Hallington and Welton-le-Wold

Ludburgh (Brackenborough, Covenham-St Bartholomew, Little Grimsby)
Bradley Haverstoe
Ashby-cum-Fenby, Grainsby, Hatcliife, Holton-le-Clay,
Irby-on-Humber, Rothwell, Swinhope, Tetney, Thoresby,
North Waltham, Wold Newton
Aylesby, Barnoldby-le-Beck, Bradley, Beelsby
Brigsley, Clee
Cabourne, Coates, Great Coates, Little Coates, North Coates,
Healing, Waithe
Manley (East)
Manton, Redbourne

Manley (North)
Alkborough, Appleby, Burton-upon-Stather, Flixborough
Roxby-with-Risby, Whitton, Winteringham, Winterton
Manley (West)
Wroot

Fig.8
Some of the Lincolnshire
slips when they were
still at the VCH store
at Egham, Surrey. They
have subsequently
been transferred to the
Lincolnshire Archives.
Author's photo.

Yarborough (South)
All parishes except Bigby

Yarborough (North)
All parishes except Wootton

Yarborough (East)
All parishes except Riby

Parts of Kesteven
Boothby-Graffoe (Lower)
Doddington (proof – prepared as a sample parish history)
Architectural Narratives for the Parts of Lindsey
Well
Corringham
Louthesk (Wold)
Ludborough
Bradley Haverstoe
Manley (3 divisions)
Yarborough (East)
Yarborough (North)
Yarborough (South)

Domesday
Introduction
Lindsey Survey Introduction
Domesday extracts
Domesday translations and notes

NOTES

1.   This article is a much revised version of the Dr Jim Johnson Memorial Lecture, delivered at
      Bishop Grosseteste University College, Lincoln, on 18 May 2010, of which a shorter version was
      given at the Lincolnshire Archives Research Progress seminar on 30 March 2019. I was Director

of the VCH 2005-10 during which I was able to access the VCH archives to provide a rounded picture of the Lincolnshire VCH project.

2.   Victoria County History Archives, Institute of Historical Research, Senate House, London (hereafter VCH), H. A. Doubleday memorandum, 7 May 1938. Lincolnshire place names used in this paper have been checked against 'Medieval Administration', in Bennett, Stewart and Bennett, Nicholas, eds, *An Historical Atlas of Lincolnshire* (2001), except for variants used in direct quotations.

3.   VCH, A12, Revd George Harvey to H. A. Doubleday, 22 April 1899.

4.   VCH A 12, Ramsay to H. A. Doubleday, 22 April 1899.

5.   VCH A 12, E. Mansel Sympson to H. A. Doubleday, 24 April 1899.

6.   VCH A 12, E. Mansel Sympson to Doubleday, Deloraine Court, Lincoln, 24 April 1899.

7.   LAO, 3/D/126, copy of the letter sent to R. W. Goulding; VCH A 44, W. O. Massingberd to Doubleday, 1 November 1901.

8.   Lincolnshire Archives Office (LAO), Longley Papers, 5/2/10, Massingberd to Longley, 14 October 1901.

9.   There was no report in the *Lincolnshire Chronicle* for 9 or 15 November 1901. My thanks to Dr Wendy Atkin for this information.

10.   *Louth Advertiser*, 17 Sept 1910.

11.   VCH, A12, Revd George Harvey to Doubleday, 22 April 1899.

12.   See, for example *Kelly's Directory of Lincolnshire*, 1905, p. 461.

13.   Charles Rawding, 2001, *The Lincolnshire Wolds in the Nineteenth Century*, Lincoln, pp. 52, 67, 111.

14.   *Louth Advertiser*, 17 Sept. 1910.

15.   LAO, Goulding Papers, 3/D/126, Massingberd to R.W Goulding, 30 Nov. 1899.

16.   *History of the parish of Ormsby-cum-Ketsby in the Hundred of Hill and County of Lincoln: compiled from original sources* (Lincoln, James Williamson, 1893); idem, *Court Rolls of the Manor of Ingoldmells, translated by William Oswald Massingberd* (Printed by Spottiswoode, London 1902); Baker, W. J., 1968, 'F. C. Massingberd: historian in a Lincolnshire parish', *Lincolnshire History and Archaeology* (LHA), 3. pp. 1–10.

17.   VCH, Box A 44, Massingberd to Doubleday, 29 Nov., 6 Dec. 1901.

18.   VCH, Box A 44, Massingberd to Doubleday, 21 Feb. 1902.

19.   VCH, Box A 12, replies to Doubleday from individuals invited to join the committee. See Appendix 1, below, for a list of the committee members. On the April 1902 meeting see *Lincolnshire Chronicle*, 11 Apr. 1902, *Stamford Mercury*, 11 Apr.1902, p. 5.

20.   VCH, Box A 44, Massingberd to Doubleday, 3, 18, 20, 24 Mar. 1902.

21.   VCH, Box A 44, Massingberd to Doubleday, 24 Mar. 1902.

22.   LAO, Goulding Papers, 3/D/126, Massingberd to Goulding, April 1902. We know that Massingberd wrote to Doubleday on 9 April reporting the meeting, and on 16 April with further names for the committee, but these letters are not in the VCH archive.

23.   VCH, A 12. Longley to Doubleday, 27 Oct. 1902; LAO, Longley Papers, 5/1/2. Doubleday to Longley, 9 May 1902, 5/1/3, Doubleday to Longley, 29 Oct. 1902.

24.   See Appendix 5 for a breakdown of the contents of volume II.

25.   This material was transferred from the VCH archive in 1965 to the Natural History Museum, where it can no longer be found.

26.   VCH, A 44, Massingberd to William Page, 19 Mar. 1908, Page to Massingberd, 20 Mar. 1908.

27.   VCH A12, R. Burton to Page, 17 Oct. 1904, Page to Burton, 19 Oct. 1904 referring to the difficulties of acquiring articles from the archaeology specialists.

28.   VCH A58, 'Memorandum for Mr Meredith', c.1920.

29.   VCH, A12, Page to the Bishop of Lincoln, 2 June 1904.

30.   VCH, A44, Page to Massingberd, 17 July 1906.

31.   VCH A12, Page to Massingberd, 5, 14 Feb., 9 Apr. 1906, Massingberd to Page, 16 July 1906; Maurice Footman to Page, 28 Apr. 1905; Page to Footman, 1 May 1905, 4 May 1906.

32. VCH A12, Page to George Collins, 17 Mar. 1905; Collins to Page, 27 June 1905.
33. VCH, A 12, Col. Alfred Welby to Page, 27 Dec. 1906.
34. VCH A44, Massingberd to Page, 13 Aug. 1906.
35. LAO, Goulding Papers, 3/D/126, Massingberd to Goulding, 15 Dec. 1906.
36. VCH *Lincolnshire*, II (1906), editorial note.
37. VCH, A 44, Massingberd to Page, 4 Jan. 1907.
38. *History of the parish of Ormsby-cum-Ketsby in the Hundred of Hill and County of Lincoln: compiled form original sources by W.O. Massingberd* (Lincoln, James Williamson, 1893).
39. VCH, H. A. Doubleday memorandum, 7 May 1938.
40. VCH, Box A 44, Massingberd to Doubleday, 27 Dec. 1901.
41. LAO, Goulding Papers, 3/D/126, Massingberd to Goulding, 14 Feb. 1902.
42. VCH, Box A44, Massingberd to Page, 23 Jan. 1902.
43. LAO, Goulding Papers, 3/D/126, 14 Feb. 1902.
44. LAO, Longley Papers, 5/1/1, Goulding to Longley, 21 Feb. 1902.
45. LAO, Goulding Papers, 3/D/126, Massingberd to Goulding, 3 Mar. 1902.
46. LAO, Goulding Papers, 3/D/126, Massingberd to Goulding, 14 Feb., 3 Mar. 1902.
47. LAO, Goulding Papers, 3/D/126, Massingberd to Goulding, 13 June 1902.
48. VCH, Box A44, Massingberd to Page, 6 Dec. 1904.
49. LAO, Goulding papers, 3/D/126, Massingberd to Goulding, 10 Jan. 1905.
50. VCH, Box A 44, Page to Massingberd, 19 Dec 1904, 3 Jan 1905; Massingberd to Page, 20 Dec. 1904, 10 Jan. 1905.
51. LAO, Goulding papers, 3/D/126, Massingberd to Goulding, 14 Jan. 1905.
52. VCH, Box A 44, Minutes of the meeting (1905 file); Box A 44, Massingberd to Page, 2, 4 Feb. 1905, Page to Massingberd, 3 Feb. 1905.
53. LAO, Goulding Papers, 3/D/126, Massingberd to Goulding, 14 Feb. 1905.
54. VCH, Box A44, Page to Massingberd, 9 Aug. 1907, including the list; E.J. Chambers to Page, 9 Sept. 1907. The list of parishes is given in Appendix 3.
55. LAO, Longley MSS, 5/2/13, Massingberd to Longley, August 1907 (no day given).
56. VCH, A 44, Page to Massingberd, 15 Aug. 1907.
57. VCH, A 44, Page to Massingberd, 18 Nov. 1907.
58. LAO, MASS 30/15, Page to Massingberd, 6 Dec 1907; H. A. Doubleday and William Page, 1902, *A Guide to the Victoria History of the Counties of England*, London, Archibald Constable, pp. 85-7.
59. LAO, Longley Papers, 5/1/4, Massingberd to Longley, 4 Jan. 1908.
60. LAO, Longley Papers, 5/1/6, Massingberd to Longley, 14 May 1908.
61. VCH, A 44, Massingberd to Page, 12 Feb. 1908; After serving curacies at Grimsby, Navenby, Epworth and Grimsby again, Foster became Vicar of Timberland, 15 miles southeast of Lincoln, in 1902. He remained here until his death in 1935.
62. VCH, A 12, Massingberd to Col. Alfred Welby, 26 Feb. 1908.
63. VCH, A 44, Page to Massingberd, 3 Mar. 1908.
64. VCH, A 44, Massingberd to Page, 11 Apr. 1908; Lincolnshire Archives, Longley Papers, 5/1/7, Dudding to Longley, 20 May 1908.
65. VCH, A 44, Massingberd to Page, 4, 7, 16 Mar. 1908; LAO, Goulding Papers, 3/D/126, Massingberd to Goulding, 14 May, 4 June 1908.
66. LAO, Longley Papers, 5/1/6, Massingberd to Longley, 14 May 1908.
67. LAO, Goulding Papers, 3/D/126, 8 Oct. 1908; R.B. Pugh, *The Victoria History of the Counties of England: General Introduction* (Oxford, 1970), 8.
68. VCH, A 44, Page to Massingberd, 15 Dec. 1908.
69. VCH, A 44, Massingberd to Page, 21 Dec 1908, Page to Massingberd, 22 Dec. 1908.
70. Pugh, *General Introduction*, p.7.
71. VCH, A44, Massingberd to Page, 16, 21 Jan. 1909, Page to Massingberd, 18, 22 Jan. 1909.

72.   VCH, A44, Massingberd to Page, 22 Mar. 1906.
73.   VCH, A44, Page to Massingberd, 15 Mar. 1909, Massingberd to Page, 26 Mar. 1909.
74.   VCH, A44, Page to Massingberd, 2 Apr. 1909.
75.   VCH, A44, Massingberd to Page, 15 Apr. 1909.
76.   VCH, A44, Page to Massingberd, 13 Aug. 1909, Massingberd to Page, 19 Nov. 1909.
77.   LAO, Longley, 5/2/19, Massingberd to Longley, 5 Feb. 1910.
78.   VCH, A12, Page to Massingberd, 19 Apr. 1910.#
79.   VCH, A12, Massingberd to Page, 20 Apr. 1910.
80.   VCH, A12, Page to Massingberd, 21 Apr. 1910.
81.   VCH, A12, Page to Massingberd, 5 May 1910.
82.   VCH, A12, Page to F. M. Burton, 26 May 1910; Pugh, *General Introduction*, pp. 8-9 provides the context but does not mention the ten county specification.
83.   VCH, A12, Welby to Page, 27 May 1910.
84.   VCH, A12, Page to Welby, 30 May 1910.
85.   VCH, A12, Welby to Page, 31 May 1910.
86.   VCH, A12, Welby to Page, 13 Sept. 1910.
87.   VCH, A12, Page to Mrs Massingberd, 1, 15 Nov. 1910, Mrs Massingberd to Page, 10 Nov., 8 Dec. 1910.
88.   VCH, A12, Page to Mrs Massingberd, 7 Dec. 1910.
89.   LAO, Goulding Papers, 3/D/117, Longley to Goulding, 1 Mar. 1912.
90.   VCH, A12, Foster to Page, 28 Aug. 1918.
91.   VCH, A12, Page to Foster, 29 Aug. 1918.
92.   VCH, A12, Foster to Page, 26 Sept. 1918.
93.   VCH Q40, includes some correspondence relating to the natural history material, from the 1950s.
94.   Appendix 5.
95.   In 1989, when the VCH published its 200th volume, the late Christopher Sturman edited *Some Historians of Lincolnshire*, which included pen portraits of Massingberd and others connected with the VCH in Lincolnshire (SLHA Occasional Paper, 9, 1992), p. 40.
96.   The list may be incomplete. It was VCH practice to print the definitive list in the first volume in each county set, but since the first Lincolnshire volume never appeared, we have to rely instead on the material in a manuscript list in VCH Archives, A12.
97.   Probably as elected at the same time as the general committee in 1902 (as reported by Massingberd to Page): VCH, A44. The list is in box A12.

PADLEY'S GREAT MAP OF LINCOLN

Rob Wheeler

J. S. Padley's 20-inch to the mile plan of Lincoln was the principal subject of a publication – Historic Town Plans of Lincoln – prepared jointly by Dennis Mills and the present author. The introduction to that work included what was known about the publication of that plan. In the two decades since that work was prepared, more has come to light, in particular about Padley's revision process and about the map's curious afterlife at a reduced scale. This paper is intended to set out this extra information. As for Padley's motives for embarking on so detailed a map, nothing new has emerged: anyone interested in this aspect should refer to the original publication.

James Sandby Padley was Lincoln's leading surveyor of the mid-nineteenth century. In 1842 he published a very detailed map of the city at 20-inch to the mile. Such detailed town plans form a recognised *genre* but usually date from the first couple of decades of the century. Lincoln's is unusually late and is even more unusual in that successive revisions were produced until the 1880s when it was superseded by the large-scale Ordnance Survey plans.

Dennis Mills had conceived the idea of publishing a reproduction of one or more of these editions. In the event the project grew into *Historic Town Plans of Lincoln*,[1] of which the greater part consisted of reproductions of all four editions of Padley's Great Map. Dennis steered the project to its successful conclusion and wrote the descriptions of Lincoln at the dates of the various maps; I led on the technical side of reproduction and handled the cartographic history, except for the two earliest maps.

The purpose of this article is to set out what has been learned about the cartographic history since then, including the manuscript drawing, the arrangements for revision, and the after-life of the 20-inch map in reduced form.

PRODUCTION OF THE 1842 EDITION

First, the manuscript drawing for the 1842 map. The card index of maps at Lincoln Central Library included a reference to an 1841 map by Padley, which could not be found. At the time we dismissed this as probably a mistake in cataloguing. Some years later, I was working on *Maps of the Witham Fens*, and the late Ray Carroll kindly lent me his notes from when he was working on his cartobibliography of Lincolnshire county maps.[2] He had originally cast his net somewhat wider. He was County Librarian at the time and had taken a photocopy of this 1841 Padley drawing (Figure 1). The original was evidently very worn, and the photocopy was not up to modern standards, but it clearly shows a manuscript version of the 1842 edition; it seems likely that this was the manuscript Padley had supplied to the engraver. There were certain differences, of which the date was the most obvious. A few additional buildings had been added to the engraved map, of which the most important was the foundry established by the newly-formed partnership of Messrs Clayton and Shuttleworth, which would within a couple of decades become Lincoln's largest industrial establishment. These additions demonstrate how keen Padley was that on its appearance the map should be absolutely up-to-date.

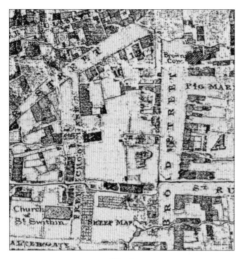

Fig.1
Extract from Padley's 1841 manuscript – a poor photocopy is all that survives.

The manuscript also helps explain an unusual feature of the printed map. This has three types of hatching of buildings for public buildings, dwelling-houses and 'outhouses' (which actually embraces all private non-residential buildings). Such a division is quite common, but what is unusual about Padley's map is that 'public buildings' include a wide range from churches to fairly modest inns. It is apparent that the manuscript used a more complex system: the Church of St Swithin in the extract is shaded (and perhaps coloured) differently from the inn on the east side of Broadgate. One suspects that the engraver warned that so complex a system was infeasible on a printed map and in consequence all the categories of public building were merged.

Because of its size – about one metre square – it was necessary to print the map from two copper plates, though the mounting of the map was so expertly done that the join is scarcely noticeable. From the similarities of surviving copies it is likely that hand-colouring of parish boundaries and the mounting, either in dissected form or varnished as a wall-map, was organised centrally. Indeed, the engraver may have arranged for this to be done in London.

Remarkably, since 2004, both copper plates have come to light (Figure 2). One had been turned over and used to surface a work bench; the reverse had become rather battered but the engraved surface was largely undamaged. That plate is now in Lincolnshire Archives. The other plate survives in private ownership.

REVISION

There can scarcely have been a worse time than 1842 to bring out an expensive new map of the city. Just a year later, the new road up Canwick Hill was extended through the Bargate Closes to complete what was almost an eastern by-pass to the city. Then, in 1846 and 1848-9, three railway lines opened, transforming the southern edge of the city. The map of 1842 must have seemed dreadfully out-of-date and in need of revision.

Surveying all the changes merely required time and effort, something that Padley could supply himself. Making the changes to the copper plates and printing new stocks would need to

Fig.2
Part of the south copper plate showing Robey's works, added for the final edition. The plate is of course engraved in mirror-image.

Fig.3
Paths on St Margaret's Burial Ground in Padley's 1851 edition.

be paid for, and Padley was suffering acute financial difficulties, following a contract to construct the Skellingthorpe reservoir which went wrong and ended in a Chancery suit.[3]

We know what Padley was doing about this in consequence of another of Dennis Mills's interests, in plans that were then in City Hall and had been prepared for various abortive sewerage schemes. Of these, the most impressive was a massive and highly detailed plan at 40 inches to the mile which had been prepared in 1849 by the engineer George Giles.[4] A reduction to the 20-inch scale subsequently came to light in Lincoln Central Library. Dennis's interest was in the politics and how they interacted with the engineering issues. My interest was in the base maps: did they represent an independent survey, or were they derived from Padley's 20-inch map?

The easiest way to show that one map is copying another is when it reproduces errors. Unfortunately, the only definite errors on Padley's 20-inch map concern parish boundaries, something the Giles plans do not show. Nor does it help that the accuracy with which details on the Giles plans have been traced is variable: sometimes quite precise, sometimes sloppy. However, one feature which stands out on the Giles plans is the arrangement of paths in the burial ground of the former St Margaret's church within the Close: a couple of paths fan out and then stop abruptly. Figure 3 explains what has happened: the paths actually carry on across the main east-west path, but on Padley's map they have been broken by the letters 'RE' of 'MARGARETS'. The Giles plans retain the break, even though the name has not been included on them. This is clear evidence that Giles was copying Padley.

A more remarkable instance can be found on South Common (Figure 4), where Padley shows a very awkward junction of paths of varying widths, the one I have labelled '1' being the widest. Giles shows the paths with the same awkward junction and again '1' is the widest. One would not expect an engineer engaged on a sewerage project to take quite so much trouble to map exact widths of paths crossing common land and well away from all his proposed sewers. But what makes this remarkable is that Figure 4 shows the *1851* edition of Padley's map. In 1842 path (1) continued to the former toll gate at the foot of Canwick Hill; in fact this was the route by which traffic from Canwick made its way to the lower High Street – hence its width. When the Canwick new road was built, a new toll gate was constructed where the Washingborough road joins. The eastern continuation of path (1) had to be destroyed to prevent travellers from avoiding the new toll gate; instead they were obliged to use path (3) – both (2) and (3) were already present as lesser paths in 1842. Path (4) seems to be entirely new; it is a dead-end of uncertain purpose.

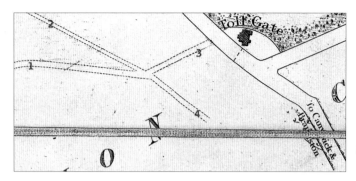

Fig.4
*Paths on South Common
in 1851 edition.*

Clearly, Giles's clerks in 1849 cannot have been copying a printed map that did not yet exist. The explanation must be that Padley was maintaining a revision model, a copy of the 1842 map marked up with the changes the engraver would need to make, and he had evidently made this available to Giles. One can find other examples where Giles's plans match the 1851 Padley and not the 1842 map: the Gourleys' brick yard at Stamp End is one such case, to be explained shortly.

Padley's revision model was a living document. One can see this because Giles's 40-inch plan is slightly earlier than his 20-inch one; and the base maps appear to have been traced independently from the revision model. This stands out most clearly in the case of the street on the western edge of the city known in 1842 as 'Besom Park' and in 1851 as 'The Park'. In 1842 this was almost undeveloped, with just a small group of houses at its southern end. Giles's 40-inch plan shows a pair of semi-detached villas added halfway up, but no other additions. His 20-inch plan shows the western side of the street almost completely built up, with just a single gap. And by 1851 that last gap had been filled.

In 1845 Padley had been appointed one of the surveyors to the Lincoln, Horncastle and Wainfleet Haven Railway and had surveyed the route from Lincoln to a point east of Horncastle. The Lincoln portion of that survey allows us to compare his 20-inch map against a survey undertaken for a different purpose. Figure 5 shows the brickyard at Stamp End owned by the Witham Navigation and leased to John and William Gourley. The boundaries of the brickyard on the railway plan are exactly the same as on the 1842 map: it is likely that Padley checked that they were unchanged and simply copied them. In contrast, within the brickyard the railway plan shows a circular feature, which is likely to be a pug-mill for mixing the clay, three pairs of rectangular structures, which must represent kilns, and two features marked by broken lines, which probably represent covered storage for bricks. The function of the two rectangular structures close to the northern boundary is uncertain. In contrast, the 1842 map showed two pairs and three single rectangular structures but none of the other features. The 1851 map made changes to the property boundaries at the west end of the site – changes that can already be seen via Giles's map of 1849 – but made no changes to the interior of the site other than deleting one of the two northern buildings.

There was logic behind this. Padley was a land-agent amongst his other activities, and he seems to have intended his 20-inch map to be used for property management. Every property that might be leased separately, be it a paddock, an isolated garden or a stable, needed to be faithfully depicted. But an industrial enterprise like a brickyard would only be disposed of as a complete business. The map needed to show its boundaries and its identity:

'Brick Yard' was good enough but there was no harm in showing a few kilns. However, the depiction of kilns did not need to be complete or up-to-date: any potential purchaser would want to satisfy himself of the condition of the kilns and the amount of brick-earth remaining on the site. It was not the function of his map to show such things. In contrast, the railway survey provided evidence that might be used by the company to argue over the valuation of any land they had taken. (The line across the south-east corner of the site indicates the limits of the area over which the promoters were seeking powers of compulsory purchase.) Thus, it was important to show that the pug-mill, the drying sheds, and two of the kilns were unaffected by the railway proposals. At most, the kiln(?) in the south-east corner would be lost but the viability of what remained would be unaffected.

This land-agent's perspective was reflected also in the way that Padley (like most other private surveyors) depicted railways. He showed earthworks and bridges because they were prominent in the landscape. He showed boundary fences because they represented property boundaries. He showed major buildings like stations, warehouses and engine-sheds either for their prominence or because they might conceivably be sold off by the railway company and be used for other purposes. But he did not show railway tracks, electric telegraphs, or any of the other features that related solely to the business of running a railway.

Throughout his life, Padley was a great admirer of the Ordnance Survey; but he never adopted their 'scientific' view of the purpose of a survey: that its job was to depict everything permanently attached to the ground. Padley's view was a good deal more practical.

Padley's Revision Model may have had other uses. Padley undertook the cartographic work for the tithe surveys for a couple of Lincoln's parishes and he may have drawn on it for those. Whether he continued to maintain it after 1851 is unknown. There were subsequent revisions of the map issued in 1868 and (after Padley's death by his partner J. M. Thropp) in 1883, but we know little about how the revision work for these was undertaken.

AFTERLIFE
Photolithography – the creation by photographic means of an image on a lithographic stone – goes back to 1826. It was discovered in 1859 that similar techniques could be used with a zinc printing plate, and the Ordnance Survey started to reproduce maps by this means. The biggest problem was obtaining a sharp image over the whole of a large plate, but the state of the art steadily improved. It would appear that Padley used this technique – engaging a

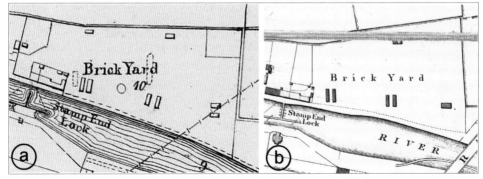

Fig.5 The Gourleys' brick yard – (a) from railway survey and (b) from 1851 edition.

Fig.6
Extract from the 1883
ten-inch map.

specialist firm, no doubt – to produce a half-size image of the 1868 revision of the 20-inch map. Now at 10 inches to the mile it was small enough to be printed as a single sheet. It was also relatively straightforward to update the printing plate from time to time with new roads or important buildings. Thus, the Arboretum was added in some detail, the County Hospital appeared in a more generalised form, and new roads had their names added in various styles of lettering. This seems to suggest a succession of revisions each printed in small numbers with the updating of the plate being done by whoever was available. The nature of the alterations suggests that this was going on in the late 1870s. The result was somewhat unappealing as a map: the photo-reduced detail was exceedingly fine, whilst the new additions could be somewhat coarse. It is not known whether it was sold commercially. The only surviving specimen was in Lincoln Central Library,[5] which was given sundry cartographic material when J. M. Thropp retired, so may have come from Padley's office.

As it happens, Akrill's Lincoln Directory for 1877, according to its title page, contained 'a new map of the City' but no copy has been found. This may provide a context for Padley's interest in producing a 10-inch reduction. However, matters are complicated by there being two parallel strands.

Padley's office appears to have cleaned off the surrounding material from the plate: the old title, the archaeological sections through the castle and city wall, and the ornate border. Their new title used fancy lettering with foliage fronds but the wording was much simpler: *Plan of the City of Lincoln*, with a date. The only specimen known is an 1883 edition in the library at Grimsby in an extra-illustrated copy of Williamson's *Guide through Lincoln* of 1881 (Figure 6). It shows 'GE & GN Railway in Course of Construction' – which is indeed an accurate statement of the state of the Avoiding Line in the early part of 1883 – but there are other features where the state of revision is less advanced. This seems to confirm the idea of a succession of editions with revision for each new one limited to the more important changes.

Meanwhile, a licence of some sort must have been granted to Charles Akrill, because his 1881 directory contains a map *From Plan of James Sandby Padley / Surveyor, 1881 / Published by / Charles Akrill, / Lincoln*. This has been redrawn, leaving out fine detail which came from the 20-inch. Public buildings are numbered rather than named, the numbers being explained in a table of reference bottom-left. Sundry updating has taken place, which is still not found on the 1883 map of the previous paragraph. For example, the Burton New Road is given that name as it climbs the hillside: it is still just 'Proposed New Road' on the 1883 map.

In both cases it only extends as far as Burton Road, the continuation eastwards having not yet been agreed. Again, Harvey Street (by the Fossdyke) is described as 'Road', as opposed to 'Proposed Road' on the 1883 plan. In contrast, the Corporation Stables, marked on the 1883 plan, never appeared on Akrill's map.

Akrill's map continued to accompany directories until 1899, with the name of the publisher changed to Akrill, Ruddock & Keyworth and then to J. W. Ruddock to reflect changes in ownership of the firm. The later versions omit the reference to Padley, along with the date. New streets are added: since the directories included a listing of occupiers street-by-street, it was important that the maps should show the streets mentioned.

Between 1899 and 1903 the map was redrawn, to cover a larger area. The new title was *Revised Map of the City of Lincoln with Bracebridge, Boultham & Canwick*. Parish boundaries within the city were omitted: they were about to be abolished anyway.[6]

What was the source for this revision? Part of the evidence comes from the names applied to some of the public buildings. Thus, what is now The Lawn is described as *Medical Lunatic Hospital*. That is the name used on the First edition of the large-scale Ordnance Survey plans, surveyed about 1885. By the 2nd edition of 1907 its preferred description was *Hospital for the Insane*. More revealingly, within the castle the new map shows *Remains of Old Prison*. Those who visit the castle now

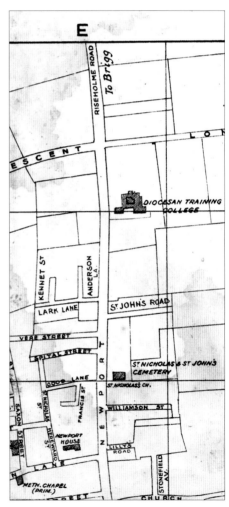

Fig.7
Newport as shown on Ruddock's revised map.

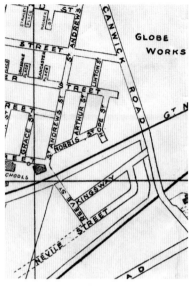

Fig.8
Nevile Street and Reeve Street,
planned in 1911 but never built –
still shown in 1931.

are impressed by the completeness of the Victorian prison; so why 'Remains of'? What happened, I think, is that Ruddock's clerk had been copying the Ordnance Survey and had run together the 'remains of' – actually referring to the Castle – and 'Old Prison'.

Perhaps the most revealing feature of the new map is the north-arrow – or rather the absence of one. Padley's 20-inch map had a north-arrow in the top-right corner, aligned with the map. The north-arrow was retained on the 1883 map. The new Ruddock map lacks one, probably because the map is not aligned precisely north-south. The Ordnance Survey plans for Lincolnshire were drawn on a Cassini projection based on the meridian of Dunnose in the Isle of Wight (1° 11′ 50″ W)[7] and away from that meridian the maps exhibit a phenomenon known as 'convergence of meridians'. As far as one can tell, Ruddock's revised plan was drawn on the same projection. The easiest way of spotting this is to observe that Newport runs parallel to the squaring on the map (Figure 7); on Padley's map it is apparent that it points a little west of north.

Of course, for the depiction of streets added since the first O.S. edition, Ruddock's cartographer was able to draw on the updates to the previous map, and updates from the men compiling the directory continued for the life of the map. Sometimes the cartographer jumped the gun, as Figure 8 shows. In 1911, a building application had been submitted for three streets off Canwick Road, immediately south of the GN&GE Jt Railway (the 'Avoiding Line'). A start was made on one of them, Kingsway, but the war intervened and Nevile Street and Reeve Street never came into existence. They remained, nevertheless, on the Ruddock map until at least 1931.

However, this is taking the account of Padley's map beyond its natural end. In reduced form, it did indeed continue to the end of the century as a directory map, but it would seem that Ruddock's maps from 1903 onwards made no use of Padley's work. Even so, for a map drawn in 1841 to be still in use in a derived form sixty years on is quite an achievement.

NOTES

1.   Mills, D. R. and Wheeler, R. C. (eds), 2004, *Historic Town Plans of Lincoln, 1610-1920*, Lincoln Record Society, Vol. 92.

2.   Carroll, R. A. (ed.), 1996, *Printed Maps of Lincolnshire, 1576-1900*, Lincoln Record Society, Vol. 84.

3.   Brook, S., Walker, A. and Wheeler, R. (eds), 2011, *Lincoln Connections*, pp. 31-42.

4.   Mills, D. R., 2015, *Effluence and Influence*. This reproduces the 20-inch version.

5.   LCL Maps 809

6.   Local Government Board Order 49039 of 1 April 1907.

7.   At first, the large-scale plans used a separate meridian for each county. This created difficulties at county boundaries and by the time Lincolnshire came to be surveyed the policy was to use common meridians for groups of counties.

INTERROGATING THE GROWTH OF A CITY: EXPLORING LINCOLN'S BUILDING APPLICATION DATABASE, 1866 – 1939[1]

Andrew Walker

This article is directly inspired by the work of Dennis Mills with regard to one particular primary source, building application plans. These are closely linked to plotting the physical development of the city of Lincoln in the later nineteenth and early twentieth centuries.

The study examines the reasons underpinning the submission of building plans in urban Britain, linked to legislative change, especially in the third quarter of the nineteenth century. Consideration is given to the survival of this primary source within Lincoln and to the development of a database containing key information drawn from these documents which is accessible on The Survey of Lincoln's website. Some consideration is given to the urban problems in Lincoln which, finally, prompted the city's leaders to adopt the public health-related permissive legislation which led to the production of the city's building plans. Due regard is paid to the limitations of the source.

The database is used to explore how building plans can be employed to illuminate various aspects linked to the growth of the city. This includes examination of the city's architects and the extent and nature of their portfolios, the changing nature of the growth of the city over time, altering tastes in terms of construction of particular residential building types, the rise of female autonomy in property development and the impact of technological change upon residential development, notably through considering the rise of the motor car.

INTRODUCTION

Dennis Mills was an active member of The Survey of Lincoln from its beginnings in 1995. He contributed regularly to the production of its publications, including the neighbourhood series of booklets, which explored the history of the city's buildings and structures, and he was also a regular contributor to The Survey's newsletter, *The Enquirer*. Dennis was also much involved in and often initiated a number of The Survey's projects.[2]

Amongst the later projects of The Survey to which Dennis contributed significantly was one relating to the city's building plans. The late David Drakes, a member of the City of Lincoln Council's Heritage Team, rescued from oblivion the Department of the City Engineer's collection of building plans and their ledgers at some time in the 1990s. This collection amounted to just under 10,000 plans. The later plans from 1932 to 1952 were sent to the Lincolnshire Archives, where they were only selectively retained. It was resolved to keep the rest at City Hall. John Herridge, then the City of Lincoln Council's Heritage Services Officer, oversaw the production of a comprehensive database providing details of these holdings. This transcription took place between 2007 and 2012 on to a Microsoft Access database, with the help of many young people on work experience and City Council apprentices.

At a point when the future of these building plans was in doubt, a small group led by Dennis decided to draw further attention to this valuable resource on The Survey of Lincoln website.

With Dennis, John Herridge, Beryl George, Geoff Tann and myself set to work producing a section of The Survey of Lincoln's website providing access to the database set up by John Herridge, and providing a range of contextual information and details of further literature about building plans more generally, together with access to a comparative piece by Dr Janet Dunleavey on the city of Worcester's building plans.[3] Following a City Hall reorganisation, the building plans of the city were transferred to the Lincolnshire Archives in 2014, where they can now be accessed.[4]

Some of Dennis's later articles, both for The Survey of Lincoln and the SLHA's magazine *Past and Present*, often co-written with his daughter, Victoria Thorpe, drew upon the content of several building plans, especially in their work on the Swan family.[5]

This article will draw upon some of the content of The Survey of Lincoln's website which examines these building plans and will undertake analysis of some of the database's content in order to demonstrate how such information can be used in exploring the development of a city. Although the potential of building plans as a research tool was advanced as long ago as 1980 by P. J. Aspinall and J. W. R. Whitehand, the number of published articles drawing upon detailed analysis of such source materials remains relatively small.[6]

THE BUILDING APPLICATION RECORDS
This series of building application records (hereafter building plans) was compiled by the City of Lincoln Engineer's Department, starting in 1866 when Lincoln rather belatedly adopted the Public Health Act of 1858. This system of building control continued in use until 1952, after which the current town planning system was initiated under the 1947 Act.[7]

The focus initially was on the sanitary aspects of development, which included a request on the application form for details of building material, distance from the frontage of the site, height of building (as a control on room heights) and the form of drainage, both rain water and waste water. In addition to new developments, alterations to existing buildings also required applications. All types of development required the submission of building plans: this included housing, factories, workshops, commercial, agricultural, educational, and religious structures.

Each completed application form was to be accompanied by the requisite number of site plans, and building plans and elevations to make it clear as to what was intended. These are attractive drawings, usually coloured. Names of architects (or builders) in addition to owners were usually attached to the plans as well as to the forms, which makes it possible to study the professional work of architects and the influence of developers. The applications were quite frequently sent back to applicants for revision, or approved with conditions attached.

NINETEENTH-CENTURY HOUSING REGULATION
During much of the nineteenth century, in many expanding industrial urban centres the quality of workers' housing was invariably very poor. In rapidly growing towns and cities, workers and their families tended either to occupy parts of older, neglected large properties in urban centres, previously the homes of middle-class residents who had moved to more salubrious suburbs, or were living in newly-built, cheaply-constructed housing, often served by rudimentary ineffective drainage systems.[8]

A common urban house type, constructed in many northern and midland industrial towns and cities, particularly in the first half of the nineteenth century, was the back-to-back terraced house. Often constructed by speculative builders, back-to-back houses were arranged in rows, with houses at the front and back, each one-room deep. The rear houses in such rows would face into courts, with shared privies and water provision. The courts were often accessed via a tunnel from the houses facing the street.[9] Court-style housing developed in the centre of Lincoln by the middle nineteenth-century in areas such as Waterside, the Drapery and the High Street.[10]

Major health problems arose as a consequence of this type of cramped building, with its ineffective sanitary provision. Cholera outbreaks, caused by infected water supplies, regularly prompted significant death tolls in such urban residential districts. It was often medical professionals who were amongst the first to draw attention to the poor quality of workers' housing. Such individuals included W. H. Duncan, Liverpool's, and Britain's, first Medical Officer of Health (appointed in 1847), and the sanitary reformer Edwin Chadwick, who was a key architect of the 1848 Public Health Act that sought to ameliorate the situation. This major piece of legislation stipulated minimum street widths and permitted local authorities to introduce higher standards relating, for instance, to the development of drainage systems and access to courts and yards.

In the 1860s and 1870s local legislation was introduced in many towns and cities to regulate residential building activity and sanitation. Gradually, this began to forbid the construction of back-to-back housing and removed some of the worst types of unsanitary housing. Much of this local legislation was informed by both the Public Health Act 1848 and the Local Government Act of 1858, the latter of which provided much regulatory detail relating to the construction of new housing. Guidelines were issued, called the Form of Bye-laws. These were used as the basis of their own local regulatory frameworks by many English and Welsh urban authorities during the 1860s. They stipulated that all carriage streets must be thirty-six feet wide; there had to be a hundred and fifty square feet of clear space at the rear of each house; and there was to be a minimum of fifteen feet distance to the next building in the case of a two-storey house.[11]

New Model Byelaws were produced in 1877 and were widely adopted, following the passing of the Conservative Government's Public Health Act in 1875. This Act required all new residential construction to include running water and an internal drainage system. The Act also compelled local authorities to appoint a Medical Officer and a Sanitary Inspector. The same year, the Artisans' Dwelling Act was also introduced. This was a central piece of permissive legislation, which enabled local authorities to implement slum clearance.[12] Through the development of this legislation, there was, as Martin Daunton has observed, a move from a residential style that was 'cellular and promiscuous' to one that was 'open and encapsulated'.[13] Courts, with communal space and shared sanitary provision were being replaced with individual houses that were private and self-contained spaces. The building controls that enabled this change, it could be argued, represented the triumph of middle-class values, with the regulations introduced and implemented by largely middle-class councillors. The sweeping away of enclosed courts and alleys, and the building of open-ended, connected residential streets, enabled not just improved health and sanitation provision but also the construction of urban residential districts that were visible for inspection and policing.[14]

LINCOLN'S BUILDING REGULATIONS

The city of Lincoln was a relatively late adopter of the 1858 Local Government Act. Other Lincolnshire places which had already implemented the legislation by the time Lincoln had done so in 1866 included Boston (1859), Sutton Bridge (1859), Barton upon Humber (1862) and Grantham (1864).[15] In early 1866 a special meeting of Lincoln's Council took place to consider the implementation of the legislation. A detailed report of the debate was published in the *Lincolnshire Chronicle*.[16] Following a four-hour meeting, the Act was adopted by seventeen votes to five. The meeting had been convened as a consequence of a requisition signed by five hundred of the city's largest ratepayers calling upon the Council to consider adopting the Act. During the debate, concerns were expressed at the city's high death rate, twenty-nine per thousand, which was six above the level at which the Government could interfere to enforce the Act.[17] It was noted that, where towns had implemented the Local Government Act, all had reduced their death rates. Several council members had, prior to the debate, visited the towns of Worthing and Croydon which had successfully implemented measures associated with the Act.

The principal advocate of the Local Government Act in the debate was Alderman Richard Harvey, a medical doctor, and three-time mayor of the city. He stated that the powers Lincoln Corporation currently possessed were not commensurate with its dignity and the wants of the town. He noted that nearly every town in the country had adopted the Act and that many populous villages had also implemented regulations relating to its contents. All of these places, he asserted, were far ahead of Lincoln as regards their powers of local government. The poor quality of the city's housing provision was highlighted and the comments of Mr Garnham, former surgeon to the city's Dispensary were introduced to the debate by Harvey, himself previously employed in this role at the Dispensary. Garnham had described the poor quality of the 'tenements' of the city, the courts uphill with homes with no back windows, the open drainage channels, and the housing with one privy for thirty people. References were made to: Sincil Street, with its courts within courts; the backyards and alleys of the Waterside; the houses on High Bridge, which were 'more fit for rabbit warrens than human habitation'; and the 'conglomerate mass of ill-built dwellings, stables and slaughterhouses' on Waterside South.[18]

The poor state of Lincoln's housing, and more particularly its sewer provision, had been the focus of earlier political attention, which had culminated in an extensive and damning report in 1849, following a cholera outbreak in the town. This report and proposed sewerage scheme was produced by the eminent civil and sanitary engineer George Giles, although his plans were not implemented.[19]

Several councillors admitted within the debate on the Local Government Act to changing their minds regarding its adoption. Alderman Ward had opposed the adoption of the Act in a Lincoln Town Council debate in 1859 but had altered his view, he stated, largely owing to the recent rapid growth of the city's population, the associated significant increase in the city's land values and builders consequently 'packing the largest possible number of houses' in these valuable spaces.[20]

The *Lincolnshire Chronicle* report explained to its readers that the thirty-fourth clause of the 1858 Local Government Act enabled the Corporation to exercise its control with respect to the levels, width, and construction of new streets and the sewerage thereof, the security of walls, the prevention of fire, the ventilation and drainage of buildings and the provision of water closets. It also stated that builders were required to submit all of their plans for examination and approval to the Corporation.

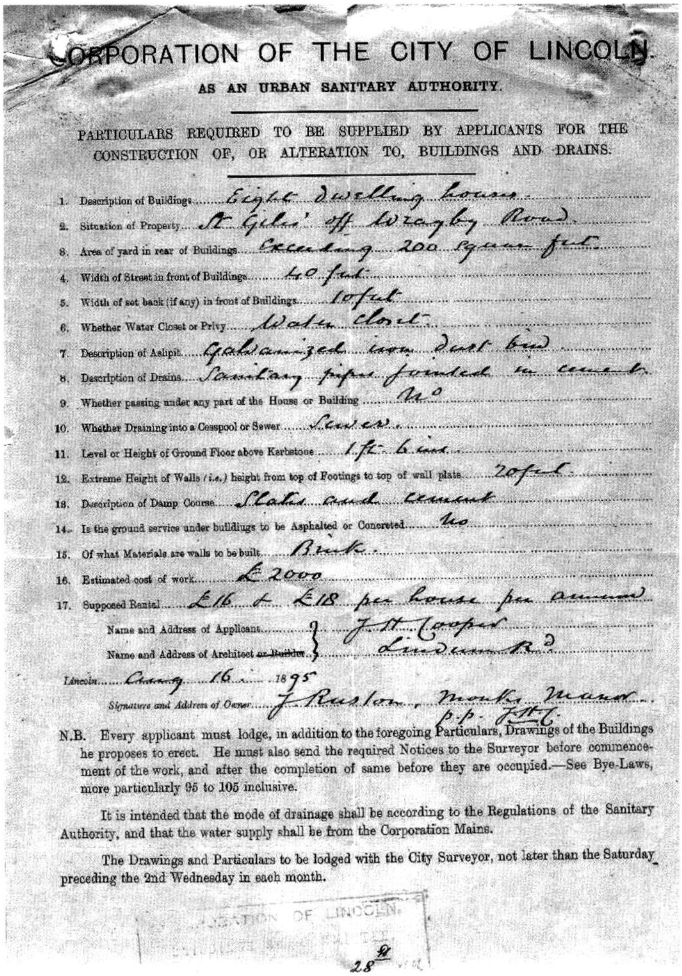

CORPORATION OF THE CITY OF LINCOLN.

AS AN URBAN SANITARY AUTHORITY.

PARTICULARS REQUIRED TO BE SUPPLIED BY APPLICANTS FOR THE CONSTRUCTION OF, OR ALTERATION TO, BUILDINGS AND DRAINS.

1. Description of Buildings...... Eight dwelling houses.
2. Situation of Property...... St Giles' off Wragby Road
3. Area of yard in rear of Buildings...... Exceeding 200 square feet.
4. Width of Street in front of Buildings...... 40 feet
5. Width of set back (if any) in front of Buildings...... 10 feet
6. Whether Water Closet or Privy...... Water closet.
7. Description of Ashpit...... Galvanized iron dust bin
8. Description of Drains...... Sanitary pipes jointed in cement
9. Whether passing under any part of the House or Building...... No
10. Whether Draining into a Cesspool or Sewer...... Sewer.
11. Level or Height of Ground Floor above Kerbstone...... 1 ft. 6 ins.
12. Extreme Height of Walls (i.e.) height from top of Footings to top of wall plate...... 20 feet
13. Description of Damp Course...... Slates and cement
14. Is the ground service under buildings to be Asphalted or Concreted...... No
15. Of what Materials are walls to be built...... Brick.
16. Estimated cost of work...... £2000
17. Supposed Rental...... £16 & £18 per house per annum

Name and Address of Applicant / Name and Address of Architect ~~or Builder~~ } J. H. Cooper, Lindum Rd

Lincoln...... Aug 16 1895

Signature and Address of Owner...... J Ruston, Monks Manor, p.p. J.H.C.

N.B. Every applicant must lodge, in addition to the foregoing Particulars, Drawings of the Buildings he proposes to erect. He must also send the required Notices to the Surveyor before commencement of the work, and after the completion of same before they are occupied.—See Bye-Laws, more particularly 95 to 105 inclusive.

It is intended that the mode of drainage shall be according to the Regulations of the Sanitary Authority, and that the water supply shall be from the Corporation Mains.

The Drawings and Particulars to be lodged with the City Surveyor, not later than the Saturday preceding the 2nd Wednesday in each month.

...ATION OF LINCOLN.

28

Fig.1 An example of a Lincoln building application form. This was approved on 29 August 1895 regarding eight dwelling houses to be built on St Giles' Avenue by architect J. H. Cooper on behalf of Joseph Ruston. (LAO MISC DON 1268. Ledger entry 2557. Reproduced with permission of Lincolnshire Archives, Lincolnshire County Council)

A few observations arising from late nineteenth-century newspaper reports are worth making regarding the list of building plans produced by Lincoln Corporation. It is clear that not all of the plans deposited, even where the buildings concerned were constructed, actually conformed to the plans. Similarly, it seems that, in some cases, buildings could have been constructed without plans being submitted and, on other occasions, where plans were deposited, these were, sometimes, considered after the point at which construction work had commenced.

Newspaper reports in Lincoln indicated that, following the implementation of the regulations, breaches of these were relatively common. Indeed, in 1882, the *Lincolnshire Chronicle* reported a story in the national publication, *The Architect*, which highlighted the fact that the byelaws of the Lincoln Urban Sanitary Authority appear as far as building regulations are concerned 'to have been a dead letter'. It seemed more common 'to violate rather than observe them.' The report noted that several people had lately been summoned by the City Police Court for infringement of some of the byelaws and had been 'let off' with a small fine. It was reported that the Deputy Town Clerk, H. K. Hebb, had observed a long list of other offenders and that if all the houses which had been erected in the last eighteen months were inspected, 'in no instance would it have been found that bye laws had been complied with.'[21]

Twelve years later in 1894, a high-profile breach of building regulations came to court, involving Charles Clarke, a tailor who had undertaken major building works on Dixon Street without submitting plans in advance. According to a *Lincolnshire Chronicle* report in 1894, it was noted that, during the court case, a clerk, John Miles, employed for twelve years by the prominent Lincoln architect Henry Goddard, had stated that it was customary for buildings in the city to be commenced before plans were deposited.[22]

Clearly, the production of Lincoln's building regulations, and the associated plans, were the result of a significant amount of reforming zeal, initially at the national level, but also ultimately, and somewhat belatedly, within the city itself. However, it is also evident that the records generated by these regulatory processes need to be treated with a degree of caution, given the concerns about the application of the local planning processes in the final decades of the nineteenth century. This needs to be borne in mind with the analysis that follows.

The concerns expressed by several councillors about the rapid growth of the city were based on significant evidence. In the three decades to 1861, the city's population was growing at about 20% every ten years. Lincoln's inhabitants in 1841 numbered just under 14,000; by 1861 the population was one short of 21,000. The implementation of the building regulations, however, was introduced at the time of the modern city's most rapid growth spurt in terms of population increase. Between 1861 and 1881, Lincoln's population grew over 77% from 20,999 to 37,313.[23]

CONSIDERATION OF THE BUILDING PLANS AND INDEX
Lincoln's Architects and Later-Nineteenth-Century Residential Development
Examination of the building plans index provides the opportunity to study the extent of the work of Lincoln's principal architects within the city itself. The impact and variety of the work of local architects in the growing mid- and later-Victorian townscape, including residential development, has not received a significant amount of attention, despite the existence of much building plan data.[24] Here, the focus is placed upon the years from the mid-1860s, when the Lincoln building plans began to be submitted, until the end of the nineteenth century, a period which, as mentioned above, coincided with significant population growth in the city. It is perhaps worth noting that the profession of architect itself was still a relatively new one. The Institute of British Architects had been founded in 1834, and architects were gradually seeking to distance themselves from direct involvement in building.[25]

The table below (see Fig. 2) indicates that several architects' names feature repeatedly among the building plans, with several individuals, such as Michael Drury and William Mortimer working both in partnership and individually. Initially, Michael Drury had worked as apprentice to one of the foremost nineteenth-century Lincoln architects, William Adams Nicholson.[26] Family names recur as well: William Mortimer, for instance, practised

Name of architect/company	Years in operation, as listed in database	Number of app's involved with during period
William Mortimer and Son	1891-1935	276
(Michael) Drury and (William) Mortimer	1870-79	148
Henry Goddard (1813-99) and Son	1867-1901	147
William Mortimer (1841-1913)	1879-91	130
(Pearson) Bellamy (1822-1901) and (John Spence) Hardy (1815-92)	1853-85	102
John Thomas Drury (1848-1914)	1871-1913	95
John H. Cooper (1847-1910)	1884-1909	93
William Watkins (1834-1926)	1864-77; 1884-94	90
Michael Drury (1832-90)	1853-71; 1879-89	84
James Whitton (1819-1903)	1866-86	40
William Watkins and Son	1894-1918	37
William Scorer (1843-1934)	1884-1901	34
Abraham Kelham (1838-73)	1867-72	31
Source: Index of City of Lincoln building plans. (www.thesurveyoflincoln.co.uk/Projects/cityba)		

Fig.2 Some Lincoln architects much involved with production of accepted building plan applications, 1866–1900.

architecture for some years with his son, William M. Mortimer, as did Henry Goddard, with his son Francis Henry, and William Watkins with his son, William Gregory, whilst another, Henry Garnham, also joined the profession, but worked in Nottingham.[27]

Several of these architectural practices undertook a wide variety of different commissions within the city: Mortimer and Son, for instance had a diverse residential portfolio including middle-class housing (latterly especially in Richmond Road in the city's West End) as well as more modest residential briefs in the lower High Street area.[28] The firm of Drury and Mortimer designed several substantial villas on South Park and Beaumont Fee.[29] Perhaps William Mortimer's most notable work in the city, however, included the Liberal Club in 1890 and the racecourse grandstand in 1897.[30]

Michael Drury tended to specialise in church building and restoration work, including the design of the Anglican and Dissenting Chapels at Lincoln's Canwick Road cemetery.[31] However, in later years he was involved largely with the design of terraced housing for workers and their families in streets such as Charlesworth Street and Foss Bank, south of Carholme Road.[32] William Watkins undertook some residential projects within Lincoln but much of his work related to more commercial buildings and public commissions, such as schools, hospitals and the Constitutional Club.[33]

Decade	Minimum	Maximum	Decadal Average	% Decadal Av'ge Increase/Decrease	% Decadal Pop'n Increase *
1860s	9 (1866)	74 (1869)	57.7		
1870s	59 (1870)	127 (1877)	93.6	+62.2	14.4
1880s	45 (1886)	148 (1884)	85.8	−8.3	11.7
1890s	79 (1890)	158 (1899)	118.1	+37.6	12.2
1900s	115 (1907)	180 (1904)	151.3	+28.1	10.9
1910s	23 (1918)	154 (1912)	70.3	−53.5	5.0
1920s	32 (1921)	182 (1924)	123.7	+76.0	5.4
1930s	95 (1931)	165 (1938)	127.0	+2.7	3.8
1940s	14 (1941)	286 (1949)	98.3	−22.6	

*Drawn from comparative census data (1861-1931) and 1939 register. (e.g. for 1870s from 1871 and 1881 census data).

Source: Index of City of Lincoln building plans, and Dennis Mills and Beryl George's census tabulations.

Fig.3 Total number of building plans accepted, 1860s–1940s.

Henry Goddard undertook business for the Dean and Chapter, for instance with work on the Precentory, and his practice also submitted plans for several new vicarages.[34] Goddard's commercial work was completed for a range of prominent local clients, including for the engineering companies of Ruston, Proctor and Company, Clayton and Shuttleworth's and William Foster and Company.[35] Much of Goddard's residential commissions were for individual projects for members of Lincoln's social elite.[36] Where Goddard produced designs for more modest properties, these tended to be relatively large projects involving rows of houses such as those on Dixon Street, and properties on Vine Street and Cheviot Street, near the Arboretum for F. J. Clarke, the chemist and city councillor, whose generally dim views of Lincoln's architects were made known in a city council meeting in October 1886.[37]

Bellamy and Hardy conducted much residential work in Newland, Portland Street and South Park, though also undertook significant commercial and public commissions such as work for the Lincoln Gas Company as well as the design of the new Corn Exchange and the Wesleyan Chapel in Bailgate.[38]

Several of the architects listed focused more on modest residential commissions. John T. Drury, of Canwick Road, undertook a substantial amount of work involving modest residential properties, sometimes described as 'cottages' and outbuildings, including bake houses, stables and pigstyes.[39] From the building plans index, it seems that James Whitton was principally engaged in small-scale residential development in the lower city, in roads such as Sincil Bank and Monks Road.[40] Abraham Kelham's work involved many small-scale 'house and shop' and 'house and stable' projects, though he undertook some recurring business for the prominent Lincoln brewer, Robert Dawber.[41]

Analysis of the building plans index during the later nineteenth century supports the case advanced by Jeremy Whitehand that, during this period, the work of local architects prevailed especially in small and medium-sized urban centres.[42] Using the details contained within the building plan database, and considering the social standing of clients and the types of work being commissioned, a clear hierarchy of architects within the city also emerges, with practitioners such as Bellamy and Hardy, Henry Goddard, William Mortimer,

William Watkins at the top and those such as John T. Drury and Abraham Kelham towards the bottom.

Building Plans and the Growth of the City

Following the introduction of the building regulation scheme in Lincoln, application numbers grew steadily, with seventy-four being received in 1869. The number of planning applications seem to indicate links not necessarily with the city's population changes but more with its economic fortunes. The impact of the First and Second World Wars on planning and building in the city also can be seen clearly from these figures. (see table at Fig. 3)

As was noted earlier, planning applications had to be made with regard to many types of building. The analysis by building type indicates that the majority of applications in most years related to residential developments, followed by industrial and commercial proposals. (see Fig. 3) From the sample of years considered, on average nearly sixty per cent of the building plans accepted related to housing and twenty-five percent to industrial and commercial developments. As a proportion of applications, house building appeared to be highest in the sample years of 1878 (74%) and 1938 (71%) and lowest during the First World War in 1918 (25%) when seventy per cent of the very low number of applications (twenty-four) were for industrial and commercial properties.

In each of the sample years, the majority of residential applications related to either the building or alteration of a single dwelling house. The number of applications for multiple houses did increase over time – though for much of the period from 1868 to 1918 very few

Year	Number/ percentage	Residential	Retail	Industry/ business	Other	Total
1868	N	28	3	11	1	43
	%	65.1	7.0	25.6	2.3	100
1878	N	74	14	6	6	100
	%	74.0	14.0	6.0	6.0	100
1888	N	30	2	13	8	53
	%	56.6	3.8	24.5	15.1	100
1898	N	89	14	32	9	144
	%	61.8	9.7	22.2	6.3	100
1908	N	67	8	36	7	118
	%	56.9	6.8	30.5	5.8	100
1918	N	6	0	17	1	24
	%	25.0	0.0	70.8	4.2	100
1928	N	91	18	18	15	142
	%	64.1	12.7	12.7	10.5	100
1938	N	130	14	22	17	183
	%	71.0	7.8	12.0	9.2	100
	Sample avge (%)	59.4	7.7	25.5	7.4	100

Source: Index of City of Lincoln building application plans. (www.thesurveyoflincoln.co.uk/Projects/cityba)

Fig.4 Types of building plans submitted in selected years, 1868–1938.

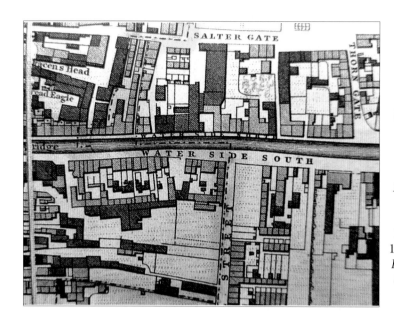

Fig.5
Extract from
1868 Padley
plan of Lincoln,
showing densely
packed courtyard
housing in the
Waterside area
of the city centre.
(Source: Mills,
D.R. and Wheeler,
R.C., eds, 2004,
Historic Town
Plans of Lincoln,
1610–1920. *Lincoln*
Record Society/The
Survey of Lincoln,
p. 69)

of these multiple applications extended beyond eight houses, suggesting that much of this residential construction was being undertaken by small builders.[43]

Where alterations were made to existing properties, the majority of these related to proposals for sanitation improvements. Additional WCs, for instance, were installed to serve the needs of residents in Meanwell Court, Waterside, in 1882, which was later to be demolished via a compulsory purchase order.[44] Most of the internal sanitary enhancements began higher up the social scale and percolated down: wash houses and bathrooms were first added in the 1880s to existing properties in uphill Lincoln, at addresses such as Winnowsty Terrace, and Yarborough Road, and in other fashionable middle-class enclaves, such as Arboretum Avenue.[45] Only later, often in the 1900s and 1910s, were such applications made for more modest properties in streets such as Newland Street West, Waterside North and Sincil Bank.[46] It was as late as 1931 that five ramshackle properties on Steep Hill (numbers 49-53) were fitted with wash houses and WCs.[47] These were owned by a clergyman, Revd N. S. Harding, who at the time was curate at All Saints' Church, Monks Road.[48]

Attempts were made to sweep away the very worst insanitary and deadly accommodation with the slum clearances of the early 1930s when a five-year programme of demolition and rebuilding took place, which planned to demolish 666 houses and build 455 new homes, rehousing 2230 inhabitants.[49] In the process, through concentrating on some residential areas off the High Street, in Sincil Street, the Waterside and The Drapery (behind The Strait and Steep Hill), many of the very worst courts and yards were destroyed.

With the coming of the byelaw housing and the implementation of the building regulation plans, the quality of new working-class housing in the city in the final third of the nineteenth century was undoubtedly superior to that built in the earlier part of the century. An analysis of building plans from one small working-class neighbourhood can shed a little additional light on residential building patterns

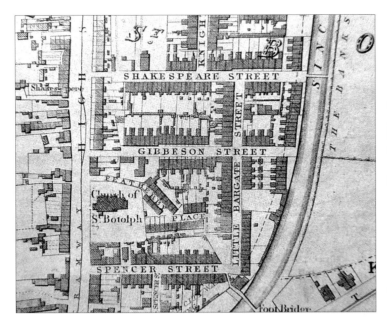

Fig.6
Extract from
1883 Padley and
Thropp plan of
Lincoln, showing
recently built open
streets of terraced
housing south east
of the High Street.
(Source: Mills,
D.R. and Wheeler,
R.C., eds, 2004,
Historic Town
Plans of Lincoln,
1610–1920.
Lincoln Record
Society/The
Survey of Lincoln,
p. 69)

BUILDING PLANS AND MICRO-STUDIES:
i) A Working-Class Neighbourhood: The Lower High Street

During the later nineteenth century there was a significant development of residential property on streets adjoining the lower High Street. This section focuses especially upon the following cluster of streets, on the east side of the southern end of the High Street, and west of Sincil Dyke. These comprise: Queen Street, Shakespeare Street, Gibbeson Street, Featherby Place, Spencer Street, Little Bargate Street and Knight Street, all of which were developed in the period roughly c.1875 to 1880: Queen Street and Spencer Street first appeared in trade directories for the year 1877; the remaining streets were listed in trade directories of 1881 (which were usually published a year earlier than their specified date). The consideration of the 1883 Padley map, reproduced from the *Historic Town Plans of Lincoln*, co-edited by Dennis Mills and Rob Wheeler, indicates the extent to which this residential building was taking place on previously undeveloped land. The plan shows quite clearly the self-contained nature of the housing provision in private spaces on open accessible streets rather than the old cellular and shared working-class accommodation found in the courts and yards that had previously been a common approach to constructing the city's working-class housing (see Figs 5 and 6).

Details of the owners and builders of properties in the streets mentioned above included in the building plans confirm that much of the area's development took place in the later 1870s. Plans for seventy-three houses were submitted between 1876 and 1879 for Shakespeare Street; and proposals for thirty-one properties on Little Bargate Street, and sixty-one on Gibbeson Street were also considered during the same years. In this period of rapid development, plans were submitted relating to these streets by a small number of owners for up to twenty properties at a time, either to be built by the owners themselves, or on their behalf by a number of Lincoln's larger building companies. The largest owner in this specific area of the lower High Street at its most rapid period of residential development appeared to be James

Fig.7
Terraced properties on Spencer Street,
Lincoln, in 2023, with double-gated
entrance for animals, built c.1871.
(Photo: Andrew Walker)

Weighell, a local builder, whose portfolio included properties in Featherby Place (including Harrison's Place) and Gibbeson Street, where he also built a blacksmith's shop and other workshops.[50] Weighell's properties were developed principally by Drury and Mortimer, local architects and surveyors, who worked closely with a number of Lincoln builders. In several cases, builders owned the land and developed it themselves. In addition to James Weighell, Samuel Horton, for instance, possessed land on Gibbeson Street and submitted plans to build thirteen houses there in 1877. Horton tended to submit his own plans for residential development rather than employ an architect.[51] As elsewhere in the city, there was also evidence of the Co-operative Society developing residential property in the area. The Lincoln Land and Building Society, based at Co-operative Hall, Silver Street, owned and built fifteen houses in Knight Street in 1877 (numbers 8-10; 16-30; and 5-15).[52] From consideration of these cases, it seems that the pattern of house building in later nineteenth-century in Lincoln was similar to that identified in Worcester by Janet Dunleavey, with some even quite modest housing designed by local architects, whilst other housing stock was more vernacular in style.[53]

ii) Middle-Class Lincoln Neighbourhoods and the Building Plans

Consideration of a rather later set of building plans in largely middle-class parts of the city in the early twentieth century, reveal how changing tastes, shifting property ownership patterns and technological advancements, can be plotted using this primary source material. Initially in this section, the register of building plans will be used to examine the appearance of both a relatively new type of residential property and owner in Lincoln's suburbs in the 1920s and 1930s.

Bungalows

The very first bungalows in the city appeared to be temporary structures, built of wood and constructed to address an acute housing shortage for newly-recruited workers and their families at Clayton and Shuttleworth's Abbey Works. According to the building control plans, ten wooden dwellings were approved in January 1920 and built subject to a permitted life of ten years.[54] Although the building control plans do not specify these as single-storey structures, in the 1921 census, they are referred to as 'Abbey Works Bungalows', and housed employees of Clayton Waggons and their families.

The first bungalow plans specifically mentioned in the building plans database were submitted in late 1920 and 1921. Over the next decade, forty-two building plans relating to bungalows were submitted in the city, mainly in the southern suburbs – with eleven built in Rookery Lane, and seven each in Doddington Road and Boultham Park Road. These tended to be built individually; there was only one application for more than one bungalow between 1921 and 1931. Several local builders became known for their bungalow construction: J. R. Halkes built ten in this period, and F. Challands constructed seven.[55] Although a significant new residential building type, many examples of which were to be built in Lincoln's suburbs in the immediate decades following the Second World War, nevertheless the bungalow in inter-war Lincoln was relatively rare: in comparison to the seventy-three building plans involving the construction of bungalows submitted between 1920 and 1939, there were 839 building plans relating to new houses.[56]

Bungalows were still a relatively new residential building style at this time. The first ones in Britain were built at Westgate on Sea in Kent between 1869 and 1870, designed by John Taylor who, with his father, also John, a fellow architect, had designed the railway stations on the Lincolnshire Loop line which opened in 1848.[57] The term 'bungalow' derived from the description of single-storeyed houses in the Bengal style which had proved popular residences for Anglo-Indians. Upon the transfer of this housing style to Britain's suburbs from the end of the nineteenth century onwards, initially these were associated with a certain Bohemian way of living. As Anthony H. King has observed, the bungalow had no stairs to mark 'proper distinction between night and day and the behaviour and activities appropriate to each.' He went on to suggest that 'the existence of bedrooms adjacent to the sitting room … introduced a potentially dangerous overlap between informal and formal, proper and improper activities.'[58]

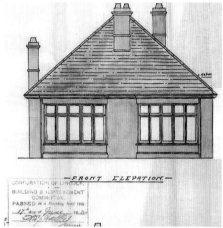

Fig. 8
Front elevation of a bungalow on Doddington Road, Lincoln, to be built for G.W. Shipley. Approved 17 June 1930. (LAO MISC DON 1628. Ledger entry 6819. Reproduced with permission of Lincolnshire Archives, Lincolnshire County Council).

Fig. 9
Semi-detached bungalows on Western Crescent, Lincoln, in 2023; plans approved on 16 February 1939. (Photo: Andrew Walker)

By the time bungalows began to be built in Lincoln, perhaps the 'raciness' of the bungalow as a building type had subsided somewhat, though a certain unconventionality could arguably still be associated with this building form in the city, as is explored below.

The Building Plans and Unmarried Women

Relatively speaking, the bungalow seemed to be a particularly popular residential building type amongst unmarried women. Of fifteen bungalows built that appeared in the Lincoln building plans in the 1920s, three were submitted by unmarried women. From the building plans data, it seemed that clusters of property owned by unmarried women

Nettleham Road 'cluster' (8)			
Year	Name	Property type	Road
1905	Miss M. Andrews	House	Mainwaring Drive
1905	Miss M. Andrews	Two Houses	Massey Road
1925	Misses M. V. Armstrong and E. M. Davies	House	Longdales Road
1926	Miss Anne Noble	House	Queensway
1928	Miss C. E. Epton	House	Haffenden Road
1929	Miss E. Ashdown	House	Massey Road
1929	Misses E. Atkinson and M. Bennett	House	Lee Road
1930	Miss E. King	House	Nettleham Road
South-east Lincoln 'cluster' (7)			
1925	Miss E. Tayles	House	Skellingthorpe Road
1926	Miss Alice Watson	House	Hykeham Road
1926	Miss M. Galbraith	House	Hykeham Road
1927	Miss Maud Annie Hides	Bungalow	Boultham Park Road
1928	Miss M. Russell	Bungalow	Boultham Park Road
1928	Miss J. Carnelly	Bungalow	Hykeham Road
1929	Miss J. Ward	House	Boultham Park Road
Source: Index of City of Lincoln building application plans. (www.thesurveyoflincoln.co.uk/Projects/cityba)			

Fig.10 Building applications for new dwellings submitted by single women, 1905–30 (17 submitted in total).

could be found in the first decades of the twentieth century uphill in the Nettleham Road area (e.g., Nettleham Road, Lee Road, Queensway, Haffenden Road, Massey Road) and south of the city centre (on Hykeham Road and Boultham Park Road). Between 1866 and 1920, unmarried females appeared to be the owners of six proposed new properties which appeared in the building plans; between 1920 and 1939, twenty-one applications for new housing were made citing unmarried women as the owners. This perhaps reflects the increasing economic power of single women, but also the fact that, owing to the loss of life during the First World War, in the years immediately following the conflict there were rather more unmarried women in the population than previously.[59]

The Motor Car and Building Plans

Unsurprisingly, the coming of the motor car began to have an impact upon the content of building plans from the upper echelons of Lincoln society by the early years of the twentieth century. Applications to build what were variously called 'motor sheds', 'motor car houses' and 'motor garages' were submitted in the first decades of the twentieth century from some of the city's most prestigious addresses. The French term 'garage' became used extensively, in preference to the other terms, to refer to domestic accommodation for cars in Lincoln, as elsewhere, by the mid-1920s, having first been employed in the city's residential building plans in 1912.[60]

Decade	No. of applications	Terminology used (in descending order of popularity)
1900-1909	7	Motor house, motor shed, motor car house, motor garage
1910-1919	30	Motor house, motor garage, garage, motor shed
1920-1929	129	Garage, motor garage, motor house, motor shed
1930-1939	225	Garage
Source: Index of City of Lincoln building plans.		

Fig.11
Total number of building applications involving motor car accommodation.

Amongst the first proposed motor-shed applications to be considered was that of the city's mayor, Councillor C. Pennell of Eastcliff Road in 1900. The city's doctors were well represented amongst the early applications for motor garages, with Dr Burgess of Canwick Road amongst the first in 1912; and the Dean and Chapter requested the construction of a motor shed in Pottergate in 1920.[61]

Some alterations to houses were requested in order to house the new motor car. Whilst today garages are regularly being converted into additional living space and bedrooms, in the early 1930s there were requests from uphill Lincoln, where space at the front of houses was at a premium for sitting rooms and dining rooms to be converted into garages.[62] Indeed, space for accommodating cars was so scarce that in 1939 a building plan application was received to convert several cottages on South Bar Square, near the High Street into a garage. Rather more common, however, was the request to convert stables into garage space. (Fig. 5) Such transformations continued to be taking place in domestic residences in the city as late as 1939.

Despite the significant increase in the number of garages within the city by the end of the 1930s, surprisingly few applications for new-build residences made reference to the construction of garages alongside the new homes. The first building control plan referring to the construction of a house and garage appeared in 1920, on Curle Avenue.[63] Only thirty-six such applications were submitted between 1920 and 1939. Many advertisements for new-build properties from the mid-1920s onwards made reference to house plots having space for garages. Few builders, however, provided new buyers with accommodation for family cars, perhaps, as Kathryn Morrison and John Minnis have suggested, because on a number of residential estates, houses with garages sold more slowly than those without.[64] Indeed, during the development of the Hunt Lea estate, just off Boultham Park Road, W. H. Hunt, the builders, described these new houses and bungalows as being 'near the Works and yet close to the Town', thereby suggesting that a car was not needed. The properties were advertised from 1s. 6d. per day and potential home owners were told 'Let your bus fare buy your home.'[65]

Where space was available, those who could afford cars purchased garages. The pages of the local press seem to suggest that if more expensive brick garages could not be bought, cheaper sectional or wooden garages were erected. Certainly, in the 1920s and 1930s, car owners valued garages in order to protect their rust-prone vehicles from the elements, and to provide

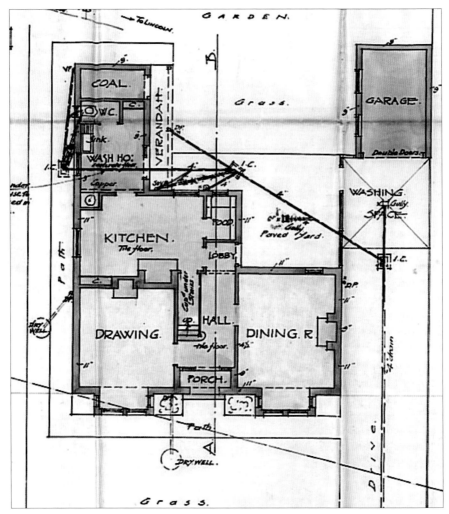

Fig.12 Plans for a new-build property on Newark Road, Lincoln, with detached garage, approved on 15 March 1926. (LAO MISC DON 1628. Ledger entry 6233. Reproduced with permission of Lincolnshire Archives, Lincolnshire County Council)

them with a reasonable chance of starting the frequently temperamental car engines on wet and cold days. As car ownership percolated down the social hierarchy, especially from the 1930s, the need for garages to protect cars prompted many who could now afford a car but lived in properties – such as terraced houses – which could not accommodate vehicles to rent nearby lock-up garages. Blocks of such structures began to appear in Lincoln from the mid-1920s near to streets such as St Catherine's Grove, the lower High Street, Dixon Street and Newport. The commercial possibilities of such developments were evidently seen by the prominent Lincoln High Street butcher, J. R. Smith, who between 1926 and 1933 submitted five separate plans for blocks of lock-up garages comprising over forty in total in the High Street and Dixon Street area.[66]

CONCLUSION

Through consideration of the surviving building plans and their invaluable index, this article has sought to demonstrate some of the ways in which this database can be interrogated to help explore the nineteenth- and early-twentieth-century development of the city of Lincoln. Through the production of similar databases using comparable information from building plans of other times, it is possible that much useful and informative comparative analysis could take place relating to a variety of aspects including an examination of the degree to which building plans were adhered to and monitored, and a comparative analysis of the extent and diversity of architects' portfolios within and between urban centres. As has been shown here, the plans and the associated database can also be employed

Fig.13
An early lean-to garage on detached property, Boultham Park Road, Lincoln, in 2023. (Photo: Andrew Walker)

to plot the pace and nature of urban development, changing residential tastes, including the increasing prevalence of particular building types, such as the bungalow, developing social trends, including increasing female autonomy with regard to property matters, and the impact of technological developments, considered here with regard to the rise of the motor car.

Dennis Mills actively encouraged myself and others to interrogate these building plans and the associated database, a primary source that he sought to ensure remained readily accessible through his skilful management of this particular project, conducted under the auspices of The Survey of Lincoln, an organisation to which he contributed so much during its first quarter of a century.

NOTES

1. My thanks are due to John Herridge and Arthur Ward for their comments on an earlier draft of this article, and to delegates at the conference held in honour of Dennis Mills in December 2021 where a version of this article was presented.

2. See the bibliography of Dennis Mills's published work later in this volume.

3. The building plans database can be accessed from The Survey of Lincoln's website: www. thesurveyoflincoln.co.uk

4. MISC DON 1268 – Plans and building plans: Lincoln nineteenth and twentieth centuries. (Lincolnshire Archives Office).

5. See also Victoria Thorpe's article in this volume.

6. Aspinall, P. J., and Whitehand, J. W. R., 1980, 'Building plans: a major source for urban studies', *Area*, 12. pp. 199-203. See also Gaskell, S. M., 1983, *Building Control: National Legislation and the Introduction of Local By-Laws in Victorian England*, British Association for Local History. For historical local case studies using building plans, see for instance: Chinnery, G. A., 1975 (for 1973), 'Nineteenth-century building plans in Leicester', *Transactions of the Leicestershire Archaeological and Historical Society*, 49. pp. 33-42; and Dunleavey, Janet, 2004, 'Suburban

residential development in Worcester during the bye law period, 1866-1969', *Transactions of the Worcestershire Archaeological Society*, 3rd series, 19, pp. 175-99.

7.   For details of the development of building regulation nationally, see Ley, A. J., 2000, *A History of Building Control in England and Wales, 1840-1990*.

8.   Residential social segregation and the geography of housing in nineteenth-century urban Britain is examined in Dennis, Richard, 1984, *English Industrial Cities of the Nineteenth Century*, especially pp. 141-85.

9.   Back-to-back and court housing are examined in Muthesius, Stefan, 1982, *The English Terraced House*, (see especially pp. 101-42); for recent case studies of specific back-to-back housing, see Timmins, Geoffrey, 2013, 'Housing industrial workers during the nineteenth century: back-to-back housing in textile Lancashire', *Industrial Archaeology Review*, 35, 2. pp. 111-27; and Wooler, Fiona, 2015, 'The excavation of nineteenth-century back-to-back housing and courts and the Kenyon Cutlery Works … Sheffield', *Post-Medieval Archaeology*, 49, 2. pp. 321-42.

10.   An examination of Lincoln's courts and yards, and especially their poor levels of sanitation, can be found in Mills, Dennis, 2015, *Effluence and Influence: Public Health, Sewers and Politics in Lincoln, 1848-50*, especially in chapter 3. pp. 29-47.

11.   Muthesius, *The English Terraced House*, p. 35.

12.   Daunton, Martin J., 1983, *House and Home in the Victorian City: Working-Class Housing, 1850-1914*. pp. 193-94.

13.   I*bid.*, p. 32.

14.   I*bid.*, pp. 266-67.

15.   Newspapers reported on the adoption of the legislation as follows: Boston (*Stamford Mercury* 13 May 1859); Sutton Bridge (*Lincolnshire Chronicle* 8 July 1859); Barton Upon Humber (*Lincolnshire Chronicle* 7 November 1862); and Grantham (*Stamford Mercury* 5 November 1864).

16.   *Lincolnshire Chronicle*, (hereafter *LC*) 2 February 1866.

17.   *Ibid.*

18.   *Ibid.*

19.   George Giles's report is reproduced in Mills, *Effluence and Influence*. pp. 48-82.

20.   *LC* 2 February 1866.

21.   *LC* 8 September 1882.

22.   *LC* 24 July 1894.

23.   Mills, Dennis and George, Beryl, 'Population', Table 1, The Survey of Lincoln website, www.thesurveyoflincoln.co.uk

24.   See, though, Whitehand, Jeremy, 1992 'The makers of British towns: architects, builders and property owners, c.1850-1939', *Journal of Historical Geography*, 18, 4, pp. 417-38; Chinnery, 'Nineteenth-century building plans in Leicester', pp. 33-42; and Dunleavey, Janet, 'Suburban residential development in Worcester', pp. 175-99.

25.   Powell, C. G., 1980, *An Economic History of the British Building Industry, 1815-1979*, p. 28.

26.   For a brief biography of Nicholson, see Van Papworth, W. A., revised by Pimlott Baker, Ann, 2004, 'William Adam Nicholson (1803-53)', *Oxford Dictionary of National Biography* (online).

27.   For more information on William Mortimer, see Tann, Geoff, 2011, 'Fresh light on William Mortimer and William M. Mortimer, Lincoln architects', *The Lincoln Enquirer*, 21, p. 7. See also Tann, Geoff 'William Mortimer and Son architects – projects database, 1879-1935' at www.thesurveyoflincoln.co.uk/Projects/mortimer; This section of the article focuses particularly on the work of these Lincoln-based architects in the city itself. For more details of some of their

work elsewhere in the county, see Pevsner Nikolaus and Harris, John, 1989, *The Buildings of Lincolnshire. Second edition.*

28. See for instance building plans, at properties at Richmond Road (ledger entry 2480, approved 13 December 1894); and Sibthorpe Street (ledger entry 2840, approved 10 June 1897).

29. For Drury and Mortimer's work at Beaumont Fee, see for instance ledger entry 649, approved 1 July 1875; and for South Park, ledger entry 349, approved 2 April 1872.

30. Pevsner, *Buildings of Lincolnshire*, pp. 521 and 509.

31. Pevsner, *Buildings of Lincolnshire*, p. 502.

32. For Michael Drury's work on Charlesworth Street and Foss Bank, see ledger entry 1314, approved 17 May 1882.

33. William Watkins's residential work included six houses on West Parade (numbers 15-25) ledger entry 1666, approved 4 February 1885. His more substantial work included the Grammar School, Upper Lindum Road, ledger entry 1558, approved 16 April 1884; isolation wards at the Lincoln County Hospital, ledger entry 1611, approved 21 August 1884; and the Constitutional Club, Silver Street, ledger entry 2509, approved 11 April 1895.

34. Henry Goddard undertook work on the precentory in 1870 and 1879 (ledger entry 183, approved 5 April 1870; and ledger entry 1052, approved 18 June 1879). Goddard's houses for clergy included St Swithin's vicarage, Lindum Terrace (ledger entry 283, approved 14 June 1871); a parsonage for Revd John Foy, vicar of St Martin's on Beaumont Street (ledger entry 414, approved 4 March 1873); St Michael's vicarage, Gibraltar Hill (ledger entry 1313, approved 7 June 1882); St Paul's vicarage, Westgate (ledger entry 1813, approved 29 August 1887); and St Peter at Gowts vicarage, Sibthorpe Street (ledger entry 2775, approved 11 February 1897).

35. See building plans for Ruston, Proctor and Co. (ledger entry 127, approved 4 May 1869); Clayton and Shuttleworth (ledger entry 925, approved 13 February 1878); and William Foster and Co. (ledger entry 1603, approved 29 July 1884).

36. Amongst other commissions for members of Lincoln's social elite, Goddard designed a picture gallery for Joseph Ruston's home at Monks Manor (ledger entry 1448, approved 6 June 1883), and a billiard room for Leslie Melville's home on Eastgate (ledger entry 1812, approved 29 August 1887).

37. Goddard was involved with a number of developments on Dixon Street (ledger entry 2280, approved 13 April 1893), and, for F. J. Clarke, work on Vine Street and Cheviot Street (ledger entry 949, approved 10 April 1878). Clarke stated that he had 'no confidence' in Lincoln's architects in a council meeting which was considering the construction of St Hugh's church and reported in the *Lincolnshire Chronicle* on 8 October 1886. This prompted defensive letters in the paper from Lincoln architects including Michael Drury on 15 October 1886, and, on 19 October 1886, from William Watkins, who described Clarke's criticism as a 'childish attack'.

38. Bellamy and Hardy's work in Lincoln included residential projects on Newland (ledger entry 332, approved 2 February 1872), Portland Street (ledger entry 926, approved 13 February 1878) and South Park (ledger entry 393, approved 5 November 1872). Work for the Lincoln Gas Company included a purifying house (ledger entry 1293, approved 22 March 1892). The Wesleyan Chapel Bailgate of 1879 and the new Corn Exchange, also of 1879 are described in Pevsner, *Buildings of Lincolnshire* on respectively pp. 516 and 523. Bellamy and Hardy's work in Horncastle has been considered by Moore, Nicholas, 2021-22, 'More buildings in Horncastle by Lincoln architects Bellamy and Hardy', *Lincolnshire Past & Present*, 126, pp 20-22.

39. John T. Drury's commissions included six cottages on Burton Road (ledger entry 1894, approved 20 March 1889), cow stables on Saville Street (ledger entry 1622, approved 10 September 1884) and a bake house on the High Street (ledger entry 1668, approved 4 February 1885).

40.   James Whitton's projects included eight houses on Sincil Bank (ledger entry 873, approved 29 August 1877) and two houses on Monks Road (ledger entry 1137, approved 7 April 1880). From 1882, James Whitton tended to be listed as the property owner, commissioning others to design and build properties – such as six houses on Turner Street, on which Whitton employed John T. Drury (ledger entry 1411, approved 21 March 1883).

41.   Abraham Kelham's projects included a house and shop at Stamp End (ledger entry 174, approved 10 January 1870) and a house and stable on Croft Street (ledger entry 269, approved 28 April 1871). He was commissioned by Robert Dawber on several occasions, including with regard to the construction of a house on Newland (ledger entry 303, approved 6 November 1871).

42.   Whitehand, 'The makers of British towns', pp. 417-38.

43.   A recent chapter by Beryl George, for instance, undertakes a close examination of building patterns in the West End of Lincoln, where small builders prevailed in the late nineteenth and early twentieth centuries: George, Beryl, 2022, 'Using the building plans database to chart the development of the West End, 1866-1914', in Walker, A., (ed.) *Lincoln's West End Revisited*, The Survey of Lincoln. pp.42-7.

44.   Building plans ledger entry 1333, approved 2 August 1882.

45.   For instance, wash houses were added, according to building plans, at properties at Winnowsty Terrace (ledger entry 1767, approved 20 October 1886); Arboretum Avenue (ledger entry 1647, approved 19 November 1884); and Yarborough Road (ledger entry 2319, approved 14 September 1893).

46.   According to building plans, WCs were added to houses in Newland Street West (ledger entry 3572, approved 13 February 1902), Waterside North (ledger entry 4059, approved 15 February 1905) and Sincil Bank (ledger entry 4071, approved 15 March 1905).

47.   Building plans ledger entry 6904, approved 21 April 1931.

48.   *Lincolnshire Echo* (hereafter *LE*) 27 May 1931.

49.   *LE* 1 December 1933.

50.   According to the building plans, James Weighell's developments included thirteen tenements in Little Bargate St (ledger entries 783 and 874, approved 27 December 1876 and 12 September 1877).

51.   Samuel Horton's building plans included one for thirteen houses on Gibbeson Street (ledger entry 903, approved 12 December 1877).

52.   See building plan, ledger entry 815, approved 28 March 1877.

53.   According to Janet Dunleavey, in contrast to Worcester's even balance between polite (i.e. architect-designed) and vernacular residential development, nearby Gloucester adopted a more vernacular approach whilst development in the middle-class suburb of Headingley in Leeds was substantially 'polite'. See Dunleavey, Janet, 2002, 'Suburban residential development, 1880-1989: polite or vernacular architecture?' *The Local Historian*, 32, 3, August. pp. 178-95. See especially p. 194. This distinction between 'polite' and 'vernacular' architecture uses R. W. Brunskill's definition, whereby developments by trained architects are deemed as 'polite architecture' and those undertaken by local craftspeople or tradespeople are identified as 'vernacular architecture'. Brunskill, R. W., 1971, *An illustrated handbook of vernacular architecture*. p. 25.

54.   The Co-operative Society's involvement in house building in Lincoln has been mentioned in Hodson, Maurice, 2006, 'The origins of street names', in Walker, A., (ed.) *Monks Road: Lincoln's East End Through Time*, The Survey of Lincoln. p. 53.

55.   Building plan ledger entry 5539, approved 12 January 1920.

56.   See Lincoln index of building plans register, 1920-1939.

57.   Brown, Andy, 2017, 'The first British bungalow', Historic England blog, www.heritagecalling.com/2017/02/24/the-first-british-bungalow/

58.   King, Anthony D., 1997, 'Excavating the multicultural suburb: Hidden histories of the bungalow', in Roger Silverstone, (ed.) *Visions of Suburbia,* Routledge, London. pp. 60 and 61. King makes reference to a farce of 1892, 'The Bungalow' by Fred Horner, which explores the ambiguities of this building type's social space (pp. 60-64).

59.   See Wall, Rosemary, 2007, 'Surplus women: a legacy of World War One?' at ww1centenary.oucs.ox.ac.uk/unconventionalsoldiers/'surplus-women'-a-legacy-of-world-war-one/; and Virginia Nicholson, *Singled Out: how two million women survived without men after the First World War.* According to Wall of the 700,000 deaths of UK combatants, a higher proportion of officers were killed than those in the lower ranks. As Rosemary Wall notes, in the UK census of 1921, there was a large gap between male and female populations, aged between 25 and 34 years, with 1,158,000 single women and 919,000 single men. Thanks to Paul Dryburgh for raising this point at the conference in honour of Dennis Mills in December 2021.

60.   Between 1900 and 1910, building plans were received in Lincoln relating to one 'motor car house', one 'motor garage', two 'motor sheds' and three 'motor houses'. In the following decade, there were applications relating to one 'motor shed', eight 'garages', ten 'motor garages' and eleven 'motor houses'. The term 'motor shed' was used for the last time in 1920, 'motor house' in 1925, and 'motor garage' in 1926.

61.   See respectively the following building plans ledger entries 3344 (12 October 1900), 5743 (11 December 1912) and 5581 (10 May 1920).

62.   See building plans for 3 James St, (ledger entry 6790, 16 February 1930) and 12 Drury Lane, (ledger entry 7114, 23 May 1933).

63.   Building plan, ledger entry 5566, 15 March 1920.

64.   Morrison, Kathryn and Minnis, John, 2012, *Carscapes: The Motor Car, Architecture and Landscape in England,* English Heritage, p. 87.

65.   *LE,* 30 April 1938.

66.   See for instance J. R. Smith's building plan for 25 lock-up garages at the rear of 69 High Street, ledger entry 6221, 15 March 1926.

'INVITING INSPECTION IN ORDER, BY FORCE OF EXAMPLE, TO GIVE AN IMPULSE TO IMPROVED CULTIVATION': J. J. MECHI'S EXPERIMENTAL FARM AT TIPTREE IN ESSEX AND NETWORKS OF IMPROVERS IN NINETEENTH-CENTURY LINCOLNSHIRE

Shirley Brook

The high quality of farming for which Lincolnshire was noted in the nineteenth century was underpinned by a culture of improvement promoted through the information environment and social networks of Lincolnshire farmers and landowners. The principal documentary source for this study is the visitors' book for J. J. Mechi's experimental farm at Tiptree in Essex, which is deposited in the British Library. Examination of the social connections of Lincolnshire visitors to Tiptree and the agricultural improvement activities in which they engaged, reveals complex inter-relationships. The suggestion is made that nominative lists, such as Mechi's visitors' book, could be considered in conjunction with other similar types of evidence to further our understanding of the social networks which promoted and sustained the improved agriculture for which the county was famous in the mid-nineteenth century. Reference is made to a study, already undertaken, in which this has been done.

At the outset of his academic career, in 1959, Dennis Mills published an article, based on his recent MA thesis, in *The East Midland Geographer*. The article was entitled 'The development of rural settlement around Lincoln with special reference to the eighteenth and nineteenth centuries'. [1] In it, Mills identified a range of factors which resulted in the dispersal of settlement on the spring-line of the limestone uplands and the clay vales north and south of the city. In his opinion, what drove this dispersal was not only enclosure but also a number of other elements within the agricultural improvements being introduced in Lincolnshire between the last quarter of the eighteenth century until the so-called 'Great Depression' in the latter part of the nineteenth century.

The festschrift, published in 2010 to mark Mills's eightieth birthday, included a chapter by the author of the present study which revisited Mills's findings in the light of new sources which were either unavailable or unknown to him at the time of his writing. These related to the availability of capital for agricultural improvements which Mills had identified as being one of the factors underlying the dispersal of settlement. [2] The current study considers another element of agricultural improvement. It takes as its focus a hitherto unexploited source, the Visitors' Book for J. J. Mechi's experimental farm at Tiptree in Essex, in order to examine the information environment and social networks within which knowledge and ideas were disseminated among the agents for change in agricultural circles.

In 1843, Philip Pusey writing 'On the Agricultural Improvements of Lincolnshire', enthused that 'Lincolnshire affords a very high example of farming'. Travelling along Ermine Street over the heath north of Lincoln in 1842 he observed 'neat enclosures, heavy turnip-crops,

Fig.1 Tiptree Hall and Farm Essex (1850–60) by William Brown of Louth. (Yale Center for British Art B1994.18.1. Public Domain Dedication CC0 1.0)

numerous flocks, spacious farm-buildings, surrounded by...lofty and crowded corn-ricks'.[3] Pusey was the first editor of the *Journal of the Royal Agricultural Society of England* (*JRASE*). The Society, its shows and its journal, played a major part in the tremendous drive for improvement which characterised mid-nineteenth century agriculture. Its membership included many members of the aristocracy and their important tenant farmers. Articles in the *JRASE* constituted the top of an information cascade about the practice and science of agriculture. Information and opinion published in the journal filtered downwards to a wider readership through reports in more popular weekly and monthly publications such as the *Agricultural Gazette, Farmers Journal, Farmers Magazine* and *Mark Lane Express*. These provided abstracts of the contents of the *JRASE* for their readers and were frequently the focus for formal or informal gatherings of farmers at which articles would be read and discussed. By this means information and ideas originating in the pages of the *JRASE* would reach all levels of the farming community. Therefore, a much larger group of people was influenced by the Society than might be assumed from the membership figures.[4]

Although the *JRASE* was extremely important in the information cascade and social interaction of nineteenth-century improvers, the example of John Joseph Mechi serves as a reminder that not all those who promoted the spread of information in nineteenth-century agricultural circles were owners of large estates or those who moved in recognised agricultural circles such as the Royal Society. Mechi was a great self-publicist but his background in trade and the perception in some quarters that he was a *dilettante* farmer meant that, although he excited much comment in agricultural circles, he was not universally accepted. He was a second-generation Italian immigrant who made his money in the cutlery trade, supplying scientific instruments, quill pen-cutting devices and razors. He made a name for himself, and his fortune, selling 'Mechi's magic razor strop'. He also patented two lighting improvements; one to illuminate shop windows and the other to reduce the effects of heat and vapours from gas and oil lamps on the atmosphere in a room.[5]

In 1841 Mechi purchased Tiptree Hall Farm in Essex. He constructed a model farmstead (Fig. 1) to serve an enterprise which directed all the latest scientific and technical innovations towards the task of bringing the poor clay soils into profitable cultivation. He invested heavily in improving his lands by paring, burning and underdraining, before deep ploughing for which steam power was used. In an article in *The Agricultural History Review*, Lesley Kinsley notes that Mechi was one of the novice high farmers who were carried away by 'guano mania'. Initially Mechi considered guano to be of prime importance in bringing his marginal heathland and poor clay soils into cultivation. He subsequently discovered, through experience, that guano was not the magic solution he initially thought it to be because it was very expensive and its long-term use compromised soil health and produced weakened and damaged crops. While continuing to use guano to begin the reclamation of his unproductive lands and as a supplementary fertilizer, Mechi turned his attention to promoting the intensive cultivation of green crops by the calculated application of both human and animal effluent.[6]

Given his farming background, the application of waste matter to the soil was a subject with which Mills was happy to engage. His chapter in *Aspects of Lincoln*, describes the establishment of a sewage farm beside Washingborough Road in the late nineteenth century.[7] At Tiptree, a system was developed whereby animal urine and solid waste were adopted as the primary substance for fertilising the land. Cattle, which were intensively fed on bought concentrates and home-grown green crops, were kept in covered sheds with slatted floors through which the manure fell to giant reservoirs beneath. Here it was diluted with water, stirred, piped to stop-taps in each field and sprayed onto the land from gutta percha hoses. Steam power was used to stir it and pump it through the pipes to the fields to maximise the harvest of green crops. These were returned to the farm to feed the cattle in the covered sheds thus beginning the cycle again.[8]

Mechi's improvements were along the lines of those put forward by the eminent agricultural writer and campaigner James Caird in High *Farming under Liberal Covenants, the Best Substitute for Protection*. This was a pamphlet 'seeking to direct attention to the prosecution of a high system of farming'. From Caird's own experience as a tenant farmer in lowland Scotland he recommended the increased cultivation of green crops in addition to corn, the heavy application of fertilisers to increase yields, and capital investment in buildings and underdraining. The influence of this publication may be gauged by the fact that it ran to eight editions. [9]

Mechi was also a great ambassador for improved farming techniques. He addressed farmers' gatherings in all parts of the country, in places as far removed as Aberdeen and Manchester, Carlisle and London. He then published the papers he delivered and a steady stream of letters, in the farming press.[10] Over a period of more than thirty-five years, there was scarcely one issue of the *Agricultural Gazette* which did not contain some correspondence from him.[11] Mechi's addresses to farmers' clubs and improvement societies were also published by him in a series of publications with variations on the title *How to Farm Profitably or the Sayings and Doings of Mr Alderman Mechi*, which appeared in a variety of editions spanning a period of nearly twenty years. In these his farm balance sheets for Tiptree Hall and a list of his 'Agricultural Library' were also included.[12]

Not content with travelling the country spreading the gospel of improvement, Mechi invited people to visit him for guided tours of Tiptree. He held an annual gathering each July to which special trains conveyed hundreds of visitors: 'peers and members of the House of Commons, civic dignitaries, men of science, heads of Government departments, engineers, writers on the science and practice of agriculture, a fair sprinkling of clergy, implement-makers, commissioners from foreign States, and a large number of farmers'.[13] They were conducted on a walk around the farm with demonstrations of the liquid manure irrigation system, views of the luxuriant crops, exhibitions of machinery, explanations of Mechi's latest innovations in cultivation and animal husbandry, and a tour of the buildings, all of which is reminiscent of Thomas Coke's sheep shearings at Holkham.[14] In addition to his open days, Mechi welcomed individuals and groups of visitors throughout the year. In doing all this he was regarded as 'inviting inspection in order by the force of example to give an impulse to improved cultivation'.[15]

The case of William Lawson, son of Sir Wilfrid Lawson Bart., of Brayton Park near Aspatria, Cumbria, who visited Tiptree in June 1861 and again in June 1864, demonstrates how influential Mechi's activities were.[16] The twenty-five-year-old Lawson returned to Cumbria full of enthusiasm for Mechi's innovative farming regimes. In response to his requests for such systems to be adopted on his father's estates he was given a farm on which to try out Mechi's ideas for himself. The farm was situated in the village of Blennerhasset, which neighboured Brayton Park and Lawson named it 'Mechi Farm' (Fig. 2a). Here he proceeded to put into practice many of Mechi's ideas for scientific and mechanised farming and also imitated him by writing a book publicising his experiences.[17] This began with a description of his travels in England, Scotland and Wales looking at model farms. He says he was especially interested in farm buildings because he planned to build for himself. He also noted the good advice given in Henry Stephens' *Book of the Farm*.[18]

Lawson commenced operations at Blennerhasset in 1862, the year after his first visit to Tiptree. He immediately embarked on a major campaign of improvement. In the first five

Fig.2 Mechi Farm, Blennerhasset, Cumbria (a) farm name; (b) original buildings including the clock tower. (Shirley Brook October 2022)

PLOUGHING BY STEAM.—TRIAL AT GRIMSTHORPE, BY LORD WILLOUGHBY D'ERESBY.—(SEE NEXT PAGE.)

Fig.3 Steam ploughing trial at Grimsthorpe. Illustrated London News, 1850. (Mary Evans Picture Library 10099560, © Illustrated London News Ltd/Mary Evans)

months three and a half miles of hedges were levelled, then upwards of thirty miles of drains were laid and stones fetched off the fields and broken for new roads and buildings. He proceeded to erect model farm buildings and install an irrigation system, a water wheel and gas manufactory. The farm buildings (Fig. 2b) had a clock tower and a laboratory with a library of 300 volumes to be lent out free of charge. The premises included a flax mill and starch mill, which aimed to exploit the good parts of diseased potatoes. There were experiments in producing gas from flax and, by 1865, gas lighting was working in the buildings.[19] This realised Mechi's vision of 'our Homesteads or Farmeries … like factories or railway stations: warmed in cold weather, lighted with gas'.[20] However, such advances were not without their problems and in August 1871 Lawson's gas manager, looking for a gas escape with a lighted candle, caused an explosion and started a serious fire.[21]

Mechi's practice of keeping cattle on boards was adopted by Lawson, with manure being collected in reservoirs and distributed in liquid form through an irrigation system. The results of his experiments with manures and cropping were set out in his book with tables of inputs and outputs.[22] The farm utilised all the latest advances in technology and steam power was used for threshing and ploughing. He began steam cultivation in 1862 with a Fowler's single engine and anchor system which he claimed to be the first in Cumbria.[23] If this claim is true it emphasises the prominent position of Lincolnshire in the hierarchy of improving counties. The evidence for this is that twelve years earlier, in 1850, a picture of a steam ploughing demonstration organised by Lord Peter Robert, Baron Willoughby de Eresby, on his Ancaster estate at Grimsthorpe, appeared in the *Illustrated London News* (Fig. 3). In 1866 Lawson exchanged his single engine and anchor system for a Fowler's double engine system whose machines he christened Cain and Abel.[24]

If anything, Lawson's enthusiasm for promoting the cause of improvement outstripped even Mechi's and his book included a chapter, written by a neighbour, entitled 'The French

Excursion'. In this, Lawson's trip to the Paris Exhibition in October 1867 is described. Blennerhasset folk were offered expenses-paid visits to the exhibition. There followed plans to construct a model farm in France using Mechi's irrigation method of farming and run on co-operative principles. The farm was to be managed by two Frenchmen with Lawson putting up the capital and Cain and Abel, his two steam engines, being exported to serve the new enterprise. However, the scheme was abandoned when Lawson saw the proposed site for the farm.[25]

Mechi also sought to promote his ideas on improved agriculture beyond the shores of Britain but, unlike Lawson who was planning a 'farm plant', Mechi invited people to come to him. He kept a visitors' book as a record of all those who came to look at Tiptree, which is now deposited in the British Library. It began with the note 'This book was kept in the Bailiff's House where visitors to the farm recorded their names after inspecting it'. [26] Its two hundred and sixty-four folios chronicle over 8000 visits to Tiptree Hall between 22 January 1846, and 22 March 22 1878. Mechi's visitors' book is a rich source of evidence and an analysis of its contents contributes to an understanding of the culture of high farming which influenced mid-nineteenth century farmers and landowners. It can also be used to identify those people from Lincolnshire who visited the experimental farm at Tiptree.

The visitors' book provides a record of the sort of people who were interested in improved farming and the periods at which their interest was greatest. It allows examination of the balance between home and foreign exposure to Mechi's 'scientific farming' ideas and enables identification of the countries of the world to which these ideas were conveyed. Its content also contributes to the development of an understanding of the interests and preoccupations of Victorian agricultural society. Some of the evidence, such as the number of visits and the country of origin of Mechi's visitors, is quantifiable, whilst other aspects, such as the insights it affords into the mid-nineteenth century world of ideas, are not quantifiable but contribute to a deeper understanding of the influences upon farmers and landowners in the mid-nineteenth century.

The entries are arranged in columns recording the date of the visit and the name and address of the visitor(s). There is also a column for remarks. Some visitors, like William Lawson, visited more than once and this is particularly true of Mechi's neighbours, many of whom came every year to his open day. Because of this it was not possible, when analysing the contents of the visitors' book, to state the exact number of people who visited the farm but rather the number of visits. A few entries recorded visits such as 'x and his farm manager (or bailiff)', 'x and sons' or 'x and friend'. These were difficult to quantify and were counted as two in each instance. There is also the possibility that some visitors did not sign the visitors' book. Such imponderables mean that the total of 8347 visits presented in Figure 4 is almost certainly an under-representation.

Figure 4 shows the temporal distribution of visits to Tiptree, providing evidence of the periodicity of interest in Mechi's experimental farm. The number of entries was greatest in 1846, the year in which Mechi began his visitors' book, when 594 visits were recorded. From 1846 to 1856 the number did not fall below 300 but in 1857 it dropped to 255 and thereafter there were generally between one and two hundred visits per year. The exceptions to this were 1862, the year of the Great International Exhibition in London, when numbers soared again to 517, and the difficult years of 1865 and 1866 when Cattle Plague restrictions

YEAR	Great Britain	Overseas	Not Categorised	All Visits
1846	576	9	9	594
1847	343	10	9	362
1848	357	1	2	360
1849	317	5	3	325
1850	475	13	7	495
1851	511	175	18	704
1852	309	21	8	338
1853	336	62	17	415
1854	353	55	10	418
1855	265	107	8	380
1856	385	80	11	476
1857	168	74	13	255
1858	139	43	9	191
1859	97	53	2	152
1860	197	83	15	295
1861	133	49	8	190
1862	186	312	19	517
1863	100	31	4	135
1864	118	36	1	155
1865	51	24	2	77
1866	46	22	1	69
1867	108	41	1	150
1868	116	36	1	153
1869	160	15	5	180
1870	85	16	0	101
1871	158	25	3	186
1872	89	20	0	109
1873	112	21	1	134
1874	136	25	7	168
1875	73	24	0	97
1876	72	20	1	93
1877	47	21	4	72
1878	0	1	0	1
TOTAL	6618	1530	199	8347

Fig.4 Annual number of visits to Tiptree Hall 1846–1878. (BL ADD 30015 'List of Visitors to Tiptree Hall')

reduced visits to 77 and 69 respectively. In 1875 the number of visits was again fewer than 100, with 97 recorded in that year, 93 the following year and 72 in 1877, which was the final full year of record.

It is unclear whether this fall in the number of visits was actual, perhaps resulting from diminishing interest in Mechi's innovative approach or from his failing health and financial difficulties, or whether it was a result of the book being relocated. A note at the beginning of the entries records that it was 'Presented (on Public Grounds) to the British Museum by J. J. Mechi May 12 1876'.[27] This conflicts with a statement on the fly leaf which says that the book was presented on 27 May of that year. It seems that Mechi, an ardent self-publicist to the last, presented his visitors' book to the museum thus ensuring a place in history for his experimental farm. What is less certain is precisely when it was presented and how further visits to the farm came to be recorded when the book was apparently lodged at the museum. As a result of these uncertainties the fall in visitor numbers in the final years should not be accorded too much significance. However, what is much more certain is the significant level of interest in Mechi's high farming systems between 1846 and 1856, the period in which Caird's *High farming under Liberal Covenants* and his survey of English agriculture were published.[28]

As the visitors' book recorded addresses it is possible to consider the distribution of home and foreign interest in high farming by categorising visits under three headings: 'Great Britain', 'Overseas' and 'Not Categorised' (Fig. 4). In addition to those giving a British address, newspaper men from British papers were assumed to be home visitors and entered in the 'Great Britain' column whilst those recording their comments in a foreign language were categorised as 'Overseas' even if they gave no address. Civil servants serving abroad were also categorised as overseas because it was assumed that they took Mechi's ideas with them to the countries in which they served, as did those who emigrated. 'Going to settle as a farmer on The prairies and shall have to thank Mr Mechi's farm for some valuable hints', wrote one visitor.[29] If there was no address, or the address was illegible, then the visit was counted in the 'Not Categorised' column. Assumptions based on the name were avoided; as has already been noted, some British people served abroad and would, therefore, be recorded in the overseas column whilst others with an overseas name, such as Mechi himself, might be naturalised and involved in British agriculture.

Home visits always exceeded overseas ones except in 1862 when there were 186 home visits and 312 from abroad, the highest number in any year. This coincided with the Great International Exhibition held in London. Numbers of both home and overseas visits were high in 1851, the year of the Great Exhibition at Crystal Palace, with 511 home visits and 175 from abroad. There was also a high number of foreign visits (107) in 1855. Other than this, visits from abroad did not exceed 100 and in many years there were fewer than fifty. However, they became proportionately more significant as time went on. Whilst the proportion of visits from home visitors diminished in the 1860s and 1870s, the proportion which were categorised as overseas visits increased. Of the total of 8347 visits to Tiptree Farm between January 1846 and March 1878, 6618 were home visits, 1530 overseas visits and 199 could not be categorised (Fig. 4).

The range of the countries from which Mechi's visitors came allows insight into the geographical extent of his influence (Fig. 5). Visitors to Tiptree came, not only from Europe, but from India, Africa, the Americas and the Antipodes and may have returned

America	Finland	Philippine Islands
Australia	France	Poland
Austria	Germany	Pomerania
Barbados	Greece	Russia
Belgium	Hungary	Sardinia
Bermuda	India	Saxony
Bohemia	Ireland	Scotland
Brazil	Italy	Silesia
Canada	Luxembourg	Spain
Cape of Good Hope	Mauritius	Sweden
Chile	Mexico	Switzerland
Croatia	Netherlands	Tasmania
Cuba	New Zealand	Venezuela
East Indies	Norway	Wales
England	Peru	

Fig.5 Countries and regions from which Mechi's visitors came. (BL ADD 30015 'List of Visitors to Tiptree Hall').

home as converts to Mechi's revolutionary farming practices. Such global dissemination of the principles and techniques of improved farming was to have a profound effect on the farmers and landowners of Lincolnshire in the final quarter of the nineteenth century when British agriculture was exposed to crippling foreign competition. Mechi, and others who so enthusiastically encouraged the exportation of British high farming across the globe, failed to realise that with their success they were sowing the seeds of misfortune and that many who 'farmed high' would soon be facing adversity in the form of competition from the very countries whose agriculture Britain had fostered.

The column in the visitors' book which recorded visitors' comments provides insights into how Mechi's innovations were regarded by this heterogeneous body of visitors and how they received his exhortation to 'improve'. It was not possible to analyse the subject categories into which their comments fell in order to identify a periodicity of interest in different aspects of agricultural improvement because there were too many diverse factors bearing upon the subjects of the comments recorded in the visitors' book. The most significant of these was the influence of each latest innovation at Tiptree: if Mechi had added a new building or purchased a new item of machinery then its novelty would incite comment. A second problem was that visitors often came in groups and influenced one another's views. By the time they had circumambulated the farm and discussed among themselves what they had seen, they had usually arrived at a shared view. Furthermore, the habit of looking at the comment of the person who headed the page and echoing it meant that the subject matter of the comment was reflecting something other than the wider preoccupations of the agricultural community.

Notwithstanding the unsuitability of the record for systematic analysis of the subject matter of the comments, individual responses can be examined in pursuit of an insight into the world of ideas inhabited by those with an interest in agriculture in the mid-nineteenth century. It is immediately apparent that many of Mechi's visitors came to learn from his example. Cornelius Maw from Crowle in the Isle of Axholme, an early visitor to Tiptree, commented that he hoped 'to benefit by the example set by Mr Mechi'. Another Lincolnshire visitor considered he had 'picked up an idea or two worth taking away' and another declared himself 'Very much pleased and instructed'. Henry Hardy of Postland commented, 'Very much pleased and shall have much to say when I get back into Lincolnshire', and a visitor from Devizes in Wiltshire went away 'Much gratified, the <u>Spirit</u> for improvement … stimulated by the example of Mr Mechi'. Joseph William Webb of Cradley near Malvern, visiting with his wife, told Mechi he was 'Very much pleased and shall put up a covered yard similar to yours', and two visitors from Essex considered 'the arrangements of the Farmery a pattern to all Landlords'.[30]

Visitors admired the 'high feeding' and 'high cultivation' and many, like Sir Tatton Sykes of Sledmere, East Yorkshire, declared themselves 'Highly gratified and pleased'. Some visitors commented on Mechi's system of keeping stock on 'stages' and in loose boxes. They praised Mechi's mode of management and mechanisation of processes. G. Thompson of the Land Drainage Company and John Dent Dent of Ribston Hall, Wetherby, Yorkshire, were amongst many who commented on the system of irrigation with liquid manure and Alexander Pitcairn, Factor for Lord Breadalbane, was 'Very much gratified with the general economy of the farm and the appliance of steam power also the efficient method of stirring the liquid Manure in the Tank by means of the small air pump'. The quality of cropping, as a result of irrigation with liquid manure and Mechi's system of thin sowing, was widely commended: 'The whole of the farm in the most productive state of any I have visited this season - particularly after a comparison of the neighbouring fields', enthused Thomas Lyall of Grantham.[31]

Not all comments were favourable and visitors sometimes took it upon themselves to offer Mechi advice. William Fisher Hobbs criticised the one-inch pipes used for underdraining and expressed dissatisfaction with the buildings; 'The buildings are not planned according to my ideas of a good Farmery the Steam Apparatus should not be in the Centre of the Yards so close to the Piggeries, Sheep Yards etc. where straw appears to be used'. A fellow Essex farmer commented '[I] think the Piggeries require more ventilation' and another visitor wrote, 'I should recommend more cleanliness and ventulation [sic] for the animals', which someone, possibly Mechi, countered by pencilling above 'I should recommend better spelling'. However, the general response was favourable; William Milford Teulon, architect, expressed 'Many thanks for the valuable hints about buildings' and Francis J. Pelham of Royal Farm, Windsor Park, considered Tiptree 'A perfect model in every respect'. 'A Model Farm: & a Model farmer' was the endorsement of one visitor from Kent.[32]

The heterogeneity of Mechi's visitors illustrates the breadth of interest in improvement within mid-nineteenth-century British society. It is, therefore, helpful to consider in more detail precisely who visited his experimental farm. Landowners such as the Duke of Rutland, Earls Grey and Macclesfield, Lords Bridport, Curzon and Rayleigh and Sir Tatton Sykes, visited Tiptree.[33] There were also farmers and members of farmers' clubs. The London Farmers' Club visited with Henry Dixon on Mechi's annual open day in July 1849. Dixon, a writer on sporting and agricultural matters, wrote under the pen name 'The Druid'. He had been to Tiptree the previous year and also attended the event in 1850 and 1851.[34] Many of those who shaped opinion in mid-nineteenth-century agricultural circles also visited Tiptree. Fisher Hobbs, who farmed nearby and was highly regarded for the quality of his cultivation, was one of the first visitors. He commented at length on the buildings and under-drainage. Henry Stephens, in whose *Book of the Farm* William Lawson found much good advice, visited in 1851.[35] Other notable visitors that year were John Bailey Denton and Chandos Wren Hoskyns, who wrote frequently for the *Agricultural Gazette*.[36]

Denton was a man of energy and determination. In the course of his working life he was identified variously as a surveyor, land valuer, land agent and civil engineer. His early career saw him involved in railway construction, his other interests being water supply, drainage, sewerage works and public health. In 1842 Denton published *What Can Now be Done for British Agriculture?* which argued that investment in underdraining and farm buildings would increase agricultural productivity and thereby offset the negative impact of loss of protected cereal prices which was the major concern of those who opposed the repeal of the Corn Laws.[37] The General Land Drainage and Improvement Company was founded under an act of 1849 to provide public money for agricultural improvement in the form of loans for owners of landed estates. Denton, who was primarily responsible for promoting the act, was put in charge as its Principal Drainage Engineer.[38] In 1864 he published *The Farm Homesteads of England: A Collection of Plans of English Homesteads Existing in Different Parts of the Country, carefully selected from the most Approved Specimens of Farm Architecture, to illustrate the accommodation required under different Modes of Husbandry.*[39] The book contained twenty-seven examples of existing farmsteads with details of the agricultural regimes they served, the size of farm and type of soil, average rainfall and distance from the nearest railway station. Lincolnshire is the only county from which two examples were chosen - another indication of its prominence in matters of improvement.

As we have seen not everyone was positive in their comments after visiting Tiptree. On the occasion of his visit with the London Farmers' Club in July 1849 Dixon ('The Druid') left the following rhyme in Mechi's visitors' book:

> There was a man and some did count him mad
> The more he spent on land (no doubt) the more he had
> (A riddle to be answered) [40]

It is unclear whether the invitation was to guess who he meant or to wait for the answer as to whether Mechi's high farming would pay. Perhaps the *double entendre* was intended.

The case of William Loft is an example of someone for whom heavy investment in a model farm and the adoption of Mechi's recommended farming methods certainly did not pay. Loft was owner occupier of an estate of around 482 acres at Trusthorpe and Sutton on the salt marsh clays near Mablethorpe. His residence was Trusthorpe Hall, known as Trusthorpe Thorpe in the nineteenth century. Loft was a leading agent for change in the Alford area. He was a committee member of Lord Yarborough's North Lincolnshire Agricultural Society, established in 1836 and, in 1838, he founded the Alford Agricultural Society of which he was first president.[41] His exposure to ideas of improvement promulgated by these societies may have led to his visit to Mechi's experimental farm at Tiptree, in August 1848.[42] Two years later, in 1850, a 'General View and Ground Plan of the Farm Buildings at Trusthorpe Lincolnshire, belonging to William Loft Esq.' was published in the *Farmer's Magazine.*[43] This was Loft's home farm which, like Lawson, he erected after his visit to Tiptree.

The life of Loft's new farming enterprise was a fleeting one. His Tiptree-inspired enthusiasm, which had resulted in the erection of a commodious mansion, tower gazebo and model farm buildings, had carried him too far. The diary of a local man records:

> Willm Loft Esqr Trusthorpe died Fridy morning 5 o'clock aged 56 May
> 13 1854. ….. He took a grate interest in agricultural persuits and built
> a modle farm after which it did not afford that amount of happiness he

expected and very much depleted his means that he had determined on selling it and taking one on rental in the southern part of the country and was in a short time going to enter in upon it. But death arested him, he was at Alford 3 days successively on the week he died. I noticed the last day how dejected he looked, and expressed my beleve that he would not live long little did I then think that he had but one day more to spend on earth.[44]

In October 1854, only four years after Loft proudly displayed his new steading in the *Farmer's Magazine*, his entire estate was advertised for sale (Fig. 6). The farm buildings were billed as 'having been recently built of the best materials in a most substantial manner, on a very complete and comprehensive scale, and upon the most approved principles of construction'. His 'newly-erected, substantially-built, and very commodious' mansion at Trusthorpe Thorpe was also included in the sale.[45] The estate did not sell and it was advertised for sale again in February 1855. This time it was to be sold in twenty-seven lots and the advertisement stated 'The steam thrashing machine and apparatus, and a considerable portion of the buildings comprising the Model Farmstead, will be sold by auction, in lots, to be removed'.[46] On the 1907 six-inch OS map only the far north-east yard and its surrounding buildings remained.

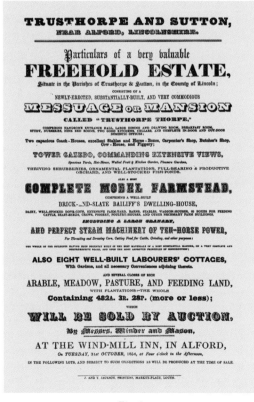

Fig.6
Sale Notice for William Loft's farm buildings at Trusthorpe (LA DIXON 20/1/11 © Lincolnshire Archives)

It is possible that they were the only ones left standing after the 1855 sale.[47]

Notwithstanding the failure of William Loft's bold enterprise and the reservations of some in the agricultural community, the overwhelming response to Mechi's farming activities was positive. The middle years of the nineteenth century were a time of great optimism for the future of British farming. There was money available through the various land improvement schemes to invest in long-term improvements and the developing disciplines of chemistry, animal physiology, plant biology, statistics, and geology afforded new understandings of how to increase inputs in farming to maximise outputs, in other words how to 'farm high'. The scientific base of high farming and the emergence of agriculture as a recognised subject of study are reflected in the visitor list at Tiptree. Charles Daubney, Sibthorpian Professor of Rural Economy, visited from Oxford in the first year of Tiptree's opening to visitors and announced himself 'Much pleased with the general arrangements of [the] system of the Farm'.[48] Thomas Tancred, one of the council of the Royal Agricultural College at Cirencester, visited in 1845, the year the college opened, and included in his lengthy remarks the comment that it was 'most encouraging to see a man with sufficient Faith in correct principles to carry them out unflinchingly in practice'.[49]

A number of architects, including Teulon and Frederick Chancellor, visited Tiptree.[50] Chancellor was a local architect, based in Chelmsford, whose plans for over fifty farmsteads survive in the Essex Record Office. These include one of the earliest examples of a covered yard and designs which provided for integrated systems within which the movement of food, litter, livestock and cereals had been carefully thought out. His comment in Mechi's visitors' book was 'Many thanks for the valuable hints about buildings'.[51] The increasing involvement of engineers, land agents and surveyors in farm building design is reflected in the number of men from these professions who also visited Tiptree.

There is evidence for the increased mechanisation of farming in Mechi's list of visitors, with Joseph Shuttleworth, Richard Hornsby and two of the owners of Crosskill's Iron Works in Beverley visiting on the same day.[52] At their Stamp End iron foundry in Lincoln, Shuttleworth and his brother-in-law, Nathaniel Clayton, developed and manufactured portable steam engines and threshing machines. Hornsby manufactured steam engines and threshing machines, as well as other agricultural equipment such as winnowing machines, seed drills and cake crushers, at his Spittlegate works just south of Grantham. At the peak of their production these two Lincolnshire firms employed over 2000 men each and exported agricultural machinery across the world.[53] In doing this, British agricultural engineers joined those who disseminated high farming ideas in contributing to the expansion of foreign meat and grain production which would so adversely affect British agriculture in the years after 1875.

Shuttleworth and Hornsby were not the only Lincolnshire visitors to Tiptree: between 1846 and 1876 there was a total of 91 visitors from the county (Fig. 7). Thomas Lyall, a farmer and auctioneer from Gayton le Wold near Louth, who visited in December 1856, would seem to be the same person as Thomas Lyall whose name appears again in June 1860 but this time with Grantham as the address.[54] There were no other names which appeared twice therefore Lyall was the only repeat visitor from Lincolnshire. There were repeat visitors from other counties including, as has already been noted, Lawson from Cumbria. George Cattle, who visited in October 1856, gave his address as 'Thorney, Lincolnshire' but Thorney is actually in Nottinghamshire so his entry was not included. Some of the names are immediately recognisable, for instance Loft, an active improver as we have seen above, who visited in August 1848. George Tomline and Captain Tomline of Riby, were early visitors to Tiptree, visiting in July 1846.[55] The Tomlines were neighbours of Lord Yarborough in the north of the county and substantial Lincolnshire landowners, with over 8439 acres at the time of the Return of Owners of Land in 1873.[56] One of their farms was occupied by William Torr, a leading tenant farmer, who was co-founder of Caistor Ploughing Society and a council member of the Royal Agricultural Society (RASE).

Other Lincolnshire landowners to appear in the columns of Mechi's visitors' book were Joseph Livesey of Stourton Hall near Horncastle, George Alington of Swinhope on the wolds, and H. S. Skipworth of Rothwell, also on the wolds.[57] Livesey visited in May 1852, and in April and December 1853 loans of over £6500 for drainage, irrigation and farm buildings on his estate at Baumber, Sturton and Hemingby were sanctioned by the General Land Drainage Company. His death from scarlet fever the following year explains why the

NAME	FORENAME	ADDRESS	YEAR
?	Edward	?	1857
Abraham	William	Barnetby le Wold	1856
Alan	Fredrick John	Worlaby, Louth	1874
Alington	George M.	Swinhope House	1854
Attenborough	Mr	Fillingham	1846
Barratt	George	Broxholme near Lincoln	1866
Belline	Charles	Lincoln	1856
Benyon	Joseph Burtt	Holbeach	1850
Bland	Thomas	Caenby, Market Rasen	1852
Broome	Edward	South Kelsey	1872
Brown	William	Horncastle	1853
Brown	Francis	Leadenham	1861
Bullen	E. J.	Claypole	1871
Chapman	H.	Edenham	1860
Clark	C. W.	Careby	1856
Clarke	George	Sheepwash, Canwick, Lincoln	1857
Codd	Francis A.	South Carlton, Lincoln	1869
Corbett	Joseph	Horncastle	1846
Dawson	Richard	Epworth	1847
Dickon	Thos	Lincs	1846
Donington	John	Whaplode Drove	1856
Dring	Thomas Boyer	Claxby, Spilsby	1854
Faulkner	Samuel	Walcott	1854
Frudd	John	Bloxholme, Sleaford	1862
Frudd	George	North Hills, Ruskington	1862
Ford, FGS	John	Market Rasen	1862
Foster	John	Owmby, Brigg	1863
Gillyatt	Charles G.	Wickenby, Wragby	1860
Goastman	Charles	Crowle	1851
Goulton	Benjamin	Gedney Marsh, Long Sutton	1856
Grant	Hannah	Farlesthorpe House	1871
Hall	John Eden	Barton upon Humber	1860
Hall	Jonas	Melwood Priory near Ferry	1860
Hardy	Henry	Postland (Crowland)	1856
Hewson	John	Tower House, Tetney near Grimsby	1853
Hillier	James	Purdies Farm, Nocton	1857
Holland	W.	Market Deeping	1868
Holmes	Lionel West	Howsham, Brigg	1847
Horberry	Thomas	Gunthorpe near Gainsborough	1860
Hornsby	R.	Spittlegate (Grantham)	1853
Ingram	William	Postland (Crowland)	1856
Jackson	Howard	The Hall, North Reston, Louth	1860
Johnson	H. A.	Louth	1847
Kempe	Jesse	Thurlby Grange (Bilsby, Alford))	1856
Laws	Henry	Kirton Sluice	1855

Fig.7 List of Lincolnshire visitors to Tiptree Hall Farm, 1846–78. (BL ADD 30015 'List of Visitors to Tiptree Hall')

Lawson	William	Whaplode Drove	1857
Lievesley	Thomas	Doddington	1857
Livesey	Joseph	Stourton Hall, Horncastle	1852
Loft	William	Trusthorpe, Alford	1848
Lyall	Thomas	Gayton Manor	1856
Lyall	Thomas	Grantham	1860
Marshall	John	Riseholme, Lincoln	1856
Marshall	J. C.	Riseholme, Lincoln	1856
Martin	William	Scamblesby	1847
Maw	Cornelius	Crowle	1846
Merrifield	Augustus	Wainfleet	1862
Moore	Henry	Kirton	1855
Mutter	William	Aswarby Park	1855
Ostler	W. J. Lely	Grantham	1857
Pilley, Junior	Samuel	Sudbrooke near Lincoln	1872
Porter	J. T. B.	Lincoln	1855
Price	F. Rockcliffe	The Manor House, West Ashby	1860
Raithby	W.R.	Grainthorpe, Louth	1847
Rawlings	Isaac	Normanton Farm (near Grantham)	1868
Richardson	William	Ashby Puerorum near Horncastle	1856
Robinson	J. W.	Frampton	1846
Robinson	George W.	Sedgebrook Manor House, Grantham	1872
Seagrave	William	Lissington, Wragby	1860
Sharp	John	Holywell	1856
Sharpley	Croft	Acthorpe (Louth)	1847
Sheir	Peter	Mile House, Heckington	1863
Shuttleworth	J.	Lincoln	1853
Simonds	Thomas	Frampton	1846
Skelton	William	Sutton Bridge	1846
Skipworth	H. S.	Rothwell House	1874
Smart	Major	Tumby	1847
Southwell	H. G.	Nettleton Lodge, Caistor	1872
Spademan	A. R.	Stamford	1874
Spencer	Thomas	Sturton-cum-Bransby, Gainsborough	1856
Thomas	William	Holbeach	1850
Tomline	George	Riby	1846
Tomline	Capt.	Riby	1846
Tooke	J. T. Hales	Scawby	1855
Turnor	Edmund	Panton Hall	1873
Ward	Thomas	Baumber	1858
Watson	John Firth	Crowle	1851
Westmoreland	Robert	Billingborough	1849
Wingate	William Brown	Hareby	1847
Wood	M.	Holbeach	1855
Wright	George	Knaith near Gainsborough	1863
Wright, Senior	Richard	Knaith, near Gainsborough	1863
Total 91			

loans were not proceeded with.[58] Although none of these men was the owner of a large estate, they were prominent in agricultural circles in their own areas, Alington seconded the resolution when the North Lincolnshire Agricultural Society was founded at Brigg in 1836 and Skipworth was one of those noted by J. A. Clarke in his prize essay on Lincolnshire, as a leading breeder of 'Improved Leicesters'.[59]

A Lincolnshire visitor who represented one of the county's largest landed estates was Edmund Turnor who visited Tiptree in July 1873 as one of a party of twenty.[60] This was some years before he inherited the Stoke Rochford estates from his father, Christopher Turnor, so he was living at Panton Hall near Wragby, the centre of Turnor's 'Mid-Lincolnshire Estate'. The Turnors were one of the county's most substantial landowning families with a holding of 20,664 acres in the year of Edmund's visit to Mechi's experimental farm.[61] In 1873 his father's estate had already borrowed almost £57,000 for improvements under the type of loan arrangements advocated by Denton. Initially the estate borrowed for underdraining, under the terms of the Private Money Drainage Act. Subsequent loans, principally for farm buildings, were taken out with the Lands Improvement Company (LIC).[62] Christopher Turnor was energetic in promoting the use of loan capital for estate improvements and, between March and December 1854, nineteen advertisements appeared in the *Lincolnshire Chronicle* and eleven in the *Lincoln, Rutland and Stamford Mercury* naming his agent, John Young Macvicar, as the Lincolnshire representative for the company. The first advertisement in the *Lincolnshire Chronicle* states that application should be made to both Macvicar and to the Hon. William Napier, Managing Director of the company.[63] In 1854 Macvicar was living at Barkwith House, Wragby, near Edmund Turnor's residence at Panton Hall. He was the architect of the distinctive farmstead plan which was adopted in all parts of the Turnors' vast estates. Wispington Farm (now Hill Farm, Wispington), one of the two Lincolnshire examples which featured in Denton's *Farm Homesteads of England*, was a Turnor farmstead designed by Macvicar.[64]

Also amongst Mechi's visitors were Lincolnshire farmers who commanded influence in their own neighbourhoods. Croft Sharpley visited in November 1847; the Sharpleys were said to farm over 12,000 acres on the wolds in the Louth area.[65] Thomas Boyer Dring of Claxby near Spilsby, who visited in April 1854, gave evidence to the 1867 Royal Commission enquiring into the employment of children in agriculture. This suggests he was regarded as one of the *cognoscenti* in his locality and was possibly known to the commissioner or moved in circles where he would be recommended as a witness. High farming was an expression of the culture of improvement which was embraced by many in the agricultural community in Lincolnshire and was reinforced and transmitted through social contact within the group. Dring was a member of the Lincolnshire Agricultural Society (LAS) and received mention in the *JRASE* as an early user of steam ploughing apparatus.[66]

Both the RASE and local agricultural societies sought to formalise the transmission of scientific knowledge and agricultural theory by promoting agricultural education. The RASE began to offer examinations in agriculture in 1870. The accounts of the LAS and Lincoln Chamber of Commerce record grants towards an agricultural science prize in the 1880s. This was usually referred to as the 'Prize for Mr Harris' Agricultural Science Class', and it seems that it was awarded to farmers or their sons who attended classes at Lincoln School of Science and Arts. In 1885 the prize was awarded to Mr F. M. Codd of South Carlton, who passed with honours. The visit to Tiptree Farm in July 1869, of Francis

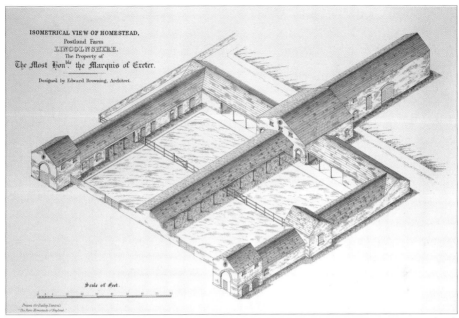

Fig.8 Isometric view of Postland Farm. (John Bailey Denton, 1864, Farm Homesteads of England, p.22 © Cambridge University Library)

A. Codd of South Carlton, is further evidence of the family's interest in informing and educating themselves.[67]

Charles G. Gillyatt of Wickenby, near Wragby and William Abraham of Barnetby le Wold, both of whom were acclaimed as sheep breeders, were other visitors to Tiptree. Gillyatt was noted by Clarke as a leading breeder of Lincoln-Leicester crosses and Abraham was recorded in the diary of Charles Nainby of Barnoldby as winning a prize at the North Lincolnshire Agricultural Society Show at Caistor in 1843, for 'a pen of 6 wonderful sucked ewes'. William Richardson of Ashby Puerorum, near Horncastle, another visitor to Tiptree, also showed sheep at the North Lincolnshire Agricultural Society Show at Caistor.[68] Christopher Turnor's tenant, William Seagrave, who occupied Manor Farm, Lissington near Wragby, visited Tiptree in July 1860, in the same party as Gillyatt.[69]

William Ingram was one of the party of thirty with whom Richardson visited in July 1856, just two days before the annual Open Day. Ingram was the tenant of the Marquis of Exeter's farm at Postland (Fig. 8) which, along with Turnor's Wispington Farm, was one of the two Lincolnshire examples in Denton's *Farm Homesteads of England*.[70] The Marquis of Exeter was patron of the Bourne Agricultural Society and also a Vice President of LAS.[71] Detail such as this contributes to the general corpus of information about notable Lincolnshire landowners, their farms and their tenants. A willingness to travel to Essex to view an experimental farm is indicative of the thirst for knowledge which characterised many of the leading improvers in agricultural circles in Lincolnshire in the mid-nineteenth century. It also suggests that there was a particular social group within the county which was identified and distinguished by shared activities such as involvement in agricultural societies, public displays of skill and

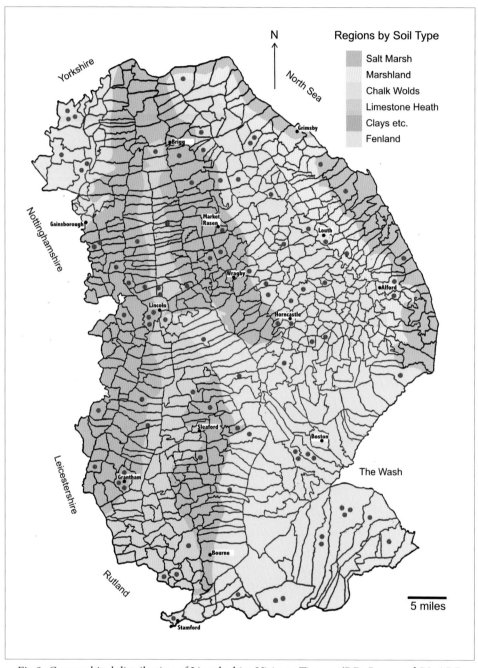

Fig.9 Geographical distribution of Lincolnshire Visits to Tiptree. (P.D. Ryan and BL ADD 30015 'List of Visitors to Tiptree Hall')

innovation in cultivation and stock keeping, dissemination of agricultural knowledge and promotion of agricultural education.

The distribution, by parish, of Lincolnshire visits to Tiptree is another aspect of Mechi's list of visitors which can be considered (Fig. 9). It is apparent that people from all land types visited Mechi's experimental farm. There was no marked concentration of visitors from clay lands who may have experienced similar problems to those encountered by Mechi on the poor clay soils at Tiptree. Men who farmed, or had an interest in agriculture, made the journey to Essex from the heath, wolds, fens, marshes and clay vales of Lincolnshire. The Isle of Axholme and the fenland area around the Wash had the greatest concentration of parishes from which more than one person visited. This may have been due to the fact that these were significant areas of reclamation and improvement in the nineteenth century. However, the same concentration was not evident on the light uplands of the heath and wolds which, equally, saw great improvement in the middle years of the century. In these areas the distribution of visitors was much more scattered.

A more probable explanation for the concentration of visitors from certain areas, albeit one which was not unconnected with local improvement activity and interest, was the presence of active local agricultural societies. Local farmers' associations were important agents in the diffusion of information locally. We have detailed information on local agricultural societies in Lincolnshire in Mona Skehel's book *Tales from the Showyard: Two Hundred Years of Agricultural Shows in Lincolnshire*. Skehel had close connections with the LAS over many years and had an intimate knowledge of its archive of material relating to the local societies it absorbed. She included a 'Register of Agricultural Societies in Lincolnshire' in this volume on the history of the LAS.[72]

In order to discover whether there were links between the presence of local societies and visits to Tiptree, names which appear in Mechi's visitors' book were studied in the context of Skehel's findings and White's 1856 directory of Lincolnshire. A connection was immediately apparent in the Isle of Axholme: Thomas Horberry from Gunthorpe and Jonas Hall from Melwood, both in Owston parish on the Isle, visited on the same day in August 1860. Owston Agricultural Society was flourishing at this time, as was the Isle of Axholme Agricultural Association which had two-hundred and sixty-five members in 1856.[73] The Owston Society came into being in 1847, the same year as the visit by Richard Dawson, a solicitor from neighbouring Epworth, and the year after the visit of Cornelius Maw, farmer, from nearby Crowle. Two other men made a joint visit from Crowle in July 1851.[74]

The fact that a local agricultural society might have come into being after people in the area visited Tiptree rather than before, does not nullify the argument for a connection between local society activity and visits to Mechi's experimental farm. In instances where visits preceded the formation of a local society, it could be that the enthusiasm for improvement generated by the visit gave impetus to the drive to found a local agricultural association. On the other hand, given that it is probable that it was out of informal associations of those interested in promoting agricultural improvement that local societies grew, it is quite possible that such informal contacts may have prompted the visit(s) to Tiptree. Either way the case can be made for a connection between visits to Tiptree and the existence of a local agricultural society. It is also important to note that the precise date of inception of many

		1850	2	1860	9	1870	0
		1851	2	1861	1	1871	2
		1852	2	1862	4	1872	4
		1853	4	1863	4	1873	1
		1854	3	1864	0	1874	3
		1855	6	1865	0	1875	0
1846	9	1856	14	1866	1	1876	0
1847	8	1857	6	1867	0	1877	0
1848	1	1858	1	1868	2	1878	0
1849	1	1859	0	1869	1		
TOTAL 91							

Fig. 10 Temporal distribution of Lincolnshire Visits to Tiptree Hall Farm, 1846–78. (BL ADD 30015 'List of Visitors to Tiptree Hall')

societies is uncertain. Skehel explains that the dates she gives are based on the first evidence she could find of a society's existence and this may not always represent the exact date of foundation.[75]

There are further instances of parishes with a concentration of visitors to Tiptree being in an area in which there was agricultural society influence. Lincoln, from whose area there was a comparatively large number of visitors, had an active farmers' club and Grantham, with three visitors to Tiptree, had an agricultural association. Horncastle, with two visitors plus one from the neighbouring parish of West Ashby, had an agricultural society for the whole of the period of Mechi's visitors' book and Bilsby and Farlesthorpe, adjoining Alford, the home of William Loft's Labourers' Society, had a visitor each. Similarly, neighbouring Kirton and Frampton, two parishes just south of Boston, which had a society for almost the whole of the nineteenth century, each had two visitors to Tiptree.[76]

The concentration of visitors to Tiptree from fenland parishes in the south of the county around the Wash, can more confidently be attributed to the influence of a strong culture of improvement among local people. This area was the home of John Algernon Clarke, who wrote about the draining and subsequent improvement of the fens in South Lincolnshire, as well as the Prize Essay on the county, in the *JRASE*. Clarke was president of the Long Sutton and District Agricultural Society founded in 1836. The society was active throughout the nineteenth century and into the second half of the twentieth century, finally becoming affiliated to the East of England Agricultural Society in 1969.[77] From within the sphere of influence of the Long Sutton society there were nine visitors to Tiptree; three from Holbeach, two each from Whaplode and Crowland, one from Gedney and one from Sutton Bridge. Those whose names appeared in White's 1856 directory were all farmers except the visitor from Sutton Bridge who was William Skelton, land steward to Guy's Hospital. Skelton made an early visit to Tiptree in May 1846.[78] Clarke himself does not appear in Mechi's visitors' book.

The double visits from Riby and Knaith were less readily attributable to connections with local agricultural associations. The two visitors from Riby in the north wolds area were the Tomlines who, as large landowners in Lincolnshire and Suffolk, would have been subject to influences beyond the level of local agricultural societies. Knaith, south of Gainsborough, also had two visitors: Richard Wright senior, a land agent, and George Wright, who visited together in May 1863. There is no evidence for an agricultural society in Gainsborough before 1873, so perhaps the incentive for the visit to Tiptree derived from Wright senior's profession.[79]

The temporal distribution of visits to Tiptree from Lincolnshire (Fig. 10) mirrors the overall pattern of visits (Fig. 4) with a high level of interest to begin with. However, unlike the overall pattern, interest from Lincolnshire was not sustained throughout the first decade; it fell away rapidly after the first two years then re-emerged in the middle of the 1850s. The year 1856 saw the highest number of people from Lincolnshire visiting Tiptree with fourteen visits, six of which were in mid-July when the Royal Show was held at nearby Chelmsford.[80] In 1860 numbers again equalled those of 1846, the first year of record, with nine Lincolnshire visitors recorded in Mechi's visitors' book.

The only female visitor to Tiptree from Lincolnshire was Hannah Grant of Farlesthorpe House near Alford, who visited with James Post of Tolleshunt D'Arcy in September 1871.[81] The same gentleman had visited earlier in the year with Mrs Tomlinson of Salt End Farm, Hedon, Hull, Yorkshire.[82] The gender profile of all the visits to Tiptree was not calculated but it can be stated that whilst the predominance of visitors were men, there were a small number of instances of women visiting. On some occasions whole families came, perhaps reflecting the widespread curiosity evoked by Mechi's system of farming. One such group commented that they 'Came expecting much from public report. It was realised fully'.[83]

In her study *Farmers, Landlords and Landscapes: Rural Britain, 1720-1870*, Susanna Wade Martins identified farmers' clubs as an important forum for the dissemination of information about improved methods of agriculture. She mentions some farmers and farmers' clubs by name and includes a table showing membership numbers of the RASE, by county, in 1854. [84] The current study has demonstrated the insights and information which can be gained from a single nominative source: that of the visitors' book for Mechi's experimental farm at Tiptree in Essex. However, much more can be discovered by comparing a number of nominative sources for nineteenth-century farming in the county. An exercise such as this has been undertaken by the author: membership lists for RASE and LAS were compared with evidence for membership of local agricultural societies; references to 'leading sheep breeders' in J. A. Clarke's Prize Essay on Lincolnshire; names of those pictured in the LAS's painting of 'Celebrated Ram Breeders'; names of those listed in the first Lincolnshire Red Shorthorn Herd Register and the list of those who visited Tiptree. The outcome was a table of a hundred and one names of Lincolnshire farmers and landowners, showing the different networks of improvers to which they belonged, thus making it possible to identify leading agents for change in the county.[85] More work of this nature would be a valuable contribution to our knowledge and understanding of the social networks of improvers in nineteenth-century Lincolnshire.

NOTES

1. Mills, Dennis, 1957, 'Population and Settlement in Kesteven (Lincs.) *c.*1775 - *c.*1885', University of Nottingham MA Thesis; Mills, Dennis, 1959, 'The development of rural settlement around Lincoln, with specific reference to the eighteenth and nineteenth centuries', *East Midland Geographer*, 11, pp. 3-15. Republished in Mills, D. R. (ed), 1973, *English Rural Communities: The Impact of a Specialised Economy*, pp. 83-97.

2. Brook, Shirley, 2011, '"The development of rural settlement around Lincoln revisited", with special reference to farm buildings and loans for improvement' in Brook, S., Walker, A. and Wheeler, R. (eds), *Lincoln Connections: Aspects of City and County since 1700*, Lincoln. pp. 91-107.

3.   Pusey, Philip, 1843, 'On the Agricultural Improvements of Lincolnshire', *Journal of the Royal Agricultural Society* (hereafter *JRASE*), 4, pp. 288-9.

4.   Goddard, Nicholas, 1988, *Harvests of Change: The Royal Agricultural Society of England 1838-1988*, p. 30; Goddard, Nicholas, 1991, 'Information and Innovation in Early-Victorian Farming Systems', in B. A. Holderness and Michael Turner (eds), *Land, Labour and Agriculture, 1700-1920; Essays for Gordon Mingay*, pp. 167-9.

5.   Creasey, John, S., 'Mechi, John Joseph (1802-1880)', c2004, in *Oxford Dictionary of National Biography*, 37, Oxford, pp. 680-1.

6.   Kinsley, Lesley, 2022, 'The significance of Peruvian guano in British fertilizer history (c.1840-1880)', in *The Agricultural History Review*, 70.2, pp. 229, 233-4, 236.

7.   Mills, Dennis, 'An "edge land": the development of the Witham valley east of Canwick Road', in Walker, A. (ed), 2001, *Aspects of Lincoln*, Barnsley, pp. 142-4. An account of the farming activities of Mills's uncle and grandfather are given in Mills, D., Summer 1996, 'The Small Farm, with Special Reference to Victorian Lincolnshire', *Lincolnshire Past and Present*, 24, pp. 7-11.

8.   'Tiptree Farm', *The Times* (hereafter *Times*), Thursday 27 July 1854, p. 9 col. f; 'Mr Mechi at Tiptree', *Times*, Monday 21 July 1856, p. 12 cols. a, b.

9.   Caird, James, 1849, *High Farming under Liberal Covenants, the Best Substitute for Protection*, pp. 6-7; 14-15.

10. There is a collection of these in the British Library Rare Books Room, in some of which the appellation is I. J. Mechi: 'Application of Town Sewage to Agricultural Fertility. Read to the Improvement Society at Leeds, 29 November, 1854', British Library (hereafter BL) CT 344; 'A Fourth Paper on British Agriculture with some account of his own operations at Tiptree Hall read before the Society of Arts, Manufactures and Commerce by Mr I. J. Mechi, 6 December, 1854' BL CT 344; 'Mr Mechi's Farm Balance Sheets also His Lectures and Papers on Farming since the publication of his former book', (1867) BL 7076 AA29; 'How I make Farming Pay. A Paper Read to the Midland Counties Farmers' Club Birmingham on April 1, 1875 by J. J. Mechi', BL CT 344; 'How to farm profitably on stiff heavy clays', n.d., BL CT 344; I. J. Mechi, 'Letters on Agricultural Improvement', n.d. BL 7074 K35.

11. Goddard, Nicholas, 1981, '*The Royal Agricultural Society of England and Agricultural Progress 1838-1880*', University of Kent PhD thesis, p. 132.

12. Mechi, J. J., various editions 1859-1878, *How to Farm Profitably or the Sayings and Doings of Mr Alderman Mechi*.

13. 'Tiptree Farm', *Times*, 1854.

14. Wade Martins, S., 2010, *Coke of Norfolk 1754–1842*, Suffolk, pp. 114, 115-9.

15. 'Tiptree Farm', *Times*, 1854.

16. 'List of Visitors to Tiptree Hall Farm', BL ADD 30015, ff. 197, 220.

17. Lawson, W., 1874, *Ten Years of Gentleman Farming at Blennerhasset, with co-operative objects*.

18. *Ibid.*, pp. 14-24; Stephens, H., 1844, *The Book of the Farm*.

19. Lawson, *Ten Years of Gentleman Farming*, pp. 39-40; 150-7.

20. Mechi, 4th edn. 1864, *How to Farm Profitably*, p. 458.

21. Lawson, *Ten Years of Gentleman Farming*, pp. 82-3.

22. *Ibid.*, pp. 221-395.

23. *Ibid.*, p. 42.

24. *Ibid.*, pp. 60.

25. *Ibid.*, pp. 212-20.

26. 'List of Visitors to Tiptree Hall Farm', f. 1.

27. *Ibid.*

28. Caird, *High Farming under Liberal Covenants*; Caird, J., 1968, *English Agriculture*, 2nd edn.

29. 'List of Visitors to Tiptree Hall Farm', f. 238.

30. *Ibid.*, ff. 11, 155, 215, 154, 22, 260, 16^v.

31. *Ibid.*, ff. 62^v, 173, 178, 75^v, 37^v, 109^v, 109, 130^v, 187.

32. *Ibid.,* ff. 9, 65, 36, 259ᵛ, 229ᵛ, 75.

33. *Ibid.,* ff. 8, 36ᵛ, 64ᵛ, 108ᵛ, 113ᵛ, 178.

34. *Ibid.,* ff. 47ᵛ, 57, 69ᵛ, 83.

35. *Ibid.,* ff. 9, 89; Lawson, *Ten Years of Gentleman Farming.* p. 18.

36. 'List of Visitors to Tiptree Hall Farm', ff. 78ᵛ, 90.

37. Denton, J. B., 1842, *What Can Now be Done for British Agriculture?*

38. Phillips, A. D. M., 'Denton, John Bailey (1814-1893)', 2004, in *Oxford Dictionary of National Biography*, 15 Oxford, pp. 856-7.

39. Denton, J. B., 1864, *The Farm Homesteads of England.*

40. 'List of Visitors to Tiptree Hall Farm', f. 83.

41. Skehel, M., 1999, *Tales from the Showyard: Two Hundred Years of Agricultural Shows in Lincolnshire*, Lincoln, pp. 119-20.

42. 'List of Visitors to Tiptree Hall Farm', f. 49.

43. 'General View and Ground Plan of the Farm Buildings at Trusthorpe Lincolnshire, belonging to William Loft Esq.', *Farmers Magazine*, 2nd ser. 22, 1850.

44. 'Diary of Robert Mason of Alford', Lincolnshire Archives (hereafter LA) Misc. Don. 1053.

45. 'Notice of Auction of Freehold Estate at Trusthorpe', LA Dixon 20/1/11.

46. 'Notice of Auction', LA PAD 3/200.

47. OS 1:10,560, Lincolnshire Sheet 58.SW, Second Edition (1907).

48. 'List of Visitors to Tiptree Hall Farm', f.19.

49. *Ibid.,* f. 21.

50. *Ibid.,* ff. 71, 259ᵛ.

51. *Ibid.,* f. 259ᵛ. More information regarding the work of Frederick Chancellor can be found in Wade Martins, S., 2002, *The English Model Farm*, Macclesfield, pp.128-9.

52. *Ibid.,* f. 128ᵛ.

53. Wright, N. R., 1982, *Lincolnshire Towns and Industry 1700-1914*, History of Lincolnshire, XI, Society for Lincolnshire History and Archaeology, Lincoln, pp. 83-5, 137-149; Redmore, K., 2004, 'The Production of Agricultural Machinery' in Bates, E., *Farming in Lincolnshire*, Heritage Lincolnshire, Heckington, pp.36-7.

54. 'List of Visitors to Tiptree Hall Farm', ff. 166ᵛ, 187. Census listings for 1851 and 1861, taken along with references to Thomas Lyall in a number of county newspapers, all point to both entries being for the same man. I am grateful to Dr Andrew Walker for investigating this and to Professor Mike Turner for comments which alerted me to my initial mis-transcription of his name.

55. 'List of Visitors to Tiptree Hall Farm', ff. 165, 49, 16.

56. 'Owners of Land, 1872-3 (England and Wales)', *British Parliamentary Papers*, C. 1097, LXXII, Part 1, 1874, p.96.

57. 'List of Visitors to Tiptree Hall Farm', ff. 107ᵛ, 134, 255ᵛ.

58. National Archives (hereafter NA), MAF66 1/8; Interview with Angela Clark (née Livesey), Great Sturton, Horncastle, Lincolnshire, 27th January 1998.

59. Skehel, *Tales from the Showyard*, p. 11; Clarke, J. A, 1851, 'On the Farming of Lincolnshire', *JRASE,* 12, p. 394.

60. 'List of Visitors to Tiptree Hall Farm', f.251ᵛ.

61. 'Owners of Land 1872-3', p. 97.

62. Brook, A. S., 2005, 'The Buildings of High Farming: Lincolnshire Farm Buildings 1840-1910', University of Hull PhD thesis, Table 8 p. 210.

63. *Lincolnshire Chronicle*, 24 March 1854 p. 8.

64. Denton, *Farm Homesteads of England*, pp.47-49.

65. 'List of Visitors to Tiptree Hall Farm', f. 36; Rawding, C. K., 2001, *The Lincolnshire Wolds in the Nineteenth Century*, Studies in the History of Lincolnshire, 1, Lincoln, p. 119.

66. 'List of Visitors to Tiptree Hall Farm', f. 131; Rawding, *Lincolnshire Wolds*, p. 188; 'Lincolnshire Agricultural Society Annual Report, 1871', Lincolnshire Agricultural Society archive, Lincolnshire Showground, Lincoln; Clarke, J. A., 1859, 'Application of Steam Power to Cultivation', *JRASE*, 20, p. 220.

67. Skehel, *Tales from the Showyard*, p. 141; 'List of Visitors to Tiptree Hall Farm', f. 236.

68. 'List of Visitors to Tiptree Hall Farm', ff. 159, 188, 166; Clarke, 1851, *JRASE*, p. 394; Charles Nainby's diary quoted in Skehel, *Tales from the Showyard*, p. 13.

69. 'List of Visitors to Tiptree Hall Farm', f. 188; Redmore, K., unpublished notes on 'Turnor Rent Books', LA 3 Turnor. (I am very grateful to Ken for sharing this information with me).

70. Denton, *Farm Homesteads of England*, pp.20-22; 'List of Visitors to Tiptree Hall Farm', f. 159; 'Mr Mechi at Tiptree', *Times*, 1856.

71. Skehel, *Tales from the Showyard*, p. 122.

72. Skehel, 'Register of Agricultural Societies in Lincolnshire', *Tales from the Showyard*, pp. 119-134.

73. 'List of Visitors to Tiptree Hall Farm', ff. 191, 191ᵛ; Skehel, *Tales from the Showyard*, pp. 129, 131.

74. 'List of Visitors to Tiptree Hall Farm', ff. 11, 30, 86ᵛ; *White's 1856 Lincolnshire*, repr. 1969, pp. 625, 629.

75. Skehel, *Tales from the Showyard*, p. 119.

76. *Ibid.*, pp. 119-20, 128-9.

77. Clarke, J. A., 1847, 'On the Great Level of the Fens, including the Fens of South Lincolnshire', *JRASE*, 8, pp. 88-133; Clarke, J. A., 1852, *Fen Sketches: being a description of the alluvial district known as The Great Level of the Fens*; Clarke, 1851, *JRASE*; Skehel, *Tales from the Showyard*, pp. 129-30.

78. 'List of Visitors to Tiptree Hall Farm', f. 7; *White's 1856 Lincolnshire*, repr. 1969, p. 862.

79. 'List of Visitors to Tiptree Hall Farm', f. 215; *White's 1856 Lincolnshire*, repr. 1969, p. 203; Skehel, *Tales from the Showyard*, p. 127.

80. Goddard, 1981, '*The Royal Agricultural Society*', Table 1, p. 35.

81. 'List of Visitors to Tiptree Hall Farm', f. 247ᵛ.

82. *Ibid.*, f. 244.

83. *Ibid.*, f. 174.

84. Wade Martins, S., 2004, *Farmers, Landlords and Landscapes: Rural Britain, 1720-1870*, Macclesfield, pp. 139-142. Unfortunately Lincolnshire has been missed off this list.

85. Brook, thesis, pp. 64-78.

2022: CENTENARY OF THE LAST LINCOLNSHIRE YEOMAN[1]

Michael Turner

Strictly speaking, the last Lincolnshire yeoman actually disappeared from view at midnight on 31 December 1925, but the act of parliament that determined this should happen was in 1922. And even then, this apparent precision only works by playing with language and the semantics of the word 'yeoman'. So to be upfront and honest, what this article will do is identify the last copyhold tenant of a Lincolnshire manor who might or might not have self-identified as a yeoman.

The year 2022 is important because it marks the centenary of the passing of the Law of Property Act in 1922. Furthermore, the last day of 1925 is important because that is the day, at the crossover between 1925 and 1926, when that law became active. From 1 January 1926 all copyhold tenants suddenly became freeholders overnight. They did not have to do anything about claiming that status, it just happened. However, if they were still copyholders just before midnight, much of the relationship between them and their lords to whom they paid their annual quit rents, remained unaltered. They still paid those rents and any other obligations that by right were the property of the lord. If they sold their property to a third party that third party would still have to pay those obligations and be admitted to the property until such time as the former copyhold tenant, though now a freeholder, or the new tenant, had agreed terms with the lord of the manor to buy out or extinguish the outstanding elements of the lords' interests by way of a compensation agreement. This continuing formal connection, until settled by such a compensation agreement, was meant to last for ten years.

But in 1935 it became evident that there were still many extinguishments to be completed and many that had not even been started, and so an extension of five years was allowed. Before that extension expired the intervention of the Second World War meant that several ongoing laws were suspended, including this extension of the 1922 Act.[2] The resumption of 'normal' business as far as the extinguishment of manorial relationships was concerned came in 1949, and a final date for the extinguishment of manorial incidents was set as the 31 October 1950. It was recognised that negotiations between lords and former tenants that had begun before the end of October 1950 would not all be completed by the appointed hour and therefore it was allowed that those negotiations that had formally begun before the clock struck would be allowed to proceed to completion. To that extent perhaps the last yeomen by the adapted definition of the term were the trustees of the will of a Norfolk man from Wymondham near Norwich who completed the extinguishment of the outstanding manorial incidents in June 1957.[3] Without the act of 1922 the final whispers of feudal tenure might still be in operation. To a modest extent they can be heard again with the scare in recent years about fracking and the overbearing attitude of some lords as to what precise elements of manorial rights still existed under their control.[4]

In one of his well-known books Dennis Mills looked at the relationship between lords and peasants in the nineteenth century. He was as uneasy about using the term peasant as I am about using the term yeoman, not least because both terms are incapable of precise definition.[5] Moreover his book and subsequent work, as well as the work of others, sparked a critical debate about what we mean by rural history in general suggesting that historians had formerly and narrowly concentrated on agricultural history and its outmoded tripartite division of activity in the countryside involving landlords, tenant farmers and labourers. Rural history was more complicated than this, and even if that tripartite division existed, its employment by historians did not easily allow a labourer also to be semi-independent with a smallholding, or a tenant to be paying a rent to one person but renting out other property to another person. In a spirited defence of his approach to rural history, Dennis pointed out that many, not all of the criticisms levelled against him had either been misinterpretations or myopic in their reading of his work.[6]

There is another reason to be cautious and hesitant with language: it carries connotations involving economic size and social status. Yeoman and peasant are both loaded with political and class sentiments. They both convey the general impression of size and humility but in the full knowledge that some of the people involved were considerable in size and income and also in social status and as far from humility as it is possible to be. And on one occasion in one property transaction, though nothing to do with Lincolnshire, even Queen Victoria was described in language that conveys an impression of small size and therefore inferior status, and yet there was nobody else of her generation who commanded a higher status in society.[7] In short there is not an adequate general term for what we are concerned with in this article. There is another issue at stake here and this is to do with the assumption that peasants, yeoman, or whatever term we use to convey small size and self-determination, misses out another important feature of the countryside, a feature that in modern parlance we would call the service providers. These were the grain merchants, the carriers, and the many professionals like country solicitors who might only be in possession of a cottage or two, or a store yard, barn, or a paddock or two for a horse. If those possessions were copyhold in tenure then they are also part of the story. With all those considerations in mind the last 'yeoman' identified in the context of this article will be the last former tenant of a manorial lord until the point at which the manorial incidents had been extinguished. For Lincolnshire, that last manorial tenants so far identified, under our hazy definitions, were five former tenants from four different manors (Crowle, Epworth times two, Fiskerton with its Members, and Moulton Dominorum), all of whom negotiated their compensation agreements with their lords before 31 October 1950 and completed them in the following three years. The very last one was W. A. T. Asplin who on 12 June 1953 (having registered the fact with the Ministry of Agriculture a week later on 20 June) finally redeemed the outstanding manorial incidents on his 35.7 acres (involving several allotments of Sims Hill Farm in Belton parish and Epworth manor, today lying to the south and within sight of the M180) and for which he paid £8 8s. 5d. He was also liable for a steward's compensation, if there was any, and also the lord's costs.[8]

There were six other compensations in England and Wales still yet to complete after Asplin completed, three in Monmouthshire, one in North Yorkshire and two in Norfolk, including the very last one in 1957. But these are the examples that passed through the hands and under the gaze of the Ministry of Agriculture and Fisheries. There were many others, in fact untold thousands, that were negotiated without the imprimatur of the Ministry and its forebears in Whitehall. If lords and their tenants could agree terms of enfranchisement and extinguishment of the manorial incidents there was no need to engage the government

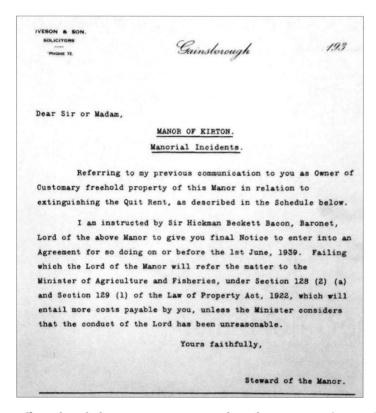

Fig.1
A blank template for a letter from the solicitor acting as Steward of the Manor inviting a customary freeholder to agree to terms of enfranchisement and extinguish the manorial incidents – issued in 1939 to some tenants of Kirton Manor and found loose leaf in the Manor of Kirton Court Roll (LAO, Bacon/Manor of Kirton/1, Ct Bk L. Reproduced with permission)

offices, though there were a succession of acts from 1841 until 1922 which those parties had to follow. (see Fig. 1) On the basis of examples from other counties where the last duties of manorial tenancy were also being played out, and assuming Lincolnshire was not so very different from those counties, there might be other former 'yeomen' in the manorial records of Lincolnshire manors yet to be identified and who stretched beyond 1953 before their formal links were finally severed, and there are surely some who evaded the obligation altogether.[9]

The wider story of the severance of copyholders and other manorial tenants from their lords and manors has been told elsewhere, at the national England level,[10] at the county level,[11] and at the institutional level in a wider study of the financial management of the Oxbridge college estates.[12] The present study offers the opportunity to honour the memory of Dennis Mills by applying an intimate microscope to a study of his home county, Lincolnshire.[13] In addition, this is an opportune moment to abandon loaded language, indulge in definition avoidance, and resort to plain speaking. So, to be precise, this article continues by looking afresh at the relationship between the tenants of manors and the final decades of the most direct relationship they had with their lords and those manors. This will be approached in two parts: first by analysing the language contained in the clauses of over 300 acts of parliamentary enclosure for Lincolnshire; and second by measuring the extent to which the copyholder remained a force in the county after enclosure by analysing his and her progress towards the severing of their direct links to their lords through the enfranchisement of their manorial tenure.

This story has said quite a lot already about the end point or points, but for every end there has to be a beginning. On the large, county-scale, canvas adopted this story needs a recognised starting or datum point. Historians, especially agricultural historians, often have resort to the county-based volumes of the *General Views of the Agriculture of* [named county] administered by the Board of Agriculture from 1793-*c*.1820. It offers very little by way of discussion of tenure, not only for Lincolnshire but also for most other counties. Thomas Stone in his 1794 report for the county advocated the enfranchisement of copyhold because the systems of fines and heriots and other manorial attachments were not conducive to general agricultural improvement. It was a comment without any evidence except that it indicates that there was a body of copyholders, of whatever collective size, still in existence. The second report for the county, written by Arthur Young, the doyen of agricultural improvement, observed that 'Tenures in this county are much copyhold in the low country, but not much in the higher land', and that was just about it.[14]

If we want a superficial but nonetheless wide ranging indication of the survival of manorial tenures before the 1841 Enfranchisement Act then one possibility with a relatively consistent format is contained in the clauses and hence the rules governing the process of parliamentary enclosure through private acts. In the context of tenure such rules of engagement were necessary because much land remained in copyhold and other tenures, and also because there was also a need to translate the intangible common rights associated with copyhold tenure into real property allotments. In this context we might think of cottage cow commons or other common rights directly attached to or associated with tangible property. This was one of the few occasions where new copyhold property was created in substitution for such rights.

For present purposes, the appropriate clauses in private enclosure acts can give a superficial feel for the presence of copyhold tenure. The enclosure movement and the debates surrounding it, especially the role of Parliament through private enclosure acts, is a well-trodden path, debated, argued about, overstated and understated in equal measures. It remains a central feature of the agrarian history of eighteenth and nineteenth-century England. In becoming a political football the enclosure debates concentrated on many questions, some of which are also important to concerns over tenure. Did it displace people from the land? Opinions rather than answers to that question can be found in highly charged debates running from Marx through to the Hammonds and on to Chambers and Mingay. The broad differences between scholars were neatly summarised by Saville who gave the conservative interpretations of Chambers and Mingay a hostile treatment. Brenner stirred up a larger hornets' nest with the wider implications for his agrarian class debate across Europe and across centuries.[15] Practical questions also arose such as did enclosure create a biddable labour force?[16] Most questions about the role of enclosure in re-shaping rural society, however, miss an important and relatively standard feature of parliamentary enclosure acts. This was the question of subsisting tenure, the presence of which can be picked up in the clauses of the acts even if the precise measurement of it only arises from laborious and meticulous studies.[17]

Before 1801 it seems safe to assume that any references to tenure in whatever guise, either directly with reference to copyhold for example, or indirectly with reference to fines or quit rents or other terms that signify a manorial interest, indicated a need to make such reference because of the circumstances of the particular enclosure. Then in 1801 the *General Inclosure Act* provided a general checklist of essential elements that enclosure bills might contain, but not necessarily all of the elements. In other words, the Act allowed special and individual tailoring of private acts according to locals needs and circumstances. The 1801 Act referred to tenure in a long paragraph containing an instruction to distinguish between 'Freehold from the Copyhold or Leasehold' when claimants were claiming rights of common.[18] To the extent that the 1801 Act was a general act designed as much as anything to tidy up the existing process, it can be assumed that it was guided by what was already in place before 1801 when bills and acts catered for the individual circumstances of parishes, villages, townships and hamlets and therefore did not necessarily all include all of the same clauses. The Act meant that from 1801 direct reference to tenure was not necessary because in stating that individual private acts were conforming to the requirements of the General Act it is assumed that such questions were not separately listed. This must be borne in mind in the analysis below with respect to private acts passed after 1801.

It is easy to suppose that country solicitors who drew up the draft enclosure bills that were presented to Parliament simply took existing acts and changed names and details appropriate to the next private bill on which they were engaged. Why not use what was a ready-made template? In practice, it was not as simple as that and after reviewing over 300 Lincolnshire enclosure acts as well as countless others in other counties, it becomes clear that many enclosure acts threw up special as well as individual circumstances. This was as true, for example, with references to tenure, as it was for any other issue attendant at enclosure. What is useful is to distinguish between the bland word that is 'tenure', meaning the relationship between a landlord and a tenant, from the specific meaning when that word is used to separate different forms of that relationship, mainly freehold as distinct from leasehold, and also from copyhold or other customary relationships. Additionally, we must be clear that this is different again from rack rent relationships. Many if not most enclosure acts allowed rack rents to fall in at enclosure with the opportunity that this gave for landlords to renegotiate their commercial relationships with their tenants.[19] In addition, more or less all acts have a clause about safeguarding special circumstances that then would not be affected by the acts, but often this clause was specifically inserted so that existing legal arrangements, especially existing wills, would not be altered by the act. The Stoke Rochford Act is a typical example. It talks about the status of existing titles. Property would be,

> liable to the same Uses and Trusts, and to and for such Uses, and the same Estates and Interests, and subject to such and the same Wills, Leases, Powers, Provisoes, Limitation, Remainders, Charges, Tenures, Rents, Services, Incumbrances, and Demands as the Lands, Interest, or Property of every such Proprietor … had been subject or liable in Case this Act had not been made... .[20]

But this is not what we mean by tenure. So, to make things clearer, we can and will discern seven distinct ways in which enclosure acts, and by presumption awards, addressed issues to do with tenure, that is tenure involving a distinction between freehold, leasehold, and manorial tenures, especially copyhold.

The first and simplest case where enclosure acts referred to tenure is where they inserted a clause stating that more or less whatever tenure subsisted on the property of a claimant just before enclosure would remain under that same tenure after enclosure. It might be almost as short and as bland a statement as that and may not necessarily elaborate further by requiring specific distinctions to be made between freehold, leasehold and copyhold. It should not imply that manorial tenures were present, and neither should it imply that they were not. Examples under this category comprise thirty-six of 302 private inclosure acts for Lincolnshire passed between 1740-1840. Three hundred and two is very nearly all of the Lincolnshire inclosure acts passed between those dates, so this is less a sample and more of an analysis of nearly the whole population of private inclosure acts for the county.[21] Just over half of those acts were passed before the General Inclosure Act of 1801.

The second discernible category of act referring to tenures did not overtly make the distinction between copyhold, leasehold and freehold nevertheless mentioned attributes that point directly to tenure other than pure freehold, tenures which we associate with manorial control of one sort or another. Most commonly these acts made provisions for customary freeholds where quit or other customary rents alone might have been the sole survival of the former more involved manorial control over the tenants. Some of these acts went so far as to offer those tenants the chance to shed the obligations they had to the manor once and for all by substituting a land transfer from their new allotments to the manor in proportion to the value of the quit rents, thereby finally securing their full freehold status. There are eighteen enclosure acts for Lincolnshire which explicitly offer this opportunity. At Huttoft in 1779 quit rents were to be substituted with a land settlement and at Freiston and Butterwick in 1808 allotments were to be set out in respect of customary quit rents, chief rents and fee farm rents. Other places had different and locally tailored provisions.[22]

The third recognisable category includes those acts specifically requesting that subsisting tenures should remain intact, but they usually did so in a longer script, usually a paragraph of twenty or more lines as against just five to ten lines in that first category. They essentially copied what I have already said but sometimes also made specific reference to the attributes of tenures or instructed that specific distinctions between tenures should be made. But they also often emphasised that the tenure follows the person and not the precise acres. So a former piece of freehold land that happens, in the allotting process, to be allotted to a copyholder became copyhold land and a former piece of copyhold land that happens to be allotted to a freeholder became freehold property. There are over forty acts which have one or other variations of this wording.

Fourthly there were acts which gave instructions that claims for property had to specify under which tenure the property was held, whether freehold, leasehold or copyhold. Moreover, those tenures would also be indicated in the enclosure award that ensued. To that extent the resulting award could act as an all-embracing township or parish title deed, at least for those parts of the township or parish that were parties to the enclosure. Twenty Lincolnshire enclosure acts fit this profile in one guise or another.[23]

Fifthly there were acts where something else was added, usually an exhortation, request, or instruction for the copyholder to be admitted afresh to his or her property at the next available court or within a specified period, often within six months. The inducement to the copyholder for doing so, if inducement we can call it, was to have the usual admission fines waived, though not it should be added the cost of parchment and the stewards' fees. However, it seems unclear why that would be an inducement to the copyholder because whoever inherited that property or to whomever the sitting tenants passed on or sold that property would have to pay the next admission fine in the usual way. The existing tenant would hardly see that as an inducement or obvious advantage. On the other hand, it would allow the lord, or more likely his or her steward, to make a single date inventory of the copyhold property associated with the manor. Another insertion in this kind of act was sometimes the instruction that future fines, rents and other customs were to remain at the levels subsisting before enclosure. The Wroot enclosure act of 1774 suggested that fines would be foregone on the first occasion after the enclosure and also that 'Quit rents, now or heretofore payable yearly by the Copyholders to the Lord of the said Manors, shall never hereafter be increased'.[24] The Frampton Enclosure Act of 1784 instructed that there would be no increase in fines for ten years for property held of the manor of Earl's Hall or Stone Hall and no increase for fourteen years for property of the manor of Multon Hall.[25] There are twelve Lincolnshire acts which carry variations of these instructions, regarding admissions or the future levels of fines and/or quit rents, most of them in or around the parishes of the Isle of Axholme. A notable exception was the enclosure act for Binbrook(e) Saints Gabriel and Mary in 1804 which allowed tenants to be readmitted within six months of the enclosure award without paying a fine but they would have to pay for parchment, stamp duty and a steward's fee.[26] A very interesting example, and the only one of its kind in the Lincolnshire collection of private enclosure acts is the act of 1830 for Deddithorpe otherwise Derrithorpe in Althorpe parish, the Isle of Axholme, and part of the royal manor of Epworth. It has a standard statement about maintaining tenures after enclosure as they had been before enclosure but it is a statement very much geared to copyhold tenure with a seriously implied threat. As such it is worth quoting reasonably fully. It invited tenants to be readmitted within six months of the completion of the enclosure or at the next available court: *without paying any Fine or other Charge, (save and except for the Stamp Duty and Parchment….and reasonable and accustomed Fees to the Steward)'* … But if people are not admitted and *'neglect or refuse to be admitted … within the Time herein-before appointed for that Purpose, then it shall and may be lawful for the Lord … to consider the Tenancy as vacant, and to take … Measures for compelling Admission to the said Copyhold Premises so allotted* … [as if a vacant tenancy caused by death]'. And if that happened the usual *'Fines, Fees, and other Payments shall be due'*. And for good measure the *'Commissioner shall by his said Award, and in and by the Map or Plan to be annexed thereto, ascertain, determine, describe, and abut the Premises which are to be and remain Copyhold'*.[27]

Sixthly, there were those instances where occasionally the acts added something much more interesting. We have in mind here the invitation to enfranchise a copyhold into freehold more or less at the same time as the enclosure, though with the appropriate compensations paid to the manorial lord. There are twenty-two enclosures in this survey which allowed enfranchisement to take place at the same time as enclosure. Apart from the specific place names and locations involved they are all quite distinctive though certain patterns can be discerned. It could be as simple as Bourn and its act of 1766 where copyholders were invited to consider enfranchisement at the same time, the payment for which would be effectively a transfer to the lord of two-thirteenths of their allotted land. These and other examples were not literally proportions based on size but rather in terms of the proportional value, in this case two-thirteenths of the value of the copyhold allotment.[28] The Morton Act of 1768 offered the same arrangement whereas the Quadring Act of 1775 was rather less generous to the copyholders requiring a transfer of one fifth of the land by value. Moreover, the tenants, at their expense, would also be required to fence the newly transferred property.[29] So this was a good deal for the lord, but less so for the tenants should they so agree to the arrangement. A deduction of one sixth became more or less the rule. In this context see the Long Sutton, otherwise Sutton in Holland Act, involving the manors of Sutton Holland, Sutton Guanock and Sutton Cranwell in 1788.[30] The same was more or less true at Gedney 1791, Langtoft 1801, and Coningsby in 1802.[31] More detail accompanied the Scotter Act of 1808 in which it was stated that the commissioners should hold a meeting at least one month before making any allotments at which all copyholders would be asked to declare in writing whether they agreed to enfranchise their copyholds at the same time.[32]

Finally, there was a seventh category, though in this case it represents those cases when tenure was either not mentioned at all or was mentioned in a sufficiently ambiguous or imprecise way as to defy the categorisations that have just been elaborated. Such cases represent 145 of 302 Lincolnshire enclosure acts which have been explored in this article. While this is the biggest category, nonetheless it does shed some light on the majority that did refer directly to tenure, a light that has shone very dimly in the scholarship of enclosure, not only in Lincolnshire, but elsewhere. In their otherwise extremely detailed explorations of Lincolnshire enclosures with their detailed maps and extracts of important data from the enclosure awards, the Russells made few references to those clauses/paragraphs in enclosure acts which address tenure. In the pamphlet on the enclosure of Holton le Clay (1763-66) Rex Russell tells us that 'After enclosure, copyhold tenants were to remain copyhold tenants under the same rents, fines and services as before enclosure', without any follow up or analytical comment. And in the compendium of enclosure landscapes covering the same place this part of the act is omitted altogether.[33] In this same volume interesting comment is made about the Scotter enclosure of 1808-20, briefly referred to in the paragraph above. The Russells observe that much land in Scotter was in copyhold held of the Dean and Chapter of Peterborough. Apparently all the tenants took up the offer in the act to consider enfranchising their property at the same time as enclosure, and they did so well ahead of the completion of the enclosure. The copyhold tenants became freeholders from 12 March 1812, the collective cost of which was a transfer of 425 acres to the Dean and Chapter.[34] In support of the Russells' approach to enclosure we must point out that their main concerns, a point emphasised in all four of their compendia books on enclosure, was landscape or rather landscape change, and so understandably other considerations were bound to take a back seat. Nevertheless, perhaps it was an opportunity missed.

The provisions, allowing enfranchisement and enclosure to occur through the same instrument, to my knowledge has never been fully articulated in scholarship, but necessarily nor has the extent to which it then actually took place. Having a permissive set of clauses in legislation is one thing, but to say it took place frequently or at all is another. It remains an intriguing issue. A partial test has been conducted for a selection of other counties of whether the invitations in enclosure acts were actually followed through in the ensuing awards.[35] The findings showed that copyhold tenures more or less slept through enclosure and the invitations to embrace enfranchisement from the manors were probably only partially taken up, if taken up at all. The real end of copyhold tenure did not come until parliament tackled it head on, and then only when they resorted to compulsory means, and even then it was not enthusiastically endorsed by lords everywhere. The dragging of feet by all actors in this field continued for eight decades until the 1920s, and even then the sound of foot dragging could still be heard. But references to property identified at enclosure both in words and on enclosure maps was often used in enfranchisement deeds as a way of locating property, sorting out ownership, and distinguishing the boundaries between different tenures, especially the freehold/copyhold boundary which otherwise had become blurred. Sometimes this was tackled at enclosure as seems to be the case at the enclosure of Thimbleby and Edlington where evidently there was a dispute between two major landowners over to which manor Edlington Common belonged.[36]

Enclosure was more or less the only way that new copyholds were created from the eighteenth century onwards. For example, when common rights were created at enclosure, that is rights attached to cottages or other property, the ensuing allotments to cover those rights necessarily were both new allotments but also registered as new copyholds. The Russells touched on this when they described the enclosure of East Keal (1773-4).[37] Alternatively, and depending on how well the commons were managed or policed, it could happen that if encroachments on a common went undetected then eventually the passage of time might legitimise such encroachments. F. M. L. Thompson touched on this when he described the encroachments that took place by common-right owners on Hampstead Heath. The 143 tenants of the manor in 1703 had grown to 300 by the early nineteenth century.[38] Amongst other things it meant that enclosure awards became an important reference point with stewards of manors when they constructed deeds and located property within deeds, especially in the subsequent enfranchisement documents. Lincoln was a county where this was used often in enfranchisement deeds, and without being over-precise about it, a casual trawl through enfranchisement records reveals at least thirty-four Lincolnshire manors in which more than one enfranchisement was located by reference to a prior enclosure award, and within those thirty-four manors over 350 enfranchisements and compensation deeds used enclosure awards to locate precisely the property in question. The top five Lincolnshire manors so to use enclosure awards for property location purposes were Bourn Abbots, Crowle, Epworth, Earls Hall in Frampton, and Long Bennington with Foston.[39] Tithe awards were also sometimes used and commonly towards the end of the nineteenth century and into the twentieth century successive editions of the Ordnance Survey were used, especially the 1910 edition.

Enclosure acts, therefore, offer a fuzzy cross section, in fact an extremely fuzzy cross section of the county at the moment when the largest single landscape change was about to take place. The summary finding is that copyhold tenure was extensive, certainly extensive enough to be visible, but that the cross section provided by enclosure was not only fuzzy, but most of it pre-dates the time when the real attack took place to convert copyhold and other manorial tenures into freehold. This attack began in earnest with extensive parliamentary debates in the 1830s, part of the more extensive reforms of organs of the State in that decade. This included franchise reform, poor law reform, local government and municipal reforms, the ending of slavery in the British Empire, the reform of church revenues including tithe commutation, and others.[40] The Cinderella reform that is overlooked to the extent that it more or less never figures in basic textbook literature was land tenure reform in the shape of the Enfranchisement Act of 1841.[41] It has also more or less evaded some of the classic or standard literature on Lincolnshire, except Joan Thirsk's work, but even in her case only briefly and very much obliquely. She has a table on the distribution of tenure across five fenland manors but based on the situation over two centuries earlier.[42] All those years later three of those manors still had very active turnovers of their copyhold tenants and eventually much enfranchisement and extinguishment of manorial incidents.

By the second half of the nineteenth century enfranchisement of copyhold must have become a highly visible revolution throughout eastern England. The ensuing deeds of transfer from the lords to the tenants as those tenants bought out their obligations to their manors were collected and rubber stamped centrally by a number of Whitehall Departments. Responsibility to oversee the process changed over time as the Copyhold Commission was subsumed by the Land Commission, then in turn by the Board of Agriculture, the Ministry of Agriculture and the Ministry of Agriculture and Fisheries. The ensuing transfer deeds are contained in three sets of records in the National Archives, MAF 9, MAF 13 and MAF 27. The first of these covers the period from the passing of the Enfranchisement Act of 1841 until the moment when copyhold as a tenure was abolished and land which otherwise was copyhold became freehold at the end of 1925. MAF 13 covers that period from 1 January 1926 until 31 December 1935 which allowed for those former copyholders who for one reason or another had not yet entered into negotiations with their lords so to negotiate and buy out their subsisting manorial incidents and complete that transfer. Finally, MAF 27 is the category which recognised that even ten years after the Law of Property Act was on the statute books, there remained some former copyhold properties that still had manorial incidents that were still active but needed extinguishment. As we have already observed, for various reasons this final extension had a final deadline of the end of October 1950, though allowing those negotiations that had begun before that deadline to proceed to completion. In England under MAF 9 there are 25,002 deeds of enfranchisement, under MAF 13 there are a further 1117 compensation agreements, and finally under MAF 27 another 458, giving a final total in the National Archives of 26,577 deeds of enfranchisement and compensation for England.

In pro rata terms if there was a perfectly even distribution of copyhold tenants across the face of England then a county the size of Lincolnshire, the second largest county in the kingdom, would be second in the list of copyhold enfranchisements. But when we look at a table of enfranchisements by county and when we look at how thickly or thinly they were spread over England we discover that far from being evenly spread the actual numbers for Lincolnshire are tiny in comparison even with a relatively small county.[43] For comparative purposes in this article, it is the counties of, broadly speaking, eastern England that illustrate how Lincolnshire is different. Most activity self-evidently took place in East Anglia and its neighbours south of the Wash and east of the extended line through the direction of the Trent. It is well known that tenure relationships in the western and south-western counties developed more towards leasehold tenure.[44] Yet we may ask whether a line through the Wash was such a dividing wall as to make Lincolnshire not proportionally represented in the national copyhold enfranchisement process.

The paucity in pure numbers and hence in consequence in terms of county density of activity in the centrally organised records now situated in the National Archives for this the second largest county in the Kingdom is surely suspicious. In fact, on closer inspection it is evident that the dividing line is more like the boundary between Lindsey and Holland/Kesteven. The county seems to divide at this boundary, but even then the actual numbers of enfranchisements are still very low for such a large county. Looked at another way, disproportionately to their sizes the other counties of eastern England from Cambridgeshire to tiny Huntingdonshire, and on to Essex and including Norfolk and Suffolk were counties awash with deeds. The answer to the puzzle is that there was more than one way to conduct enfranchisements. There is also a question as to whether lords and tenants could agree or not over enfranchisement. Why would a tenant for life, who may have invested a large sum of money in taking up the tenancy in the first place in terms of an entry fine (depending on the individual manorial conventions for entry fines), willingly pay another large sum of money to enfranchise that copyhold property when by staying as a tenant he or she simply had to pay mostly trivial payments in quit rents to the lord, once a year? Moreover, the bulk of copyhold property by the eighteenth and nineteenth centuries was copyhold of inheritance which allowed tenants to sell their property, or to mortgage it, make gifts of it, or bequeath it in wills to family members, charities or complete strangers. In terms of day to day living and in nearly everything but name, they were already more or less freeholders. They had an asset of some value while the lord was encumbered with a potential asset whose potentiality would only be realised if they could sell their stake in that asset (the manorial incidents), and use the resources in other ways. It was only when the law changed and enfranchisement became compulsory in 1858 if one or other party, lord or tenant, wished it to happen, that the move to enfranchise copyhold tenure accelerated.[45] For example, 30.7% of the enfranchisement deeds for England in MAF 9, covering the period 1841-1925 occurred in the first ten years after the passing of that 1858 act. The equivalent proportion for Lincolnshire enfranchisements was only 18.5%.[46] The 1860s were the busiest years in modern copyhold enfranchisement history, especially in eastern England, but this was not the case in Lincolnshire.

The enfranchisements held in the National Archives and administered directly through the instruments of law provided for them required specific language which holds a clue. They stated whether the lord and the tenant agreed or did not agree to proceed with enfranchisement. Many, though certainly not all, enfranchisements indicated disagreement. This could be disagreement of two sorts, disagreement over the terms offered by the lord (implying agreement over enfranchisement *per se*) or disagreement plain and simple. The usual reason for disagreements was over the lord retaining or not retaining certain rights, usually mineral rights. As often as not tenants tried to avoid the added expense of buying out those rights, though where that happened it may also have meant more extensive objections to enfranchisement. From a national sample of enfranchisements taken from MAF 9 involving 3800 enfranchisements, nearly 1800 clearly indicate whether or not there was agreement or disagreement over enfranchisement. The ratio of agreement to non-agreement is 1:2.69. As a national sample this necessarily includes Lincolnshire. When Lincolnshire is removed from the sample the revised national ratio drops to 1:2.48. Lincolnshire on its own is 1:4.7, for every agreement there were nearly five disagreements.

Evidently there was a lot of disagreement in the county. But there were ways round grievances and general objections, ways to smooth out the lord to tenant relationship over this issue. A case in point is the enfranchisement history of Crowland. At the time that most of the copyholds in the manor were enfranchised the lords were Henry Edwards Paine and Richard Brettell, partners in a legal firm located in Chertsey in Surrey. Their interest in manors stretched far and wide and were as representative as any of a new type of manorial lord, people climbing the social ladder from the world of commerce and business enterprise. Their manorial interests stretched from Yorkshire in the north to Hampshire and Sussex in the south, and from East Anglia across to Oxfordshire. Crowland was the most important manor they acquired. They purchased it following an auction in London on the 30 October 1885. The manor was advertised as 2185 acres of good productive arable and grass and about 400 houses. The combined estimated rental value was £6500 per annum. There were over 170 tenants on the court roll and average entry fine income from 1870-85 was £450 p.a..[47] Crowland was formerly the seat of Lord Normanton. Before the auction the proposed sale was described as a 'great inconvenience' to the copyholders, whatever that means. Evidently Normanton was a good lord establishing a stable relationship with his tenants, a relationship which was about to be disrupted. But why was the sale felt necessary?[48] On its announcement it caused 'considerable anxiety' to the local copyholders who 'feared that the manor may fall into the hands of a speculator who would speedily press for compulsory enfranchisement'.[49] This became a profoundly prescient comment: it was more or less what happened. The *Grantham Journal* questioned why now (October 1885) was the chosen time for selling the manor and putting the copyholders to so 'great a trouble just when they were least able to bear it'. Lord Normanton reportedly no longer felt secure in his ownership because of speculation that future governments might consider more generally the confiscation of property.[50] The background to this was a general, widespread and persistent depression in agriculture, severe enough for the government to conduct a Royal Commission. It eventually reported in the mid-1890s but reflected on the state of the industry in the 1880s. Add to this economic background the rumours and speculation that some kind of property grab or nationalisation was possible, inflamed by the writings of the American economist and social activist Henry George.[51] More to the point, in Lincolnshire generally, as in much of eastern England, there was a real agricultural depression.[52]

The advertisement for the manor sale played up the attractiveness of the property and the harmonious local relationships with the tenantry. It commented on the comfort of those tenants in their cottages, observing that there was a spacious and productive piece of land (a garden) attached to each cottage. The bidding went from £8000, then by increments of £100, stopping at £12,100. The seller wanted more and so the property was 'bought in', or effectively withdrawn from sale. Subsequently a 'gentleman' who attended the auction, privately offered £13,050, and that became the selling price.[53] Whether the 'gentleman' in question was Paine or Brettell, or their representative is not clear, but the fears that the tenantry felt about the change of lord were about to be realised.

A manorial court was held in May 1886. A document attached to the surviving Crowland enfranchisement papers (Fig. 2) commented that 'the worst fears of the public had been realised to the extent that the owners of the manor were determined on enfranchisement'.[54] The tenants faced the option of paying a large lump sum to buy out the manorial incidents or settle for an annual rent charge, redeemable further down the line at twenty-five years purchase. Those who 'recently [may have] paid heavy admission fees and fines' to enter the property in the first place way have felt particularly aggrieved, even though this was standard practice and properly developed by a succession of copyhold enfranchisement acts. Nonetheless, when enfranchisement arrived one day in an otherwise undisturbed and insular community of tenants, it must have been something of a shock. The new lords convened manor courts in May and November 1886 with a new steward in the chair, a man from Essex. To residents it must have felt like their stable traditional world had been turned upside down, and in this case by a group of complete strangers from several counties distant. The steward received surrenders, granted admissions, and arranged enfranchisements in the normal way, but it was a meeting that took four days.[55] Evidently, the main purpose of the court and the reason for its long duration, was to issue notifications of enfranchisement.[56] The steward had been doing this anyway shortly after the manor had changed hands.

At the next court in November 1886 it was reported that about three quarters of the copyholders had already voluntarily agreed to enfranchisement, but it was also suggested that the lords and steward had made this 'tax' on the peasantry 'as light as possible' by generous financial arrangements, observing that three quarters of the enfranchisements were made

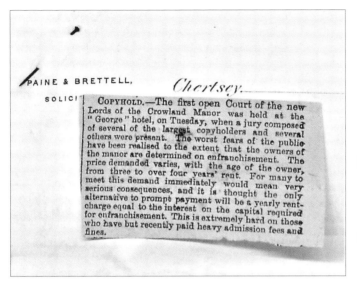

PAINE & BRETTELL,
SOLICIT

Chertsey

COPYHOLD.—The first open Court of the new Lords of the Crowland Manor was held at the "George" hotel, on Tuesday, when a jury composed of several of the largest copyholders and several others were present. The worst fears of the public have been realised to the extent that the owners of the manor are determined on enfranchisement. The price demanded varies, with the age of the owner, from three to over four years' rent. For many to meet this demand immediately would mean very serious consequences, and it is thought the only alternative to prompt payment will be a yearly rent-charge equal to the interest on the capital required for enfranchisement. This is extremely hard on those who have but recently paid heavy admission fees and fines.

Fig.2
Newspaper report of the Crowland Manor Court meeting of 1886 (Peterborough Standard 8 May 1886, p.7, c.6) found with loose leaf enfranchisement deeds of 1885–1886 (LAO, CROWLAND MANOR 5. Reproduced with permission)

and completed under voluntary arrangements.[57] In consequence only a small proportion of the subsequent Crowland enfranchisements involved the London-based administering bodies, the Land Commission which had subsumed the Copyhold Commission in 1883, and the Board of Agriculture which subsumed the Land Commission by 1889. Only twenty-three Crowland enfranchisements passed through the hands of those bodies. They involved a rent charge or *Certificate of Charge*, which was effectively a loan at four per cent until such day that the former tenants could pay off their debt. As a conveyance those deeds required endorsement by the Land Commission. They had to be rubber-stamped centrally and consequently became part of the MAF 9 collection. Otherwise, there is every reason to suppose that they may never have appeared in the central records. The tenants could treat the four per cent loan like a rent.[58]

The remaining enfranchisements were conducted without direct recourse to the London-based Commissions, and there were a lot of them for this extensive manor. They suggest that the new lords tried hard to relieve the financial pressures facing the tenants, but still treated the process in business terms. Eighteen of those tenants were charged a nominal sum because they had enjoyed 'peaceable quiet and uninterrupted possession … for upwards of twelve years', and in one case for twenty years. For another seventeen tenants the lords allowed payment by instalments, a not uncommon arrangement. Those instalments varied between two and six payments.[59] The lords waived the charge for the poor allotment.[60] There followed a further 252 enfranchisements, first under the lordship of Paine with Brettell, and then involving Paine alone when Brettell died. The very last enfranchisement was completed by Paine's trustees after he died. But while offering good terms to some tenants, the lords nonetheless treated the whole process very much on business terms, and very much in a way to recoup their initial outlay on the purchase of the manor. In the first year of their lordship Paine and Brettell completed 178 enfranchisements. Another forty-one followed by the end of the decade. It was a front-loaded exercise with 87% completed within four years. It looked like a snatch and grab, but unlike other lords, Paine and Brettell retained the lordship, continued to admit new tenants and receive annual quit rents as the size of their manor shrank. Mind you, in about half of those late cases the eventual enfranchisements took place within a year of the new tenants having entered. The advantage to the lords of such haste was that they received two payments; the initial entry fine, followed quickly by the notice to enfranchise. Crowland may not have been typical but it is one example of Dennis Mills's *Lords and Peasants* in action.

What this one example illustrates is that an overwhelming proportion of the Crowland enfranchisements never reached the London-centred registration agencies – and the same can be said for Lincolnshire manorial enfranchisements in general. This means that contrary to the otherwise major national register of enfranchisement deeds, for some counties the best source of investigation will be in the local rather than the national repositories. Crowland is a perfect example of this. So, however amicable or not the relationship between lord and tenant nonetheless that relationship is sometimes best uncovered by local investigations. This task of investigation has been made easier by the completion in June 2022 by the Manorial Documents Register (hereafter the MDR) of its online index or register. The register is centrally administered by TNA, but the listed manorial records are mostly not in the National Archives but overwhelmingly for most manors in local archives. The last two counties to be included on the register include Lincolnshire.[61] The completion now allows a modest statistical comparison of survivability to be made across counties. The premise is that survivability is indicative of the persistence of manorial tenure.

The 1841 Enfranchisement Act allowed manorial courts no longer to sit. Business could be conducted out of court. Fortunately, many courts decided to continue with the age-old traditions and so after this date court books remain full of familiar business, of the surrenders of tenants and the admissions of new ones, the register of mortgages of manorial property where necessary, the appointments of officers, and the transcriptions of the required deeds of surrender, admission and enfranchisement in a standard format. The court book or court roll remained the legal register of such business. And even the 1922 Law of Property Act which abolished copyhold tenure required that such deeds had to be recorded even after that act became law on 1 January 1926. Copyhold tenure may have been abolished, and all otherwise not yet enfranchised copyhold property had become freehold on 1 January 1926, but if tenants and lords had still not entered into enfranchisement arrangements nonetheless they still had to do so, but using different instruments known as *compensation agreements* for the *extinguishment of manorial incidents*. Manorial court books therefore continued the task of registering these transactions until such time as such registration was no longer required, and as we know, that moment was in October 1950. The end of manorial tenure therefore was not 1922, neither was it 1925, but really it was 1950. And even then manorial court books, technically, were still needed to register those last compensation transactions, and also to record subsequent transactions associated with outstanding mortgages, certificates of charge, and other legal instruments.

Careful use of the MDR will allow us to see just to what extent the Lincolnshire manors, in the context of manors in other counties, continued to operate.[62] In doing so we can point to two conclusions: firstly, the MAF records as a register of the end of manorial tenure is only part of the story, and in the case of Lincolnshire very much the junior partner in the story, as it is also in many other counties; and secondly, as a proportion of manors that survived with traditional tenure relationships between lord and tenant well into the twentieth century, Lincolnshire is about midway in a county hierarchy for such survival.

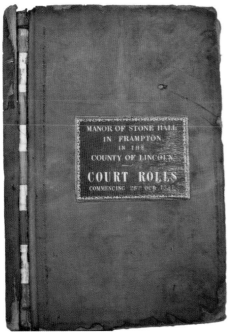

Fig.3
Front cover of the Court Roll of the Manor
of Stone Hall in Frampton, 1887–1902
(LAO, BRA 235/1/2/D5. Reproduced with
permission)

To demonstrate this, a simple sorting system to interrogate the MDR register based on a few rules has been developed. The MDR itself gives a list of forty-two search terms of which the two appropriate to this study are *court books* and *court rolls*. And since the message from this article is survivability of the manor as a landlord the search has been confined to a period beginning with the lead-up to the first enfranchisement act of 1841, and ending after 1950 when the final abolition of manorial incidents in turn came into force. The chronology of investigation, therefore, extends back to 1820 to allow for overlap with the period of enclosure enactments and their immediate aftermath, and forward to 2000 to see what evidence remained of as yet unfinished business between lords and their former tenants. I should add that in some parts of the country, for the period in question, the term 'court roll' was used even to describe what in actual fact was a large tome or book of several hundred pages. (see Fig. 3) In the relatively recent past under investigation it rarely meant an actual roll of parchment and when it did it was usually a flat or folded sheet of paper or parchment and rarely for a run of years sufficient for this survey. Which brings us to another rule of investigation, only those books or rolls with a continuous run of at least ten years is included in this survey.

With these rules in place there are scattered through the archives of this country nearly 4900 manors with court books and rolls covering the period from *c.* 1820 to c.2000. That is not to say that there are *c.* 4900 actual documents. There are many more than this. For example, Epworth manor can boast twenty-nine books covering the period 1841-1933 and Crowland seven books for 1841 to 1897 and enough other material to take the story of manorial business to the 1930s. It is not unusual for Lincolnshire manors to have four, five, six or more court books for the period in question even if many of these huge tomes are called rolls.[63] In numerical terms, the East Anglian counties have the largest survival rates with Norfolk heading the field on 679 manors represented, followed by the other East Anglian counties of Suffolk (438) and Essex (430). The two south coast counties of Sussex (336) and Kent (205) come next before two other eastern England counties Hertfordshire (199) and Cambridgeshire (169) follow. This emphasis on the east of England counties does not come as a surprise given the literature on manorial and tenure history of the early modern period which has been recited over many years.[64] In this exercise Yorkshire is counted as three counties with three main record collecting 'agencies'. It is only when Yorkshire is reconstituted as a single entity that there are enough surviving manors with court books to put the county in the top ten.[65] Lincolnshire as one county (ignoring its three divisions) has but eighty-one manors within the chronology under study with surviving court books obeying the sorting conventions adopted, placing it in twenty-first place in a list of forty-one counties. But Lincolnshire and Yorkshire are huge counties and so in terms of density of survival, which may or may not be correctly taken as a proxy for the survival of manors and their business in general, Lincolnshire is in the bottom four in terms of the density of survival, whether per total area or per total number of parishes.

Perhaps Dennis Mills's peasants, I have called them yeomen, did disappear fairly rapidly after enclosure. But we can paint some variation in this picture. Many more of them when they did eventually succumb to the wishes of their lords to redeem their manorial incidents and claim their freeholder status did so without direct recourse to the London agencies set up to administer and monitor the process. For those overseen directly by these agencies or commissions there are 453 Lincolnshire enfranchisements in MAF 9 and eighty-eight compensation agreements in MAF 13 and 27. The average size of these properties taken together was sixteen acres (17.7 acres before 1926 and 7.5 acres after 1925). But not all copyhold or former copyhold owners were owners of land alone. Most were in receipt of land and associated building, and many only owned buildings, especially cottages. Therefore, a different way to look at average size is to consider only those owners in receipt of land alone or land with buildings attached. When we do this with the MAF samples the average sizes rise modestly to 18.4 acres (19.3 acres before 1926 and 12.0 acres after 1925). But the survival of court books and associated unfinished manorial business indicated by the survival, especially late survival of court books indicates that the MAF collections were not the only route to enfranchisement. From just a sample, admittedly probably a large sample of surviving court books, and in this particular sample all available in Lincolnshire Archives Office, there are enfranchisements and compensation agreements which were negotiated privately. At the latest count I have extracted details from 1534 enfranchisements and 1420 compensations. The average size of property from them is 7.7 acres for enfranchisements and 9.7 acres for compensation agreements. When adjusted to include only those examples with land or land with buildings, those average sizes increase to 9.7 and 12.5 acres respectively. These are sizes too small to act as family farms alone and indicate either that other property was rented or owned (as freeholds for example), or the copyhold and former copyhold was rented to others. Moreover, Lincolnshire we are told was a county where small-scale farming was a feature, 'Smallholdings numerically were in the majority, 74 per cent of the county's holdings being 50 acres or less in 1870'.[66] And in specific areas, the Fens and the Isle of Axholme for example, the average size was smaller still.[67]

Here then is the Lincolnshire peasant or yeoman, not quite big enough for most of them to be wholly independent, perhaps not valuable enough (using acreage size as a proxy for value) for lords to chase too hard in the late nineteenth and early twentieth centuries, in contrast to those tenants who were twice as large and therefore more or less twice as valuable when it came to financial return to the lord, and therefore worth pursuing earlier rather than later in the process, as demonstrated in the MAF 9 examples. By accident the example that may 'prove' this rule allows our very last identified Lincolnshire yeoman still standing by 1953, Mr Asplin, to have the last word. He was huge by comparison, but only thirty-five acres in reality.

NOTES

1.   The research for specifically county Lincoln material buried in this chapter was carried out at The National Archives (hereafter TNA) mainly in the Ministry of Agricultural and Fisheries

records all of which bear the shorthand MAF, Lincolnshire Archives Office (hereafter LAO), and in the Borthwick Institute at the University of York. My thanks to personnel at all of these archives for their help and guidance.

2. *Law of Property Act,1922,* (or Act to assimilate and amend the law of Real and Personal Estate, to abolish copyhold and other special tenures), 12 & 13 Geo V, c. XVI; *Law of Property Act (Postponement),* 1924, 15 Geo V, c. IV; *Law of Property (Amendment) Act,* 1924, 15 Geo 5, c. V; Postponement of Enactments (Miscellaneous Provisions) Act, 1939, 3 & 4 Geo VI, c. II; *Manorial Incidents Extinguishment Order,* Statutory Instruments, 1949, no. 836.

3. TNA, *Extinguishment of Manorial Incidents Series II* (1936-1957), MAF 27/4/59, Wymondham of the Queen (Norfolk), Representatives of Henry Percy Standley (deceased), 20 June 1957.

4. Many lords think they still own mineral rights on former copyhold property, and indeed many of them do, but by no means all of them. The *Land Registration Act,* 2002, Eliz II, c. IX, allowed those lords who thought they still owned certain rights to register them by 12 October 2013.

5. Mills, D. R., 1980, *Lord and Peasant in Nineteenth-Century Britain,* pp. 43-63. On the terminology see Beckett, J. V., 1984, 'The peasant in England: a case of terminological confusion?', *Agricultural History Review,* 32.2, pp. 113–23. See also Hoyle, R.W. 2016, 'Introduction: recovering the farmer', in Hoyle, R.W. (ed.), *The Farmer in England, 1650-1950.* pp. 1-42.

6. Mills, D. R., 1990, 'Peasants and conflict in nineteenth-century rural England: a comment on two recent articles', in Reed, Mick and Wells, Roger (eds), *Class, Conflict and Protest in the English Countryside, 1700-1880.* chapter 8, pp. 115-120.

7. She was a tenant of Lords Hold Manor in Hackney in east London and when in 1849 her legal representatives bargained with William and Daniel Tyssen, the lords of the manor, to enfranchise her copyhold property (the language that was used), that is to buy out the lord's interest in her tenancy (mainly compensation for the lords' loss of future admission charges and future annual quit rents), she is entered on the deed of enfranchisement as a tenant. TNA, *Middlesex Enfranchisement Deeds and Awards,* MAF 9/173/29, Enfranchisement, Manor of Hackney (The Lords Hold Manor), re The Queens Most Excellent Majesty, 16 October 1849.

8. These five last remnants in TNA, MAF 27/3, 66, 67, 72, 73 and 74.

9. Elsewhere, and based only on a casual trawl through the recently completed Manorial Documents Register (hereafter MDA) to which register Lincolnshire was one of the last two counties to be entered (in June 2022), there were at least 112 active court books from 1949 onwards, of which 11 still seemed to record business after 1960 with the last listed of Balneath Manor in Sussex with a court book for the period 1876-1995, East Sussex and Brighton and Hove Record Office, ACC 7633/1. This is notwithstanding Laxton and over thirty other places recognised as still having active courts through the *Administration of Justice Act,* 1977, Eliz II, c. 38, Part II, Section 23, pp. 13-14 and Schedule 4, part III, pp. 31-3.

10. Turner, M. E., 2009, 'The demise of the yeoman *c.* 1750-1940', in John Broad (ed.), *A Common Agricultural Inheritance,* (Reading), pp. 83-103; Turner, M. E., 2020, 'In search of the Nottinghamshire yeoman', in Gaunt, Richard A. (ed.), *Church Land and People: Essays presented to John Beckett,* The Thoroton Society Record Series, 50, Nottingham. pp. 229-46; Turner, M. E., 2000, 'Corporate strategy or individual priority? Land management, income and tenure on Oxbridge agricultural land in the mid-nineteenth century', *Business History,* 42.4, pp. 1-26.

11. Turner, M. E., 2020, 'In search of the Nottinghamshire yeoman'. pp. 229-46.

12. Turner, M. E., 2000, 'Corporate strategy or individual priority? ...pp. 1-26.

13. But I also more closely worked with him nearly 40 years ago when we edited a book of essays together on a shared interest, Turner, M. E. and Mills, D. R. (eds), 1986, *Land and Property: The English Land Tax 1692-1832,* Gloucester.

14. Stone, Thomas, 1794, *General View of the Agriculture of the County of Lincoln,* p. 95; Young,

Arthur, 1813, *General View of the Agriculture of Lincolnshire*, pp. 23-4, where he also talked about leaseholds of one description or another.

15.   Chambers, J. D. and Mingay, G. E., 1966, *The Agricultural Revolution, 1750-1880*, especially pp. 88-104; Hammond, J. L. and Hammond, B., 1927 (4th ed.), *The Village Labourer 1760-1832*; Saville, J., 1969, 'Primitive accumulation and early industrialisation in Britain', *The Socialist Register*, 6, pp. 247-71; Brenner, R., 1976, 'Agrarian class structure and economic development in pre-industrial Europe', *Past and Present*, 70, pp. 30-75; Aston, T. H. and Philpin, C. H. E., (eds), 1985, *The Brenner Debate: agrarian class structure and economic development in pre-industrial Europe* (Cambridge). See also Mingay, G. E., 1968, *Enclosure and the small farmer in the age of the Industrial Revolution*, London and Basingstoke.

16.   Adopting Neeson's language in Neeson, J. M., 1993, *Commoners: Common Right, Enclosure and Social Change in England, 1700-1820*, Cambridge. p. 30.

17.   See the study based on the three south midlands counties of Oxfordshire, Northamptonshire and Buckinghamshire, and also the East Riding of Yorkshire in Turner, 'The demise', especially pp. 89-91.

18.   *An act for consolidating in one act, certain provisions usually inserted in acts of inclosure*, 1801, 41 Geo III, c. 109, para VI.

19.   *An act for dividing, allotting, and inclosing … Caistor*, 1796, 36 Geo III, p. 24 is a case in point with care taken to exclude those leases involving fines. In other words, this was a provision specifically related to rack rent tenancy.

20.   *An act for dividing, allotting, and inclosing … North Stoke and South Stoke, otherwise Stoke Rochford*, 1796, 36 Geo III, c. 101, p. 24.

21.   The true number is 313 including acts passed before 1740 and some public acts which have been omitted. See the Lincolnshire chronology of enclosure acts in a national (English) context in Turner, M. E., 1980, *English Parliamentary Enclosure*, Folkestone. Appendix 1, p. 176.

22.   *An act for dividing, inclosing, and improving … Huttoft*, 19 Geo III (1779), p. 11; *An act for embanking the salt marshes … in Freiston and Butterwick … and for inclosing the same*, 1808, 48 Geo III, p. 27.

23.   For example see *An act for dividing, allotting, and Inclosing … Barrow*, 37 Geo III (1797), c. 57, pp. 10, 43; *An act for inclosing lands … Carlby*, 1804, 44 Geo III, c. 40, pp. 17-19.

24.   *An act for dividing and inclosing … Wroot*, 1774, 14 Geo III, c. 55, pp. 18-19.

25.   *An act for dividing and inclosing … Frampton*, 1784, 24 Geo III, c. 26, pp. 33-34.

26.   *An act for inclosing lands in Binbrooke St Gabriel and Binbrooke St Mary, 1804*, 44 Geo III, c. 44, pp. 15-16.

27.   *An act for dividing, allotting, and inclosing…Deddithorpe, otherwise Derrithorpe, in … Althorpe in the Isle of Axholme, 1830*, 11 Geo IV, c.11, para XXXVII.

28.   *An act for allotting, dividing, inclosing and draining … in Bourn*, 6 Geo III (1766), c. 52, pp. 7-8; and amending act of 1772, *An act for dividing, inclosing, and draining … the Cow Pasture … [and for amending the act of 1766] … in Bourn*, 1772, 12 Geo III, c. 62, pp. 5-8.

29.   *An act for dividing and inclosing … Morton*, 8 Geo III (1768), c. 41, p. 8; *An act for dividing and inclosing … Quadring*, 1775, 15 Geo III, c. 70, pp. 29-31.

30.   *An act for dividing and inclosing … Long Sutton otherwise Sutton in Holland*, 1778, 28 Geo III, c. 54, pp. 16-18.

31.   *An act for dividing and inclosing … Gedney*, 1791, 31 Geo III, c. 49, pp. 15-18; *An act for dividing, allotting, and inclosing … Langtoft and Baston*, 1801, 41 Geo III, c. 78, p. 22; *An act for dividing, allotting, and inclosing … Coningsby otherwise Conesby*, 1802, 42 Geo III, c. 119, para XXXI.

32.   *An act for inclosing lands … Scotter*, 1808, 1808, 48 Geo III, c. lxxxi, para XXXV.

33.   Russell, Rex C., 1972, *The Enclosures of Holton-Le-Clay1763-1766, Waltham 1769-1771, and*

Tetney 1774-1779 (WEA, Waltham Branch), p. 8; Russell, Eleanor & Rex, 1987, *Parliamentary Enclosure and New Lincolnshire Landscapes* (Lincolnshire County Council: Lincolnshire History Series No.10), pp. 93-97.

34.   Russells, *New Lincolnshire Landscapes*, p. 168.

35.   An exercise first presented as Turner, M. E., 1998, 'Enclosure re-opened', *ReFRESH*, 26, p. 3; also Turner, M. E. and Beckett, J.V., 1998, 'The lingering survival of ancient tenures in English agriculture in the nineteenth century', in F. Galassi, F., Kauffman, K. and Liebowitz, J.(eds.), 1998, *Land, Labour and Tenure: The Institutional Arrangements of Conflict and Co-operation in Comparative Perspective* (Proceedings B2, XIIth International Economic History Congress, Madrid), pp. 110-11.

36.   Identified by Russell, Eleanor and Rex, 1985, *Old and New Landscapes in the Horncastle Area* (Lincolnshire County Council, Lincolnshire History Series, no.7), pp. 22-3, quoting *An Act for dividing and inclosing ... Thimbleby and Edlington*, 1778, 18 Geo III, c. 43, p. 11

37.   Russells, *Old and New Landscapes Horncastle*, p. 42.

38.   Thompson, F. M .L, 1974, *Hampstead: Building a Borough, 1650-1964*, pp. 15, 132-150, 300-1.

39.   The top five Lincolnshire manors so to use enclosure awards for property location purposes were Bourn Abbots, Crowle, Epworth, Earls Hall in Frampton, and Long Bennington with Foston: LAO, Bourn Manorial 12-14, Bourn Abbots Court Books, 1884-1937; Crowle Manor Compensations CM 12/3/18 and Crowle Manor Papers, CM11/1-3, Draft Enfranchisements, 1859-1925; 2 TGH 4/B/41, Epworth Court Book, 1922-1925; JEBB 1/13 & 14 Earls Hall in Frampton, Court Books, 1856-1926; LARCO/1/2/1/14-15, Long Bennington and Foston-with-Members Court Books, 1891-1931. Including some in TNA MAF 9 and MAF 27.

40.   As in, *An Act to amend the Representation of the People in England and Wales*, 1832, 2 & 3 Wm IV, c. XLV; *An Act for the Amendment and better Administration of the Laws relating to the Poor in England and Wales*, 1834, 4 & 5 Wm IV, c. LXXVI; *An Act to provide for the Regulation of Municipal Corporations in England and Wales (or the Municipal Corporations Act)*, 1835, 5 & 6 Wm. IV., c. LXXVI; *An Act for the Abolition of Slavery throughout the British Colonies*, 1833, 3 & 4 Wm IV, c. LXXIII; *Tithe Commutation Act*, 1836, 3 & 4 Wm IV, c. LXXXIII.

41.   With the rather obscure title that is never used, *Act for the Commutation of certain Manorial Rights in respect of Lands of Copyhold and Customary Tenure, and in respect of other Lands subject to such Rights, and for facilitating the Enfranchisement of such Lands, and for the Improvement of such Tenure*, 1841, 4 & 5 Victoria, c. XXXV but instead is known as or referred to as *The Enfranchisement Act, 1841*.

42.   Thirsk, Joan, 1957, *English Peasant Farming: the Agrarian History of Lincolnshire from Tudor to Recent Times*, London: Routledge and Kegan Paul. p. 43.

43.   For a map showing the English position, a map that measures the number of enfranchisements and extinguishments in the MAF series of records see, Turner, M. E., 2000.

44.   For which we may look no further than the contributions by Christopher Clay, as in Clay, C., 1980, '"The greed of Whig Bishops"? Church landlords and their lessees, 1660–1760', *Past and Present*, 87, pp. 128–57; Clay, C., 1985, 'Landlords and estate management in England', in Thirsk, Joan (ed.), *The Cambridge Agrarian History of England and Wales, Vii (1640-1750), Agrarian Change* (Cambridge), pp. 189-230; Clay, C., 1981, 'Lifeleasehold in the western counties of England, 1650–1750', 29.2, pp. 83–96.

45.   *Act to amend the Copyhold Acts*, 1858, 21 & 22 Victoria, c. XCIV.

46.   Based on the collection of deeds in TNA in MAF 9 and isolating the period 1859-69 inclusive.

47.   *Lincolnshire Chronicle*, 1885, 'Sales by Auction: Manor of Crowland', 6 October, p. 4.

48.   *Stamford Mercury*, 1885, 'Stamford Division: re Sale Crowland Manor', 23 October, p. 6.

49.   *Stamford Mercury*, 1885, 'Crowland: Manorial Rights', 9 October, p. 4.

50. *Grantham Journal*, 1885, 'Spalding: Sale Crowland Manor', 24 October, p. 8.

51. For example, George, Henry, 1879, *Progress and Poverty* (New York); Taylor, Anthony, 2010, 'Richard Cobden, J.E. Thorold Rogers and Henry George', in Cragoe, Matthew and Readman, Paul (eds), *The Land Question in Britain, 1750-1950*, London and Basingstoke. esp., pp. 158-61.

52. On the 1880s agricultural depression see, *Royal Commission on Agriculture*, 'First Report of Her Majesty's Commissioners Appointed to Inquire into the Subject of Agricultural Depression: Minutes of Evidence with Appendices', BPP, 1894, C. 7400, XVI, Parts I-III; 'Second Report', BPP, 1896, C. 7981, XVI, 'Minutes of Evidence', BPP, 1896, C. 8021, XVII (1896); 'Final Report', BPP, 1897, C. 8540, XV, 'Appendix', C. 8541, XV. See also Perry, P. J., 1974, *British Farming in the Great Depression, 1870-1914*, Newton Abbot; Thompson, F. M. L., 1991, `An Anatomy of English Agriculture, 1870-1914', in Holderness, B. A. and Turner, M. E., (eds), *Land, Labour and Agriculture, 1700-1920*, pp. 211-40.

53. *Stamford Mercury*, 1885, 'Crowland: Value of Land in Lincolnshire', 6 November, p. 4.

54. Printed commentary headed 'COPYHOLD' in LAO, Crowland/5, *Enfranchisement Agreements 1885-1888*.

55. From hundreds of court books inspected over a large area of mainly eastern and northern England, most business was usually completed in one, or at most two days.

56. *Stamford Mercury*, 1886, 'Crowland: Manor Sale', 14 May, p. 4.

57. And 'tax' was the word used, *Lincolnshire, Rutland and Stamford Mercury*, 1886, 'Crowland: General Court', 19 November, p. 4.

58. TNA, MAF 9/155/52-74, *Enfranchisement Deeds* re Crowland Manor, Lincolnshire. Only one of those enfranchisements took place under Lord Normanton (in 1876). Two enfranchisements were not settled until 1906 and 1913. Paine was still the Lord but Brettell had since died.

59. Also the case on another Paine and Brettell manor at Whaplode, LAO, Whaplode Abbatis /14 *Enfranchisement Agreements, bundle 1885-88*.

60. LAO, Crowland Manor/8, *Enfranchisement Agreements, 1886-1921* and Crowland manor/5 & 6, *Enfranchisement Agreements, 1886-89*, deeds in bundles, and Crowland Manor/11, Ct Bk, 1870-1880, for cross checking admission dates.

61. All appeared in June 2022 and can be investigated on the TNA website on: Manorial Documents Register - Archives sector (nationalarchives.gov.uk)

62. Lincolnshire was one of the last three English counties (along with Cornwall and Durham) to be entered on the register, and then as recently as June 2022.

63. Lincolnshire Archive Office, *Epworth Manor Court Books, 2 TGH 4/B/16-44, 1841-1933; Crowland Manor Court Books, Enfranchisements and Assorted Papers, 1841-1929, CROWLAND MANOR /5-9, and 2-CROWLAND MANOR/6-12*. A word of warning however, the MDR is a wonderful resource but it does not always pick up all of the material that is available.

64. See the references to Clay's work cited earlier.

65. 275 manor court books formed respectively from the three Ridings of East Yorkshire (76), North Yorkshire (94) and West Yorkshire (105).

66. Brown, Jonathan, 2005, *Farming in Lincolnshire 1850-1945*, Studies in the History of Lincolnshire 2. pp. 58-9.

67. Generally described in *ibid.*, pp. 58-66.

'WIZARDS OF THE SOIL': CONSTRUCTING AND CHALLENGING THE INSTITUTIONAL RHETORIC OF AN ASYLUM FARM, LINCOLNSHIRE COUNTY ASYLUM, 1852-1902[1]

Sarah Holland

Lincolnshire County Pauper Asylum opened in 1852, a response to the 1845 County Asylums Act. Thirty acres were set aside for the farm upon which patients worked. Patient work was a central tenet in the move from mechanical restraint to moral and occupational therapy from the late eighteenth century through the nineteenth century. Individually and collectively, asylums and mental hospitals constructed elaborate narratives and rhetoric pertaining to the curative and remunerative value of their farms. However, these narratives were often challenged by the experiences of patients working on the land. Using annual reports and case notes, this article explores the construction of an institutional rhetoric about the asylum farm and the conscious or unconscious challenges posed by the experiences of patients thereon. By examining the use of farm work at the Lincolnshire County Asylum, an institution which had a high proportion of patients from agricultural and rural backgrounds, and the connections between the institutional rhetoric and the experiences of patients both within and outside of the asylum, this article adds a further dimension to our understanding of rural life and health in the county of Lincolnshire.

From 1845, under the County Asylums Act, all counties had to make provision for 'pauper lunatics' which gave rise to the building of new county asylums across England. Many of these asylums had farms, and the use of patient labour thereon was a central tenet in the move from mechanical restraint to moral and occupational therapy from the late eighteenth century through the nineteenth century.[2] Therapy, self-sufficiency and profit were often not perceived by asylums or mental hospitals as mutually exclusive objectives, but rather as complementary partners integral to institutional success.[3] Individually and collectively, these institutions constructed elaborate narratives and rhetoric pertaining to their curative and remunerative value. However, these narratives were often challenged by the experiences of patients working on the land. Although accounts of patient labour were generally narrated by medical superintendents and thus mediated through an institutional lens, the actions and reactions of patients to work were recorded in case notes. These provide valuable insights into how individuals navigated and experienced institutional spaces. Non-linear narratives and indifference to work, coupled with complex interconnections with occupational identities and rural society, come to the fore. The tensions and competing narratives are particularly apparent through a close analysis and comparison of the extent to which the farm or farm labour was foregrounded in annual reports and case notes. This article focuses on the Lincolnshire County Pauper Asylum between 1852 and 1902 as a lens through which to explore the construction of an institutional rhetoric about the asylum farm and the conscious or unconscious challenges posed by the experiences of patients thereon.

Fig.1 Lincolnshire County Pauper Asylum opened in 1852 at Bracebridge Heath, two miles south of Lincoln. It remained a mental health facility (later known as St John's Hospital) until its closure in 1989. The buildings are now used as private apartments. (A.Walker)

Lincolnshire County Pauper Asylum opened in 1852, a response to the 1845 legislation.[4] The institution was located at Bracebridge, two miles south of Lincoln. (Fig. 1) It was described in a local directory as occupying an 'elevated and healthy' site, with forty-five acres of land and accommodation for 250 patients. Thirty acres were set aside for the farm, which was 'partly cultivated by spade husbandry' to give 'healthy employment to many of the patients'.[5] Moreover, 'a considerable quantity of ground-work' was 'intentionally left as a means of occupation for the male patients on their arrival'.[6] This emphasis on manual work for patients not only represented a wider movement from mechanical restraint to moral therapy but also had pecuniary benefits for the institution.[7] Therapy and profits both featured prominently in the annual reports and other official accounts of the institution. It is important to acknowledge that the categorisation of the 'insane' was complex and fluid during the nineteenth century. Admissions to pauper lunatic asylums encompassed 'insanity' and 'idiocy'.[8] Up to a quarter of the pauper insane were retained in workhouses.[9] The patient population of the Lincolnshire Asylum was equally complex, and it is beyond the remit of this article to explore this fully. Patient narratives are derived from a detailed study of the male case books from the 1860s.[10] Case notes became obligatory after the 1845 Lunacy Act, fulfilling varied medical, bureaucratic and legal functions, and became increasingly detailed offering insights into the lives and experiences of patients. Patients are referred to by their first name and the initial of the surname in order to provide some anonymity and yet retain their identity beyond that of merely being a patient within the asylum.[11]

Dennis Mills's multifaceted research interests, especially his work on village differentiation and public health, have intersected with mine.[12] His book, *Lord and Peasant*, was pivotal to my doctoral research on rural communities in the Doncaster district which resulted in my first book, *Communities in Contrast*.[13] I was delighted to be invited to speak at the conference in honour of Dennis Mills in December 2021 and subsequently to contribute to this special edition of the journal. His work on public health in Lincoln interconnects with my current research on health and the countryside and highlights some important issues for consideration here.[14] Firstly, Mills highlighted that sanitary reform required an understanding of topographical features.[15] The location of asylums was determined by various factors including its 'healthy' character determined by geology, geography and topography with a particular focus on water supply, drainage and sewage arrangements.[16] Secondly, his work emphasised the relationship between politics, ideologies, finance and society underpinning Victorian sanitary reform.[17] Again, legislation, ideas about the land and farm work, the role of the poor law and internal economies played an important role in asylums and their agricultural endeavours. Thirdly, his work drew attention to the tensions regarding public health and the various stakeholders involved.[18] Asylums were complex and highly bureaucratic entities, scrutinised nationally by the Lunacy Commission and locally by the Visiting Committee, with the Medical Superintendent and sub-committees overseeing the various activities undertaken. Local agriculturalists and ratepayers also expressed opinions on the operation of these institutions, and the acquisition of land, hiring practices or the cost of maintenance had the potential to be sources of conflict in the locale. By examining the use of farm work at the Lincolnshire County Asylum, an institution which had a high proportion of patients from agricultural and rural backgrounds, and the connections between the institutional rhetoric and the experiences of patients both within and outside of the asylum, this article adds a further dimension to our understanding of rural life and health in the county of Lincolnshire.

CONSTRUCTING THE INSTITUTIONAL NARRATIVE: 1854

In the first annual report of the Lincolnshire County Lunatic Asylum (1854), the Medical Superintendent, Edward Palmer, wrote extensively about the institutional farm. Not surprisingly, institutions sought to present favourable critiques of their endeavours, and in this respect, Palmer was no different. The narrative he constructed about farming coalesced around three key components: admissions and occupational background, the use of patient labour and pecuniary benefits of the farm. These were indicative of the nature and preoccupations of annual reports, recording admissions, patient work and the internal economies of the institution. The reports had an external audience who were increasingly concerned about the purported rise in lunacy and the increased poor law expenditure which affected rates. This was augmented by the newspaper media who reprinted extracts from the annual reports, together with minutes of meetings of visiting committee and other matters of interest to ratepayers, and thus amplified the voice of the institution. Indeed, a much-condensed version of the 1854 annual report was printed in the *Lincolnshire Chronicle*, prefaced by the line 'The following extracts from the last report of Dr Palmer, the superintendent of this institution, may prove interesting to our readers'.[19] With verbatim extracts printed by the media, the same voice was articulated using varied mediums for different audiences, constructing and communicating ideas accordingly.

Palmer's first reference to farming was in connection to asylum admissions. He wrote:

> As would be expected in a county whose population is essentially agricultural, the admissions have included a large number of farm-labourers, their wives and families. From the healthful and unexciting nature of its employment, it

might be supposed that such a population should enjoy a larger immunity from insanity than that of manufacturing counties, but such does not appear to be always the case.[20]

He drew attention to an enigma that preoccupied alienists during the nineteenth century: the enduring notion of a healthier countryside (compared to urban and industrial society) and yet statistical evidence that suggested differential rates of lunacy in town and country were not as clear-cut as presumed. In 1829, Sir Andrew Halliday, a Scottish physician, had argued that insanity appeared 'more prevalent in the agricultural districts than amongst the manufacturing population'.[21] Many sought to counter this claim in a debate that lasted over a century.

Palmer then provided comparative statistics of the proportion of 'insane paupers' in different counties and a discussion thereof:

> The proportion of insane paupers to the population of Lancashire is as 1 to 1083, in the West-Riding of Yorkshire as 1 in 1176, and in Staffordshire as 1 to 1079; while in Lincolnshire it is as 1 to 806 – a proportion which, it is believed, is largely attributable to hereditary predisposition. In many of the cases received from the towns the mental disorder has been distinctly traceable to habits of intemperance and dissipation; but in those coming from the rural districts of the county such causes have been comparatively rare, and a congenital want of mental power to resist ordinary excitants and depressants has appeared pretty generally to have been the 'fons et origio mali.[22]

A distinction was drawn between types of mental disorder and their causes to explain the differential rates of 'insane paupers' in different counties. Classification, such as this, became an important factor in the debate about rising lunacy with concerns about the accumulation of chronic lunatics, those deemed incurable, intensifying from the middle of the nineteenth century onwards.[23] The debate about hereditary predisposition in the countryside was prevalent amongst alienists at this date. At Lincoln, the role of hereditary insanity was revisited in 1901 as the number of patients had grown exponentially and plans to enlarge the institution were discussed. Opposition to this proposal included a communication from the Gainsborough Guardians who suggested rather than enlarging the institution 'a farm should be bought, and suitable buildings be erected thereon, so that the harmless lunatics might be separated from the others, and partially earn their own living'.[24] Although classification within institutions was not always clear and distinct, and sometimes arbitrarily applied, the move to distinguish between 'lunacy' and 'mental deficiency' saw the creation or expansion of specific institutions, including land colonies.[25] This section of Palmer's annual report was reprinted verbatim in the local newspaper. Although the institutional farm was not mentioned at this stage, it provided foundational context to discussions about patient labour and occupational background in subsequent years.

The second reference Palmer made to farming was specifically about the role of the institutional farm and patient labour. In 1847, John Conolly, a prominent alienist, asserted that work relieved monotony, preserved bodily health and improved the mind.[26] Work, if carefully selected and managed, was deemed to have curative and restorative properties, as well as pecuniary benefits for the institution.[27] This was what Palmer alluded to when he wrote 'The great advantages arising from the useful occupation of the Patients, especially in out-door labor, are too well known to require any comment'.

He continued:

> spade husbandry applied to 10 acres of ground: besides which, almost 10 acres of potatoes have been planted and dug, and 9 acres of barley and oats harvested and prepared for market. For the whole of this work no paid labourers were engaged; the Patients, under the direction of the Farm-bailiff and Gardener, have been the true wizards of the soil

The evocative use of 'wizards of the soil' positioned patient labour as performing a transformative role on the land. The focus here was on the clearance and cultivation of the land rather than the health and wellbeing of patients – in part because the 'great advantages' were supposedly already established. This section was also reprinted verbatim in the local newspaper, perhaps to reassure ratepayers that this was a cost-effective initiative.

The annual report however elaborated on the role of patient work. Palmer wrote:

> But, however profitable the labor of lunatics may be made to appear, due regard has always been paid to the facts that they are all more or less the subjects of bodily infirmity, and that labor, of whatsoever kind, can only be useful to them in proportion as it increases or maintains their bodily health and diminishes their mental excitability. The number of hours employed in daily labour by the Patients will, therefore, be found considerably less than those of an ordinary workman, but it has been ample to meet the curative and palliative indications in that direction, and left sufficient time of the use of other agents of almost equal importance in their treatment.[28]

This echoed the sentiments of the Lunacy Commission, a public body established by the 1845 Lunacy Act to oversee asylums, that stated patients should only be employed where it was in their own interests rather than those of the institution.[29] Moreover, a connection was drawn between physical and mental health. Pioneering medical figures, such as William Ellis at Wakefield and John Conolly at Hanwell, advocated outdoor labour as beneficial to both body and mind.[30] Conolly also highlighted greater recovery rates from work on the farm compared with those engaged in workshops on account of being more active and various.[31]

Palmer's third reference to the farm directly addressed its financial contribution to the institution. He wrote:

> The farm will naturally not be expected to have been very productive during its first year; but after clearing all expenses it is found to leave a small balance to profit, and from its present forward state it promises to form a valuable feature in the economy of the Asylum for the future.[32]

This assertion regarding the farm's financial contribution to the institution and his previous one that foregrounded the needs of patients over their productive labour might seem incompatible. Nevertheless, as poor law institutions, asylums were considered to have a responsibility to the ratepayers. The institutional narrative therefore posits the long-term viability of the venture and aligns the farm as central to the financial position of the institution.

An overlapping but distinct narrative was published in the *Asylum Journal* in 1854. The *Journal* (later the *Journal of Mental Science*) was the mouthpiece of alienists, founded to provide a forum for debate and to exchange ideas or practice for superintendents of county lunatic asylums.[33] Extracts from selected annual reports were reprinted with editorial commentaries, together with features written specifically for the *Journal* by Medical Superintendents about their institutions or other matters they considered to be of potential interest or relevance to others in the field. Palmer's 'Description of the Lincolnshire County Asylum' opened with a brief history of the institution including an account of the location. It noted that it was 'an elevated and healthy locality, two miles south of Lincoln' comprising forty-five acres:

> at the commence of the Lincoln Heath (now enclosed throughout and covered with productive farms) and consists of rich loam with a large admixture of decomposed oolite and a trifling quantity of sand lying on a subsoil of loose porous rammil, and succeeded by several beds of oolite. The natural drainage is consequently complete, and this in connection with the elevated position of the site renders it at once healthful and advantageous for agricultural purposes.[34]

The suitability of locations was extensively discussed in the *Journal*, with particular attention to topography, geography, water supply and drainage.[35]

In his article for the *Asylum Journal*, Palmer went on to write about the scale and scope of the farming operations:

> about thirty acres available for husbandry, nearly the whole of which have already been brought under cultivation. The spade has been applied to ten acres, and a large amount of labour expended in clearing the estate from foul and rank weeds which had accumulated on its surface during the six years of neglect which had preceded the purchase of it by the magistrates. The same amount of labour on land already cleared would almost suffice to drive away the plough altogether, and it is anticipated that this will ultimately be effected.[36]

This was clearly connected with the 'Wizards of the Soil' statement made in the first annual report and reprinted in the local newspaper, which hinted at the overall profitability of the estate. Palmer went on to give a detailed description of the farm buildings where he stated there were 'stalls for ten cows, sties and yard-room for about forty pigs, stables for carts and carriage horses, coach house, cart shed, granary, &c' and noted 'all of which are arranged in the most improved method. They are placed with the gas works at the north-east of the grounds, and are under the management of a bailiff, who with his wife occupies the entrance lodge'.[37] This report positioned their land holding as akin to a model farm, with a focus on the practicalities of farming from a business and management perspective. The use of patient labour, foregrounded in the annual report, is secondary in this article, although Palmer highlighted the relationship between farming methods and the scope for patients to work on the farm.

These themes were all revisited to a greater or lesser extent in subsequent annual reports. Accounts were moulded to adapt to specific objectives or concerns, which further nuanced the institutional narrative. The most prominent and recurring strands were those concerning the economic contribution of the farm and the role of patient labour. At different times, these strands were positioned as being either intrinsically linked or separate and distinct, privileging one or the other dependent on context and purpose of the narrative. A further strand interwoven into the reports and thus shaping the institutional narrative addressed the position of either the farm or the institution within the wider rural and agricultural setting.

THE DEVELOPMENT OF THE INSTITUTIONAL NARRATIVE: 1855-1901

The farm was not mentioned by Palmer in the second annual report (1855), but the Chair of the Visiting Committee, Robert Sheffield, referred to the role farm size played in the economics of asylums. This was part of a wider discourse which argued that farm work could contribute to lowering the cost of maintenance per patient, especially as asylums were considered more costly than the workhouse.[38] In discussing the cost of maintenance, a matter of constant consternation, Sheffield wrote that 'no two Asylums are similarly circumstanced in many leading financial matters', noting that 'some, like the North and East Ridings, are aided by extensive farms'. He went on to conclude that the Lincolnshire County Asylum had been 'conducted with strict and scrupulous economy'.[39] This was republished in the *Lincolnshire Chronicle* with the preface 'The following documents deserve the attention of all our readers'.[40] Institutional finances were subject to intense scrutiny and there was a pre-existing rhetoric regarding the accountability of poor law officials to ratepayers.[41] The institutional farm was positioned as pivotal in this discourse. Where profits from the farm proved elusive, the rhetoric was moulded accordingly. Farms were heralded as having the potential to lower the cost of maintenance per patient, yet this was somewhat simplistic in underestimating the role of management, institutional accounting processes, and labour costs. Nor was it consistently applied. A year later, the productivity of the farm was foregrounded by the Chair of the Visiting Committee, noting both that it was 'cultivated chiefly by the manual labor of the patients' and that 'now a sufficient balance has been accumulated to maintain the necessary stock in hand, the entire profits of the Farm will in future be carried to the relief of the Maintenance Account'.[42] Underpinning this narrative of profitability was a tacit acknowledgement, that the financial investment necessary to commence farming operations would take some years to show as credit in the institutions accounts.

Equally important and dominant was the narrative that situated the economic contribution of patient labour as secondary to the curative and therapeutic benefits. Palmer's discussion of farm labour included several statements that referred to the 'useful occupation' of patients and how 'the industry of the patients continued unabated'.[43] It is not clear at this point whether he was alluding to the utility of the work in terms of economic contribution, therapeutic work or the management of patients. As in the first annual report, he also specifically mentioned the occupational background of patients, noting the majority were 'derived from the agricultural class'. He even asserted that the farm profits would have been the greatest yet if the potato crop had not failed. However, Palmer's foremost argument in this report regarding patient labour was that it 'should always be kept subservient to the real objects of an Asylum, and be apportioned both in degree and duration to the mental and physical requirements of each case. Without attention to these considerations, an increase of land becomes an increased calamity to the unfortunate patients, and their place of abode little more than a mortuary... '.[44] This was aligned to the rhetoric established by Palmer in his first annual report and by the Lunacy Commission a few years earlier. The judicious selection of patients and work, ensuring a suitable alignment between the two, and the careful management of patient labour were discussed more widely by alienists during the nineteenth century.[45]

Palmer, in his discussion of admissions, positioned the institution within the surrounding rural and agricultural environment. In addition to his explicit references to occupational background and work on the farm, he also discussed wider contextual factors linking location to admissions. Commenting on the causes leading to admission, Palmer noted (in the fourth annual report) that twenty-seven patients (39.7% of all admissions) had 'either meditated or attempted suicide', acknowledging that this was 'very common amongst opium-smoking people'. What is particularly interesting about this discussion is the historical reflection he offered about 'the habitual use of opium' in Fen countries on account of malaria or ague.[46] Opium was consumed or smoked for a range of reasons, including to treat the symptoms of malaria. Many contemporaries connected improved drainage with the disappearance of malaria.[47] Palmer wrote that the ague had been 'endemic in the fens before a complete system of drainage and tillage had swept the miasmata from their surface'. This correlation has subsequently been argued to be insufficient or incomplete, highlighting the importance of changes in farming and land use.[48] However, Palmer's explanation was also more nuanced as he mentioned that 'Richly cultivated farms intersected by a network of dikes now occupy the sites of the stagnant lakes and fermenting marshes, and Ague as an endemic is banished from the County'.[49]

Palmer was not however primarily interested in the environmental, landscape and agricultural factors at play in the rise and demise of malaria, but the continued indulgence in opium and the mental disease arising from this. The fact he reflected on the former not only demonstrated that this was a preoccupation during the period but also showed evidence of Palmer positioning the institution actively within its rural and agricultural setting. Of opium indulgence, Palmer wrote of 'its deep degenerating influences on mind and body (affecting not only individuals but their posterity)' and 'the great difficulty in removing its cause, viz.: – that of breaking the habit of using this poison'. He specifically mentioned children 'commonly drugged with it in the cradle', and there is evidence of opium having been used to quieten the offspring of female agricultural workers.[50] Palmer argued this led to 'a degenerate and half-imbecile offspring to add to the criminal and insane population', and ultimately to a suicidal form of insanity.[51]

Further reference to the surrounding landscape was made by Palmer in his discussion of recreational activities for patients. Here he noted the benefits of 'sending patients to walk beyond the limits of the Asylum'. The idea of nature and the wider landscape as having a therapeutic effect was prevalent during the nineteenth century, and consideration was given to this notion when choosing the location for new asylums.[52] Palmer stated that although 'the scenery in the immediate neighbourhood has no claim to the picturesque', even 'a simple roadside walk, or a scramble across the fields relieves the monotony of Asylum life, and mitigates the feeling of coercive confinement'.[53] He added 'A few of the patients were also sent into the Lincoln Fair, where they conducted themselves with perfect propriety, and thoroughly enjoyed both its gingerbreads and wonders'.[54] The institutional narrative thus positioned the institution as integrated into the landscape and rural life, negotiating the relationships between institution and the countryside and between the countryside and the town.

One of the main products in which asylums aimed to be self-sufficient was milk. This extended beyond mere supply and demand dynamics, with the importance of fresh, safe milk highlighted, although cost and availability were often foregrounded. The Chair of the Visiting Committee, G.K. Jarvis, reported in the sixteenth annual report (1869) that they hoped 'soon to be able to supply milk to the Asylum from the produce of land in their own occupation; and by so doing to avoid a heavy charge, at present amounting to nearly £500 a year, and constantly increasing'.[55] They proposed purchasing the land currently occupied by

Edward Clarke, tenant of White Hall Farm, who supplied milk to the asylum. This had cost implications but as Jarvis noted 'The impossibility of obtaining good milk at a reasonable cost, or even at all in sufficient quantity, from the neighbourhood of Lincoln, will compel the Visitors to provide it from their own farm; and in order to enable them to do this, the possession of a grass-field on the hillside, now occupied by Mr Clarke, and in which his cows are kept in the summer months, would be of the greatest value'.[56] Patterns of land acquisition were motivated not only by the impetus to provide work for patients but also by the demand for fresh milk and the prohibitive costs of purchasing sufficient quantities elsewhere.

The inherent tensions between profits and patient labour were not only evident in, but also helped to shape, the institutional narrative. G. K. Jarvis discussed patient labour in relation to farming type in the tenth annual report (1863). He noted that the institution had forty-five acres, thirty of which were cultivated 'about one-third as Kitchen-Garden, and the rest in the production of Farm Crops'. He explained that:

> The latter portion is not cultivated by the spade, but with ploughs and horses in the usual way of farming. The average number of male patients capable of working on the land is 50. It is expected that by changing the system from the plough to the spade as the number of patients increases, ample employment may still be found for them to meet the views of the Commissioners, especially as no facility at present exists for renting or purchasing more land'.[57]

By 1867, the Commissioners in Lunacy report noted that thirty acres were now 'under spade cultivation'.[58] This suggests that institutional farms and attendant farming practices were underpinned by the rhetoric surrounding patient labour. The 1860s was a period of agricultural innovation with a focus on mechanisation. Over time some asylums and mental hospitals developed model farms, with considerable investment in land, buildings, equipment and pedigree stock.[59] Nevertheless, at the outset, the rhetoric of patient work was so compelling that 'spade husbandry' was heralded as desirable.

The beneficial effects of farm labour were reiterated in the seventeenth annual report (1870). Palmer wrote that:

> Farm-labour has continued to be the chief, as it is the most healthful and curative, employment of the male Patients, the majority of whom being drawn from the agricultural class, know but little of any other kind of labour, and always seek their customary occupation with the earliest dawn of convalescence.[60]

As in the first annual report, Palmer highlighted the occupational background of patients, but also drew connections to work within the institution. Farm work, he asserted, was requested by agricultural workers. He went on to explore the benefits attributable to farm work to a range of patient types:

> A large number of the chronic cases also of every form of insanity, are found to forget themselves, as it were, when engaged in husbandry, and to work with a skill and steadiness truly remarkable; while not a few imbecile and inactive Patients become busy in some trifling work on the land, and are both healthier and happier for their exertions. Indeed, all the Patients have derived more or less recreation of the most salutary kind, either as workers or observers, from the farming and gardening operations carried on.[61]

Indeed, according to Palmer, the benefits extended beyond merely the patients who worked on the farm or in the gardens, indicative of wider therapeutic landscapes.[62]

The 1870 report also highlighted the remunerative value of the farm, noting that the additional land occupied by the institution would 'enhance the material resources of the institution, and permit of progressive improvements without increasing the weekly-rate'.[63] In 1875 the Commissioners in Lunacy remarked that 'The farming operations continue to be satisfactory, and have resulted in a considerable profit to the Institution'.[64] Likewise, in the same annual report, the Medical Superintendent noted that 'profits arising from the Farming operations were again satisfactory'.[65]

The multiple strands that comprised the interwoven institutional narrative were emphasised in a feature about Bracebridge Asylum, printed in the *Lincolnshire Chronicle*, the fifth in series of 'tours round Lincoln's institutions'.[66] It noted that 'many of the male patients are given employment on the farm which is connected with the institution, and there they find healthy occupation'. It went on to state that patients 'take a very great interest in their work, and the quality of the produce shows the care and attention which is bestowed upon the farm'. The scale of the farm was addressed, noting it was 'very large' and covered 'several scores of acres of land'. The supply of fresh produce to the institution was also mentioned, alongside the employment of non-patient labour. It stated that the farm 'provides vegetables for the institution, and a certain amount of the milk consumed is supplied by cows on the farm. In addition to patients, a number of workmen are employed on the land'.[67] The construction and reconstruction of an institutional narrative over half a century repeatedly positioned the farm as pivotal.

PATIENT NARRATIVES – A CHALLENGE TO THE INSTITUTIONAL RHETORIC

The patient voice is not actively present in the institutional narratives constructed about farm work within the annual reports. To understand the institutional farms and patient labour thereon, it is crucial to look beyond the institutional narrative and seek the patient perspective. This was often recorded, albeit in official and mediated sources, such as case notes. To a certain extent these reflected institutional preoccupations. Nevertheless, they recorded patient actions and reactions. The ways in which patients negotiated, navigated, and even contributed to the narration of, their experiences were varied and are crucial to an understanding of patient labour. Patient experiences often diverged from the prevailing institutional narrative. This is particularly evident in non-linear patient narratives, through unsuccessful or unexpected outcomes and refusal to work.[68] A close examination of patient case notes enables the historian to understand the ways in which patient experiences of farm work challenged the institutional rhetoric.

According to Palmer, the suitability of patients to undertake work was aligned to their occupational backgrounds. He asserted that the agricultural classes sought 'their customary occupation with the earliest dawn of convalescence, healthier and happier for their exertions'.[69] Some patients undoubtedly expressed these sentiments, seeking the familiar and potentially reassuring in an otherwise disorienting situation.[70] For others, this prospect provoked strong emotions. Gideon A, an agricultural labourer, was admitted to the Lincolnshire Asylum on 23 April 1864, with mania and delusions. His mother was noted as stating he was 'very restless, and endeavouring to overcome the evil influences which he believes beset him. At times he is violent and threatening'.[71] Families played a key role in decisions over the treatment and management of relatives, including provision of information upon admission and readmission.[72] Two months later, an entry in his case notes stated he 'appeared depressed; talks despondingly. Does little work'.[73] A clear association between work and recovery was made in the case notes, perhaps not unsurprising within the context of the prevalent institutional rhetoric. A willingness to work was translated as progress in the recovery of a patient. With regard to Gideon, his case notes suggested this occurred five months after his admission, as he was noted to be 'in improved condition of body and mind' and 'employs himself occasionally in the ward'.[74] A similar correlation was noted in March 1865 with reference to him being 'industrious in the wards' and 'in good bodily health'.[75] The mind and body were closely interlinked in nineteenth-century psychiatry, and connections between mental state and bodily health were frequently made in case books and the work of alienists.[76] On both occasions explicit mention is made in his case notes of Gideon's refusal to work on the farm. This appears to contradict Palmer's assertion, as this agricultural labourer did not seek his 'customary occupation' at any stage, and indeed actively refused to do so. Perhaps it was this explicit contradiction that made it worthy of recording. This highlights that case notes were the product of interactions with the patient and record traces of the patient 'voice'. Gideon's refusal was indicative of how patients could narrate and navigate their experiences within the institution. Rather than representing a reassuring and familiar presence, work could trigger negative reactions and associations. Moreover, by consciously or unconsciously resisting the institutional narrative, there may have been some awareness that work was often imposed with little input from the patient.

The experiences of many patients challenged the institutional rhetoric that farm work was healthy and curative. Case notes provide many examples of non-linear, indifferent or even negative outcomes.[77] Matthew D was noted to be 'somewhat better, both mentally and bodily' but 'Does very little work' on 25 June 1864.[78] An entry that seemed more aligned to Palmer's views was made on 25 September 1864 'has lately been induced to do a little light work in the fields, since when, he has been much better in mind & body'. Even here the idea of being 'induced' to work would suggest patients were not actively requesting to work. Subsequent entries however noted he did little work and he died on 6 October 1868. Work was only one component of life within the institution and many other factors affected health and overall outcomes. Patient narratives were not linear, and the fact that a patient worked on the farm and was seemingly much improved did not mean they were recovered.

John J, an agricultural labourer, who was admitted on 8 December 1864, had a similarly ambivalent attitude to working on the institution's farm. The language of his case notes again suggest that work was imposed rather than sought, and in this instance that work had a detrimental impact. Less than a month after admission, it was noted that 'For several days, while in the ward, he continued comparatively cheerful & communicative, but as soon as he was sent to work on the farm, he became exceedingly dejected and held down his head & would not speak a word'. Firstly, he was 'sent to work' and secondly, he became 'dejected'. John's relationship with work was charted through his case notes. By 25 March 1865 it was noted that he was 'slightly better in mind' and worked 'reluctantly but less so than formerly'. Then on 29 March 1866 he was working regularly in the fields although 'occasionally throws himself down on the floor'. This non-linear account of patient labour culminated in 1867 when it was noted that he did not work and there were no subsequent references to work or the farm.[79] Other patients were noted as requiring greater persuasion or supervision to enable them to work on the land. Stephen B's case notes stated he 'works in the fields, requiring however much persuasion to do so'.[80] Similarly it was noted that Matthew H 'continues to work on the farm, but requires much looking after, as he is disposed to loiter, pick fruit, & prevent the other patients working uninterruptedly'.[81] The institutional rhetoric that patient labour was transformative underestimates the role of attendants, and in some cases paid farm workers (non-patient labour), in working alongside patients. Attendants were often expected to work with the patients rather than 'merely order them to work', and this was a recurring discourse in the *Journal of Mental Science* with emphasis placed on 'the gain to the workers' rather than the 'work to be done', not merely being 'task masters' and the importance of leading by example.[82] The ongoing tension between the idea and reality surrounding patient work and the farm perhaps reflected the unwavering institutional rhetoric and commitment to work in spite of inconsistent or negatives outcomes.

Just as the institutional narrative positioned the institution within a wider rural setting, so did patient accounts. For example, John L's case notes suggest a sense of community and responsibility arising from his work on the farm. On 25 June 1864 it was observed that he 'continues to be a very useful and trustworthy assistant to the farmer'. Then on 25 September 1864 further reference to work and the relationship between the asylum and the town were mentioned. The entry noted that John 'Works well, and appears quite happy. On Sunday afternoon generally visits the farmer at his cottage, when he joins the family circle and conducts himself with undeviating propriety. He is a great favourite with the farmer and his acquaintances. Goes to town eight or nine times weekly, and continues to show himself worthy of the trust. Conversation very childish'. John's experience of institutional life was shaped by his work on the farm, his relationship with the farm bailiff's family and opportunities to go beyond the confines of the institution's physical boundaries. The case book makes further references to work on the farm and in the gardens. However, this was not without incidence which reflected both his physical and mental state. For instance, following an incidence of gout, it was noted that 'while employed at the farm-yard' on 27 August 1866, he had made a deep cut into his foot. The patient voice was recorded in his noted, with John stating his 'foot was rotten and would never do him any good'. He continued to work on the farm and in garden but would die in the asylum on 6 March 1875 aged fifty-nine years.[83]

A distinctive case was that of Robert G who was admitted to the Lincolnshire County Asylum on multiple occasions from the late 1850s onwards. His case notes focus on a series of delusions relating to property, trade and money. Medical superintendents showed a growing interest in delusions, as reflected in lengthy entries in case books. Although generally no attempt was made to understand or interpret the basis of these delusions, they were often grounded in previous experiences of patients prior to admission.[84] This is particularly apparent in the instance of Robert, whose delusions were occupation and place specific. They not only related to past experiences but also derived from intermittent time spent at home during a long period of confinement within the institution. Case notes thus present the challenge of disentangling assumptions about delusions from realities that provide a link with life before admission. What makes this case more unusual is the preservation of the patient voice through his handwritten notes that were appended to the casebook to corroborate the alleged delusions.

Robert was a shoemaker who lived in the village of Bassingham.[85] He was first admitted in December 1858 and discharged as recovered in April 1859.[86] However he would be readmitted in May 1864 with 'mania' after which his life was dominated by long periods of incarceration until his death in 1878. On admission in 1864, Robert's case notes detailed his behaviour and alluded to his delusions. For example, 'Incoherent talk. Is constantly walking about, seldom sleeps', 'His wife and daughter state they are afraid of him' and 'Says his wife and son will be transported' were noted alongside comments such as 'States he has ordered six Journeymen to help him (He has nothing to do, but a little mending). Also says, he is going to open a public house, and is obtaining the necessary signatures. Is busy with circulars about shoemaking' and 'Has ordered leather, ironmongery so enough to last a shop his life'.[87] Such statements suggest his judgement about work was being called into question which had financial implications and affected his family. Subsequent entries noted that he 'works well in the shop [shoemaker's workshop] and conducts himself with propriety' and characterised his behaviour as 'eccentric' following an escape.[88] Once he was considered 'more rational in conversation and conduct' he was discharged on trial on 25 March 1865 for three months.[89] However, on 25 May 1865 he was 'reported to be troublesome and idle at home' and on 15 June the casebook entry was 'Is said to have delusions to the effect that he has property, people owe him money. Has offered property for sale to various persons'.[90] On the 23 June he was once again detained 'much to his surprise'. Further case book entries refer to his industriousness and work in the shoemaker's shop. He was discharged again on 7 January 1867 as 'recovered' but was readmitted on 30 April. This pattern of discharge and readmission continued, with another discharge 'as recovered' on 9 January 1871 and a further readmission on 6 March 1871. Robert remained in the asylum then until his death on 10 June 1871.[91]

Notably, the patient voice and his preoccupation with trade during this period were preserved. Accompanying Robert's case notes was a printed circular announcing a new branch of the York Tanning and Currying Company in Lincoln, dated 29 March 1865.[92] Handwritten notes pertaining to three different issues had been added to this. The first were a set of rules for a boot and shoe club, undated, outlining membership fees and benefits.[93] Mutual aid of this kind was not uncommon through the nineteenth century often taking the form of friendly societies and providing support in times of illness and difficulty. The second were particulars for 'a most desirable freehold property' in the 'improving village of Bassingham' to be sold by auction on 17 July 1865, with the contact address of Mr J. Pacey of Bassingham. The third was a request stating 'I should like to see you on Friday and bring Mr Butcher Rogers with you'. The Medical Superintendent saw sufficient significance in this document to retain it, perhaps with further input from the family, that helped to shape the case notes.

At the heart of this narrative is Robert, who clearly retained a strong occupational identity and whose occupation had perhaps triggered the alleged delusions. He worked in the shoemaker's workshop at the asylum and spent intermittent time at home between admissions. Non-institutional sources provide insights into his life before and between admissions.[94] A couple of years before his first admission, the *Lincolnshire Chronicle* cautioned readers that a 'Jeremy Diddler' had been 'victimising the tradesmen of Bassingham and vicinity to an unusual extent, and in a rather clever manner'. A 'Jeremy Diddler' referred to the literary character who borrowed but did not repay money.[95] The report went on to state that he had paid 'sundry visits to most of the brewers, grocers, shoemakers, millers, &c., around, as was evinced by the anxiety of several of the above tradesmen'.[96] As a resident shoemaker, Robert would have been acutely aware of this incident if not directly affected. This may have been the catalyst for the constant preoccupation with property, money and trade thereafter. The delusionary behaviour outlined in the case notes seem to suggest an underlying anxiety fuelled by real life experience. Indeed, money worries, real or imagined, were a known source of distress which could lead to mental disorders.[97] To some extent, we may never entirely disentangle Robert's delusions from his life experiences, but his case highlights two important points. Firstly, patients, as noted earlier as well, could narrate their own institutional experiences through actions and reactions and via written accounts. Secondly, delusions were often rooted in real life experiences and relating to strong occupational identities. Although removed from home, Robert was still very much a part of rural society. Aside from the rural location of the institution, he retained a strong occupational impulse perpetuated by intermittent periods of time spent back at home in Bassingham. Whereas the institutional narrative positioned the asylum and the farm within their wider rural and agricultural setting as part of a positive rhetoric, the realities of the countryside and rural living were more complex. Poverty, ill health and occupational triggers underpinned the admissions of at least some of those from rural and agricultural backgrounds.

CONCLUSION

The institutional rhetoric positioned these farms as having a transformative impact, with medical, moral and economic motivations and outcomes intertwined. This narrative was the product of multiple voices, seemingly synthesised into a coherent account, constructed as both an internal and external dialogue of particular interest to other alienists and the ratepayers. It was predominantly shaped by the accounts of the Medical Superintendent and the Visiting Committee, with local newspapers amplifying certain elements. The rhetoric firmly situated the asylum, the farm and farm work within a wider context, underpinned by the enduring notion of a healthy countryside and interconnected with the occupational background of patients. The ways in which patients interacted with outdoor spaces extended beyond farm work to include walks around and beyond the asylum estate, picnics or visits and were interwoven into these institutional narratives. Although mediated by the Medical Superintendent, case notes presented the patient experience of farm work or connections with the countryside and life outside the institution, which challenged the carefully constructed institutional rhetoric. Indifference to work, inconsistent outcomes and complex interconnections with life outside of the asylum rooted in strong occupational or locational identities, which could become the basis of delusions, present a more nuanced account of farm work. Most significantly they provide insight into the patient perspective of farm work and rural life both within and beyond the confines of the institution.

NOTES

1. The archival visits that form the basis of this work were made possible by the award of an EC grant from Sheffield Hallam University. The author thanks the anonymous referees for their comments and Dr Andrew Walker for co-ordinating this edition.

2. Philo, Chris, 2004, *A Geographical History of Institutional Provision for the Insane from Medieval Times to the 1860s in England and Wales,* Lampeter. p. 477; Laws, Jennifer, 2011, 'Crackpots and basket-cases: a history of therapeutic work and occupation', *History of the Human Sciences,* 24:2, pp. 65-81; Scull, Andrew T., 1993, *The Most Solitary of Afflictions: Madness and Society in Britain, 1700-1900,* London. pp. 183-4.

3. Ernst, Waltraud, 2016, 'Introduction', in Ernst, W. (ed.), *Work, Psychiatry and Society, c. 1750-2015,* Manchester. pp. 1, 23.

4. Palmer, Edward, May 1854, Description of the Lincolnshire County Asylum', *Asylum Journal,* 1:5, pp. 73-75.

5.   White, William, 1856, *History, Gazetteer and Directory of Lincolnshire,* Sheffield. p. 96.

6.   Palmer, 'Description of the Lincolnshire County Asylum', p. 73.

7.   There were two Asylums in Lincoln. The earliest was the Lincoln Lunatic Asylum (opened 1820), which was heralded by John Conolly, a prominent alienist, as being 'the first in which the idea of wholly abolishing mechanical restraint was adapted in the most unqualified manner, and acted upon with success'. See *Asylum Journal,* 1:11 (February 1855), pp. 164-6.

8.   Jarrett, Simon, 2020, *Those They Called Idiots: The idea of the disabled mind from 1700 to the present day,* Reaktion Books. pp. 12-14, 216-218.

9.   Miller, Edgar, 2007, 'Variations in the official prevalence and disposal of the insane in England under the poor law, 1850-1900', *History of Psychiatry,* 18:1, pp. 25-26.

10.   Gender shaped experiences of work within institutions, with female patients generally assigned to work in the laundry or kitchen and male patients to the workshops or outdoor labour including the farm. There were exceptions, and work in the gardens was undertaken by male and female patients.

11.   Holland, Sarah, 2021, 'Narrating and Navigating Patient Experiences of Farm Work in English Psychiatric Institutions, 1845-1914', in Hanley, Anne and Meyer, Jessica, (eds), Patient Voices in Britain, 1840-1948, Manchester. p. 127; Wallis, Jennifer, 2017, *Investigating the Body in the Victorian Asylum. Doctors, Patients, and Practices,* p. 34.

12.   The scale and scope of Dennis Mills's work is examined in A. J. H. Jackson's article 'The "Open-Closed" Settlement Model and the Interdisciplinary Formulations of Dennis Mills: Conceptualising Local Rural Change', *Rural History,* 23:2, 2012, pp. 121-136.

13.   Holland, Sarah, 2019, *Communities in Contrast: Doncaster and its rural hinterland, c. 1830-1870,* Hatfield.

14.   For further discussion of psychiatric institutions and farm work see Holland, 'Narrating and Navigating Patient Experiences of Farm Work' and Holland, Sarah, *Farming, Psychiatry and Rural Society, England 1845-1955* (Routledge, forthcoming).

15.   Mills, Dennis, 2009, 'Public Health, Environment and Surveying', *Social History of Medicine,* 22:1, pp. 153-163.

16.   Philo, Chris, 1987, '"Fit localities for an asylum": the historical geography of the nineteenth-century "mad-business" in England as viewed through the pages of the *Asylum Journal*', *Journal of Historical Geography,* 13:4, pp. 398-415, p. 406.

17.   Mills, Dennis, 2009, 'Local Studies in Sanitary Reform: the importance of the engineering aspect – Lincoln 1848-1850', *The Local Historian,* 39:3, p. 207; Mills, Dennis, 2015, *Effluence and Influence: public health, sewers and politics in Lincoln, 1848-50,* Society for Lincolnshire History and Archaeology.

18.   Mills, *Effluence and Influence,* pp. 14-18.

19.   *Lincolnshire Chronicle,* 28 April 1854, p. 3. The *Lincolnshire Chronicle* was a Conservative newspaper as discussed in Mills, 'Local Studies in Sanitary Reform', p. 207.

20.   *First Annual Report of the Lincolnshire County Lunatic Asylum* (1854), pp. 6-7.

21.   Sir Andrew Halliday, 1829, *A Letter to Lord Robert Seymour, with a report of the number of lunatics and idiots in England and Wales,* London. p. 55.

22.   *First Annual Report of the Lincolnshire County Lunatic Asylum* (1854), pp. 6-7.

23.   'The Accumulation of Chronic Lunatics in Asylums. Questions of further Accommodation', *The Asylum Journal,* 1:13 (May 1855), pp. 193-9.

24.   *Lincolnshire Chronicle,* 26 July 1901, p. 5; *Lincolnshire Echo,* 25 July 1901, p. 3; *Stamford Mercury,* 2 August 1901, p. 5.

25. Holland, *Farming, Psychiatry and Rural Society.*

26. Conolly, John, 1847, *On the Construction and Government of Lunatic Asylums and Hospitals for the Insane,* London. p. 77.

27. Laws 'Crackpots and basket-cases', p. 68; Philo, *A Geographical History of Institutional Provision for the Insane,* p. 594.

28. *First Annual Report,* pp. 7-8.

29. Holland, 'Narrating and Navigating Patient Experiences of Farm Work', p. 130.

30. Conolly, *On the Construction and Government of Lunatic Asylums,* p. 79; Steven Cherry, 2003, *Mental Health Care in Modern England,* p. 66; Philo, *A Geographical History,* p. 594; Parr, Hester, 2007, 'Mental Health, Nature Work and Social Inclusion', *Environment and Planning,* 25, p. 541.

31. Philo, *A Geographical History,* pp. 601-2; Holland, 'Narrating and Navigating Patient Experiences', p. 132.

32. *First Annual Report,* p. 16.

33. Philo, '"Fit localities for an asylum"', pp. 398-415.

34. Palmer, 'Description of the Lincolnshire County Asylum', pp. 73-74.

35. Philo, '"Fit localities for an asylum"', p. 406.

36. Palmer, 'Description of the Lincolnshire County Asylum', p. 74.

37. *Ibid.,* p. 75.

38. Miller, 'Variations in the official prevalence and disposal of the insane', p. 32.

39. *Second Annual Report of the Lincolnshire County Asylum* (1855), p. 5.

40. *Lincolnshire Chronicle,* 18 May 1855, p. 2.

41. Shave, Samantha A., 2017, *Pauper Policies: poor Law practice in England, 1780-1850,* Manchester. p. 41.

42. *Third Annual Report of the Lincolnshire County Asylum* (1856), p. 4.

43. Ibid., p. 16; *Fourth Annual Report of the Lincolnshire County Asylum* (1857), p. 15.

44. *Second Annual Report* (1855), pp. 15-16.

45. 'Second Notice of the Eighth Report of the Commissioners in Lunacy', *Asylum Journal,* 1:10 (January 1855), p. 148; 'The Annual Reports of the County Lunatic Asylums', *Asylum Journal of Mental Science,* 2:17 (April 1856), pp. 266-7; 'The Annual Reports of the County Lunatic Asylums', *Asylum Journal of Mental Science,* 3:22 (July 1857), pp. 479-481.

46. *Fourth Annual Report* (1857), p. 12.

47. Williamson, Tom, 2005, 'The disappearance of malaria from the East Anglia Fens', in Barona, J.L., and Cherry, S., (eds), *Health and Medicine in Rural Europe 1850-1945,* pp. 249-251.

48. *Ibid.,* pp. 252-262.

49. *Fourth Annual Report* (1857), p. 13.

50. *Ibid.;* Williamson, 'The disappearance of malaria', p. 249.

51. *Fourth Annual Report,* p. 13.

52. For more on the location of asylums, including issues of seclusion, see Philo, '"Fit localities for an asylum"'.

53. *Third Annual Report* (1856), p. 16.

54. *Ibid.*

55. *Sixteenth Annual Report* (1869), p. 7.

56.   *Ibid.*, pp. 7-8.

57.   *Tenth Annual Report* (1863), p. 5.

58.   *Fourteenth Annual Report* (1867), p.10.

59.   Holland, *Farming, Psychiatry and Rural Society.*

60.   *Seventeenth Annual report* (1870), pp. 14-15.

61.   *Ibid.*, p. 15.

62.   Hickman, *Therapeutic Landscapes*, p. 98.

63.   *Seventeenth Annual Report* (1870), p. 15.

64.   *Twentieth Annual Report* (1875), p. 7.

65.   *Ibid.*, p. 15.

66.   *Lincolnshire Chronicle*, 10 April 1909, p. 6.

67.   *Ibid.*

68.   Holland, 'Narrating and Navigating Patient Experiences', p. 126; Andrews, Jonathan, 1998, 'Case Notes, Case Histories, and the Patient's Experience of Insanity at Gartnavel Royal Asylum, Glasgow, in the Nineteenth Century', *Social History of Medicine*, 11:2, pp. 255-81; Kelly, Brendan D., 2016, 'Searching for the Patient's Voice in the Irish Asylum', *Medical Humanities*, 42:2, pp. 87-8; Chaney, Sarah, 2016, 'No "Sane" Person Would have any Idea: Patients' Involvement in Late Nineteenth-Century British Asylum Psychiatry', *Medical History*, 60:1, pp. 37-9 .

69.   Annual Report of Committee of Visitors to Lincoln County Lunatic Asylum including extracts by the Medical Superintendent 1869, cited in *Stamford Mercury*, 10 June 1870, p. 6.

70.   Holland, 'Narrating and Navigating Patient Experiences', pp. 136-8.

71.   Lincolnshire Archives, Hosp St John's 2/13/1, Male Case Book, Entry 1404.

72.   Bartlett, Peter and Wright, David, 1999, 'Community care and its antecedents', in Bartlett and Wright (eds), *Outside the Walls of the Asylum: The History of Care in the Community, 1750-2000*, pp. 4-5; Suzuki, Akihito, 1999, 'Enclosing and disclosing lunatics within the family walls: domestic psychiatric regime and the public sphere in early nineteenth-century England', in Bartlett and Wright (eds), *Outside the Walls of the Asylum*, pp. 117-118; Long, Vicky and Brown, Victoria, 2018, 'Conceptualizing work-related mental distress in the British coalfields (c. 1900-1950)', *Palgrave Communications*, 4:133, pp.5-6; Smith, Cathy, 2013, 'Family, community and the Victorian Asylum: a case study of the Northampton General Lunatic Asylum and its pauper lunatics', *Family and Community History*, 9:2, pp. 109-124.

73.   Lincolnshire Archives, Hosp St John's 2/13/1, Male Case Book, Entry 1404, 25 June 1864.

74.   *Ibid.*, 25 September 1864.

75.   *Ibid.*, 25 March 1865.

76.   Wallis, *Investigating the Body*, p. 4; Browne, W.A.F., 1864, *The Moral Treatment of the Insane: A Lecture,* London; Medico-psychological Association for Great Britain and Ireland, 1889, *Handbook for Attendants on the Insane*, London. p. 124.

77.   Holland, 'Narrating and Navigating Patient Experiences', p. 140.

78.   Lincolnshire Archives, Hosp St John's 2/13/1, Male Case Book, Entry 839, 25 June 1864.

79.   Lincolnshire Archives, Hosp St John's 2/13/1, Male Case Book, Entry 1478.

80.   Lincolnshire Archives, Hosp St John's 2/13/1, Male Case Book, Entry 1102, 25 June 1864, 25 March 1865.

81.   Lincolnshire Archives, Hosp St John's 2/13/1, Male Case Book, Entry 1333, 25 June 1864.

82.   *Journal of Mental Science*, 29:125 (April 1883), p. 97; *Journal of Mental Science*, 29:126. (July 1883), pp. 285-6; *Journal of Mental Science*, 34:147 (October 1888), p. 440.

83. Lincolnshire Archives, Hosp St John's 2/13/1, Male Case Book, Entry 206; *Lincolnshire Chronicle*, 12 March 1875, p. 5.

84. Holland, 'Narrating and Navigating Patient Experiences', pp. 141-142.

85. The National Archives, HO 107/615/5, Census Enumerators' Book, Bassingham, 1841; Kelly, W., 1849, Post Office Directory of Lincolnshire, 1849, p. 2976; The National Archives, HO107/2136, Census Enumerators' Book, Bassingham, 1851 census.

86. The National Archive, Lunacy Patients Admission Registers, 1846-1912, December 1858.

87. Lincolnshire Archives, Hosp St John's 2/13/1, Male Case Book, Entry 1423, 21 May 1864.

88. *Ibid.*, 25 September 1864, 25 December 1864.

89. *Ibid.*, 25 March 1865.

90. *Ibid.*, 25 May 1865, 15 June 1865.

91. *Ibid.*, 23 June 1865, 25 September 1865, March 1866, 21 September 1866, 7 January 1867; The National Archive, Lunacy Patients Admission Registers, 1846-1912, 30 April 1867 to 9 January 1871; The National Archive, Lunacy Patients Admission Registers, 1846-1912, 6 March 1871 to 10 June 1878.

92. Lincolnshire Archives, Hosp St John's 2/13/1, Male Case Book, Entry 1423, inserts.

93. *Ibid.*

94. For more about how non-institutional sources challenge the partiality of 'institutionally-generated records' see Wright, David, April 1997, 'Getting Out of the Asylum: Understanding the Confinement of the Insane in the Nineteenth Century', *Social History of Medicine,* 10:1, p. 149.

95. 'Jeremy Diddler' in Dibble, M., Stringer, M.J. and Hahn, D., (eds), 2013 online 3rd edition, *The Concise Oxford Companion to English Literature*, Oxford University Press.

96. *Lincolnshire Chronicle*, 19 October 1855, p. 5.

97. Holland, *Farming, Psychiatry and Rural Society.*

CO-OPERATION IN THE FACE OF CONFLICT: THE LINCOLN SOCIETY AND THE FIRST WORLD WAR 1914–1915

Andrew J. H. Jackson

The First World War has been extensively documented and much studied. Nonetheless, there was still scope remaining for the centenary years to stimulate fresh exploration and the discovery of a great deal that was alternative, unfamiliar, and challenging. The home-front experience attracted particular and long-overdue attention. Meanwhile, another history, that of the co-operative movement, has generated considerable general survey and analysis as well. However, it has left neglected deep local study, and understanding of the complexities, nuances, and contradictions borne out in individual society contexts. This article, on the Lincoln Co-operative Society, brings these two lines of historical study together. It yields both new insight on the First World War at home, and different perspectives on the shifting nature and enhanced significance of co-operation at this time of crisis, local, national, and international.

INTRODUCTION: 'WAR AND CO-OPERATION AT HOME AND ABROAD'[1]

From the mid-nineteenth century until the early twentieth, the co-operative movement steadily expanded. It was rooted in the ideal of providing unadulterated food stuffs at a fair price for its members, and attending to their broader economic, social, and cultural well-being. Co-operation established itself as a strong dimension of the wider labour movement in Britain and elsewhere. The scope of its retail and production operations diversified, and the length and sophistication of its supply chains advanced. Local societies also developed their education, leisure and outreach, with the intention of supporting the physical, material, and political advancement of its membership. The Lincoln Society followed suit from the 1860s, finding a footing around a retail-centred model, growing its member numbers, adding branches, but also gradually diversifying into other forms of economic and social provision.

The First World War provided a great test for the movement as a whole and for individual societies. This is a detailed study of one society over two of the wartime years, 1914 and 1915. These saw two sharp shifts, which brought both unwelcome jarring and sense of unease, but also unexpected opportunity and unique contribution. International co-operation, politically and philosophically, had to reconcile itself with conflict, one that was not of the making of the social classes who it aimed to serve. Economically, its relatively independent socialist and community-self-help trading model had to align itself with a more corporate and centralised management of the national economy. The dynamics of these major transitions have to be understood at the local level and how they were understood, accepted, and applied in practice by individual societies and members. The life and work of the Lincoln Society is preserved in an extensive archive and provides a special and illuminating opportunity for such investigation.

> War, the enemy of progress, the sum-total of all evil, the last relic of barbarism, has suddenly sprung upon us, in such a manner that for its vastness, the like was never known before in the history of the world. Perhaps the one gleam of

Fig.1
Central Stores, Lincoln
Co-operative Society,
Free School Lane and
Silver Street, Lincoln
(front cover, Quarterly
Record Editions, 1914–
1915). (Source: courtesy
Lincoln Co-operative
Ltd).

> hope in this dark hour is that the effects of this conflict may be so far-reaching,
> and its toll of human sacrifice so great that never again will the working-classes
> of all countries allow themselves to be drawn into such a catastrophe.[2]

It was this declaration that greeted the readers of the Lincoln Co-operative Society's news-sheet in the Autumn of 1914. The First World War presented the co-operative movement with a series of major challenges, locally and more widely. How would the employees, members, and customers of local societies contend with the considerable stresses and anxieties brought by war? Would co-operation be able to keep up the pursuit of its national and international ideals, and achieve the greater representation, influence, and integration that it was seeking, but now during a time of fierce global conflict and domestic emergency?

The reports published by the Lincoln Equitable Co-operative Industrial Society (LECIS), together with its accompanying news-sheet, the *Quarterly Record*, articulate the various and changing responses of co-operation to the conflict, at its onset and through the war years themselves (Fig. 1). Indeed, the period saw the *Quarterly Record's* final years, with the last edition ending with the Winter quarter, 1919. The articles contained in it show shifts between different spheres of attention: the international, the national, and the local. In addition, the content also conveys the concerns relating to a range of evolving and contrasting areas of political, economic, and social priority. The document, as a primary source, provides rich insight into how the war was perceived and experienced, and how it was faced at the level of a local society in Lincolnshire, by national co-operation, and by co-operative endeavour world-wide. The publication expresses how co-operators sought to come to terms with the war and to engage with its conduct, and to tackle critical moments when the cause and position of co-operation were called into question and appeared threatened.

The First World War imposed various demands upon society and the economy, many of them considerable. For most of the population the onset of the conflict came as both a great shock and surprise. The nation was far from ready, in both practical or psychological terms. This said, as the crisis established its course, it also opened up unexpected opportunities in some quarters. The impact of the war has attracted considerable attention from historians and commentators more broadly.[3] Perspectives and interpretations are numerous and diverse, among which are a set of prominent and critical questions. Was the war welcomed, for example, or at best accepted? How did it facilitate the hopes and ambitions of some sections of society, but thwart others? Did the intervention of a world war at this moment in the twentieth century speed, divert, or distract forms of advancement that were in evidence before August 1914? More specifically, had the working classes and labour interests achieved a stronger position and greater influence by the closing months and in its immediate aftermath?

Similar queries run though histories of co-operation. As both a business and movement, it shared in shouldering the strains, while also seizing new possibilities where they presented themselves.[4] Co-operation's involvement in production, distribution, and supply of food and other commodities was already well developed, as was its stance as a protector of the well-being of working-class consumers. Yet, the need arose for co-operators to grow and develop their operations, and to participate within an economic regime that fell subject to more comprehensive management by government, local and central. The position of the movement politically and socially came under closer external scrutiny as well as internal self-evaluation, so much so that it decided to assume more formal parliamentary representation in the defence of its members' interests, as employees, consumers and citizens. Co-operation was progressive in calling for, and modelling, approaches to price control and rationing, but found itself ignored and pushed to the margins by the strength of private-trader influence in government. On the matter of taxation, co-operators felt themselves to be singled out for unfair treatment.

Co-operation's place in the labour movement as a whole would also be re-assessed, as the war prompted new arrangements for the representation of trades unions and ushered in new levels of militancy – including within co-operative business operations. Organised labour had expanded considerably and now expected far more by way of the management of the economy and social reform during the war years and in the years to follow. Furthermore, the extension of conscription exposed societies to additional pressures. Societies were very proactive in supporting the war effort and enlistment, although, as the war rolled on, the departure of personnel to the Front would place their functioning under ever greater strain. The advancement of women, in politics and the economy, was also reflected in co-operative custom and practice in this period. Female employment expanded, the Guilds extended their external political outlook and strengthened their campaigning position. Women also rose to more influential roles in local and national government as the representatives of co-operation. Through the war years, co-operative media and propaganda activities played an essential role, in local societies, and on the larger political stage.

The Lincoln Society was just over fifty years of age at the outbreak of the First World War. In many respects it would simply carry on meeting, and benefitting from, the well-established and growing demands of an expanding, industrialising, and developing city and its hinterland. In other respects, the pace of change would accelerate or activities would be considerably delayed or disrupted.[5] Retail would continue to dominate its operations, although the Society would further diversify its production, processing and distribution activities. New Coulson Road premises were opened on 16 October, 1915, the Society's twenty-third branch store (Fig. 2). It would also extend its provision beyond foodstuffs and expand its involvement in the agriculture and housing sectors. Through each of the five years of war, different pressures emerged and grew. Meanwhile, fresh opportunities arose and were taken, to the advantage of both the local society and co-operation as a whole. These were explained to local members through updates provided in the 'Half-yearly Report and Balance Sheet' (HYBS). These were published in early January and July each year, and, at mid-points between, in the 'Quarterly Report and Cash Account' (QRCA) issued in early April and October. Inserted into all of these publications was an edition of the *Lincoln Co-operative Quarterly Record (LCQR)*. A striking feature of the editorship of the *Quarterly Record* was its sampling, balancing, and conveying of news, whether from the international scene, the national domain, or the Society's local and regional setting. This is an examination of the second half of 1914, and the whole of 1915. Over this time the repositioning of the Lincoln Society and the wider movement was rapid, intense, and dramatic.

1914: 'FOR KING AND COUNTRY'[6]

> What vacant chairs and anxious hearts there have been this festive season…
> To all our homes, where anxious ones are bravely bearing great burdens, employees and members alike, the Society as a whole, from the centre to the circumference, as with one voice express to you their indebtedness for the patriotism and devotion your brave lads are now showing.[7]

Shortly after Christmas 1914, this message went out to the members of the Lincoln Society in its *Quarterly Record*. The city and the county were settling into the likelihood of a longer conflict. The response of the population to the outbreak of war was complex, and indeed its character shifted through the opening months of the conflict through to the year's end.[8]

In the first instance, the country's entry into the war secured sufficient acceptance by politicians and from the national media. However, this was not without strong expressions of regret from many quarters that this major catastrophe had not been averted. History today rather plays down the idea of a universally felt urge to rush to the colours, with eager recruits charged up, heady with enthusiasm and a sense of adventure. There was a euphoric reaction among some certainly, but also much reluctance and reticence among many others faced with the prospect of whether to join up or not. Recruitment tended to follow pre-war patterns in terms of the sectors of society from which from the military traditionally formed its ranks. Through the autumn and winter, various military reverses or heroic defensive stands, together with news of the fate of the Belgian population, prompted fresh rounds of enlistment. The mood, though, was more generally one of a sober-minded and collective sense of duty and the sharing of patriotic concerns for the security of the nation and its people, as opposed to jingoistic fervour. Moreover, the language of mobilisation also reached for religious reference points, to notions of sacrifice and of having God on one's side.

On the home front, meanwhile, the first five months of the First World War did require some rapid responses from various organisations and groups, the co-operative movement included.[9] This said, there remained the general expectation that hostilities would be brief and any disruption made manageable. The idea that it would be 'business as usual' was accepted. Co-operation, and the economy and society in Britain more broadly, responded with this assumption in mind. There was panic buying in the first instance, but this eased, and the Co-operative Wholesale Society (CWS) and local societies played a role in steadying supply of essential commodities and prices. Indeed, its hand in the control of distribution and price levels, and the maintenance of quality, meant that it would attract larger membership numbers, a trend that would continue through the war years. Co-operation would express its support for the war effort, reflected in the reinstatement of the allowances and re-employment guarantees that it had put in place for the Boer War, and the receipt of

Fig.2 Former branch store, Coulson Road, Lincoln.

early government orders to supply the armed forces.

However, the CWS felt that it could step back from an opportunity to take up national representation, as offered through an invitation to join a new Prices Advisory Committee set up by the Asquith government. Such external activity was seen as not permissible within the narrow constraints of the role of its Board members. This would prove a major strategic error on the part of the movement, and with considerable ramifications nationally and locally during the war years. Before 1914 was out, co-operators found themselves failing to receive invitations to join a Royal Commission on Sugar Supplies and a Grain Supplies Committee. More promising, though, was the growing of bonds with the wider labour movement through the War Emergency Workers' National Committee (WNC). This body was established by the Labour Party and trade unions, and its membership would admit representatives of the Co-operative Union (CU) and the Women's Co-operative Guild (WCG). The Committee would give advice to government through the war on matters of prices and supply.

In the first instance, it was a despairing report that confronted the *Quarterly Record's* readers in the early Autumn of 1914. Much of the front page is given over the outbreak of the war. Shock and regret predominate:

> It has been stated that this is not a war of peoples; that the German people did not want war, and probably this was so. We have sufficient faith in the good sense of the majority of middle and working class people in both this country and Germany, to believe that if the bonds of sympathy and understanding which the co-operative and democratic movement of both countries are endeavouring to weave had only had the opportunity to grow stronger, this war would have been impossible.[10]

The article turns to reflect back, with wistfulness and anguish, on the meeting of the International Congress in Glasgow in August 1913, when the 'highest point of enthusiasm' had met the submission of a resolution on 'Co-operation and international peace'. A German delegate had stressed the ideals of friendship, solidarity, and unity among co-operators, and the realisation and accomplishment of 'that great work for the peace of the whole world, and the resolution was carried with 'Germans, French, Russians, Serbians, Britons, and Austrians, vying with each other in their intense earnestness'. The fear, though, was 'the baneful system of conscription', and how this might compel 'the same delegates' to 'meet each other in deathly conflict… they are by a military system made into deadly enemies… International Co-operation and Trade Unionism will get a serious set-back as the result of this war'. The article concludes:

> We dare not think what International Co-operation will be like at the end of this strife, we can only hope. Probably all progressive movements will be thrown back for a generation, and when peace reigns again throughout the land of Europe, may it be a peace made permanent by the bonds of International Fellowship of Co-operation, so strong that the militarism of any country is not powerful enough to break it.

By early January 1915, the tone of the *Quarterly Record* had shifted from the position of horror and alarm that it had expressed three months earlier. Discussion of the war would remain on the front page but had been pushed towards the bottom of the second column. The co-operative movement accommodated itself with the national crisis and had been actively supporting and encouraging enlistment. In an article entitled 'For King and Country', the *Quarterly Record* draws on prevailing attitudes towards the promotion of recruitment, including a collectively shared patriotism, a sense of duty, and the need to defend the homeland:

> England's call has met with a magnificent response from all classes and conditions of the people: 'cook's sons,' and 'duke's sons,' are comrades in arms fighting one common foe… Our gallant fellows, impelled by the one sacred call of duty, have laid down the pen, have left the counter, the stables, the mill, the buildings, and the farm for the motherland. They have enlisted under the flag that stands for freedom and liberty… Already the price is a terrible one, but the liberties we enjoy to-day have been won by blood, we must hold fast that which has been so nobly won.[11]

It is clear from the outset the level of support of the Lincoln Society for those taking up arms locally. Reporting on those that had left for service, and the first reports of injuries, if not yet fatalities, the account declared: 'As a Society we are immensely proud of them, we know they will do their duty, and play their part well, and thus do something to bring this terrible war to an end'. The piece continues: 'and the good wishes of all our readers will follow them with a prayer for their speedy return'. The article, though, is caught rather ambivalently, not yet wishing to lose sight of its international hopes and visions:

> If, when peace comes, militarism in Europe is hopelessly broken, and all nations work for the common weal, then a new day will dawn in which our children and future generations will enjoy a liberty even this land has yet known.

Critical to opinion forming was the fate of Belgium. The October report refers to a contribution to a relief fund for Belgium. However, by January the Management Committee reported on the establishment of a fund and, citing one case, that: 'we took immediate action and prepared an unoccupied house on Newark Road, for their reception. Mr. and Mrs. Moorgat, of Antwerp, with a family of four children, arrived on December 23rd, and are highly gratified at your kind consideration'.[12] The *Quarterly Record's* third article devotes some length to the matter of Belgium, and includes a number of individual and personal accounts of families being housed by co-operative employees:

> The debt that all civilised countries owe to Belgium, cannot be adequately put on paper, hence the hearts of the peoples of these countries have been sorely stricken at the terrible calamities through which the Belgian people have, and are now passing. Fire and sword (and worse things still) have done their work, and in scores of thousands these people are looking to other lands for succour.[13]

The positioning of the co-operative movement internationally, in the immediate and longer term, is reflected upon further in January 1915 in an article reproduced from the national publication, the *Co-operative News,* for the Lincoln Society's members. It recognises the spiralling of 'the price of food and other necessities of life', observing that the 'most serious, of course, is the advance in the price of bread, because this hits hardest the very poor'. The account explains the background in terms of the destruction of shipping and the disruption of supply, and the impact on shipping and commodity prices. It expresses a mindfulness of the need for future reconciliation and restoration. However, the article is concerned at the prospect of the capitalist gains that might be achieved in securing and then perpetuating greater national dominance of trade: 'the idea of permanently destroying German trade, not merely during the war, but after the war, so much talked about by our yellow press, would, if it were possible, only rebound to the capitalist interest'.[14]

For the October 1914 edition, consideration of the international scene dominated the *Quarterly Record's* front page. The place of co-operation at home is relegated. In the lead article of the October's news-sheet, the impact of the war at home is confined to a single and relatively perfunctory paragraph. This said, it is quite assertive, and reflects the wider picture: 'The suddenness of the conflagration created something like a panic throughout the country', and fears were abounding in relation to sustaining levels of supply and demand, and the likelihood of shortages and spiralling prices. However, 'the Co-operative movement throughout the country saved the situation', with the report referring to societies that had ceased or reduced the facility for advance ordering, or had managed demand through other means, such as limiting the number of orders placed per week, and declining to supply to, or to admit, new members.[15] Nationally, the business of the CWS had increased. Although profits in some areas were being limited by wage rises, 'all the departments are in a healthy condition'.[16]

Locally, the Lincoln Society reported that 'the great European War has been uppermost in all our minds during the greater part of the quarter, and has affected very considerably the usual smooth working of the Society'. It had to contend with price rises and rash buying but could reassure members that: 'as far as supplies were concerned we were, as a Society, exceptionally well placed. We have advanced prices only where it was absolutely necessary'.[17] Moreover, the loss of draft horses for deliveries was being met with the addition of further motor vehicles. The role of the Lincoln Society in the local economy receives further elaboration in a discussion of bread pricing: 'We are the largest dealers in bread in the city, and have always controlled the prices, and it has been no uncommon thing for the bakers to approach the Committee, urging the necessity of raising bread'. Co-operative outlets had continued with established practices of selling in standard weights, but varying prices in line with the cost of flour. Other traders, by contrast, had switched to fixing prices, but were masking fluctuating production costs by reducing the loaf weights, and not that transparently. City co-operators could only but take up their customary cause of protecting the honest customer: 'Knowledge is power, and we believe the public have only to learn the facts, to condemn the new system'.[18] The article continues by notifying readers of a Select Committee Report, with recommendations relating to the standardisation of bread weights, and the weighing and clear pricing of products at the time of sale.

By the New Year, 1915, co-operators could be even more emphatic about the movement's domestic contribution. A report places the satisfactory trading position of the Lincoln Society in the context of its national economic significance: 'Never before has the movement had such an opportunity, but it has proved itself worthy, and the Government in many ways have found the "Great" Wholesale of immense benefit in this critical period of our history'. Government contracts had been negotiated through the CWS for clothing, boots, and other items, and the movement could 'rejoice in a prestige we never had before'.[19] The Half-yearly Report of 6 January 1915 brought to a close the business of the year 1914.[20] For the Lincoln Society, and its operations on the home front, there had been a broad sense of business being as usual. The *Quarterly Record's* leader opens with the title 'Allies still advancing', but in fact follows with a report of the Secretary on 'Another year of splendid progress'. The war was 'responsible for many things, positive and negative', but, on balance, could be set in the context of a celebration of what had been the most successful trading year in the Society's fifty-three years, and a strong decade of advancement since 1904. Many areas of growth could be evidenced, including: 'our Society has the distinguished honour of being foremost in taking co-operation into the county districts', together with greater investment through the Educational Department: 'music, books, gymnastic exercises, nursing, &c., catered for all, and relieved considerably the monotony and drabness of many a life'. Domestic supply concerns had translated into an expansion of membership and custom, and, with this, the wider place of the movement, locally and nationally: 'From the highest paid official to the youngest employee… all are allies in a great cause, in a peaceful revolution which is doing much to regenerate the workers of our land'.[21]

Elsewhere there is little other reference to the war in the early January 1915 *Quarterly Record*, except a further contribution a relief fund for Belgium, the restoring of bread deliveries, and the departure of some staff to take up service in the army. Coverage is generally to be expected, with short pieces commending co-operative trade practices and services, listing meetings of the Women's Guilds, summarising the provision of the Education Department, and including news of other societies in the country. Moreover, there is little sign in the Society's advertisements of the impact of the war on the supply of consumer commodities through its Central Store. The Outfitting & Ready-Made Department drew attention to new designs and being 'well up' in certain sporting ranges, and with a 'large stock' in 'fancy goods', The Tailoring Department was also encouraging advance orders, including in the 'latest colours'. Furthermore, The Drapery and Millinery Department could announce:

> our half yearly clearance sale, which we trust, as usual, will be effective in clearing all Surplus last Season's Stocks so as to give us good Space for our new deliveries of Spring Goods: these were bought early and consist of the Newest and Latest of the early Spring Novelties. We would earnestly ask you to call and inspect our New Stocks; they will be both well-varied and abundant, and for value unexcelled.

1915: 'NOT BUSINESS AS USUAL'[22]

> The difficulties of providing adequate labour according to the demands of our growing business is ever increasing, and we expect it will get worse sooner than better, we therefore respectfully ask your assistance whenever possible by trading at your nearest branch, carrying home your own goods, as far as able, and in various other ways that will occur to you. It would help us considerably, if, where it could be done, our members would make their purchases at other than the ordinary times when our shops are crowded.[23]

By the end of the second full year of the conflict, the readers of the *Quarterly Record* were becoming more familiar with announcements on mounting challenges to supply and demand, and regular appeals to participate in voluntary measures to alleviate shortages and pressures. More generally, through 1915, co-operation adapted further to the political, economic and social adjustments required of a country at war.[24] Its organisation was integrated well into the economy through processes of production, procurement, distribution, and retail. This meant that the movement was very well placed to respond, but it was becoming clearer that the scale of the conflict would no longer be met with a mindset of 'business-as-usual'.

Various accommodations and compromises were arrived at between government and labour interests. Parties would endeavour to settle disputes through arbitration rather than by striking, while trade unions would permit the dilution of skilled labour forces along with the admittance of female workers. Undertakings were agreed to ensure that pre-war practices would be reinstated at the end of the conflict. Negotiations with the Amalgamated Union of Co-operative Employees (AUCE) had arrived at equal pay for women employed through the CWS and other societies. This said, they would be required to join a union while employed, and with the expectation that substituted workers would not be retained after the war. At the same time, the CU set mechanisms for the negotiation of hours and wages levels from the local to the national levels. However, such measures would not be adequate to ease all tensions that would mount through the war years, including recourse to strike action.

Co-operative operations would also be increasingly hampered by procurement and supply issues, from the centre to the stores, as international shipping suffered greater losses at sea. Co-operation could contend with this to some degree, in terms of managing distribution and prices. given the role of the CWS in the supply chain between overseas producers and local retailers. Nonetheless, co-operation, as a movement and as a trader itself, was sensitive to the struggles of its working-class consumer base and stepped up its campaigning for greater government-managed rationing at a time of rising food prices and their impact on household budgets. Particularly significant was the tracking of staple-commodity prices, working with the WNC, and informing both the government departments and the general public.

An important reverse, though, was suffered with the imposition of Excess Profits Duty (EPD). The measure was greeted by the movement initially, given the Duty's introduction as a response to widely held indignation sparked by evidence of private-trader profiteering. However, co-operation failed to bring the retraction of the EPD's inclusion of dividend payments to its members. The taxation of the dividend, of what was a mechanism intended to assist and encourage saving in working-class households, was seen as a major blow to one of co-operation's core principles and practices. Co-operators felt that their societies were already making a significant contribution through the Duty, and it was fair and appropriate to reduce the specific tax liability on the dividend. Societies, typically, achieved this through reducing the level of dividend payments by lowering of prices closer to the cost price.

For the *Quarterly Record* of April 1915, the war re-occupies its position as the subject of the lead article. The leaning of the content here is far more resolved and focused, with less ambivalence and *caveat*. It is set at some distance from the tone of the October 1914 leader.

> Our brave lads from all parts of the town and country, from cottage and mansion, democrat and aristocrat, are nobly responding to their country's call, and standing shoulder to shoulder in one common cause against one common foe... we consider the response magnificent, and of which any Society would be justly proud. The history of one of our Society contains many glowing records, and among the best will be the readiness with which they obeyed the call of duty at the time of greatest crisis in our history as a nation.[25]

The service of the Society, eight months into the conflict, justified the call for the creation of a roll of honour. The account lists the names of sixty-nine former employees who had enrolled but with, at the time of writing, no fatalities, if with one prisoner of war in Germany. The report of the Education Secretary at this time noted that 'some have left our classes and gone to fight for our King and Country in the lands across the seas, including a former Junior Choir member and recent recipient of the Victoria Cross: we trust that other of our boys may become heroes, not only on the battlefield but in the battle of life'. The report was of the view that the Education Department's classes had a role to play in securing the advancement of its young members and, as needed in the current time: '"England expects that every man this day will do his duty," and at this time we shall include the women who are nobly bearing their part'.[26]

The *Quarterly Record* for October 1915, in a graver tone, had to return discussion of the course of the war to the position of lead article. The Society was confronted with its first fatality. It is one of what would follow as a series of notices of the deaths of former employees in active service at the Front. The publication, however, was not without its eye on the wider and longer-term vision and hopes for the future. A contrasting perspective from overseas is provided in a long article of more than one page dedicated to co-operation in Russia. It is an international insight that reminds readers of the advance of the movement globally, in spite of the current military crisis. It celebrates the growth in the number of local societies, reaching 37,000, and passing the total present in Germany. Moreover, the author estimated that members and their families probably accounted for one third of the population. There is no explicit message in the form of a call to British co-operation to adopt features of the Russian model in Britain in wartime.

The same article, though, proceeds to stress the significance of the levels of government intervention and partnership that had developed, including the direction of state finance through the local co-operative credit societies, and the approval of the formation of co-operative unions. Furthermore, relationship with the state had extended itself to local government, with the forming of partnerships and the offering of credit through co-operative credit societies: 'The high prices of necessaries, speculation on the part of small tradesmen and the war have all contributed to the appreciation of the part played by the co-operation movement'. Involvement and engagement in munitions production had also developed: 'Its straight-dealing has won the confidence of organisations for supplying the army, and numerous orders are now placed with the societies'. The author goes on to discuss the productive capacity of co-operative societies, their credit-raising value, and their charitable and relief functions. More generally, the piece concludes: 'We express our earnest hope that the light of Co-operation may illuminate those remote corners of Russia which until now have remained in utter darkness'.[27]

Through 1915, the *Quarterly Record* considers the management of national affairs, and the role of co-operation. The July *Quarterly Record*, for example, gives a clear expression of the more prominent place of women in the movement and the building influence of the women's guilds. A report of a Lincoln delegate attending the Women's Guild Congress in Liverpool in that year observed 'Naturally the war largely occupied the thoughts of the congress, and ways and means of obtaining a permanent peace'. The President's speech had acknowledged the gains in the employment conditions of women, and the role of the Guilds in the advancement of the education of women through the Guild. Indeed, the report added pointedly: 'Perhaps too much importance was attached to the idea that, if the women of Europe had a greater share in local and Imperial government, the danger of war would disappear', and, referring to Ruskin's writings, that: 'the women of Europe could prevent war to-morrow if they wished, by exercising quite other methods than having a share in the government'. The account also turned to current and practical action in relation to a debate on co-operation and prices:

> Organisation, by means of co-operation, to get more complete control of food products, would enable the co-operative societies to control prices and bring them within more reasonable limits than is possible at present. Speakers, one after another, pointed out how the co-operative societies in their own districts had done a great deal indeed to keep the greed of the private trader within limits.

The article's author, 'ER', could add that the 'Lincoln delegates were very pleased to think that their own Society had done much to keep down prices in their own town'.[28] The same edition of the *Quarterly Record* also reports on the national Annual Congress of co-operatives, noting with regret the absence of foreign delegates. There is little by way of discussion of the content of the proceedings of the meeting. However, the report did reflect the position of the movement at this point in the war on the issue of more formal political engagement. A general aversion to this continued to prevail, with the gathering declining, 'by a very large majority', any direction towards greater political-party affiliation. Nonetheless, the Congress did debate its engagement in the management of the economy, with 'How far can the Co-operative movement control prices' as topic. Moreover, it returned to its wider and future significance, with: 'The future policy of the movement after the war from an International standpoint'.[29] Moreover, an article in the subsequent edition of the *Quarterly Record*, on the opening of a new branch store, was capitalised upon as an opportunity to remind co-operators of the greater war that they were fighting:

> The allies of thrift and industry are moving on, occupying new ground, and ever waging war against monopoly, trusts and unfair competition. Truly a bloodless revolution is taking place in our midst, and instead of desolation, peace, happiness and contentment follow in its train. May we have more of it.[30]

The new headway being achieved by the movement was being enjoyed across the country. As 1915 came to a close, the *Quarterly Record* made reference once again to quarterly reports of the CWS. Sales had increased by twenty-six and thirty-six percent, although it was recognised that these were actual rather than in real terms, given the increase in prices, nonetheless, 'when all allowances are made, the CWS is evidently steadily progressing, in the likes of banking, flour, cocoa and chocolate, and boots and shoes.[31] Furthermore, co-operation's ongoing contribution to the economy through a second year of war had earned due political recognition:

> It has been tested in many ways and has stood the ordeal well… The clasped hand has been real, a brotherhood has been fostered, that will endure when peace comes. The Government has at last realised what a power the movement is, and when the history of these times are written, the story will be told how prominently a part Co-operation played in the greatest crisis the old country has ever had to meet.[32]

Moreover, the course of 1915 had finally dispelled the idea of a wartime regime that could enjoy 'business as usual'. An extended analysis of the general economic conditions concluded: 'Never in the memory of business men has there been such difficulties of keeping up supplies as during the year 1915'. Various causes are ascribed, including the loss of vessels to enemy action at sea, the cancellation of contracts by suppliers experiencing the impact of higher freight charges, labour shortages, the scarcity of raw materials, the redirection of import shipping to safer, but more distant ports, and greater insurance charges. The article also incorporates a series of extracts from trading journals, 'full of their lamentations and complaint as to ever growing troubles in carrying on business'; three tables of statistics, listing the increase of freight charges from New York, and from the River Plate; and figures illustrating the increases in food prices over the last year. The article concludes: 'in addition to the ghastly work of the war that is claiming those nearest and dearest to us, in every household we are paying the toll in another way, and shall continue to pay for this barbarous crime to humanity to the end of our days'.[33]

Through 1915, the quarterly and half-yearly reports, together with the *Quarterly Record,* conveyed to local co-operators how the war was affecting the Society's trading and other activities. At the end of the first quarter of 1915, the Management Committee could note in positive terms the continuing prosperity for its trade, and Lincoln's engagement in producing for the war effort:

> The War, while causing much sorrow and anxiety, has brought to the Society a large increase of trade of a special kind, notably in the Tailoring Department in the shape of Government Orders. Already we have made and delivered 450 overcoats, 1215 Hospital Gowns, 465 Service Suits and 300 pairs of Breeches. It is gratifying to learn that complete satisfaction has been given with the work done.[34]

At the end of the next quarter of the year, the Management Committee reported similarly, emphasising further growth in trade and membership. Its progress was also represented in the declaration of a £5000 contribution to a War Loan through the CWS, in response to a national appeal from Government. It was a 'transaction which, apart from patriotic motives, will be a profitable investment for a portion of the Reserve funds of the Society'.[35] The *Quarterly Record* could bring a close to the year in good spirit, making reference to its support for the war, and the ongoing co-operative effort: 'Sacrifices have been made of which we are all proud… the one thought has been to fight for the flag that demotes freedom wherever it goes'. In business terms, benefits had clearly arisen locally: 'we have had a very successful year. A large increase of members, and a vastly growing trade', if with the *caveat* that 'expenses have gone up very considerably, the heaviest being for labour, the enhanced prices of living necessitating higher pay'.[36] Co-operators were also having to accept a widening in the incidence of shortages.

By early 1915, members were forewarned that they must accustom themselves to selecting from existing stock within a narrower range. Advertisements echo this. The Drapery and Millinery Department, in smaller font towards the end of a feature, added: 'Owing to the War deliveries of certain good are very difficult and, in some cases, impossible. Under these circumstances we must ask our members kind forbearance.'[37] There are also remarks on shortages or delays in the advertisements of the Outfitting & Ready-Made, Tailoring, and Furnishing & Hardware Departments. An advertisement of the Boot & Shoe Department was most explicit, and impressed upon customers the need for early orders:

> Labour conditions are causing great concern in Boot Manufacturing Centres. This serious fact, occurring at a time when certain leathers are both Scarce and Dear, has brought about conditions of shortage in Footwear which is without parallel in the Boot Trade.[38]

Such advertisements continue in this manner through 1915, giving notice of the impact of wartime conditions. Others, meanwhile, speak of measures taken to alleviate shortages or where possible, offer reassurances. The Outfitting & Ready-Made Department, for example, stressed that 'we have made extensive purchases EARLY ON, in view of the great rise in the prices of all kinds of goods'; while the Tailoring Department was could still 'supply you at the old prices.'[39]

Disruption was also being experienced in relation to the Society's social and cultural activities. An early 1915 report of the Education Department noted the loss of an instructor to military service and the requisitioning of the gym facilities for military training needs.[40] Other support for the war effort, though, could be reported in more positive terms. The proceeds of a Junior Choir Concert, for example, were being donated for the 'comforts of the soldiers' in the Northern Hospital, Boultham Hospital and 4th Battalion, the Lincolnshire Regiment, at the Front: 'Nothing could be more cheering than to see the children doing their bit to cheer the soldiers who have so bravely fought for us.'[41]

CONCLUSION: 'WE HAVE COME OUT QUITE WELL'[42]

Throughout the war, articles in the Lincoln Society's *Quarterly Record* appeared reflecting on how much its status and role had been advanced. This is a discussion of the first couple of years of the First World War only. The circumstances of this time acted as a catalyst in the transformation of the Lincoln Society and co-operation more broadly. The 1914-18 war was a great test for the movement. It brought considerable advances, but also drew attention to areas of challenge that would have to be confronted in subsequent decades. If the years up to 1914 can be regarded as something of a golden age of expansion, the years of the First World War allowed a deeper embedding of co-operation socially, politically and economically, and locally and nationally.[43] It had demonstrated convincingly that it could operate both as a successful trader under demanding and competitive market conditions, and remain a conscientious and persuasive protector of its consumers, as well as its employees and members.

For the Lincoln Society more specifically, it had entered the second decade of the twentieth century in a more mature state, both consolidating and expanding its activities. This trajectory was maintained, and indeed accelerated during the early war years. Its place as a political representative, employer, and provider of services would grow and diversify significantly. It is difficult to discern how much publications like the *Quarterly Record* were read, and how far members and customers felt themselves to be part of a national or even international movement. For the Society's leadership and management at least, as they expressed themselves through the *Quarterly Record* and other reports, the war demanded a vision of local co-operation that was positioned operationally and culturally on a wider stage. The significance and role that the publication had established for itself before 1914 was posed a more urgent and graver task. The publication was a multi-layered media form, informing its membership on the national and international scene, as well as that on its doorstep. It was also a sophisticated mode of propaganda, articulating the thought and practice of the wider co-operative movement, the continuing and the shifting. The world of the Lincoln co-operators had never been more assailed by, but also advanced by, general political and economic forces.

NOTES

1.   *Lincoln Co-operative Quarterly Record (LCQR)*, 'War, and co-operation at home and abroad', October 1914, 5.

2.   *LCQR*, 'War, and co-operation', 5.

3.   K. Adie, K., 1914, *Fighting on the Home Front: The Legacy of Women in World War One*, London; Bourne, J., 2014, 'The Midlands and the First World War', *Midland History*, 39, 2, pp. 157-62; Pelling, H., 1963, *A History of British Trade Unionism*, Harmondsworth: Penguin. pp. 149-66; Fussell, P., 1975, *The Great War and Modern Memory*, Oxford; Gregory, A., 2008, *The Last Great War*, Cambridge; Paxman, J., 2014, *Great Britain's Great War*, Harmondsworth; Van Emden, R. and Humphries, S., 2017, *All Quiet on the Home Front: An Oral History of Life in Britain during the First World War*, London; Sheffield, G., 2017, *World War I: 100th Anniversary Commemorative Edition*, London; Winter, J., 2009, *The Legacy of the Great War: Ninety Years On*. Missouri; Winter, J., 2014, *Sites of Memory, Sites of Mourning: The Great War in Cultural History*, Cambridge.

4.   McCabe, C., 2009, 'Irish railwaymen and the retail co-operative movement, 1917-23', in Black, L. and Robertson, N., *Consumerism and the Co-operative movement in Modern British History: Taking Stock*, Manchester. pp. 110-18; Hilson, M., 'The consumer co-operative movement in cross-national perspective: Britain and Sweden, *c.* 1860-1939', in Black and Robertson, *Consumerism*, pp. 76-81; N. Robertson, 'Co-operation: The Hope of the Consumer? The co-operative movement and consumer protection', in Black and Robertson, *Consumerism*, pp. 222-39; Thompson, D. J., 1994, *Weavers of Dreams: Founders of the Modern Co-operative Movement*, Davis, CA. pp. 100-102; Wilson, J. F., Webster, A. and Vorburg-Rugh, R., 2013, *Building Co-operation: A Business History of the Co-operative Group, 1863-2013*, Oxford. pp. 150-65.

5   Bruckshaw, F. and McNab, D., 1961, *A Century of Achievement: The Story of Lincoln Co-operative Society*, Lincoln: Lincoln Co-operative Society. pp. 54-9; Jackson, A. H. J., 2015, 'The Lincoln Cooperative Society, Silver Street and Free School Lane', in Walker, A. (ed.), *Lincoln's City Centre: North of the River Witham*, Lincoln. pp. 51-4; Jackson, A. J. H., 2016, 'The co-operative movement and the education of working men and women: provision by a local society in Lincoln, England, 1861-1914', *International Labor and Working Class History* 90. pp. 32-6; Jackson A. J. H. and Kent, H., 2016, 'The Lincoln Co-operative Society and the Lower High Street', in Walker, A. (ed.) *Lincoln's City Centre: South of the River Witham: From High Bridge to South Park*, Lincoln. pp. 60-1; Middleton, A., 2011, *150 Years of Lincolnshire Co-operative*, Lincoln: Lincolnshire C-operative Ltd, 43. pp. 68-71.

6.   *LCQR*, 'For king and country', January 1915, 11.

7.   *LCQR*, 'For king and country'.

8.   Adie, *Fighting on the Home Front*; Beckett, J., 2014, 'Patriotism in Nottinghamshire: challenging the unconvinced', *Midland History*, 39, 2. pp.185-201; Beeching, N., 2014, 'The provincial press & the outbreak of the war: a Unionist view in Worcestershire', *Midland History*, 39, 2, pp. 163-84;

Bell, S., 2014, 'Soldiers of Christ arise: religious nationalism in the East Midlands during World War I', *Midland History*, 39, 2, pp. 219-35; Fussell, *The Great War*, pp. 3-5; Middleton, *150 years*, p. 69; Sheffield, *World War I*, pp. 6-41; Winter, *Sites of Memory*, pp. 205-7.

9.   Robertson, 'Co-operation', pp. 223-4; Wilson, Webster, and Vorburg-Rugh, *Building Co-operation*, pp. 152-6.

10.   *LCQR*, 'War, and co-operation', 5.

11.   *LCQR*, 'For king and country', 5-6.

12.   Half-yearly Report and Balance Sheet (HYBS), 'Committee's Report', January 1915, 2.

13.   *LCQR*, 'Our Belgian friends', January 1915, 11.

14.   *LCQR*, 'Prices and freights – how the people are being robbed – co-operation and party politics', January 1915, 12.

15.   *LCQR*, 'War, and co-operation', 5.

16.   *LCQR*, 'C.W.S.', October 1914, 5.

17.   Quarterly Report and Cash Account (QRCA), 'Committee's Report', October 1914, 2.

18.   *LCQR*, 'Size bread v. bread by weight', October 1914, 6.

19.   *LCQR*, 'Our "Great" Wholesale', 111, 11.

20.   HYBS, January 1915.

21.   *LCQR*, 'Allies still advancing: another year of splendid progress', January 1915, 10.

22.   *LCQR*, '"Business Not as Usual"', January 1916, 10-11.

23.   HYBS, January 1916, 2.

24.   McCabe, 'Irish railwaymen', pp. 110-18; Robertson, 'Co-operation', pp. 223-5; Wilson, Webster, and Vorburg-Rugh, *Building Co-operation*, pp. 154-8.

25.   *LCQR*, Our roll of honour', April 1915, 7.

26.   *LCQR*, 'Educational Department', July 1915, 10.

27.   *LCQR*, 'The development of co-operation in Russia by Professor V. Totomianz (Moscow)', January 1916, 11-2.

28.   *LCQR*, 'Impressions of the Women's Guild Congress held in Liverpool, 1915', July 1915, 10.

29.   *LCQR*, 'Impressions of congress, July 1915, 10-11.

30.   *LCQR*, 'Allies advancing: opening of the new branch on Coulson Road', October 1915, 5.

31.   *LCQR*, 'Remarkable figures', January 1916, 11.

32.   *LCQR*, '1915', January 1915, 10. See: Robertson, 'Co-operation', pp. 223-4; Wilson, Webster, and Vorburg-Rugh, *Building Co-operation*, pp. 154-8.

33.   *LCQR*, '"Business Not as Usual"'.

34.   QRCA, April 1915, 2.

35.   HYBS, July 1915, 2.

36.   *LCQR*, '1915', 1916, 10.

37.   QRCA, April 1915, 6.

38.   QRCA, April 1915.

39.   HYBS, July 1915.

40.   *LCQR*, 'Educational Department', April 1915, 8.

41.   *LCQR*, 'Educational Department', October 1915, 6.

42.   *LCQR*, 'Our Society after three years', October 2017, 6-7.

43. Robertson, 'Co-operation', pp. 222-35; Wilson, Webster, and Vorburg-Rugh, *Building Co-operation*, pp. 165-202.

DENNIS MILLS : A BIBLIOGRAPHY

Shirley Brook*

THE PLACE OF PUBLICATION OF BOOKS IS LONDON UNLESS OTHERWISE STATED

1950–1959

(with J. P. Cole and J. C. Crossley) 'Recent Soviet atlases', *Geographical Journal,* 122 (1955), pp. 282-84.

'The USSR: A reappraisal of Mackinder's Heartland Concept', *Scottish Geographical Magazine,* 72 (1955), pp. 144-53.

(with J. P. Cole) *English Guide to the Soviet Geographical Atlas for Teachers in Middle Schools,* Nottingham (1956).

'Regions of Kesteven devised for the purposes of agricultural history', *Lincolnshire Architectural and Archaeological Society, Reports and Papers,* 7.1 (1957), pp. 60-82.

Population and Settlement in Kesteven (Lincs.) c.1775 - c.1885, MA Thesis, University of Nottingham (1957).

'Lincolnshire farming regions', *East Midland Geographer,* 9 (1958), pp. 41-43.

'A bibliography of post-war work relating to the geography of Lincolnshire', *Lincolnshire Architectural and Archaeological Society Reports and Papers,* 7.2 (1958), pp. 175-83.

'Enclosure in Kesteven', *Agricultural History Review,* 7 (1959), pp. 82-97.

'The development of rural settlement around Lincoln, with specific reference to the eighteenth and nineteenth centuries', *East Midland Geographer,* 11 (1959), 3-15. Republished in *English Rural Communities: The Impact of a Specialised Economy,* edited by D. R. Mills (1973), 83-97.

'The poor laws and the distribution of population, *c.*1600-1860, with special reference to Lincolnshire', *Transactions and Papers of the Institute of British Geographers,* 26 (1959), pp. 185-95.

1960–1969

Land Ownership and Rural Population: With Special Reference to Leicestershire in the Mid-19th Century, PhD Thesis, University of Leicester (1963).

The Early History of Meldreth, Melbourn, Cambridgeshire, (1965).

'English villages in the eighteenth and nineteenth centuries: A sociological approach. Part I: The concept of a sociological classification', *Amateur Historian,* 68 (1965), pp. 271-78.

'English villages in the eighteenth and nineteenth centuries: A sociological approach. Part II: A survey of the main types of source material', *Amateur Historian,* 7.1 (1966), pp. 7-13.

'Integration (of Geography) with the humanities', *Times Educational Supplement,* May 25, 1967, p. 1804.

The English Village, (1968).

'Middle school teachers' training in Geography', *Times Educational Supplement,* March 28, 1969, p.1028.

1970–1979

'The geographical effects of the Laws of Settlement in Nottinghamshire: an analysis of Francis Howell's Report, 1848', *East Midland Geographer,* 5.1-2 (1970), pp. 31-38. Republished in *English Rural Communities: The Impact of a Specialised Economy*, edited by D. R. Mills (1973), pp. 182-191.

(with Andrew Learmonth *et al.*) *Political, Historical and Regional Geography,* Bletchley (1972).

'Francis Howell's Report on the operation of the Laws of Settlement in Nottinghamshire, 1848', *Transactions of the Thoroton Society of Nottinghamshire,* 76 (1973 for 1972), pp. 46-52.

(ed.) *English Rural Communities: The Impact of a Specialised Economy* (1973).

(with Ray Thomas and John Collins) *The Spread of Cities,* Milton Keynes (1973).

'The christening custom at Melbourn, Cambs', *Local Population Studies,* 11 (1973), pp. 11-22. Republished in *Population Studies from the Parish Registers*, edited by Michael Drake, Matlock (1982), pp. 36-47.

'The peasant tradition', *Local Historian,* 11 (1974), pp. 200-206.

'Starting points for local history teachers', *Times Educational Supplement* February 15, 1974, p. 65.

(with Andrew Learmonth and Brendan Connors) *Population Resources and Technology,* Milton Keynes (1975; repr. 1976).

'A social and demographic study of Melbourn, Cambridgeshire, *c.*1840', *Archives,* 12 (1976), pp. 115-20.

An economic, tenurial, social and demographic study of an English peasant village, Social Science Research Council, HR 3932 (1977).

'The peasant culture', *New Society,* April 7, 1977, pp. 10-12.

'The quality of life in Melbourn, Cambridgeshire, in the period 1800-50', *International Review of Social History,* 23 (1978), pp. 382-404.

'The residential propinquity of kin in a Cambridgeshire village, 1841', *Journal of Historical Geography,* 4 (1978), pp. 265-76.

'The technique of house repopulation: experience from a Cambridgeshire village, 1841', *Local Historian,* 13 (1978), pp. 86-97.

'The Court of Arches and church rates disputes as sources of social history', *Bulletin of Local History East Midland Region,* 14 (1979), pp. 1-11.

1980–1989

Aspects of Marriage: An Example of Applied Historical Studies, Milton Keynes, (1980).

Lord and Peasant in Nineteenth Century Britain (1980).

'The false widows of Melbourn: A cautionary census tale', *Journal of the Cambridgeshire Family History Society,* 3.1 (1981), pp. 3-5.

(with Carol G. Pearce) *Census Enumerators' Books: An Annotated Bibliography of Published Work Based Substantially on 19th Century Census Enumerators' Books,* Milton Keynes (1982).

'The significance of land tax assessments', *Local Historian,* 15 (1982), pp. 161-65.

'Rural industries and social structure: Framework knitters in Leicestershire, 1670-1851', *Textile History,* 13 (1982), pp. 183-203.

(ed. with J. Gibson) *Land Tax Assessments c.1690-c.1950*, Plymouth (1983; repr. with minor amendments and additions, 1984).

'Family background: The significance of family and demographic history for the general historian', *Times Educational Supplement*, (9 April 1982) p. 27.

(with Brian M. Short) 'Social change and social conflict in nineteenth-century England: the use of the open-closed village model', *Journal of Peasant Studies*, 10.4 (1983), pp. 253-62. Reprinted in *Class, Conflict and Protest in the English Countryside, 1700-1800*, edited by Mick Reed and Roger Wells (1990), pp. 90-99.

A Guide to Nineteenth-Century Census Enumerators' Books, Milton Keynes (1984).

(with Philip Aslett *et al.*) *Victorians on the Move: Research in the Census Enumerators' Books 1851-1881*, Buckingham (1984).

'The nineteenth century peasantry of Melbourn, Cambridgeshire', in *Land, Kinship and Lifecycle*, edited by Richard M. Smith, Cambridge (1985), pp. 481-519.

(*et al.*) 'Sustaining rural communities', in *The Changing Countryside*, edited by John Blunden and Nigel Curry (1985), pp. 162-202.

(ed. with Michael Turner) *Land and Property: the English Land Tax 1692-1832*, Gloucester (1986).

'Early land tax assessments explored, 1: Rutland, Cambridgeshire and Lincolnshire', in *Land and Property: the English Land Tax 1692-1832*, edited with Michael Turner, Gloucester (1986) pp. 189-203.

'Survival of early (pre 1780) land tax assessments', in *Land and Property: the English Land Tax 1692-1832*, edited with Michael Turner, Gloucester (1986) pp. 219-234.

'Country matters', *History Today*, 36, 9 (September 1986) pp. 5-7.

(with Carol Pearce) 'Researching in the Victorian censuses: A note on a computerized, annotated bibliography of publications based substantially on the census enumerators' books', *Quarterly Journal of Social Affairs*, 2.1 (1986), pp. 55-68.

'A Lincolnshire guide to the nineteenth century censuses', *Lincolnshire History and Archaeology*, 22 (1987), pp. 25-29.

'Peasants and conflict in nineteenth-century rural England: a comment on two recent articles', *Journal of Peasant Studies*, 15.3 (1988), pp. 395-400. Reprinted in *Class, Conflict and Protest in the English Countryside, 1700-1800*, edited by Mick Reed and Roger Wells (1990), pp. 115-20.

'A "directory" of Lincolnshire medical men in the late eighteenth century: Two original sources', *Lincolnshire History and Archaeology*, 23 (1988), pp. 59-62.

(with Carol Pearce) *People and Places in the Victorian Census: A review and Bibliography of Publications Based Substantially on the Manuscript Census Enumerators' Books, 1841-1911*, Historical Geography Research Series, 23, Bristol (1989).

(ed.) *Twentieth Century Lincolnshire*, History of Lincolnshire Series, 12, Lincoln (1989).

'The revolution in workplace and home', in *Twentieth Century Lincolnshire*, (ed.) History of Lincolnshire Series, 12, Lincoln (1989), pp. 18-36.

(with Joan Mills) 'Occupation and social stratification revisited: The census enumerators' books of Victorian Britain', *Urban History Yearbook* (1989), pp. 63-77.

1990–1999

The Knights Templar in Lincolnshire, Sleaford (1990; rev. edn. 2009).

(with Ruth Tinley) 'The people of Swinderby in 1771 and 1791: A study in population mobility', *Lincolnshire History and Archaeology,* 26 (1991), pp. 7-11.

'The rise and fall of the English village: or rural planning and technological change', *Lincolnshire Past and Present,* 3 (Spring, 1991), pp 18-21.

'Village history in the Scopwick area', *Lincolnshire Past and Present,* 9 (Autumn, 1992), p. 15.

(ed. with P. Baumber) *Kirkby Green and Scopwick: Historical Sketches of two Lincolnshire Parishes,* Scopwick (1993).

(ed. with Jeremy Gibson and Mervyn Medlycott) *Land and Window Tax Assessments,* Birmingham (1993; 2nd edn., 1998; updated Bury, 2004).

'County Seats of the Gentry', in *An Historical Atlas of Lincolnshire,* edited by Stewart Bennett and Nicholas Bennett, Hull (1993; repr. Chichester, 2001), pp. 106-07.

'Dispensaries and hospitals to 1937', in *An Historical Atlas of Lincolnshire,* edited by Stewart Bennett and Nicholas Bennett, Hull (1993; repr. Chichester, 2001), pp. 128-29.

'Local history on the council agenda', *History Today,* 43, 12 (December 1993).

(with Michael Drake) 'The census, 1801-1991', in *Studying Family and Community History, Nineteenth and Twentieth Centuries, 4, Sources and Methods: A Handbook,* edited by Michael Drake and Ruth Finnegan, Cambridge (1994), pp. 25-56.

'Community and nation in the past: perception and reality', in, *Time, Family and Community: Perspectives on Family and Community History,* edited by Michael Drake, Oxford (1994), pp. 261-85.

(with Ruth Tinley) 'Population turnover in an eighteenth-century Lincolnshire parish in comparative context', *Local Population Studies,* 52 (Spring, 1994), pp. 30-38.

'Heritage and historians', *The Local Historian,* 24.4 (1994), pp. 225-228.

'The founding fathers of the City School, Lincoln', *Lincolnshire Past and Present,* 21 (Autumn, 1995), pp. 7-8.

(with Kevin Schûrer) *Local Communities in the Victorian Census Enumerators' Books,* Oxford (1996).

'The Fawcetts of Lincolnshire and the development of the medical profession', in *Lincolnshire People and Places: Essays in Memory of Terence R. Leach (1937-1994),* edited by Christopher Sturman, Lincoln (1996), pp. 162-67.

(with Joan Mills) 'The holy well and conduit, Canwick', *Lincolnshire Past and Present,* 23 (Spring, 1996), pp. 3-5.

'The small farm with special reference to Victorian Lincolnshire', *Lincolnshire Past and Present,* 24 (Summer, 1996), pp. 7-11.

(with Michael Edgar and Andrew Hinde) 'Southern historians and their exploitation of Victorian censuses', *Southern History,* 18 (1996), pp. 61-86.

(with Joan Mills) 'Prehistoric barrows in the Witham valley at Canwick', *Lincolnshire Past and Present,* 29 (Autumn, 1997), pp. 3-5.

(with Joan Mills) 'Farms, farmers and farm workers in the nineteenth century census enumerators' books: a Lincolnshire case study', *Local Historian*, 27 (1997), pp. 130-43.

(with Joan Mills) 'A case study at Canwick of the enduring influence of monastic houses', *Lincolnshire History and Archaeology*, 33 (1998), pp. 47-54.

'More information on the Fawssett family of Holbeach, Horncastle, Louth etc', *Lincolnshire Past and Present*, 33/34 (Autumn/Winter, 1998), p. 24.

'Trouble with farms at the Census Office: An evaluation of farm statistics from the censuses of 1851-1881 in England and Wales', *Agricultural History Review*, 47 (1999), pp. 58-77.

(with Paul Hudson) 'English emigration, kinship and the recruitment process: Migration from Melbourn in Cambridgeshire to Melbourne in Victoria in the mid-nineteenth century', *Rural History*, 10 (1999), pp. 55-74.

2000–2010

'Wigford in the nineteenth century', in *Wigford: Historic Lincoln South of the River*, edited by P. R. Hill, The Survey of Lincoln Series, 1, Lincoln (2000) pp. 26-29.

(with M. Edgar) 'Social history in Lincoln's Victorian residential streets', *Local Population Studies Society Newsletter* (September 2000) pp. 4-10.

(with Maurice Hodson) 'A Lincoln scene about a century ago', *The Lincoln Enquirer*, 1 (October, 2000).

Rural Community History from Trade Directories, Aldenham (2001).

'An "edge-land": the development of the Witham valley east of Canwick Road', in *Aspects of Lincoln: Discovering Local History*, edited by Andrew Walker, Barnsley (2001), pp. 134-46.

(with Joan Mills and Michael Trott) 'New light on Charles de Laet Waldo-Sibthorp, 1783-1855', *Lincolnshire History and Archaeology*, 36 (2001), pp. 25-37.

'A common question: were Wigford, Canwick and Bracebridge part of a single early estate?', *Lincolnshire Past and Present*, 44 (Summer, 2001), pp. 7-11.

'Proposed historical atlas of Lincoln 1610-1920', *The Lincoln Enquirer*, 4 (April, 2002), p. 2.

A Walk Round Canwick, the Lincolnshire Estate Village of the Sibthorps: with Enclosure Map of 1787, Branston (2003).

'Brayford Villa: where was it, what was it, when was it?', *Lincolnshire Past and Present*, 51 (Spring, 2003), pp. 3-7.

'Where was it?', *The Lincoln Enquirer*, 5 (April, 2003), p. 4.

(with Rob Wheeler) *Historic Town Plans of Lincoln, 1610-1920*, Lincoln Record Society, 92, Woodbridge (2004).

'Defining community: a critical review of "community" in *Family and Community History*', *Family and Community History*, 7.1 (2004), pp. 5-12.

'A "Tech" school for Victorian Lincoln', *Family and Community History*, 7.2 (2004), pp. 129-40.

'The Lincoln atlas', *The Lincoln Enquirer*, 7 (November, 2004), pp. 3-4.

The People of the Steep Hill Area of Lincoln About 1900: An Illustrated Social Study, Lincoln (2005).

(with Timothy H. M. Clough) *The 1712 Land Tax Assessments and the 1710 Poll Book for Rutland*, Rutland Local History and Record Society Occasional Publication, 7, Oakham (2005).

'"Recollections" of the Romans in Canwick village', *Lincolnshire Past and Present*, 59 (Spring, 2005), pp. 3-6.

(with Rob Wheeler) 'Some peregrinations of Lincoln race course', *Lincolnshire Past and Present*, 60 (Summer, 2005), pp. 6-12.

'Recusancy and declining gentry fortunes: evidence relating to the Forsetts of Lincolnshire', *Recusant History*, 27.3 (2005), pp. 321-32.

'Lowering Cross Cliff and Canwick Hills', *The Lincoln Enquirer*, 8 (May, 2005), pp. 4-6.

My Life as a Coder (Special), D/MX 919781,1952-54, Branston (2005).

'Population, 1801-1901', in *Monks Road: Lincoln's East End Through Time*, edited by Andrew Walker, The Survey of Lincoln Series, 2, Lincoln (2006) pp. 16-17.

(with Joan Mills) 'Pregion's progress: The life and times of a Lincolnshire yeoman family, 1570 to 1773', *Lincolnshire History and Archaeology*, 41 (2006), pp. 7-17.

'William Watkin's house and the Lincoln Register of Plans and Buildings', *Lincolnshire Past and Present*, 63 (Spring, 2006), pp. 3-6.

'Canwick (Lincolnshire) and Melbourn (Cambridgeshire) in comparative perspective within the open-closed village model', *Rural History,* 17.1 (2006), pp. 1-22.

'Housing at the turn of the twentieth century', *The Lincoln Enquirer*, 11 (November, 2006), pp. 2-3.

'Titus Kime, entrepreneur of Mareham le Fen 1848-1931, and the Eldorado Potato Boom of 1903-1904', in *All Things Lincolnshire*, edited by Jean Howard and David Start, Lincoln (2007), pp. 139-150.

'The Cow Paddle, Lincoln, 1855: a plan, a cemetery, a boiling copper and a furnace', *Lincolnshire Past and Present*, 67 (Spring, 2007), pp. 7-10.

(with Rob Wheeler) 'Interpreting the 1:2500 County Series', *Sheetlines,* 78 (April, 2007), pp. 45-48.

'Cartographic Treasures', *The Lincoln Enquirer*, 12 (April, 2007), pp. 3-5.

(with Rob Wheeler and Matthew Woollard) 'Some comparative perspectives on two early-Victorian registrars of births and deaths in rural Lincolnshire in the context of national legislation' *Local Population Studies*, 79 (Autumn, 2007), pp. 8-22.

'The building of Monson Street', *The Lincoln Enquirer*, 13 (November, 2007), pp. 4-6.

'Recording and interpreting moffreys: hermaphrodite cart/wagons of Eastern England', *Folk Life: Journal of Ethnological Studies,* 46 (2007-8), pp. 99-122.

'Monson Street courts and clearances', *The Lincoln Enquirer*, 14 (May, 2008), pp. 2-5.

'Rasen Lane', in *Uphill Lincoln I: Burton Road, Newport and the Ermine Estate*, edited by Andrew Walker, The Survey of Lincoln Series, 5, Lincoln (2009), pp. 51-54.

'Population growth in North Lincoln', in *Uphill Lincoln I: Burton Road, Newport and the Ermine Estate*, edited by Andrew Walker, The Survey of Lincoln Series, 5, Lincoln (2009), pp. 58-59.

'The Giles engineering family', *Root and Branch*, 36.2 (West Surrey Family History Society) (2009), pp. 57-60.

'Public health, environment and surveying', *Social History of Medicine,* 22.1 (2009), pp. 153-63.

'A "Valentine" – no not that sort!' *The Lincoln Enquirer*, 17 (November, 2009), pp. 4-5.

'Local studies in sanitary reform – the importance of the engineering aspect, Lincoln 1848-50', *The Local Historian,* 39.3 (2009), pp. 207-17.

'The steps leading from the Stonebow to Waterside North, Lincoln', *Lincolnshire Past and Present*, 77 (Autumn, 2009), pp. 12-14.

2010–2020

'George Giles, civil engineer and the Great Northern Loop line: Peterborough-Spalding-Boston-Lincoln-Gainsborough', *Great Northern News*, no. 170 (March/April 2010), pp. 8-11.

'St Giles' Avenue', in *Uphill Lincoln II: The North-Eastern Suburbs*, edited by Andrew Walker, The Survey of Lincoln Series, 6, Lincoln (2010), pp. 44-46.

'Where were George Giles and Motherby Hill?', *The Lincoln Enquirer*, 19 (November 2010), pp. 2-5.

'Signals Intelligence and the Coder Special Branch of the Royal Navy in the 1950s', *Intelligence and National Security*, 26, 5 (2011), pp. 639-655.

(with Joan Mills) *Traditional Farming in Branston*, Branston (2011).

'One third of us might have been Wrens', *East-West Review*, 11, 2, (2012), pp. 5-9.

'Soviet General Staff Maps of Lincoln, 1984', *The Lincoln Enquirer*, 23 (November 2012), pp. 6-8.

'The training of linguists for war: Coulsdon, 1952-54. Part I', *Local History Records*, 73 (November 2012), pp. 3-13.

'Brayford Pool and George Giles' Sanitary Report of 1849', in *Brayford Pool: Lincoln's Waterfront Through Time*, edited by Andrew Walker, The Survey of Lincoln Series, 8, Lincoln (2012), pp. 17-18.

'The training of linguists for war: Coulsdon, 1952-54. Part II', *Local History Records*, 74 (February 2013), pp. 3-12.

(with Victoria Thorpe) 'The Cornhill residence of the Henry Swans and Robert Swan the elder', *The Lincoln Enquirer*, 25 (November 2013), pp. 2-5.

(with Chris Page) 'Derby Grounds', in *Boultham and Swallowbeck: Lincoln's South-Western Suburbs,* edited by Andrew Walker, The Survey of Lincoln Series, 9, Lincoln (2013), pp. 7-9.

'Some watery accidents', *The Lincoln Enquirer*, 25 (November 2013), p. 11.

'Getting into the Navy in 1952', *Lincolnshire Past and Present*, 94 (Winter 2013-14), pp. 7-10.

'Joint Services' schools for linguists, 1951-60. National Servicemen preparing for war as Russian linguists' (2013). Accessible at: www.royalnavyresearcharchive.org.uk/JSSL.htm#.Y9LrSsnP02w

(with Victoria Thorpe) 'The career of Robert Swan the elder and his uphill residences', *The Lincoln Enquirer*, 26 (May 2014), pp. 4-6.

(with Victoria Thorpe) 'Taking the census in Lincoln Minster Close in 1841', *Lincoln Record Society News Review*, 5, (September 2014), p. 3.

(with Victoria Thorpe) 'The houses of the contemporaries of Robert Swan the elder', *The Lincoln Enquirer*, 27 (November 2014), pp. 2-4.

(with Victoria Thorpe) 'Servant-keeping households in the Minster Close', in *Lincoln's Castle, Bail and Close*, edited by Andrew Walker, The Survey of Lincoln Series, 11, Lincoln (2015), pp. 51-53.

(with Beryl George) 'The population of Lincoln', *The Lincoln Enquirer*, 29 (May 2015), pp. 4-6.

Effluence and Influence: Public Health, Sewers and Politics in Lincoln, 1848-50, Lincoln (2015).

(with Joan Mills) 'An early eighteenth-century pre-enclosure estate rent roll: Branston, *c.* 1740', *Lincolnshire History and Archaeology*, 51 (2016), pp. 141-146.

(with Victoria Thorpe) 'The Victorian farm labourers of Mere Oaks Cottages in Branston Parish', *Lincolnshire Past and Present*, 108 (Summer 2017), pp. 7-8.

(with Victoria Thorpe) 'The clerical Swans, the building of bridges and the peopling of the Bargate Closes', *The Lincoln Enquirer*, 33 (May 2017), pp. 2-5.

(with Victoria Thorpe) 'John Swan and Stonefield House, Church Lane' *The Lincoln Enquirer*, 34 (November 2017), pp. 2-5.

(with Victoria Thorpe) 'John Swan of Stonefield House', *Lincolnshire Past and Present*, 110 (Winter 2017-18), pp. 18-21.

(with Victoria Thorpe) 'Robert Swan II, Quarry House', *The Lincoln Enquirer*, 35 (May 2018), pp. 7-9.

(with Victoria Thorpe) 'Bothy boys', *Lincolnshire Past and Present*, 112 (Summer 2018), pp. 13-18.

(with Victoria Thorpe) 'Where the children of Robert Swan II and Lucy Swan went to live', *The Lincoln Enquirer*, 36 (November 2018), pp. 2-5.

'The people of Branston in 1881 and the building of the railway', *Lincolnshire Past and Present*, 116 (Summer 2019), pp. 25-27.

'Schoolboy memories of some Lincoln streets in the 1940s', *The Lincoln Enquirer*, 38 (October 2019), pp. 3-6.

(with Joan Mills) 'The enigmatic Dame Anne Chesshyre, Lord of Branston Manor', *Lincolnshire Past and Present*, 118 (Winter 2019-20), pp. 15-16.

'The Revd Adrian Gustavus Devereux-Quick', *Lincolnshire Past and Present*, 119 (Spring 2020), pp. 11-13.

* With assistance from Andrew Walker for the entries from 2010 onwards.

THE HISTORIC ENVIRONMENT IN LINCOLNSHIRE 2018: ARCHAEOLOGY AND HISTORIC BUILDINGS

Edited by Richard Watts

The notes below cover archaeological work and surveys of historic buildings carried out in Lincolnshire largely as a result of development managed by the planning system. The work was carried out between 1 January and 31 December 2018. Most historic environment work carried out in the county is funded by developers and their input is duly acknowledged. Full reports of this work have been deposited with the appropriate Historic Environment Record where they are available for consultation. A summary list of archaeological work for which the results are either entirely, or substantially, negative will be made available on the SLHA website rather than being published in this journal. Assistance in the preparation of these notes was provided by Alison Williams of the HER in the Places Directorate of North Lincolnshire Council, and by Louise Jennings, the Heritage Officer for North-East Lincolnshire Council. In addition, the society is publishing here a series of notes, compiled by Lisa Brundle, on archaeological objects found in Lincolnshire that have been reported to the Portable Antiquities Scheme during 2018.

ABBREVIATIONS

AAL	Allen Archaeology Ltd
AHC	Austin Heritage Consultants
APS	Archaeological Project Services
ASWYAS	Archaeological Services WYAS
CA	Cotswold Archaeology
CAC	Caroline Atkins Consultants
FLO	Finds Liaison Officer
HAL	Headland Archaeology Ltd
HE	Historic England
HER	Historic Environment Record
HFA	Humber Field Archaeology
LCC	Lincolnshire County Council
LCNCC	The Collection, City and County Museum, Lincoln
LHA	*Lincolnshire History and Archaeology*
MAG	Magnitude Surveys Ltd
MAS	Midland Archaeological Services
NELC	North-East Lincolnshire Council
NELMS	North-East Lincolnshire Museum Service, Grimsby
NH	Neville Hall
NLC	North Lincolnshire Council

NLM   North Lincolnshire Museum, Scunthorpe

OAE   Oxford Archaeology East

PAL   PCAS Archaeology Ltd (Saxilby)

PAS   Portable Antiquities Scheme

PCG   Pre-Construct Geophysics

SAS   Souterrain Archaeological Services Ltd

SUMO   SUMO Geophysics

WA   Witham Archaeology

YAT   York Archaeological Trust

Belton: Belton Brickworks, SE 7859 0567. Report in the HER at NLC.

A magnetometry survey was conducted by MAG to inform proposed development on land at the former Belton Brickworks site. Linear magnetic anomalies consistent with the remains of medieval ridge and furrow were identified across much of the site, as well as a number of former field boundaries. The survey also identified anomalies thought to reflect natural geological processes and more modern activity.

Belton: Thorne Road, Sandtoft, SE 7429 0822. Report in the HER at NLC.

Five trial trenches were excavated by YAT to inform proposed residential development on land off Thorne Road, Sandtoft. The investigation identified a clear series of ditches, all relating to the previous subdivision, drainage and use of the area for agricultural purposes. The excavated features corresponded well with a series of linear cropmarks noted int his area on earlier aerial photographs. However, barring a single fragment of post-medieval brick, finds or dating material were not recovered from the vast majority of the features,. It was thus not possible to determine the origins or phasing of the various features identified with any certainty.

Belton: Westgate Road, SE 7748 0734. Report in the HER at NLC.

Ten trial trenches were excavated by ASWYAS to inform proposed residential development on land off Westgate Road. The investigation identified a number of archaeological features, mostly thought to represent former boundary and drainage ditches. Pottery recovered from the fills of these ditches indicate a late Iron Age and Romano-British date for this activity. The remains of two large pits were also identified towards the northern end of the site. A mixture of thirteenth and fourteenth century medieval pottery was recovered from their fills, thus indicating some form of medieval activity was also occurring in this vicinity.

Bottesford: Moorwell Road, Yaddlethorpe, SE 8790 0657. Report in the HER at NLC.

A magnetometry survey was conducted by PCG to inform proposed development on land to the south of Moorwell Road, Yaddlethorpe. The survey recorded a limited number of linear magnetic anomalies in the central and western parts of the site, possibly representing the remains of buried ditches. These features did not share the alignment of the current and recent boundaries on the site, suggesting a relatively early origin, although an alternative explanation as cultivation marks could not be discounted. Other magnetic anomalies recorded elsewhere on the site were thought to all be reflective of natural geological processes or modern services and recent use of the site as horse paddocks.

Broughton: Little Crow Solar Park, SE 9401 1001. Report in the HER at NLC.

A magnetometry survey was conducted by SUMO to inform the proposed construction of the Little Crow Solar Park. Most of the recorded geophysical anomalies were thought to relate to modern services and agricultural activity or to natural geological fracturing in the underlying limestone, although evidence of a former ring ditch feature was identified. A number of linear magnetic anomalies thought to be the remains of former ditches were also recorded, along with several other linear trends of uncertain origin.

Broughton: Little Crow Solar Park, SE 9947 0715. Report in the HER at NLC.

A series of investigations comprising archaeological field walking and archaeological monitoring and recording was conducted by CA in advance of the proposed construction of the Little Crow Solar Park.

The archaeological field walking was conducted across three areas totalling just over 53 hectares and comprising roughly 25% of the total proposed development area. The survey recorded over 19kg of artefacts, most of which were of post-medieval and modern date. The more significant finds were all recovered from the south of the site, and included pieces of worked flint, dating from the Neolithic and Bronze Age periods. An assemblage of twelfth to sixteenth century medieval pottery was also recovered, possibly associated with the nearby site of Gokewell Priory, a Cistercian holding established in the twelfth century and suppressed at the Dissolution of the Monasteries. A small assemblage of Roman material was also recovered, comprising sherds of locally made greyware pottery and fragments of abraded ceramic building material, possibly pieces from Roman roof tiles or tegulae.

The subsequent archaeological monitoring and recording was conducted during the excavation of test pits for ground investigation and drainage works. These works confirmed the sequence of topsoil deposits overlying buried soil layers and bedrock at various depths across the site but did not identify any significant archaeological features.

Archive at NLM, Accn code LCRO.

Coleby: Dovecote Lane, SK 9777 6039. Report No.4823 in the HER.

A programme of archaeological monitoring and recording was conducted by PAL during groundworks for the construction of four new dwellings on land off Dovecote Lane. The monitoring recorded an early twentieth century demolition layer, overlying and clearly associated with the partially surviving foundations of a limestone building which had previously occupied the site. The investigation also recorded the remains of a series of quarry pits and an associated access ramp. Whilst the exact date of these quarry pits was uncertain, they had been backfilled by the mid-nineteenth century, and clearly pre-dated the post-medieval buildings in this area.

Archive at LCNCC, Accn no. 2017.111.

Covenham St Bartholomew: Birketts Lane, TF 3428 9469. Report No.6231 in the HER.

An earthwork survey was conducted by WA prior to proposed residential development on land off Birketts Lane. Remains of poorly preserved medieval ridge and furrow were recorded in the north-eastern part of the site. These remains comprised six parallel earthwork ridges, separated by low troughs, and all aligned on a south-west to north-east axis. The highest ridge on the southern side of the group measured 0.32m in height, while the remainder were between 0.1-0.2m in height. The longest earthwork measured 104m from end to end and was located towards the south of the group.

Archive at LCNCC, Accn no. 2018.36.

Croft: Church of All Saints, Church Lane, TF 5094 6186. Report No.6098 in the HER.
A programme of archaeological monitoring and recording was conducted by NH during the excavation of service trenches for new drainage at the Church of All Saints. No archaeological features were recorded, although a small quantity of re-deposited, disarticulated human remains were revealed. All of the remains were reburied in the churchyard at the end of the investigation.

Archive at LCNCC, Accn no. 2018.99.

Crowle: Manor House, Church Street, SE 7713 1293. Reports in the HER at NLC.
Eight trial trenches were excavated by MAS over two phases of investigation, to inform proposed residential development on land at Manor House, Church Street. The investigations revealed a number of features and deposits, all thought to relate to the post-medieval use of the site. The recorded features comprised a variety of shallow pits, post-holes and linear features, all likely to be associated with agricultural activities. The investigation also recorded small remains of brick foundations and more extensive demolition debris clearly associated with the later post-medieval former structures on the site. An assemblage of late post-medieval and twentieth century ceramics and glass fragments was recovered, but no evidence relating to the medieval manor house thought to have formerly been on the site was revealed.

East Halton: Halton Marshes, TA 1513 2177. Report in the HER at NLC.
A programme of archaeological monitoring and recording was conducted by AAL during drainage works on a wetland habitat compensation area at Halton Marshes. The works exposed a sequence of topsoil overlying naturally accumulated silty clays, typical of a coastal saltmarsh environment. A single linear feature running along a broadly north-west to south-east alignment was recorded cutting through this sequence in the southern part of the site. No dating material was recovered from the fill of the feature, and its date and origin remain unknown, although an association with the known nearby location of a Second World War barrage balloon site may be possible.

Archive at NLM, Accn code EHHM.

East Kirkby: Sandilands, Fen Road, TF 3341 6196. Report No.6177 in the HER.
A programme of archaeological monitoring and recording was conducted by NH during groundworks associated with the construction of a new residential dwelling on land adjacent to Sandilands, Fen Road. The investigation revealed a number of features thought to be associated with medieval and post-medieval settlement activity in this area. These features included two linear ditches, joined in a T-shaped intersection, which were thought to represent part of a former medieval field system or enclosure. Four sherds of late twelfth to mid-thirteenth century pottery, all from the same vessel, were recovered from the fill of the north to south aligned ditch, providing a probable date for these features. The remains of two likely medieval refuse pits were recorded to the north-east of the ditches, with a single sherd of mid-twelfth to thirteenth century pottery also being recovered from the fill of one of the features. Also recorded during the investigation were the remains of a posthole of unknown date, and the remains of a (probably) eighteenth century pond at the south-western edge of the site.

Archive at LCNCC, Accn no. 2016.207.

Fiskerton: Orchard Road, TF 0468 7206. Report No.6437 in the HER.

A programme of archaeological monitoring and recording was conducted by NH during groundworks associated with the construction of a new residential dwelling and garden store on land off Orchard Road. The remains of a large pit of likely late medieval date were located towards the southern edge of the site. A single sherd of late fifteenth to mid-sixteenth century pottery was recovered from the fill of the pit, along with a redeposited fragment of Roman brick. A further redeposited sherd of third to fourth century Roman pottery was found in the topsoil deposit. Two short lengths of roughly constructed stone walls were also recorded during the investigation, at the western edge of the site. The walling was thought to have formed part of the foundations of an earlier structure of unknown (though likely medieval or later) date on the site.

Archive at LCNCC, Accn no. 2018.170.

Gayton le Wold: High Street, Biscathorpe, TF 2179 8479. Report No.6137 in the HER.

A programme of archaeological monitoring and recording was conducted by PAL during groundworks for the construction of an investigative oil well and temporary access track, on land off High Street, Biscathorpe. Whilst no archaeologically significant deposits or features were encountered, residual finds of a late Neolithic flint scraper and an early Roman pottery sherd were recovered. The prehistoric flint was a well-fashioned side and end scraper with secondary working on the distal end and one lateral edge. The Roman sherd was abraded and difficult to identify with certainty but appeared to be in a transitional gritty ware type fabric, probably dating to the later first to second century.

Archive at LCNCC, Accn no. 2018.162.

Grimsby: Claremont House, Welholme Avenue, TA 26662 08657. Report in the HER at NELC.

Two trial trenches were excavated by PAL to inform proposed residential development on land within the grounds of Claremont House, Welholme Avenue. The remains of a large cut feature, some 5m wide, was recorded in the northern trench. The feature is thought to have formed part of a drain known to have been culverted in the mid to late nineteenth century and depicted on later nineteenth century mapping of this area. The original cutting of the drain could not be dated, and it may be possible that it had formed part of a drainage network associated with the nearby medieval Wellow Abbey.

Archive at NELMS, Accn code CHGE17.

Healing: Larkspur Avenue, TA 2110 1096. Report in the HER at NELC.

A programme of archaeological monitoring and recording was conducted by AAL to inform proposed residential development on land off Larkspur Avenue. The works exposed more extensive remains of a first to fourth century Roman settlement, previously identified from geophysical survey and trial trenching conducted in this area in 2014. These features included a series of enclosures forming part of the south-south-east to north-northwest ladder settlement. Pottery recovered from the fills of many of the enclosure ditches dated from the second to fourth centuries, with the finds indicating the settlement was in continuous occupation throughout this time. A number of other pits, ditches and gullies clearly associated with the main ditches of the ladder settlement were also investigated, with similar finds being recovered. Other features recorded during the monitoring included a large pit containing a number of dumped and burnt deposits, including potential kiln furniture and wasters. Part of a ring ditch was also recorded, only half of which was visible, with the other half having been truncated by a later furrow. Domestic waste and material were recovered from features across the site, with oyster shells and bones from a wide range of different animals being included. In addition to large quantities of Roman greyware pottery, a number of high status Samian ware fragments were also found. Pieces of fired clay and daub, regular tile and imbrices were also recovered, along with iron nails, an iron knife and slag fragments, suggestive of metal working and industry in the vicinity.

Archive at NELMS, Accn code GRIMS: 2019.007.

Holbeach: Holly Lodge, Spalding Road, TF 3480 2486. Report No.6152 in the HER.

A programme of archaeological monitoring and recording was conducted by NH during groundworks for the construction of seven new residential dwellings at Holly Lodge, Spalding Road. The remains of two intercutting pits were recorded in the area of one of the house plots. Two pottery sherds from mid-fifteenth to mid-sixteenth century Toynton type jugs were recovered from the fill of the earlier pit, indicating a late medieval date for the origin of these features. A fragment of late post-medieval roof tile also found in the pit fill was thought to be a later intrusion.

Archive at LCNCC, Accn no. 2017.200.

Humberstone: South Sea Lane, TA 3106 0489. Report in the HER at NELC.

A magnetometry survey was conducted by AAL to inform proposed residential development on land off South Sea Lane. The survey identified the remains of medieval ridge and furrow cultivation across large parts of the site, along with a potential enclosure feature close to the western edge. The enclosure was roughly square in shape and appeared to be respected by the ridge and furrow, suggesting it may have been a contemporary settlement feature. A few more amorphous magnetic anomalies, thought to possibly represent former pits, ponds or soil-filled hollows, were also recorded during the survey. Areas of magnetic noise recorded around the edges of the site were thought to be the result of modern disturbance, although it was noted that this could potentially be masking more ephemeral archaeological features in those locations.

Inner Humber Estuary: Rapid Coastal Zone Assessment Survey. Report in the HER at NLC.

An aerial investigation and mapping project was conducted by HE as part of a wider research programme assessing the heritage assets of England's coastline. The survey was focused on a 256 square kilometre strip of riverine and coastal land along the Inner Humber Estuary, between Sunk Island and Grimsby in the east, to Trent Falls in the west. The survey comprised the study of the wide range of current and historical aerial photographs, digital imagery and LiDAR date for the study area. It aimed to identify, record and map the extensive variety of archaeological sites visible as earthworks, cropmarks and structures, revealing the complexity of an historic landscape reaching back from modern times to prehistory. It provided enhanced data on an extremely large number of previously recorded and new sites, ranging from Second World War defences, post-medieval brick manufacturing sites and industry, medieval settlements and agricultural patterns, and prehistoric occupation, alongside coastal features such as shipwrecks, jetties and fishing structures.

Immingham: Highfield House, Stallingborough Road, TA 1803 1364. Report in the HER at NELC.

Thirty-three trial trenches were excavated by APS to inform proposed residential development on land at Highfield House, Stallingborough Road. The trenches were targeted to investigate a number of geophysical anomalies recorded by magnetometer survey, conducted in 2017. The trenching confirmed the presence of significant settlement activity in the western part of the site. Although thought to be of Roman date during the geophysical survey, the trenching discovered this activity to be of medieval to early post-medieval date, with a large number of ditch, pit and post-hole features being excavated. The clustering of some of these features suggested that there had been two main phases of occupation on the site, one in the north and the other in the south. The evaluation also revealed the eastern edge of a probable further settlement area continuing towards Stallingborough Road. The settlement activity declined markedly towards the eastern end of the site, suggesting this area was unsuitable for extensive human activity at the time, either due to these areas being more prone to flooding or use for other activities such as farming. A range of Saxo-Norman, medieval and early post-medieval pottery was recovered from the site, with other artefacts including ceramics, animal bone, iron nails and a near-complete Beverley orange-ware pottery vessel.

Archive at NELMS, Accn code GRIMS: 2017.031.

Immingham: Mill Lane, TA 1706 1486. Report in the HER at NELC.
A magnetometry survey was conducted by ASWYAS in advance of proposed development on land off Mill Lane. Whilst the majority of the recorded magnetic responses were thought to be clearly associated with modern ploughing and field drains, some anomalies of possible archaeological origin were recorded. These included what were thought to represent the remains of a potential ring ditch in the east of the site, and a possible rectilinear enclosure in the south-east. Further potential archaeological anomalies included a number of linear and curvilinear trends, and some probable pit features.

Keadby with Althorpe: Keadby II Combined Cycle Gas Turbine, SE 8231 1174. Report in the HER at NLC.
A series of investigations comprising trial trenching and borehole survey was conducted by HAL to inform the proposed construction of a replacement power station on land to the north-west of Keadby.

Whilst the trial trenching did not reveal any archaeological features, it did expose a series of alluvial layers, most likely derived from deliberate warping episodes, overlying extensive peat deposits. It was thought that a combination of changes in the course of the river Trent, the warping episodes and the twentieth-century development of the area may have removed any archaeological features that might have previously been present in this area.

The borehole survey confirmed the sequence of alluvial layers thought to derive from warping episodes, overlying extensive peat deposits across most of the site. Fourteen sediment cores were extracted from the boreholes with a smaller selection sub-sampled for palaeo-environmental assessments and radiocarbon dating. Initial examination of the cores revealed a tripartite character to the peat deposits, with the middle part best described as wood or reed-peat, and the upper and lowers parts comprising silty peat (or peaty silt, depending on the proportions in particular locations). Wood within the peat was well preserved, with a variety of material from small twigs to larger branches. The uniform nature of the material across the site and lack of evidence for thicker areas suggest that the peat was unlikely to derive from the infilling of palaeochannels but was rather part of a more extensive floodplain wetland, with the woody character possibly suggesting alder carr. Two radiocarbon dates obtained from plant macroscopic remains recovered from the basal part of the peat indicate formation started during the late Neolithic to early Bronze Age. Given the depth of peat deposits, it seems likely that waterlogged conditions prevailed in this area throughout the Bronze Age, which would accord well with palaeo-environmental records from elsewhere in the region. Analysis of the macroscopic plant remains in the basal deposits support the interpretation of a likely woodland carr environment in this locality. Plant remains in the middle and upper part of the deposits suggest this environment later developed into an open rush/sedge/reed marshland, with little nearby woodland. This environment at the wetland-dryland interface would have formed a rich habitat and resource for exploitation by later prehistoric settlers, though with settlement most probably situated on slightly higher ground beyond the immediate floodplain.

Archive at NLM, Accn code KELI. Full report published in *LHA*.[1]

Keelby: South Street and Stallingborough Road, TA 1660 1027. Report No.4659 in the HER.

A series of investigations comprising trial trenching and auger survey was conducted by APS to inform proposed residential development on land at South Street and Stallingborough Road.

The trial trenching recorded the remains of three probable former drainage ditches of uncertain date, which likely marked the area around former pasture land or paddocks. No dateable material was recovered from the ditches, however, and their exact origin remains uncertain. The trenching also recorded a circular pit of probable twentieth century date, from which part of a modern battery and a small number of cattle bone fragments were recovered.

The subsequent auger survey comprised the augering of ten holes across a partly silted up ditch still visible in the field as an earthwork and thought to be associated with medieval settlement activity in this area. The survey established that the fills of the ditch extended to a depth of up to 0.45m from its current surface level.

Archive at LCNCC, Accn no. 2018.103.

Langton by Wragby: Hoop Lane Farm, TF 1449 7524. Report No.6221 in the HER.

A magnetometry survey was conducted by PCG to inform the proposed construction of a new swimming training facility on land at Hoop Lane Farm. Widespread remains of medieval ridge and furrow were identified across the site, as well as a possible curvilinear ditch-like feature at the western edge of the surveyed area. The ridge and furrow remains were identified as a series of parallel linear magnetic anomalies, aligned on a roughly south-west to north-east axis.

Subsequent trial trenching conducted in this area in April 2019, confirmed the presence of medieval ridge and furrow remains across the site but found no trace of the possible curvilinear feature.

Lincoln: Westbrooke Road, SK 9576 6953. Report No.6275 in the HER.

A programme of archaeological monitoring and recording was conducted by PAL ahead of the third phase of residential development on land at Westbrooke Road. The remains of two intercutting linear ditches were recorded, one of which appeared to be on the same north-east to south-west alignment as a similar linear feature recorded in the previous 2017 phase of development. The other ditch ran on a roughly east to west alignment, and was cut by the first ditch, and was therefore stratigraphically earlier. The alignment of both features was different to the field pattern shown on late nineteenth-century mapping of this area, and it was thought likely that the ditches predated the post-medieval drainage and enclosure activities here. No dating material was recovered from either of the features, however, and their origins could not be determined.

Archive at LCNCC, Accn no. 2019.182.

Nocton: Nocton Wood House, TF 0717 6444. Report Nos.6384 and 6507 in the HER.

A series of investigations comprising magnetometry survey and trial trenching was conducted by APS to inform the proposed construction of a new agricultural reservoir on land north of Nocton Wood House.

The magnetometry survey identified only a few anomalies, most of which were thought to relate to recent agricultural activity, although it did locate a small linear anomaly at the eastern edge of the field. The anomaly corresponded well with a former field boundary of probable post-medieval date that is depicted in this area on historic Ordnance Survey maps.

The subsequent trial trenching confirmed the presence of the former field boundary of post-medieval date, along with two linear ditches at the eastern edge of the site. The linear ditches ran parallel to each other, on a roughly east to west alignment. Their position and alignment corresponded well with cropmarks previously identified by the National Mapping Programme, which were thought to represent the remains of a probable medieval hollow way. The later post-medieval field boundary ditch was approximately 2.3m wide, and had a late post-medieval ceramic field drain in its base.

Archives at LCNCC, Accn nos. 2018.10 and 2018.166.

Norton Disney: Fields Around Roman Villa Site, SK 859 602. Source Documents in the HER.

A programme of archaeological field walking was conducted by the Norton Disney History and Archaeology Group, as part of an ongoing community history project investigating the late prehistoric and Roman archaeology around the villa site. Fragments of Roman tile were collected from the surface of the main villa site field, with the fragments thought to comprise pieces of floor tile and possibly flue-liner material. Several large blocks of slag were also recovered from the edges of the fields to the immediate east and south-east of the villa. Analysis of samples taken from the blocks strongly indicated that they were pit-type iron smelting slags of probable mid-Iron Age date, suggesting that the smelting of significant quantities of iron was being conducted somewhere in this vicinity at that time.

Reepham: Fiskerton Road, TF 0431 7365. Report Nos.4826 and 6217 in the HER.

A series of investigations comprising magnetometry survey and trial trenching was conducted by PAL to inform proposed residential development on land off Fiskerton Road.

The magnetometry survey recorded no clearly defined features of archaeological origin but did identify some faint magnetic anomalies possibly reflecting previous human activity in the south-east corner of the site.

The subsequent trial trenching confirmed some of those anomalies as the remains of archaeological features of probable Roman date, along with truncated remains of medieval ridge and furrow across much of the site. The probable Roman features comprised the truncated remains of a narrow ditch or gully, and a ditch or elongated pit. A few pieces of Roman tegulae and late first- to early second-century Roman pottery were recovered from these features and the overlying subsoil. The medieval furrows were all aligned on a roughly north-north-west to south-south-east axis, but all had been cut into by modern agricultural activity. A single sherd of pottery from a thirteenth-century Nottingham Glazed ware jug was recovered from one of the furrow fills. The jug had burnt or misfired copper-green glaze and applied scale and strip decoration.

Archive at LCNCC, Accn no. 2018.183.

South Ferriby: Winteringham Ings to South Ferriby Flood Alleviation Scheme, SE 9838 2116. Report in the HER at NLC.

A magnetometer survey was conducted by HAL to inform proposed improvements to the existing flood defences between Winteringham Ings and South Ferriby. The majority of the magnetic anomalies recorded were thought to be indicative of former shorelines, inlets and widespread estuarine alluvial deposits spread across the wider area. A number of post-medieval clay extraction pits and brick manufacturing sites were recorded, including the remains of three possible former brick clamps. It was thought likely that a linear magnetic anomaly also recorded during the survey may represent a continuation of a medieval causeway known to cross this area, although this suggestion remains tentative. The surveyors also noted that the strong magnetic responses from the widespread alluvial deposits and estuarine features could be masking other, more subtle archaeological features which may be present here.

South Killingholme: Hornsea Offshore Wind Farm Project Two, TA 1482 1670. Reports in the HER at NELC.

A series of investigations comprising trial trenching and set-piece excavation was conducted by AAL along the route of the Hornsea Two electrical cable. The investigations were largely focused to the south of the areas investigated by the previous works for the Hornsea One cable route, with the later areas of investigation closer to South Killingholme. A similar pattern of archaeological features was revealed, with many of the features possibly being continuations of the extensive areas of prehistoric and Romano-British settlement activity previously identified. This activity comprised a number of intercutting linear features and several phases of enclosure, with further boundary ditches nearby. Finds recovered from many of the features included a range of Iron Age and Roman pottery sherds and ceramics, with small quantities of animal bone, and an unidentified copper alloy object. Medieval remains overlying some of these features included traces of former agricultural activity, including areas of ridge and furrow, and associated field boundaries. A possible continuation of the medieval moated enclosure previously investigated was also recorded during the set-piece excavation.

Archive at NLM, Accn code HOWF.

Stallingborough: Mauxhall Farm, TA 192 131. Report in the HER at NELC.

A magnetometry survey was conducted by APS to inform the proposed installation of a renewable energy scheme on land adjacent to Mauxhall Farm. The survey identified a number of potential archaeological features, including several rectilinear enclosures of possible late prehistoric or Roman date, to the south and east of Mauxhall Farm. This area lies in close proximity to the marine alluvium layers of the adjacent tidal flats and a possible connection for the enclosures with former salt-making activities was postulated. Remains of medieval ridge and furrow, and a number of former trackways were also noted as earthworks across parts of the survey area. The survey also recorded other magnetic anomalies clearly relating to more recent field drains and services in this area.

Archive at NELMS, Accn code STMF18.

Stallingborough: Stallingborough Interchange, TA 201 133. Report in the HER at NELC.

Twenty-four trial trenches were excavated by OAE as part of a second phase of investigations to inform proposed development at the Stallingborough Interchange site. The trenches followed the first phase of investigation, conducted in 2017, and exposed more of the extensive Roman settlement activity here. Evidence suggested that the settlement site had developed over three successive phases, with the main focus of the settlement being agricultural. Some potential industrial activity was also recorded, with evidence of kilns and craft activities nearby. Later activity on the site was again recorded, with the remains of medieval ridge and furrow noted across parts of the investigated area.

Stow: Stow Park Road, SK 8801 8186. Report No.6072 in the HER.

A programme of archaeological monitoring and recording was conducted by NH during groundworks for new residential development on land south of Stow Park Road, Stow. No features of archaeological interest were uncovered, although three redeposited sherds of thirteenth-century pottery were recovered from the plough soil. Two of the sherds were from thirteenth-century Nottingham Light-bodied Glazed ware jugs, with one being from a medium-sized jug, and the other being from a small jug with a bright copper-green glaze. The third sherd was from a thirteenth to fourteenth century Lincoln Glazed ware jug with a reduced glaze.

Archive at LCNCC, Accn no. 2017.37.

Surfleet: 61-71 Seas End Road, TF 2704 2874. Report No.2554 in the HER.

Three trial trenches were excavated by APS ahead of proposed residential development on land between 61-71 Seas End Road. The remains of a late medieval ditch, a post-medieval ditch and a pit of unknown date were identified.

The medieval ditch was aligned on a north-west to south-east axis, running perpendicular to the nearby river Glen, and was thought to have possibly functioned as a former land boundary. A few sherds of fifteenth- to sixteenth-century Toynton Late Medieval ware and Bourne D-type ware pottery were recovered from the lower fills of the ditch, along with a few fragments of animal bone. The animal bone assemblage comprised single fragments from horse, cattle and sheep/goat. Further sherds of Toynton Late Medieval ware pottery were recovered from the upper fill of the ditch, along with a single sherd from a probable jar of South Lincolnshire Shell and Iron Ware fabric, dating from the eleventh to thirteenth centuries.

The post-medieval ditch was aligned on a north-east to south-west axis, running parallel to the nearby river Glen, possibly serving as a former flood defence. A few fragments of post-medieval brick were recovered from the fill of the ditch, along with two clay tobacco pipe stems of late seventeenth- to early eighteenth-century date.

The pit was roughly oval in shape and was located at the south-western edge of the site. No significant dating material was recovered from its fill and its origins and function remains uncertain.

Archive at LCNCC, Accn no. 2018.60.

Tattershall: Church of the Holy Trinity, Sleaford Road, TF 2122 5755. Report No.6340 in the HER.

A programme of archaeological monitoring and recording was conducted by NH during the construction of a new brick buttress and associated underpinning works to the southern churchyard wall at the Church of the Holy Trinity. The groundworks revealed a graveyard soil with several disarticulated fragments of human bone, and a late nineteenth- or early twentieth-century cremation burial, contained within a stoneware jar and surrounded by a cist made from four bricks. This cremation pit was itself cut through an earlier, east to west aligned inhumation burial of uncertain date and a heavily truncated, east to west aligned linear gully. This gully ran a couple of metres to the south of the current churchyard wall, and on the same alignment, and was thought to be the remains of an earlier medieval churchyard boundary or drainage feature. The cremation and inhumation burial were left in situ during the works, and the disarticulated human bone fragments were collected for reburial.

Archive at LCNCC, Accn no. 2018.180.

Tealby: 36 Cow Lane, TF 1536 9050. Report No.2494 in the HER.

Four trial trenches were excavated by NH to inform proposed residential development on land to the rear of 36 Cow Lane. A single linear feature of unknown date was located but could not be fully investigated as it extended below the safe limit of excavation. It was thought possible that the feature may have functioned as a former drainage ditch, perhaps of post-medieval origin. No associated finds of dating material were recovered and the date and function of the feature remain uncertain.

Archive at LCNCC, Accn no. 2018.56.

Tetney: Tetney Golf Course, TA 3064 0060. Source Documents in the HER.

The remains of a prehistoric log coffin were discovered during the digging of a pond at Tetney Golf Course. The coffin was recovered from the site of a probable Bronze Age barrow that had been largely buried by alluvium until its exposure during the works. The finding of the coffin was reported to officers of Historic England, who secured the site and commenced a more controlled excavation of the barrow with assistance from staff of the University of Sheffield. Approximately half of the barrow mound was removed and recorded during the works, with the remains of the waterlogged timber coffin being recovered, together with associated human remains and artefacts. The coffin was believed to be of late Neolithic or early Bronze Age date, and had been set into the underlying clay, with the Bronze Age barrow being constructed over the site at a later date. Evidence of a second burial within the mound was also identified during the excavation. The finding of the coffin was believed to be of national importance and prompted detailed analysis of aerial photographs and Environment Agency lidar data for the barrow cemetery known to be in this area. It allowed the locations of the individual barrows to be mapped with greater accuracy, and also identified a group of four previously unrecorded barrows, to the west of the main group. The main barrow cemetery site was later designated as a Scheduled Monument in August 2021.

Thornton Curtis: Station Road, TA 0934 1806. Report in the HER at NLC.

Two phases of magnetometry survey were conducted by AAL to inform proposed residential development on land off Station Road. The surveys identified a number of potential archaeological features, mainly in the northern and central parts of the site, although magnetic noise in the southern and south-eastern areas may have masked some archaeological responses. The recorded features included a number of parallel-aligned linear features, possibly representing the remains of an earlier course of the road between Thornton Curtis and Thornton Abbey. The survey also recorded a number of possible enclosure features, thought to be associated with the linear feature, and possibly representing the remains of medieval settlement or agricultural boundaries. However, it should be noted that this site has been used as a nursery for growing plants in recent years and some of the recorded anomalies may relate to much more recent activity.

Trusthorpe: Wreck Fragment, Trusthorpe Foreshore, TF 5180 8356. Report No.6465 in the HER.

A programme of tree-ring analysis was undertaken by HE, on samples taken of oak timbers from a fragment of a wrecked vessel. The fragment, found washed up on the foreshore at Trusthorpe after heavy storms in Spring 2018, was comprised of five close-set frames or ribs, and four hull planks closed by caulking. Tree-ring analysis indicated that all of the sampled timbers were likely to be co-eval and were probably felled at some point shortly after 1815. This would suggest that the vessel they belonged to was of early to mid-nineteenth-century date, although its identity, and the main wreck location, remain unknown.

Whaplode: Mill House Farm, Drove Road, Shepeau Stow, TF 3090 1220. Report No.6102 in the HER.

A programme of excavation was conducted by NH during groundworks for the construction of two new residential dwellings at Mill House Farm, Drove Road, Shepeau Stow. The remains of two twentieth-century drainage ditches were identified in plot 4, with more significant remains identified in the area of plot 3. These features comprised the remnants of a north-east to south-west aligned ditch and a pit or possible hearth. The ditch had a shallow and truncated profile, and was completely ploughed out in places, although it continued beyond the limits of the monitored area. The pit was ovular in shape and extended beyond the northern limit of ground reduction. It contained a fill of burnt or vitrified clay fragments, suggesting a possible function as a hearth or a small rubbish pit. No finds or dating evidence were recovered from the fills of either feature, thus, their date and origins remain unknown.

Archive at LCNCC, Accn no. 2017.131.

Willoughby with Sloothby: Spring Farm, Hasthorpe Road, Sloothby, TF 48777 70353. Report No.2497 in the HER.

An earthwork survey was conducted by SAS to inform the proposed construction of a new poultry unit, feed silo, and road access on land south-west of Spring Farm, Hasthorpe Road, Sloothby. What were originally two adjoining medieval ridge and furrow fields were surveyed and recorded. The western field had earthworks of north to south aligned ridge and furrow, whilst those in the eastern field were aligned on an east to west axis. The distance between the furrows was between 8-9m on average.

Archive at LCNCC, Accn no. 2017.221.

Winteringham: High Burgage, SE 9327 2190. Report in the HER at NLC.

A magnetometry survey was conducted by AAL to inform proposed residential development on land off High Burgage. The survey identified several features of archaeological interest, including a large number of linear, curvilinear and amorphous features in the eastern half of the site, thought to likely represent the remains of former enclosure and boundary features, along with potential settlement activity. Areas of medieval ridge and furrow remains were also identified in the north-west and south-east corners of the site as parallel, linear magnetic anomalies. A large linear magnetic anomaly, running east to west across the centre of the site was thought to be the remains of a former palaeochannel, recorded on historic Ordnance Survey maps as a drain or stream. An earthwork mound noted in the north-east corner of the site did not closely correspond with any of the recorded geophysical anomalies, although a nearby strong magnetic anomaly may have been associated. Previous interpretations of the mound feature had been as a barrow or windmill mound, but no conclusive evidence or interpretation of the feature could be offered by the survey.

HISTORIC BUILDING RECORDING IN LINCOLNSHIRE 2018

Aylesby: Manor Farm, Main Road, TA 2020 0760. Report in the HER at NLC.

A programme of historic building recording was conducted by NH to inform the proposed conversion to residential use of former farm buildings at Manor Farm, Main Road. The surveyed structures comprised a north to south aligned range of attached buildings, thought to date from the early nineteenth century onwards. The structures were largely single-storey and built of red brick. The earliest part of the range is thought to be the central barn, which is open fronted to its east, suggesting it functioned as an animal shelter or storage space of some kind. Mid to late nineteenth-century alterations and extensions added the stables and coach-house structures to the south and converted the northernmost compartment of the barn for use as smithy. Further alterations conducted in the mid-twentieth century changed parts of the internal layouts of these structures and added further outbuildings to the north and south, of which only the northern outbuilding now survives.

Archive at NELMS, Accn code GRIMS: 2018.001.

Bardney: Bardney Sugar Factory, TF 1134 6873. Report No.6386 in the HER.

A programme of historic building recording was conducted by LCC to create a record of the industrial archaeology and heritage of parts of the old Bardney Sugar Factory prior to their demolition. The survey recorded the main factory building, the main office, the hostel, the canteen, and many of the outbuildings.

Plans to build a sugar beet factory in Bardney began in 1925 and land for the factory site was purchased in 1926. The Lincolnshire Beet Sugar Company Ltd was registered in January 1927, with construction of the factory beginning shortly afterwards. The factory was one of the first of its kind in the country and came into operation on 10 October 1927. In the early years of operation beets were primarily delivered to the factory by rail, and by barges on the river Witham. Three daily trains also brought factory workers to and from Lincoln in time for shift changes until the line closed in the 1960s. During the Second World War, German and Italian prisoners-of-war from the camp at Potterhanworth were brought to work in the factory, and logs show that some of their wages were paid in cigarettes. All the windows and ventilation had to be covered during the 'Blackout', to prevent the factory from becoming a bombing target during the war. The company also brought in workers from Ireland and continued to do so until 1976. Regular expansion and improvements were made to the factory and surrounding infrastructure as production levels increased. The company purchased accommodation and a sports field in Lincoln, and the Lincsgran Sports and Welfare Club was formed in 1930. The club held regular social and sporting events, as well as an annual 'Beet Ball' for employees and their families. Operations increased, and new products were developed and packaged on site from the 1980s. The Bardney factory began to produce golden syrup and black treacle in 1980, and other flavours of syrups were produced starting in 1989. The closure of the sugar beet processing facilities was announced on 23

January 2001. The final delivery of beets was made on 30 January 2001, and the final shift in the processing facilities was on 9 February 2001. The Finished Products and Packaging Plant continued to operate after the closure of the processing facilities. In the seventy-four years that the factory was in operation, 29.6 million tonnes of beets were processed, and 4.1 million tonnes of sugar were produced. Most of the machinery was dismantled and shipped to factories in Russia once beet processing ended at Bardney.

The main factory building was built of red brick, with over forty windows on each floor to allow plenty of light to enter. The building was of five storeys, but with only four floors, with a large open lifting shaft in the centre. Several steps in the production process took place within the walls of the main building, including slicing the sugar beet, and the diffusion and drying processes. Control panels were installed when the sugar production process was automated. The laboratory space, used to check the quality of the sugar, was also located in this building. Breakrooms and toilets were located on all floors to cater to workers' needs.

The main administrative office was constructed in 1973, designed in the Brutalist style of the time, and was built of concrete with the exterior clad in brown and grey flint. An interesting feature of the design is the 'moat' that surrounds the building. The interior looked like a typical 1970s office, with some modernisation. The main floor had the reception, an open floor office area, personnel manager office area, plant room clocking area, first aid room and computer room. The first floor had various smaller offices and two conference rooms.

The hostel was located to the north of the main building, and was built in 1969 to house temporary, foreign factory workers, replacing the use of Nissen huts previously on the site. The two-storey, double pile building was constructed out of yellow-brown brick, with two gabled roofs. There were fourteen dormitory rooms, a large recreation room, a laundry and several toilets and bathrooms split over the two floors. The sugar factory ceased using foreign workers in 1976, and the number of people using the hostel decreased. Some of the rooms on the top floor were converted into office space to house the Agricultural Research and Development department.

Belton and Manthorpe: Woodyard, Belton House, SK 92934 39633. Report No.6214 in the HER.

A programme of historic building recording was conducted by APS to inform the future use of the sawpit and Dutch barn at the Woodyard, Belton House. The sawpit is a Grade II listed structure dating to the early to mid-nineteenth century, while the Dutch barn dates to the early to mid-twentieth century.

The first depiction of the sawpit is on a Belton House estate plan of 1883, where it is shown with adjoining buildings on the east side and the south-east corner. These adjoining buildings had been removed by 1971, leaving the main sawpit structure standing alone. The sawpit was built using brick laid in English Garden Wall bond and has double door openings on the north and south elevations. The east elevation has seven contemporary brick buttresses along its length. The middle portion of the western elevation is open at ground level and has a timber supported weatherboarding panel covering the upper third of the opening. There is also later brick infill at the northern end of this elevation, which contains an unglazed window opening. Only a small portion of the timber framed roof survives at the northern end of the building, and this is covered in pantiles. The interior of the building is a single open space, dominated by the large brick lined pit dug into the floor of the room. The pit measured 9.75 x 3.5 x 1.97m deep, and has large wooden joists across it, supported by timbers that are resting on stone bases. There is an iron bar that runs over the pit for the length of the building at eaves height, which is thought to have been part of a lifting system to move timbers into place.

The Dutch barn is located on the western side of the Belton Estate woodyard, and is constructed with a steel and timber frame, clad with corrugated iron with some timber walling. The eastern elevation is open, the lower third of the northern elevation is open, the southern elevation is partially infilled with timber and the western elevation is partially infilled with corrugated sheeting. The interior of the barn is a single space open to the roof, and at the time of recording, was being used as a timber store.

Archive at the National Trust.

Caistor: Brigg Road, TA 11063 02689. Report No.6083 in the HER.

A programme of historic building recording was conducted by HFA to inform the conversion to residential use of former farm buildings on land to the west of Brigg Road. The group of surveyed buildings was comprised of a central barn and cow shed, with later ranges added to each side creating a U-shaped arrangement. The central building is thought to date from the mid to late nineteenth century, being first depicted on the first edition, six inch Ordnance Survey County Series map. The later east and west ranges were mid-twentieth century additions which appear to have been used as piggeries and storerooms. All the buildings were single storey, built out of a mix of red-orange and reddish pink brick laid in English Garden Wall bond, Scottish bond or Stretcher bond, depending on the phase of construction. The central block had a gabled roof of pantiles, whilst the west wing had a mono-pitched roof of modern corrugated asbestos sheet. The east wing was roofless at the time of recording. A small section of brick walling in the eastern elevation of the west wing matched that of the central range. It was, therefore, thought likely that this mid-twentieth century west range was a re-build of an earlier structure in this location.

Archive at LCNCC, Accn no. 2018.38.

Crowle: Manor House, Church Street, SE 7711 1295. Report in the HER at NLC.

A programme of historic building recording was conducted by MAS to inform the proposed demolition and redevelopment of the site of former farm buildings at the Manor House, Church Street. The surveyed structures comprised a north to south aligned range of attached buildings, thought to date from the eighteenth century onwards. The structures were largely of two storeys, built of red brick laid in English Garden Wall bond. The earliest part of the range was at the southern end, which functioned as a former threshing barn, with large opposing doors to the east and west elevations. The southern bay of this structure had been altered to incorporate a cart store. A large granary space would have formerly been present above the threshing floor, although this was no longer extant due to the collapse of the upper-storey floor and roof structure.

Attached to the northern end of the former threshing barn was a series of stables, tack rooms and stores, again of two storeys, although access to the upper storey could not be safely achieved. The internal walls on the ground floor had been lime plastered, and a variety of earth and brick floors were present in the various compartments. Some fixtures and fittings relating to the original use of the building were still present, notably the stalling in the stable area and various hooks and racks within the tack room.

Also recorded in the survey was a small pigsty, possibly contemporary with the eighteenth-century threshing barn and stables, and a later nineteenth-century lean-to attached to the northern end of the stables.

Archive at NLM, Accn code CWDV.

Crowle: The New Trent Inn, Ealand, SE 7841 1126. Report in the HER at NLC.

A programme of historic building recording was conducted by CAC to inform the proposed demolition and redevelopment of the site of the former New Trent Inn at Ealand. The building is thought to date to the mid-nineteenth century, and initially served as a private dwelling, before opening as a beer house in about 1863, when it was known as Ealand House. The building was further developed, with the addition of eastern and western extensions by 1885, by which time it was then known as Robinson's Hotel after its then owner. The name of the building was changed to the New Trent Inn in 1892; by its then owner Thomas Dymond, who also owned the nearby New Trent Brewery.

At the time of the survey, the building was in very poor condition with almost all of the timber elements including floor joists having been stripped, along with most of the former slate roof. Access to the interior of the building was consequently limited and hazardous, although some detailed recording could still be conducted, with a ground plan of the building being drawn up. The structure is thought to have been built of locally produced, hand-made bricks, largely covered by twentieth-century render.

Archive at NLM, Accn code CWDU.

Holbeach: Woodhouse Farm, Hurn Road, TF 37765 26452. Report No.6065 in the HER.

A programme of historic building recording was conducted by NH to inform the proposed demolition of the farmhouse and outbuildings at Woodhouse Farm, Holbeach. The farmhouse and outbuildings date to the late nineteenth century, with some modern alterations and additions. The buildings had been derelict for several decades, with the interior of the farmhouse too unsafe to allow full recording.

The farmhouse was a two-storey building with a gabled roof covered with modern concrete tiles. The building had been covered with modern concrete rendering, and all the window and door openings were boarded up. The main elevation faced south with a single door opening on the ground floor and two windows on either side, with five windows on the upper floor. The eastern elevation had no openings, and the northern elevation was mostly obscured by twentieth-century extensions. The western elevation had a single door opening and a window on the ground floor, and two windows on the upper floor.

The first outbuilding was a single storey former garage, and had a flat roof covered with modern corrugated iron sheeting. The interior was divided into two rooms. The structure was built in brick, laid in English Garden Wall Bond. The southern elevation had a single door, and two larger garage-door openings, and the western elevation had a single window opening. A small modern breezeblock extension was built onto the northern elevation.

The second outbuilding was built off the eastern elevation of the first outbuilding and was a single-storey building with a flat roof covered with modern roofing felt. The southern and eastern elevations were covered with modern concrete rendering, and the northern and western elevations were of brick laid in English Garden Wall Bond. The southern elevation had four door openings and a single window. The interior had four rooms, one of which may have been used as a stable.

Archive at LCNCC, Accn no. 2018.21.

Lenton, Keisby and Osgodby: The Tithe Barn, Ingoldsby Road, TF 0256 3028. Report No.6540 in the HER.

A programme of historic building recording was conducted by FCD Architecture to inform the proposed conversion to residential use of a group of structures now known as the Tithe Barn at Lenton. The group comprised a complex of three buildings which originally formed part of the working farm buildings of Church Farm, being a former threshing barn, wagon shed and livestock holding barn.

The former threshing barn is the oldest structure on the site, being of likely early eighteenth century origin. Built of roughly coursed local limestone, the structure features a hipped pantile roof and formerly had a granary space to the upper loft floor (although this was no longer extant at the time of survey). The building had large opposing double doors in the main elevations, allowing carts to pass through. Some twentieth century alterations to the structure were noted, including the insertion of an internal timber framed partition, creating two small rooms at the eastern end.

The former wagon shed was thought to date between 1873 and 1886, based on historic map evidence. The structure was single-storey, built of red brick with a pitched pantile roof, with three bays to the north-eastern side, allowing carts and implements to be stored inside. Although now open-fronted, hinge pins and reinforcing stone quoins were present at the middle bay, indicating it originally had heavy doors attached, allowing tools and small implements to be locked away.

The former livestock barn and shelter is thought to have been constructed in two phases, based on historic map evidence. The earliest, northern part of the building, is thought to date between 1856 and 1873 with the southern part being added at some point between 1873 and 1886. The structure was single-storey, and built of red brick with a pitched pantile roof. The northern part of the structure was enclosed, whilst the southern part was largely open-fronted. Brick walls to the east and south of the building would have created an adjacent crewyard.

Archive at LCNCC, Accn no. 2020.68.

Moulton: Clifden Farm, TF 30773 23310. Report No.1992 in the HER.

A brief programme of photographic recording was conducted by G.R. Merchant to inform the proposed conversion to residential use of a number of former outbuildings at Clifden Farm. The surveyed buildings comprised a large barn at the southern end of the farmstead, with a smaller barn to the western side, and a range of attached outbuildings to the north. All of the structures were thought to be of probable mid-nineteenth-century date, and all were single-storey, built of coursed brick and featured pitched, timber-framed roofs covered by corrugated sheet metal. The large southern barn was comprised of a single general purpose space. Two sunlights had been cut into the south-facing pitch of the roof, and there was evidence of a blocked opening in the upper half of one of the gable ends. The smaller, western barn showed evidence of having been painted or whitewashed inside, at least to the lower half of the walls, suggesting it had functioned as a livestock shelter. The northern outbuildings were largely open-fronted and probably functioned as cart-sheds and stables for horses or shelter for cattle, as evidenced by the presence of a hay trough in one of the bays.

Nettleham: 19 East Street, TF 00871 75578. Report No.4850 in the HER.

A brief programme of historic building recording was conducted by Kingsmead Design to inform the proposed conversion of an outbuilding behind 19 East Street. The building is single-storey, and constructed of coursed limestone, with a pitched, timber-framed roof covered in red clay pantiles. It was thought likely that the structure dates to the mid-nineteenth century based on mapping evidence and appears to have been largely used for storage. The eastern elevation has a set of double wooden doors to the north and is open near the centre of the elevation. There is a hayrack on the exterior wall near the south end of the elevation. The western elevation has no openings and was in poor condition at the time of recording, having partially collapsed. An extension had been built off the northern elevation, but this was no longer structurally sound and was demolished as part of the conversion. The exposed northern elevation has a single goods door.

Northorpe: Village Hall, Manor Road, SK 89436 97165. Report No.6094 in the HER.

A brief programme of historic building recording was conducted by APS in advance of the proposed conversion to residential use of the former Village Hall, at Manor Road. The building dates to the mid-nineteenth century and was originally used as a school room. It is single-storey, and primarily constructed of coursed limestone with a slate roof and later brick alterations. The southern elevation was the main façade, with four bays containing windows and a sign that reads 'County Library'. The eastern elevation has a large arched window and features a plaque that reads 'National School 1846'. This elevation also had some twentieth-century brick alterations, with an older doorway blocked with bricks and a new doorway inserted. The western elevation had been rebuilt using red brick and had a large arched window. The main wall of the northern elevation had been rebuilt in red brick and two phases of extensions extend from this elevation. The extensions were built in yellow brick and limestone. The interior of the hall was divided into the north and south ranges; the north range was divided with twentieth-century partitions, while the south range was one large room.

Somerby: Grange Farm, TA 06687 06218. Report No.3196 in the HER.

A programme of historic building recording was conducted by AAL to inform the proposed conversion to residential use of a former farm building at Grange Farm. The surveyed building is a two-storey former cart-shed with hayloft, being the sole remnant of a larger, formerly U-shaped complex of farm buildings, though to date from the mid to late nineteenth century. The surviving structure was built out of red brick, laid in English Garden Wall bond, and featured a pitched roof covered with corrugated cement sheeting. The south-eastern end of the building was single-storey, with a mono-pitched roof. The main frontage of the building was the north-east facing elevation, which featured a sliding door in the mono-pitched section, and two arched doorways on either end of the main two-storey part. Between the two arched doorways were five open-fronted cart bays, above which were two windows and two pitching holes, indicating that the upper floor was used as a hayloft. Modern sheds attached to the south-western elevation largely obscured that part of the structure. At the time of the survey, the building was being used as office and storage space, with the ground floor divided with modern breezeblocks and used as stabling.

Archive at LCNCC, Accn no. 2018.92.

South Killingholme: Killingholme North Low Lighthouse, TA 1777 1844. Report in the HER at NLC.

A programme of detailed photographic recording and structural survey was conducted by AC Archaeology and Howarth Litchfield Architects to inform proposed management, repair and refurbishment works to the Killingholme North Low Lighthouse. The structures were built in 1851, to the designs of William Foale, and comprise a four-storey, round and tapered lighthouse tower, with an attached two-storey lighthouse keeper's house. The structures are brick-built, smoothly rendered to the tower, and roughly rendered to the house. The tower features a ribbed dome with scalloped eaves, whilst the house carries a slate roof. Later, single-storey extensions have been added to the left and rear of the house. The lighthouse was used as a signal station for trawlers until 1920. It was subsequently occupied as a residential property until recent years. It is intended that the structure be used as an office and store after remedial repairs are completed, with the longer term objective to return the structure to residential use.

Spridlington: Ha-Ha Wall, Spridlington Hall, TF 00704 84920. Report No.6055 in the HER.

A programme of historic building recording was conducted by AHC as part of a wider programme of conservation and conversion works to Spridlington Hall. This particular survey focused on a ha-ha wall, located on the southern and western sides of the Hall. The exact date of the ha-ha's construction is not known, although documentary evidence suggests a date between 1950 and 1967. The ha-ha provided a physical barrier between the Hall gardens and the adjacent field, without interrupting the views from the house. It represents an interesting, later addition to the setting of the Hall. The wall is thought to have been built from re-used material, largely using red bricks set on the diagonal to create a diamond or squared-herringbone pattern, with the headers as the finished surface. The majority of the wall is topped with chamfered or saddleback coping stones, with some sections having concrete coping stones. There are four bastions of various sizes on the south and south-eastern sides of the ha-ha. The wall had previously extended further to the north-west but was altered during the construction of the tennis court in that area.

Archive at LCNCC, Accn no. 2018.33.

Stow: 6 Sturton Road, SK 88218 81882. Report No.6077 in the HER.

A programme of photographic recording was conducted by Alice Gray in advance of the proposed demolition of an outbuilding to the rear of 6 Sturton Road. The recorded building is a single-storey brick structure of probable nineteenth century date, with a pitched roof covered with corrugated asbestos or concrete sheeting. The structure was thought to have been bigger when originally built, based on its depiction on the second edition 25" Ordnance Survey County Series map, but episodes of demolition have reduced it to its current size. The building appears to have had a variety of past uses, including storage and as a piggery. The southern elevation had built-out recesses in the lower portion of the wall, above which were chutes that were open to the interior of the building, allowing food to be passed down to pigs. The western elevation had largely been rebuilt with modern concrete breezeblocks. The northern elevation appeared to be a more modern addition to the outbuilding, built in brick with a mono-pitched roof covered with clay pantiles. The western portion of this elevation had a large opening and was completely open to the west. This area was probably used for coal or wood storage. The eastern portion of the elevation is thought to be an old toilet, later being used for storage. The eastern elevation of the outbuilding had a large double door opening. The outbuilding had one large internal space, which had been used as a garage and as storage in more recent years.

Sturton by Stow: Red Lion Inn, Marton Road, SK 89016 80339. Report No.2145 in the HER.

A programme of historic building recording was conducted by PAL to inform the proposed demolition of the former Red Lion Inn at Sturton by Stow. Historical records show that the building had been operating as a public house from the late eighteenth or early nineteenth century. However, some of the internal fabric and features noted during the recording of the structure may suggest an earlier construction date or rebuilding. These features were located in the south range and comprised a stone plinth and oak 'A' frame roof, suggestive of an encased timber frame in this part of the building. Recording during the demolition process identified further timbers in the street-frontage side, suggesting that part had also begun as a timber-framed structure. The building was comprised of a variety of construction materials, as it stood at the time of recording, reflecting the extensive later alterations and extensions that had occurred. These alterations included the application of an external white render to cover the variety of building materials and produce a unified external appearance. Other significant alterations included the replacement of the entire first floor and relocation of the staircase in the late twentieth century. Demolition of the building had been completed by the end of April 2019, and the site is now occupied by a Co-op convenience store.

Archive at LCNCC, Accn no. 2019.12.

FINDS REPORTED TO THE PORTABLE ANTIQUITIES SCHEME IN 2018

Compiled by Dr Lisa Brundle

The following objects have been reported to the Portable Antiquities Scheme (PAS) during 2018. In some cases the objects were found in previous years but only reported to the PAS during 2018. Full descriptions of all finds recorded by the PAS are available via their online database (www.finds.org.uk). The finds described here are only a selection of the finds of note from Lincolnshire. A total of 6412 finds were reported to the scheme from Lincolnshire in 2018, which have been recorded by the Finds Liaison Officers (FLOs), and in some cases by PAS interns, student placements or volunteers under the guidance of FLOs. The reported finds ranged in date from the Palaeolithic to modern periods, although were predominantly dated to the Roman, medieval and post-medieval periods.

PREHISTORIC

Blyton: Iron Age bracelet, found while metal detecting. PAS record no. NLM-6B397B.

A fragment of a copper-alloy bracelet dating from the fifth to early third century BC. It is one half of a bracelet made in two parts with paired lugs with holes of diameter 3mm at one end as one half of a hinged fastening, and a short, pointed lug at the other end, perhaps a more battered relict of the same device. There are nine bulbous or drum-shaped segments separated by plain collars. Each segment bears a moulded chevron around the external three quarters of its circumference, with the inner side smooth to lie against the skin of the wearer. The moulded decoration resembles 'chip carved' work, though not formed in that way.

ROMAN

Alford: Roman gold aureus, found while metal detecting. PAS record no. LEIC-35CCA5.

A Roman gold aureus of Augustus (31 BC-AD 14), dating to the period *c.* 2 BC-AD 4 (Reece period 1). Obverse: CAESAR AVGVSTVS DIVI F PATER PATRIAE / laureate head right.

Reverse: C L CAESARES (in exergue), AVGVSTI F COS DESIG PRINC IVVENT depicting Gaius and Lucius Caesar facing resting hands on a shield, behind each shield a spear, above on left a simpulum, right, and on right a lituus, left. Mint of Lyon.[2] Recorded by Wendy Scott (Leicester and Rutland FLO) and Andrew Brown (Assistant Finds Adviser and Treasure Curator for Iron Age and Roman coins).

Asgardby and Howell: Roman nail cleaner, found while metal detecting. PAS record no. LIN-82B0F4.

A re-used fragment of a copper alloy snake-headed bracelet dating to the Roman period *c*. AD 43-250. The fragment consists of one of the terminals and bears a stylised snake design. The terminal forms the head of the snake. The head is oval in plan and plano-convex in section. A possible groove runs around the perimeter of the terminal which might indicate the mouth. The eyes are possibly indicated by what appear to be two worn punched circles, but the entire head is very worn. The hoop of the bracelet has been straightened and modified at the break with the addition of a v-shaped notch. This notch is consistent with the terminals of other nail cleaners, though the present example appears to be the first instance of a bracelet being converted to a nail cleaner recorded on the PAS database. The object has a dark brown patina. See for parallel Eckardt and Crummy.[3] Recorded by Adam Daubney (Lincolnshire FLO) and Sally Worrell (National Finds Advisor, PAS).

Roxby cum Risby: Roman strap fitting, found while metal detecting. PAS record no. NLM-55C37D.

A cast copper-alloy openwork fitting of plano-convex cross-section with a pair of integrally cast discoid-ended fixing pins projecting from its flat back. On its display side, it comprises a U-shaped figure with flared ends from which a pair of waisted trumpet-ended and addorsed continuations project; the appearance is of a figure-of-eight with top truncated. This is set above a stepped base. Extensive traces of white metal plating appear on the display side. The finder kindly cites SUR-278166 as a close parallel, which is a fitting of a form thought to be associated with Batavian auxiliary cavalry serving in the Claudian invasion of the first century. As their best-known exploit during the invasion was the execution of a contested river crossing, of either the Medway or the Thames, the discovery of such a fitting on the southern bank of the Humber may shed light upon the Roman crossing of the river *c*.AD70. Recorded by Martin Foreman (North Lincolnshire FLO).

Roxby cum Risby: Roman steelyard weight or figurine, found while metal detecting. PAS record no. NLM-6B99F4.

A cast copper-alloy figurine in the form of a cockerel rendered in schematic form, with a slightly elongated bowl-shaped body, curled tail feather, short, curved wings on top of the body whose outer edges project slightly beyond it, and a small comb down the centre of the head. A bill appears merely as the narrower end of the sub-triangular or conical head. The feet are integrally cast along with the rest, though separated by a gap which extends into the body of the bird, and there is no attempt to model claws; the feet end in slightly expanded 'pods' which join each other. The bird balances on its feet, though an integrally cast loop springing from the back retains a single pointed hook for the figure's suspension. The hook is made from drawn wire with a separate strip wrapped around its upper end. Two stamped hollows appear on the wing on one side of the body, but this texturing is not symmetrical. Recorded by Martin Foreman (North Lincolnshire FLO).

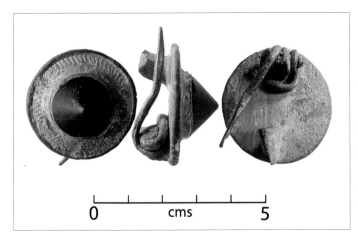

Fig.1
A Roman gilded copper-alloy disc brooch, c.AD 200–350, circular in plan, with a central boss made of a dark gemlike material. The fastening mechanism is complete, consisting of a sprung pin and catch-plate.
(LVPL-833A86).

Temple Bruer: Roman brooch, found while metal detecting. PAS record no. LVPL-833A86.

A complete Roman gilded copper-alloy disc brooch, *c.*AD 200-350 (Fig. 1). The brooch is circular in plan, with a central boss made of a dark gemlike material. The boss is conical, and the base of the boss is raised 1.8mm above the surrounding surface. A slightly raised rim forms the outer circumference of the brooch and enough gilding survives to recognise a repetitive pattern of 'S' shapes just inside this edge. On the reverse, there is some white metal coating remaining and the fastening mechanism is complete, consisting of a sprung pin and catch-plate.[4] Recorded by Megan Hall (University of Chester student placement, Cheshire, Greater Manchester & Merseyside).

Winteringham: Roman figurine, found while metal detecting. PAS record no. NLM-36FA1E.

An incomplete cast copper alloy figurine representing Eros/Cupid, probably dating from *c.*AD 200-350 and from a group representing Venus and her attendants, rendered in Classicised naturalistic style (Fig. 2). This suggests manufacture in a Romanised provincial context. The subject is depicted as a naked winged boy, left arm extended with an open palm, and the right arm bent at the elbow with the forearm horizontal and fingers and thumb curled to accommodate an object, now lost. The legs are parted as if striding forward, with the sole of the left foot flat, and the right foot formerly brazed to a separate base by a spot below its forepart. The facial features are finely modelled, with large deep-set almond-shaped eyes with drilled dots representing the pupils. The soft lines between nose and mouth are clearly defined, as are full and unparted lips below a broad snub nose. Lightly curling hair obscures the ears entirely. A pair of narrow hair braids passes from around a small frontal topknot back along the centre line of the head, with short tresses falling to either side. Though the facial features approach a cherubic ideal, they convey a slightly adult appearance viewed face-on, and the neck appears short and thick. The torso is straight-sided, with over-emphasised sunken circular navel and appropriately diminutive genitalia. A slightly flattened rear aspect to the hips emphasises small firm curving buttocks, while the legs are perhaps more developed than those of an infant, and short in proportion to the rest of the body. Recorded by Martin Foreman (North Lincolnshire FLO).

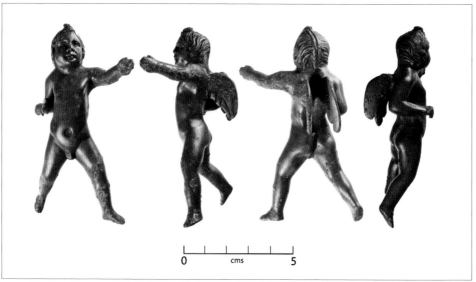

*Fig.2 A Roman cast copper-alloy figurine of a naked winged boy representing Eros/
Cupid. Probably dating from c.AD 200–350 and from a group representing Venus and her
attendants. (NLM-36FA1E).*

EARLY MEDIEVAL

Caistor area: early medieval pin, found while metal detecting. PAS record no. LIN-CD7507.

An incomplete copper-alloy early medieval (early Anglo-Saxon) pin dating to c.AD 500-680
consisting of a cross-shaped plate with two surviving crescentic or pelta-shaped collared
lobes (Fig. 3). The collars of the two surviving lobes comprise of transverse bands in a
raised square. The third lobe is now missing. The collar of the missing lobe has a different
design: with two longitudinal bands over four transverse bands; notably this collar appears
to be a later repair which was soldered onto the plate and subsequently broke again in
antiquity. Where the crescentic lobes converge is a central raised boss with a copper-alloy
pellet, surrounded by pairs of raised bands in a lozenge form with concave sides. Three
sub-rectangular longitudinal moulded bands are positioned where the plate meets the pin
shaft. Below here are two transverse grooves. The pin shaft is sub-rectangular and tapers to a
rounded point. The head is bent slightly backwards, though it is unclear whether this is post-
depositional damage or an intentional original feature perhaps to allow the pin to function
more effectively when worn. This pin parallels Ross's cross-headed type.[5] The crescentic
lobes closely parallel an example from Breach Downs in Kent dating to the seventh century
(British Museum accession no. 1855,0521.1). Recorded by Lisa Brundle (Intern, Lincolnshire
PAS).

Newark area: early medieval coin, found while metal detecting. PAS record no. DENO-FCA770.

A silver early medieval penny of the Vikings minted in the name of St Peter of York (c. 905-
927) (Fig. 4). Phase 3, Sword/Cross issue (North 555), minted in York, c. 921-927. The reverse
legend differs from the example recorded in North.[6] This coin has also been recorded on the

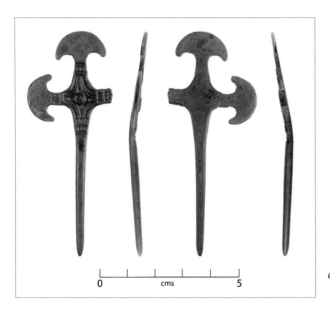

Fig.3
An early medieval copper-alloy pin in the form of a cross-shaped plate with two surviving crescentic lobes, dating to c.AD 500–680. (LIN-CD7507).

Corpus of Early Medieval Coin Finds: EMC number: 2018.0435. Recorded by Alastair Willis (Derbyshire and Nottinghamshire FLO) and John Naylor (Ashmolean).

Threekingham: early medieval Urnes-style mount, found while metal detecting. PAS record no. LIN-FA6943.

A late Saxon copper alloy Urnes-style mount dating to *c.*AD 1000-1100. The mount is circular and openwork. The frame is just over 1mm thick and contains within it a quadruped shown in profile going left, with its head looking back over its body and biting its tail. The body of the animal is slender and muscular, and the legs are relatively thick to the body. The neck is slender, as is the head. The tail is long and curves outwards and then back above to its mouth. The beast is joined to the frame at the top by four further tabs of copper alloy. The reverse is undecorated. There are no obvious attachment points or fittings. Recorded by Adam Daubney (Lincolnshire FLO).

Fig.4
A silver early medieval penny of the Vikings (c.905–927) minted in the name of St Peter of York (DENO-FCA770).

Torksey area: early medieval Irish mount, found while metal detecting. PAS record no. LIN-9BCF25.

Fragment of an Irish early medieval enamelled copper alloy mount or strap end dating to the eighth century. The object is formed of a flat, thick, trapezoid terminal broken across its narrowest end. The terminal is also trapezoid in section, narrowing towards the top. The front of the object is decorated with a rectangular perimeter of reserve metal, which extends in the centre towards the break, thus forming a 'T' shaped perimeter. The recessed areas around and within it appear to contain degraded enamel; patches of it are brown-burgundy in colour. Recorded by Adam Daubney (Lincolnshire FLO).

Waddingham: early medieval hanging bowl escutcheon, found while metal detecting. PAS record no. LIN-65EE1A.

An early medieval cast copper alloy escutcheon from a Late Celtic hanging bowl of Bruce-Mitford Type B or C dating to *c.*AD 650-700.[7] The escutcheon is circular, slightly domed, and would have been set into a circular frame with integral hook. The convex front is decorated with a developed multi-spiral trumpet design. The design has a central spiral with six outlying spirals and is strikingly similar to examples from Winchester and Cumbria.[8] The recessed cells between the triskeles are filled with degraded enamel that is now greenish-brown in colour. Recorded by Adam Daubney (Lincolnshire FLO).

MEDIEVAL

Linwood: medieval brooch, found while metal detecting. PAS record no. DENO-7ECEEA.

An incomplete and broken copper alloy medieval buckle dating to *c.* 1200-1500. The outer edge of the frame is in the form of a pair of conjoined confronted harpies gardant. The buckle is missing its pin, strap bar and part of its frame. The object comprises two pieces of the same artefact, without a direct join. A large knop depicts a humanoid head with an incised eye and wearing a flattened hairstyle or a hat. This would have originally joined a

Fig.5 A copper-alloy/iron knife handle, probably dating to the sixteenth century. One side depicts a male figure possibly working at a desk or bench. The other side has a depiction of a seated woman wearing a wimple. A child's head looks over her left shoulder. (NLM-D3A281).

matching head/knop which is missing with a recent break. The buckle frame is composed of two hybrid creatures facing one another, which have been identified elsewhere as harpies (see below). They have slender necks and raised arms or forelimbs which are truncated and broken and may have attached directly to each other. The hind legs appear equine with sharp elbow joints and possible hooves, but contemporary depictions of harpies suggest that the legs were intended to be bird's legs. Wings are shown folded over and behind the legs with feathers indicated with incised lines. There is a distinct separation between the two halves of the body to distinguish between the human half and the bird half. Such a distinction is seen in some contemporary depictions. Recorded by Meghan King (Derbyshire and Nottinghamshire FLO).

POST-MEDIEVAL

Muckton: post-medieval knife handle, found while metal detecting. PAS record no. NLM-D3A281.

An incomplete copper-alloy, iron and mineral-preserved organic [?wood] knife handle, probably dating to the sixteenth century (Fig. 5). The tang passes into ?wood, now impregnated with ferrous corrosion products from the tang. A pommel or cap has probably been lost, as is the blade. The handle is sheathed with a tapered hexagonal section sleeve bearing a panel of incised decoration on each of its facets. One panel bears a rear view of a male figure partly turned to the left, possibly working at a desk or bench. His straight hair is partly covered by a soft hat; he wears puffed or slashed sleeves, and a garment with a cross-hatched panel across the upper back, perhaps quilting or leather. The hem of his jacket or tunic appears in the lower part of the image. At the base is an object with a passing resemblance to a closed helmet of medieval style, or to a satchel. The opposite broad panel carries a depiction of a possible woman seated, again with her back to the viewer, with a wimple over her hair and wearing a garment with puffed or slashed sleeve, and with vertical and horizontal panels on the back of her garment. A child's head looks over her left shoulder while the woman gazes upon it. Recorded by Martin Foreman (North Lincolnshire FLO).

Near Spilsby: post-medieval helmet, found while metal detecting. PAS record no. LIN-E0B301.

An incomplete iron 'lobster pot' helmet from the English Civil War (Fig. 6). The helmet is formed of two plates folded over at the top. A triangular visor survives, but the bars are missing. The visor is riveted to the helmet by a dome headed rivet on either side. The visor still moves. The tail survives largely intact but is damaged in places. There are ten rivets set around the perimeter, six of which retain a rectangular washer of sheet copper alloy on the interior. All but

Fig.6

An almost complete iron 'lobster pot' helmet from the English Civil War. The armourer's mark HK (Henry Keene) survives on the visor. (LIN-E0B301).

one rivet is dome-headed; the remainder has a deep slot across the centre. The armourer's mark HK - for Henry Keene - is visible on the visor. Keith Down (Assistant Curator of European Armour, Royal Armouries, Leeds) kindly examined the helmet and provided the following comments: Often known today as a 'lobster pot' due to the resemblance of the embossed neck-guard to a lobster's tail, this type of helmet was worn by light cavalry, known as harquebusiers, from *c*.1630 until *c*.1690. However, based on the shape of the skull, the presence of a comb, the size and angle of the peak and the shape of the neck-guard, this particular helmet can be dated to *c*.1645-1650. In addition, the peak has been stamped with a maker's mark comprising a conjoined 'HK'. This mark can be identified as being that of the London armourer Henry Keene (d.1664) who was active during the British Civil Wars. Recorded by Adam Daubney (Lincolnshire FLO).

NOTES

1.   Scholma-Mason, O., Bailey, L. and Dalland, M., 2022, The Archaeology of a Dynamic Landscape – Archaeological Works at Keadby Windfarm, in *Lincs Hist & Arch,* Vol 52 (2017/18), pp. 81-95.

2.   Sutherland, C. H. V. and Carson, R. A. G, (eds), 2nd Edition, 1984, *Roman Imperial Coinage*, Vol. I, Spink. p. 55, no. 206.

3.   Eckardt, H. and Crummy, N., 2008, *Styling the body in Late Iron Age and Roman Britain: a contextual approach to toilet instruments*. Instrumentum Monograph 36. p. 136, fig. 79.

4.   Mackreth, D. F., 2011, *Brooches in Late Iron Age and Roman Britain*, Oxford, Oxbow books. British; plate 3.b3.

5.   Ross, S., 1992, *Dress pins from Anglo-Saxon England: Their Production and Typo-Chronological Development*. Unpublished PhD thesis, University of Oxford. pp. 241-2, fig. 5.26.

6.   North, J. J., 1994, *English Hammered Coinage, Vol 1, Early Anglo-Saxon to Henry III c. A.D. 600-1272*, Spink. p. 116; 55.

7.   Bruce-Mitford, R. L. S. and Raven, S., 2005, *A Corpus of Late Celtic Hanging-bowls with an Account of the Bowls Found in Scandinavia*. Oxford University Press. 11.

8.   *Ibid.*, 14; Fig F.

BIBLIOGRAPHY

This list aims to include as many 2019 titles as possible that came to the attention of the editors and were published since the last volume of Lincolnshire History & Archaeology. *Titles that have received reviews in the Society's quarterly magazine* Lincolnshire Past and Present *are shown with the relevant issue number in brackets at the end of the entry. Not all the works listed were actually sent in for review purposes.*

A select bibliography of books relating to the county published in 2019:

ACTON, Mark and ROBERTS, Stephen, *Charles Seely of Lincoln: Liberalism and making money in Victorian England*, Kindle Direct Publishing, London. 2019. 61pp. £4.99. **(LP&P 115)**

ANNETT, Roger, *RAF College, Cranwell. A centenary celebratio*n, Air World, Barnsley. 2019. 376pp. £30.00.

AUSTIN, Richard and RADFORD, David, *Boston: the small town with a big story*, Cherry Tree Books, Boston. 2019. 120pp. £12.95. **(LP&P 117).**

BLACKWELL, John and WHEATMAN, George, *Sponge man to president: 45 Years of ups and downs with Boston United: the John Blackwell story*, Chris Cook Print, Boston. 2019. 160pp. £15.00.

BROWNLOW, Robert, *Escritt and Barrell: auctioneers and estate agents, Grantham. A history, 1861-1920*, Grantham Civic Society, Grantham. 2019. £7.50

CROOK, Ruth, ed., *Notes on Grantham by a Victorian lady*, Grantham Civic Society, Grantham. 2019. 56pp. £4.00.

CUMMINGS, Marcus and MARSHALL, Chris, *St James' Church, Louth: the stained glass*, C. J. Marshall, Louth. 2019.

DAVIES, Christopher, *A – Z of Stamford places, people, history*, Amberley Publishing, Stroud. 2019. 96pp. £15.99.

DAVIES, Christopher, *Stamford history tour*, Amberley Publishing, Stroud. 2019. 96pp. £8.99.

GURNHAM, Richard, *The story of early Louth – from its origins to the Reformation*, Pines Publishing, Louth. 2019. 186pp. £16.99. **(LP&P 119)**.

HONEYBONE, Diana and HONEYBONE, Michael, *Against the odds: the survival of the Spalding Gentlemen's Society*, Shaun Tyas for the Spalding Gentlemen's Society, Donington. 2019. 54pp. £8.00**. (LP&P 117).**

HOSKIN, Philippa, *Robert Grosseteste and the 13th-Century Diocese of Lincoln: an English bishop's pastoral vision*, Brill Books, Leiden. 2019. 260pp. £93.00.

JENNINGS, Anthony, *The Bourne identity: articles on buildings, heritage and conservation*. First published in the Bourne Local, Bourne Civic Society (in association with Shaun Tyas), Bourne and Donington. 2019. 152pp. £14.95. **(LP&P 117)**.

KING, Paul, *Railways of north east Lincolnshire. Part two. Stations*, Pyewipe Publications, Grimsby. 2019. 112pp. £18.95.

LEWIS, Carenza, SCOTT, Anna, CRUSE, Anna, NICHOLSON, Raf and SYMONDS, Dominic, *'Our Lincolnshire': exploring public engagement with heritage*, Access Archaeology, Archaeopress, Oxford. 2019. 269pp. £55.00, and available as an open-access PDF.

McENTEE-TAYLOR, Carole, *A history of women's lives in Scunthorpe*, Pen & Sword History, Barnsley. 2019. 184pp. £14.99.

MEERES, Frank, *The story of the Fens*, Phillimore, Andover. 2019. 256pp. £14.75.

MOYES, Michael, *Eyeless in Cleethorpes: the life and art of Peter Brannan, RBA*, Matador, Kibworth Beauchamp. 2019. 96pp. £12.00.

NORTH SOMERCOTES & DISTRICT STUDY GROUP, *Yan tan tethera, a study of a Lincolnshire marsh village*, North Somercotes & District Study Group, North Somercotes. 2019. 144pp. £10.00. (**LP&P 119**).

ORR, Colin, *Letters from Lincoln: the Penroses of North Hykeham, 1858-73*, Lulu Press, Morrisville, USA. 2019. 331pp.

PINCHBECK, John, *Grantham at work: people and industries through the years*, Amberley Publishing, Stroud. 2019. 96pp. £15.99.

PRYOR, Francis, *The Fens: discovering England's ancient depths*, Head of Zeus, London. 2019. 436pp. £25.00.

ROBERTS, Stephen, *Lincoln in 1837*, Kindle Direct Publishing, London. 2019. 49pp. £3.99. (**LP&P 121**).

ROSE, Chris, *Dancing in their uncouth fashion: a look at the survival of the Morris dance in Lincolnshire and Nottinghamshire*, Ivy Farm Press, Newark, 2019. 97pp. £5.00.

SENTANCE, Neil, *Ridge and furrow: voices from the winter fields*, Little Toller Books, Beaminster, 2019. 96pp. £12.00.

STAMFORD ENDOWED SCHOOLS, *Stamford School Chapel: eight hundred years of St Paul's Stamford*, Stamford Endowed Schools Foundation, Stamford. 2019. 16pp. Freely available open-access publication.

WALKER, Andrew (ed.), *George Boole's Lincoln, 1815-49*, The Survey of Lincoln, Lincoln. 2019. 80pp., £8.50. (**LP&P 118**).

WRIGHT, Graham, *A small boy in a small country town. A personal history of Sleaford and the Wright family: the early years, 1945-57,* Graham Wright, Sleaford. 2019. 296pp.